D1264327

Freedom, Modernity, and Islam

Modern Intellectual and Political History of the Middle East
Mehrzad Boroujerdi, *Series Editor*

Freedom,
Modernity,
and Islam

Toward a Creative Synthesis

RICHARD K. KHURI

Syracuse University Press

First Edition 1998
98 99 00 01 02 03   6 5 4 3 2 1

Publication of this book is made possible by a grant
from the Muhammad El-Hindi Foundation.

The paper used in this publication meets the minimum requirements of
American National Standard for Information Sciences—Permanence of
Paper for Printed Library Materials, ANSI Z39.48-1984. ∞™

Library of Congress Cataloging-in-Publication Data
Khuri, Richard K.
Freedom, modernity, and Islam : toward a creative synthesis /
Richard K. Khuri. — 1st ed.
p.   cm.—(Modern intellectual and political history of the
Middle East)
Includes bibliographical references (p.   ) and index.
ISBN 0-8156-2698-3 (alk. paper)
1. Islam and state—Islamic countries.
2. Islam and politics—Islamic countries.
3. Islamic countries—Politics and government.
4. Islam—20th century. I. Title. II. Series.
BP173.6.K53   1998
323.44'0917'671—dc21   97-25578

Manufactured in the United States of America

In memory of
Albert Habib Hourani
(1915–1993)

and to
my mother and father

Liberations have always led to servitude at another level.

—*Jean Baudrillard*[1]

• • •

Are you sure that were you given freedom, you would be able to live freely?

You get drunk with the word that names it, you defend it even on behalf of your foe, you die for its sake. But when it is yours, can you stand it?

I see you lost in your freedom, as though you do not know what to say.

And this is the hard and dreadful problem: Freedom reveals, exposes this emptiness within us, this real and abysmal wasteland, as though chains suited it, even enslavement and persecution, because they conceal it and provide excuses for crying out against suppression and tyranny. . . .

Today, faced with the wave of "liberation" gushing through the world, I have resolved to find out why I am unable to celebrate this wedding "till the end," and I discover that what bridles my joy is this desert, this dull, hackneyed, impoverished, lethal emptiness, the emptiness of what lay beyond liberation.

Does this mean that I am against liberation? Certainly not. . . . But I would hate for it to take its course in a barren land, for one to leave prison only to end up in a grave.

Were I a tyrant, I would not condemn suppression, but would have told those who questioned me: "I do this to protect them from discovering their emptiness, I do this as a service to them, so they would go on longing for that which, were they fulfilled, would kill them with triteness."

But the painful truth is that the tyrant does not suppress in order to protect the suppressed from discovering emptiness and triteness, but because he is still more trite and empty himself.

—*Unsi al-Hajj*[2]

• • •

Man . . . both longs for freedom and fears it. The paradox of liberation is that in order to preserve freedom and to struggle for it one must, in a sense, be already free, have freedom within oneself. . . . Ancient taboos surround man on all sides and fetter his moral life. In order to free himself from their power man must first be conscious of himself as inwardly free; only then can he struggle for freedom outwardly. . . . The awakening of creative energy is inner liberation and is accompanied by a sense of freedom. Creativeness is the way of liberation. Liberation cannot result in inner emptiness—it is not merely liberation from something but also liberation for the sake of something. And this "for the sake of" is creativeness. Creativeness [for its part] cannot be aimless and objectless. . . . It does not move along a flat surface in endless time but ascends toward eternity.

—*Nikolai Berdyaev*[3]

Richard K. Khuri received his doctorate in philosophy from the University of California at Berkeley. He lives and writes in the Washington, D.C., area, where he has taught and lectured at several universities, including Georgetown University and the Catholic University of America. He is affiliated with the Council for Research in Values and Philosophy. The subjects of his scholarly articles include modern cultural history of the Middle East, the philosophy of art, and the philosophical evaluation of contemporary scientific thought. This last area is the focus of his current research. He has also written several literary and critical essays for the international daily, *al-Hayat*. He is a recipient of the Freedom Award, conferred on him by the IIAS in August 1997.

Contents

Preface

In 1984 my brother and parents moved to London. This gave me the occasion to travel there more frequently, especially that I could still enjoy long breaks from my work as a doctoral student in the United States. On one of those trips in late 1985, I met Albert Hourani at a large gathering at his brother Cecil's house. From then on, lunches, teas, and dinners with him became a regular treat. More often than not, we were alone together. On one such occasion, in the summer of 1988, at an Italian restaurant not far from the British Museum, I informally shared with him several scattered ideas that had been brewing within me for many months. Some were philosophical, while others concerned the Arab Muslim world. In a casual manner belied by the sparkle in his eyes and his decisive tone, he urged me to write them down for him to examine. Within a fortnight, I was back with a twenty-page "abstract." A few days later, over tea in his tranquil and understated garden, he declared that in the abstract lay the germ for several books worth writing. Anyone who knew him well would appreciate that no more encouragement was needed. He proceeded to point out where the proposed work could be corrected, enriched, or otherwise improved. He then glided across the garden and the kitchen toward the library upstairs, only to reemerge from the dimness moments later with half a dozen books for me to borrow and read through. Before long, I began to work on my own book.

Those unforgettable exchanges with Albert—unforgettable for an atmosphere so special in how far it went beyond the ostensible scholarly and intellectual context—continued with every subsequent visit to London, until I appeared with a rough draft in the summer of 1992. He then left for Italy. Shortly after his return, having read the manuscript, he called me to come over to his house. No sooner had we begun to talk than I realized his health had been failing. Between coughs and wheezes, he went over my work with great care and detail, overflowing with suggestions that would improve it (not least of which was his insistence that I familiarize myself with the mystical thought of Ibn ʿArabi). Many times, I pleaded with him to allow me to leave so that he could rest. He rejected my pleas so firmly that nothing short of rudeness on my part would have cut short our discussion. When I left several hours later, I was overcome with sadness. My flight back to Virginia was booked for the following morning, and I feared I would not see him again. We exchanged a couple more letters before his death in January 1993.

With every change that I made, I tried to imagine Albert's reaction. And so I ended up with a harder task than that he had so kindly, generously, and unobtrusively set for me, and I can only hope that he would have been happy with the result.

The ideas that I was to share with Albert Hourani in the summer of 1988 had not grown and begun to crystallize coincidentally by then. Nine months earlier, at a dingy Persian café in Berkeley, when I had let out my thoughts regarding what had seemed like an imminent upsurge in the global spread of democracy, and I had ingenuously asserted that this might yet *undermine* freedom, my good friend Vedat Milor, who has since gone on to teach sociology at Brown University, reacted with infectious enthusiasm. He assured me that he had "never" encountered an approach like mine to the issues we were considering, and that it would be a shame if I failed to pursue the matter any further. There was, he believed, a completely original work in the making. I mention such details not in the name of self-aggrandizement, but only because nothing less would have diverted me from the more traditional areas of philosophy to which I had devoted myself.

Vedat also introduced me to the writings of Ernest Gellner. Although I have since developed my ability to see Gellner's work in a more critical light, it did show me that one can write about the Arab Muslim world in a colorful and imaginative fashion and yet display ample erudition. Vedat and his wife, Linda, then read the same "abstract" mentioned earlier and shared some preliminary remarks with me. Finally, I was to join them in Turkey in the fall of 1988, where I was to gain my first exposure to the scents, tones, and flavors of a non-Arab Middle Eastern country. Such was the intensity and uncanny warmth of what I imbibed, above all in Istanbul, that it would take the better part of a Proustian volume to do it justice. It is enough to say here that my thoughts, from then on, could reach their "objects" with a special intimacy, something that would later be reinforced as I read the works of Mardin, Hodgson, and Berque.

Şerif Mardin has also been crucial in the shaping of this book. Albert Hourani had introduced us at Cambridge University in the winter of 1989. He deftly brought us together for a few moments despite the commotion caused by the simultaneous attempts of hundreds of thinkers and scholars gathered there from near and far for his exquisite Tanner lectures to steal a few words with one another afterward before rushing back to their other professional duties. I was amazed that Mardin should remember me from this shortest of meetings and call me the following summer to ask if I would like to participate in a workshop he would chair the following December in Washington, D.C. It transpired as the occasion for me to present some of my work to a lively, friendly, distinguished interdisciplinary group of intellectuals (which reflects Mardin's admirable disdain for artificial boundaries when the breadth and depth of the subject at hand demand this). There were memorable exchanges with Seyyed Hossein Nasr, Roy Mottahedeh, Malise Ruthven, Engin Akarli, and Yusuf Ibish as a blizzard unfolded beyond the large picture window in the conference room atop the Bender Arena at the American University. Those exchanges helped shape my work at an early stage. Şerif and I have since become friends. Every conversation has been a delight, never repeating itself, always driven by a thoughtful man whose utterances often refract the riches that lay behind them.

That I had the privilege to get to know Seyyed Hossein Nasr better because of that snowbound workshop was but one of its felicitous by-products. We have met several times over the past four years. Seyyed Nasr is not one to discourage younger thinkers from focusing on difficult subjects while gently reminding them that their reflections ought to be backed with solid scholarship. In the comfort of his spacious office or over lunch at the faculty club at George Washington University, I have been able to probe metaphysical themes freely and sound him out on the limits to which the criteria for Islamic legitimacy can be taken. He is an example of how open a religious man can be to religions other than his, indeed an affirmation that a truly religious man can best exude such openness—for of what worth is it when the lukewarm show tolerance toward what they are inherently indifferent to?

Seyyed Nasr has since formed the "Washington Consortium for Islamic Studies," which he has kindly invited me to join. I have thus been able to meet several accomplished scholars, but this was after I had completed my manuscript. So although my interactions with them have often been fruitful, to mention them here would amount to dropping names. Majid Fakhry, however, is my neighbor and we have had a number of enjoyable outings and interesting conversations that have at least indirectly affected some of the contents of this book.

Someone who would surely be a key member of the consortium had he stayed in this area is James Piscatori. He was the first younger person whom Albert Hourani thought of when considering who, once I moved to the Washington, D.C., area, might take the strongest interest in my project. Our first meeting in Russell Square (London) was filled with verve and laughter. Subsequent meetings here and in Baltimore kept up the good spirits. Only the remoteness of the south of Wales and his incurable tendency to overwork himself, such is the excess of his generosity, have prevented James from continuing his watch over my work. But his extremely positive reaction in the initial stages was more than enough.

· · ·

As I turn to acknowledge those who have contributed to the philosophical content of my book, what better person to mention than my
close friend from long ago, Habib Malik? We have also been very good
enemies to each other, for we agree on just enough fundamental principles to dispute almost everything else. After many long sessions of vigorous argument in August 1989, which often went on late into the night, I
resolved to give my book an explicit philosophical dimension and framework that went well beyond the domain of the Arab Muslim world. It
always lay somewhere in my heart that the book ought to be philosophical, for philosophy is what I love the most. But years of grappling with
an academic-philosophical environment at the University of California at
Berkeley that by and large seemed to care little for philosophy itself had
taken their toll by way of a despondency that would thankfully fade
away as my participation in George McLean's seminars, held on the
campus of the Catholic University, became more and more active (of
which more shortly). That I returned to philosophy with the same spontaneity that had led me to study it formally at the highest level, I owe in no
small measure to Habib.

What about Father McLean, then? Quite simply, the seminar cycles
that he has periodically held, which group mostly professors together,
many of them from other countries—China, Lithuania, Austria, Nigeria,
Peru, and the Philippines, to mention only a few—have been an extraordinary forum for the unfettered presentation of ideas relating to some of
the most urgent issues facing the contemporary world, such as the moral
and cultural implications of global democratization (and modernization)
or the interplay between freedom and democracy. In particular, Father
McLean's ability to draw out hidden depths in one's thoughts is no less
subtle and sensistive than Hourani's. And he certainly does not clamp
down on boldness and originality. In his company and that of the good
and learned people gathered for his seminars, the philosophical core of
my book was first sketched and articulated, above all in the paper that I
read in the spring of 1991 in which I tried to clarify the difference between
freedom and unfreedom in metaphysical terms.

Among the many persons that I have met through Father McLean,
special mention must be made of Professors Ji Shu-Li, Heinz Holley,
László Tengelyi, Yu Xuan-Meng, and Joseph Donders. Ji Shu-Li, from
the University of Shanghai, opened the floodgates in his critique of the
persistent and creeping imposition of norms only partly valid in the
physical sciences on all walks of life, in China as well as in the West (and
elsewhere). This propelled my participation to the point where McLean
urged me to prepare and contribute a paper on science and values in the
context of the relentless drive to democratize, when a few weeks earlier
he did not even know me! It is thanks to Habib that I was there at all, for
he had told McLean about me and persuaded him to have me join the

seminar as an observer. This was in the autumn of 1990. More than two years later, as an active member of those seminars, I was to meet Heinz Holley (Johannes Kepler Universität Linz), László Tengelyi (Eötvös Lo-ránd University in Budapest), and Yu Xuan-Meng (Shanghai Academy of Social Sciences). Heinz and László eagerly drew upon the intellectual treasures of central European culture as we struggled to arrive at a fair definition and assessment of modernity. My critique of modernity has thus become more nuanced. Yu Xuan-Meng is one of the most genuine thinkers I have ever met. How refreshing it was to stammer our way through recondite fields without the slightest regard for formal trifles. He built invisible but powerful bridges buttressed by his personal interpreta-tion of the masterpieces of ancient Chinese thought and wisdom, bridges that I have yet to cross often enough to no longer fear the abysses they span. Father Donders, a jolly and humane missionary from Holland, and a regular member of the seminars, is a font of gemlike anecdotes that shed light on the elusive effort to approach other peoples empathically. And Osman Bilem provided additional perspectives on cultural develop-ments in Turkey since 1800.

Although Paul Feyerabend, who sadly died in 1994, did not know about this book, he did have much to do with some of what eventually went into it. To portray him here would take us too far afield. Besides, he has done the job himself in his recently published autobiography. Suffice to say that he reawakened a youthful interest in science that had vanished in the dreariness of many among the courses that I had to complete for my engineering degree (before I decided to commit myself to philoso-phy). As is well known, his philosophy of science is highly controversial. But no one can question the learning behind it, the brilliance with which it is expressed, and his admiration for those exceptional individuals who have made science what it is (as opposed to the technicians who trundle about their laboratories and algorithms, which the public often confounds with science). In his emphasis on the art in science, on how its most illustrious exponents have always leaped with their imagination, in how much more lay behind it than the dim and dull picture drawn up by the large contingent of mechanically minded modernizers, he has made an invaluable contribution toward the restoration of the dignity of all human endeavors—and that of the beings who undertake them. It has been my good fortune to have taken part in many of his graduate seminars, and for him to have become one of my doctoral thesis advisers. Having been his teaching assitant more than once, I have been privy to his pedagogical methods at every level of university instruction. A good Feyerabend lecture had the aura of a great recital, a residue perhaps of his boyhood aspiration to become a tenor at the opera.

Hans Sluga, the main adviser for my doctoral thesis, also merits grati-tude. He allowed me to write my dissertation in the spirit of a budding philosopher. When I set out to write this book, I therefore already had the experience of giving my thought free rein, then ordering it into an extended work that would meet the approval of able and demanding judges. Charles Taylor and Aryeh Kosman showed me, the one in his philosophy, the other in his unique approach to ancient Greek thought, how a philosopher could advance within esoteric domains without sacrificing rigor or clarity. Alas, their tenure as visiting professors was all too brief.

A word of thanks, too, for those at Syracuse University Press who helped in the publication of this book, especially Cynthia Maude-Gembler, John Fruehwirth, Tom Seller, Mehrzad Boroujerdi, and all those who work so hard to make room for such books in a busy and complex market.

My mother and father have been exemplary in their support. At the very least, I ought to mention that they have never done anything to stifle my curiosity. On the contrary, in their company, the world has often seemed worthy of a lifetime of exploration, be it on the political, geographical, scientific, musical, or literary planes. They have not wished that my life be forced down banal byways, for they have consistently treated me as though I could do better. It would be nice if this were but the first installment in a long oeuvre of gratitude. Whether I shall be up to it remains to be seen. When I came close to losing faith some years ago, my brother Raymond intervened decisively. Now is the time for him to know how much it has meant. My sister Doris also deserves my thanks.

The list of family and friends to whom I indirectly owe so much regarding this work is blessedly long, but belongs in an autobiography that I have not earned the right to write. They surely know themselves. Among them are several close Muslim friends who, over many years, have shown how very far their spirit of brotherhood extends to those from other religions who neither fear nor look down on them.

In this more personal vein, however, may I take the liberty to recall how Odile Hourani infused my dinners with Albert and her at their home with her spry wit. In her love of well-wrought things past, she embodies the subject for which they both have shared an enduring passion.

I may also finally turn to Hania. To say that my wife has been patient and pleasant throughout years of work with uncertain practical consequences is to understate her virtues. Among them are those that emanate from what used to be signified by a four-letter word, with an *l* and a *v* in it, that has been abused unto uselessness.

Falls Church, Virginia   Richard K. Khuri
August 1, 1995

Introduction

The travails that thwart the attainment of the good life in the contemporary Arab Muslim world are almost cruelly many. A short list includes Bangladeshis ever in doubt whether their land shall feed or drown them, Afghans led to absurd fratricide soon after a heroic and successful war of liberation against the Soviets, Iraqis pained beyond tears by an unusually callous and violent despot, Lebanese bullied into silence amid free-falling living standards, Palestinians still mostly deprived of their homes and long mistreated by their brethren, southern Sudanese starved and terrorized by northern fanatics, and unemployed Algerian young men whose rage and despair make some of them dream of sweeping the streets of New York City while schoolgirls who dare seek an education have their throats slit. The freedom longed for by those faced with such injustice can hardly extend beyond its most obvious dimensions: freedom constitutionally guaranteed by elected governments, and freedom to believe and say what they please and attain modest material comfort. Most people in the Arab Muslim world therefore think of freedom from war, poverty, fanatics, or the secret police, the kind of freedom many of them live vicariously in television programs imported from the United States or those in its cultural orbit.

There is no doubt that the peoples of the Arab Muslim world deserve freedom from want and abuse. For this, they and those abroad who empathize with them ought to strive without pause. However, prolonged, widespread, and severe injustice has prevented those involved in the struggle against it from seeing that there is more freedom to be sought than the freedom from want and abuse. Here unexpected problems may arise as they have already arisen elsewhere. For given the present political, economic, and cultural realities of the world, one can envisage what will follow the anticipated liberation. The dominant global trends are clear. They enable one to legitimately wonder whether freedom, as people everywhere think or are made to think about it, has a strangely hollow feel. What if the freedom won pertained to a very limited aspect of each human being, with the rest quietly left to wither? What if the dream and all the pain, courage, and sacrifice to realize it were to dissipate in the consumer "paradise" and the frantic impersonal work needed to sustain it? What if the cultures in which freedom can go far in depth and meaning were to fall apart, only for the fragments to be picked up and marketed as packaged nostalgia? Who would the newly free be, and what would their freedom amount to?

Such fears have been monopolized by extremists and fanatics in the public arena. They have also been exploited by despots, plutocrats, and those who allege that the Arab Muslim world is congenitally incapable of economic or technological advance. It must therefore be firmly stated at the outset that the arguments advanced in this book ought not by any stretch of the imagination serve as apologia for such people and their odious deeds. On the contrary, the intention here is to deepen the freedom that they obstruct. The reasonableness of the foregoing questions is affirmed as part of a broad contribution toward a more substantial freedom, one more commensurate with human nature and potential, and certainly one not inconsistent with freedom from want and abuse. In contrast with the demagoguery of those who feed greed or frenzied cries for cultural authenticity, the aim here is to portray freedom in a manner worthy of human beings and examine the relevant possible contributions of both Islam *and* modernity.

How much modernity contributes to freedom depends on the condition in which modernity finds itself, and on how well it is understood or appreciated. The history of modernity begins with various factors, among them that human beings wished to assert themselves in a dignified manner as the free individuals they believed they were, and that this freedom was in the end a spiritual concern. If these be understood as among modernity's original motives, then much that today passes for modernity represents a trivialization and diminution of its historical scope. This is a worldwide problem. As far as the Arab Muslim world is concerned, the problem is magnified by the whole question of "modernization." On which modernity is modernization based—that which revitalizes or that which trivializes human freedom? If modernization programs are based on the second, then theirs is at best a shallow contribution to the freedom of individuals in the Arab Muslim world.

When reform-minded individuals in the Arab Muslim world speak of modernization, what they have in mind is modernity as they have known and encountered it over the past century or so. What they and their adversaries call "modernity" is therefore the usually trivialized and diminished version of modernity that has predominated in our time. The failure to appreciate the true scope of modernity on both sides, reformist and traditionalist, results first in the effort to implement modernization programs that do not add substantially to the freedom of the individuals concerned, and may even take away from it, and hence second in hostility toward modernity.

In a world dominated by a trivialized and diminished version of modernity, it is admittedly difficult to regain comprehension of modernity's original scope. But it is important that this be done if one has an interest in the more encompassing conception of freedom that informed some of modernity's greatest thinkers and inspired people to sacrifice mightily for its attainment. It is especially important if one wishes to break out of one of the worse vicious circles that have afflicted the Arab Muslim world, namely, that which begins with the attempt to impose a shallow modernity, which is followed, as we shall see, by a revolt in the name of an equally shallow version of Islam.

To better appreciate how modernity can contribute substantially to freedom, it will then be necessary to first show how it has failed to do so. Part of this failure lies in how modernity has become identified with reason and rationality, how these have become identified with science, and how science has become identified with mechanism. In many parts of the world, to modernize effectively means to mechanize. But because whatever is mechanized is entirely predictable, and perfect predictability is entirely contrary to freedom, it follows that the more people and their society become mechanized, the less free they are. The way back to freedom lies partly in showing how poorly mechanism represents science, how poorly science represents reason, and how much more there is to modernity than what can be rationally justified. Science for its part will (briefly) be shown as an activity that transcends the scope of reason when it reaches the highest level, that is, when we deal with science from the standpoint of those who advance it rather than those who reiterate those advances in laboratories or behind their computers. Reason too will (also briefly) be shown to have comprised far more than the elementary logical operations to which it has been reduced, and in its broadest form will be seen as open to the transcendent ideas and realities that have guided the best modern thought and activity.

If one imagines what lies within each human being as a series of concentric circles, then the smallest may be filled with mechanical activity, a larger one with mundane science and reason, one much larger with all that science and reason could encompass, and a very large one indeed with all that has been comprehended by modernity at its peak. Freedom will hence be defined in terms of how fully a human being is permitted to flourish as a whole. The larger the "circle" within a human being covered by freedom, the more truly free one is.

A better appreciation of modernity will then reveal it as irreducible to what either mechanism, science, or reason can tell us. Science and reason themselves must also be understood for what they can be irrespective of any reductionism. With a broader view of science, reason, and modernity, based on what has been thought and done, a broader context can be established for freedom, one that provides far more scope for the individual human being to flourish as a whole. At this point we can speak of freedom. Also at this point, an authentic convergence can be found between modernity and Islam.

Just as the shallow version of modernity that currently predominates makes it difficult for us to retrieve modernity's full scope, so does the shallow conception of freedom that accompanies it obscure the extent of the domain of human freedom. A book whose central theme is freedom ought to present as rich a conception of it as possible. Only then would it make sense to consider where modernity and Islam stand with regard to their respective contributions to freedom.

We may distinguish between two kinds of freedom. To clarify the distinction, let us present two hypothetically extreme worlds. In the first kind, there is great occupational mobility and an endless variety of opinions and consumer goods; in the second, there are serious economic and political limitations. In the first, however, individuals are unattached to people and places, friendless with their relatives far away, and live and work in impersonal buildings; but in the second, they are surrounded with family and friends, live in familiar neighborhoods over generations, and have a strong sense of identity and purpose. The first world, for all the dazzle, is hollow; the second, for all the warts, full. The first presupposes materialistic, self-interested human beings; the second considers them beings with a spiritual dimension who take a natural interest in their communities.

If we take the foregoing two worlds as theoretical limiting cases, then one way to look at each society and the freedom that prevails in it is by seeing to which it is closer. There is little doubt that the present wave of modernity is creating environments that presuppose self-interested, materialistic individuals, environments that in the future will favor and spawn individuals in the image of those presuppositions. On the other hand, Islamic societies, whatever the extent of their difficulties and shortcomings, are modeled on a worldview that attaches great importance to spirituality and community. This is not to say that Islam is incompatible with *any* version of modernity, nor does it suggest that whatever today bears the name "Islamic" is immune to materialism and self-interest. But the shallow version of modernity now in vogue, and Islam as traditionally articulated and practiced (an Islam that still resonates), do contrast neatly as suggested here.

The two kinds of freedom that must be explained to understand the respective emphases of the prevalent version of modernity and Islam have been called "negative" and "positive" freedom. "Negative" freedom is defined in terms of the removal of as many barriers as possible in the way of the realization of plans made by individuals, whether they act alone or in voluntary association. Originally, when the scope of modernity was far broader than today, it was assumed, and sometimes taken for granted, that the individuals who made those plans were rational, had a good will, and had the interests of the whole of humanity at heart. But through a process that we have just begun to understand, modernity gave birth to practices and institutions that steadily eroded those qualities and ended up favoring individuals with a self-interested, materialistic bent. Thus today, liberation through removal of as many barriers as possible is not to enable individuals to express their freedom as moral beings and form stable and prosperous communites, but to carry out plans that reflect a materialistic, self-interested outlook.

If negative freedom concentrates on the removal of barriers so that individuals may realize their plans, "positive" freedom concentrates on the *quality* of those "plans." It is better not to think of plans, but of all that a human being does given the freedom to do whatever one wishes. How free is an individual when his actions reflect a very limited range of his humanity? How free, for instance, is a human being driven to act and think mechanically most of his waking hours, and then spend the remainder passively, in a state of near vegetation? From the standpoint of positive freedom, what matters is the range of an individual's humanity that is expressed in one's desires, beliefs, feelings, thoughts, words, and actions. An individual in whom the full human range is well developed is far more able to exercise her freedom, and so be far more free, than one in whom most of that range has suffered neglect. The former individual, for instance, does not get carried away by fashionable desires nor mimics feelings that are commercially induced, but has strong and genuine feelings and can reflect on her desires and order them according to a clear view of what must be done to become the best possible human being.

Positive freedom, then, is a measure of how free individuals really are. This measure is patently exposed when the liberties characteristic of modern democracies have been won. Only an intellectual élitist, however, would maintain that individuals will cultivate the greatest extent of their humanity if left to their own devices. Usually, whether individuals are pulled toward the full range of their humanity or channeled along narrow domains within it depends on their environment. A family or a society that cherishes human life as a whole is more likely to nurture individuals who will care about the full range of their humanity than one that does not. Positive freedom is hence also about the sustenance of an environment that adequately nurtures human life in all its fullness. It pertains to the human being as a complex totality, with emotional, intellectual, and spiritual needs besides the material needs already acknowledged. Thus anonymity and impersonalism would constitute severe limitations on freedom. For part of what it is to be human is precisely to be treated as a person and given a sense of familiarity with one's peers other than the feigned familiarity of clusters of individuals who address one another on a first-name basis but do not exude the least personal considerations.

Positive freedom is therefore profoundly linked with the debate over what it is to be human and, based on that, with what it is that makes humans flourish.

It is clear that modernity as we mostly run into it today is far more closely associated with negative than with positive freedom, whereas the reverse is often the case within Islamic circles. *But the attainment of freedom requires emphasis on both its negative and positive dimensions.* In the absence of a view that takes individuals to have moral and spiritual concerns that enlarge the scope of their humanity and reflect well on their communal existence, the reduction of freedom to its negative aspect entails indifference to how much of their humanity individuals cultivate. Such reduction encourages them to channel their lives along narrow domains. That this was not so at an earlier stage of modernity is because common moral and spiritual values were widely recognized, at least unofficially. But the more unofficial the recognition became, the more apparent it was that morally and spiritually, people lived on borrowed time. As increasingly powerful public and private institutions treated individuals as though they were primarily self-interested and materialistic, more and more individuals conformed with that image. Thus in our contemporary world, we can no longer suppose that when individuals are guaranteed negative freedom, they will go on to live in a manner worthy of their humanity.

Conversely, if negative freedom were ignored for the sake of positive freedom, then nothing would prevent a group of self-appointed guardians with a powerful dogma or ideology from taking over a society and forcing everybody to follow "the best way" to express their freedom. Pluralism is therefore essential to ensure that no self-appointed guarantors of positive freedom take too much upon themselves and become oppressors.

Hence, if modernity should recall the positive aspect of freedom present at its origins and articulated by some of its greatest thinkers, then Islam should pay more attention than it has to negative freedom for it to remain a bulwark of moral and spiritual support and not be tempted toward theocracy.

There is no a priori reason for the rejection of theocracy. In the Middle Ages, it might well have been the best among the available choices. What makes theocracy a bad idea today has mostly to do with profound social, political, and economic changes that have become reflected in the modern state. The power available to the state today is unprecedented. So is the complexity of the affairs that it has to manage. Although these affairs may bear in varying degrees on moral and spiritual life, their management demands a thoroughly secular style. Clerics, Muslim or otherwise, who directly involve themselves in running a state thus risk a grave threat to the frame of mind in harmony with their calling. Moreover, with the vast power at their disposal, the temptation to abuse it grows proportionately. On both counts, the clerics would fail the faithful. In our terms, they would undermine freedom negatively and positively.

When we turn to Islam in particular, we find that theocracy today is likely to sap its moral and spiritual vitality. It is useful to keep in mind—and this will be argued in the book—that the original doctrine that links Islam with the state did not pertain to anything like what the state has recently evolved into, but to a state so small as to be better thought a community. For doctrinal and pragmatic reasons, and for the sake of the moral and spiritual interests of Muslims and those who live among them, Islam must distance itself from the modern state.

However, the modern state has shown itself to be inadequate where Islam is best, namely, with regard to the inner life of a society, to what really holds it together, to the emotional, moral, and spiritual fabric of life. In these domains, Islam like other great religious traditions has very much to offer. If the state ought to guarantee negative freedom, with which all must comply, then those who work in the name of Islam ought to play their part in the creation of an environment worthy of human beings and their freedom.

Islam in the past has given rise to vibrant, cohesive communities, in which individuals have readily found their moorings and sense of purpose. This effort has been spearheaded by two groups: the scholars and jurists, who meticulously studied, applied, and sometimes carefully revised the laws that would perpetuate the paradigm Muslim community, for which different Muslim sects and schools of law had different definitions; and the mystics, who, especially when scholars and jurists were co-opted by the state, were propelled into the role of informal spiritual leaders, and at all times helped carry the faithful to new heights and capacities to experience the fullness of being. Both groups remain influential throughout the Arab Muslim world. Their heritage forms one of the principal sources for whatever positive freedom will take hold there in the future. It is therefore important not only to recapture Islam's long history of significant contributions to the positive freedom of the faithful but also to point out a current generation of thinkers steeped in that history and aware of the modern condition as well, so that a new and effective synthesis may be forged to set the appropriate framework for freedom in the Arab Muslim world. Both the historical and contemporary dimensions will hence be amply discussed.

Whatever the great potential of Islam with regard to freedom, however, it will not have escaped the attention of many people that those Muslims who today most actively pressure the state into creating a more coherent and purposeful environment often advocate specific measures that do not constitute more substantial freedom. How, one may ask, do the ban on alcohol, the closure of cinemas, the silencing of musicians, the exaggerated veiling of women, or the murder of alleged apostates contribute to freedom? They do not. They represent a trivialization of Islam's potential to contribute immeasurably to freedom. This is the mirror image of the trivialization that currently sweeps through modernity. Several Muslims anguished over the moral chaos and spiritual vacuum that seem to await them have already unknowingly been stripped of the ability to delve into their faith to break out of the cycle of trivialization.

But Muslims who yearn for more coherence and purpose, yet find themselves unable to call up the rich cumulative resources of Islam, have also been distanced from it for internal reasons. Thus, we shall see that the victory of orthodoxy in the Middle Ages and the rise of state-sponsored Islam have had a deleterious effect. Only exceptional Muslims can effectively draw on their tradition and steer it toward a convergence with what must be done today and in generations to come.

Traditional Islam itself has also unwittingly and indirectly led to some of the deprivations that prevail in our time. For instance, it has been noticed that Muslims are often passive in the face of despotism. This passivity goes back to the old custom based on a controversial interpretation of a Qur'anic verse that enjoins Muslims to obey those in authority. The custom became cherished in the classical Islamic era and thereafter because of the frequency of internecine warfare and, later, foreign invasion. Any stability, save for the most unimaginably cruel, was preferred to a breakdown of order. But it will be argued that this custom has become anachronistic and, given the nature and power of the modern state, self destructive. The failure of Muslim scholars and thinkers to appreciate how drastically historical developments can alter the effective meaning of certain Islamically sanctioned injunctions has therefore deprived Muslims of their freedom, sometimes to an astonishing degree. But the task of Muslim intellectual and spiritual leaders ought to be made easier by the fact that those injunctions typically involve controversial interpretations of Qur'anic verses, interpretations that have definitely become falsified because their application seriously harms the welfare of Muslims, which no Muslim can believe is the intention of the Qur'an.

The causes for the lack of freedom in the Arab Muslim world that may directly or indirectly be attributed to prevalent interpretations and applications of Islam can then be seen in the victory of orthodoxy and the ensuant ossification. As a result, the ability of thinkers within the Arab Muslim milieu to challenge modernity with a viable alternative or synthesis has been compromised.

Three relevant developments that have contributed to undermine freedom can thus be pointed out: (1) the general shallowness (and fanaticism) of those who wage war against a trivialized modernity in the name of Islam, (2) habitual passivity in the face of despotism, and (3) a continued insistence that Islam become intertwined with the modern state, which in its nature and structure can only adversely affect an Islam theocratically intertwined with it and so harm the community of believers. But the reader will only be led to these later in the book, against a backdrop of the great expansion of the realm of freedom, positively understood, that has been possible under Islam, and which is the font of any real freedom that Muslims are to enjoy once more, and any real tolerance that they may show toward the non-Muslims in their midst.

If the vicious circle of trivialization and hostility into which both Islam and modernity have been drawn is one of this book's principal themes, then a more important theme is perhaps that of the broader view of both Islam and modernity and how it may release them to mutually reinforce each other to better serve the cause of freedom and make human life worthy of its potential. The freedom of individuals depends on the breadth and depth of their world. If it is limited and deformed by a trivialized modernity, based on a near caricature of freedom, reason, and science, or by a trivialized Islam, based on a near caricature of the first community of Muslims and the manner of its applicability over time, then however much choice an individual may or may not have, one's freedom would not go very far. If, on the other hand, modernity were to free itself from the shackles of criteria that mostly relate to economic efficiency, technological advancement, and consumerism, and were to return to its rootedness in a broad vision of human nature, then freedom would grow from that identified with an abundance of choice within a narrow domain to that characterized by an abundance of possibility within an infinite domain. Freedom would grow toward the same end, but from a different beginning, were those who act in the name of Islam to understand the difference between what is traditional and what is static, and the corresponding difference between a dynamic past and an invariant past. What is sufficiently valuable and profound to endure does so precisely because it is dynamic, because it is such that it can merge with and shape individuals and communities across temporal and geographical boundaries. Yet to transcend these boundaries does not mean to remain the same in the trivial sense of sameness, in the sense that dress and grammar and artistic styles ought to remain the same. Whatever is truly eternal can be expressed over and over again, each time anew, in a manner that makes it familiar to those who encounter it. To deny the eternal that ability is to reduce it to the fetishes of an illusory past.

Freedom is thus diminished by a trivialized modernity that offers an abundance of illusory choices and a trivialized Islam that limits itself to an illusory past. It is restored when the past is freed from the fears that freeze it and when modernity fixes its gaze more on what choices truly further human life than on maximum choice for its own sake.

On such high ground, there can be a genuine and fruitful meeting between modernity and Islam, and meaningful freedom for all concerned. This book is mostly about that high ground and what is involved in its reconstitution on both sides.

There are signs that the present confrontational stance between Islam and the West, which is far from being their sole mode of interaction, may develop into open conflict. This confrontation, however, is really between the political leadership of a trivialized modernity and the Islamic movement that has become its mirror image. Both sides stand to lose. The more ground gained by a trivialized modernity, the less free those who live within its world—and this is a global predicament. Similarly for those who suffer the proportionate Islamic reaction. It remains to be seen whether modernity and traditions everywhere, and not just in the Arab Muslim world, will metamorphose peacefully into their broader aspects, or whether this can only come about catastrophically.

Were Islam for its part allowed to regain its verve and scope among those who populate the bleak landscape described in the opening paragraph of this introduction, then at least despair, anger, and hatred would be mitigated. And were the bleakness to finally give way to freedom from want and abuse, then a resplendent Islam could build on the euphoria and ensure that the hard-won liberties do not fade into the indulgence of the whims or fancies that faintly color the lives of the atrophied.

. . .

The principal themes that may be extracted from the foregoing overview, and which unify the contents of this book, are the following:

1. How much freedom there is depends as much on the removal of obstacles in the way of human activity as on the quality of that activity after those obstacles have been removed. In technical terms, it depends as much on its negative as on its positive aspect.

2. For freedom to be exercised in a manner worthy of human beings and their potential, there must be an appropriate environment. The exercise of freedom is not context free.

3. Freedom has been severely restricted for those committed to a reductionistic and by now trivialized version of modernity. It has been likewise restricted for those in the Arab Muslim world for whom centuries of orthodoxy have entailed limited or programmed thought and action at many levels. It has become even more restricted for those caught in the vicious circle set in motion by a reductionistic modernity imposed on the Arab Muslim world by both internal and external powers, and a corresponding Islamic reaction that in the intensity of the confrontation loses sight of the depth and scope of Islam.

4. Were modernity to regain its original spirit, the conditions for freedom would be tremendously improved. A similar change would result from an authentic renewal of Islamic vibrancy, for much freedom had been possible within an Islamic framework.

5. Because the encounter between Islam and modernity is destined to continue, as are the two fated to become further intertwined, the best context for freedom would be in place against the backdrop of a viable, original synthesis between Islam and modernity (and indeed, wherever local traditions remain vital and resonant, between those and modernity. The themes stated here have global import were the argument transposed from Islam to any other similarly encompassing local tradition, and appropriately adjusted).

It can be readily seen that the freedoms at the forefront of the present global democratization are not given priority within the perspective defined by the five themes just stated. This is not to say that those freedoms are trivial, but that they will be trivialized if the deeper freedom emphasized throughout this book, and the worldviews that make it possible, are ignored.

It is impossible to divide the foregoing five themes among individual chapters given the manner in which they are interrelated. However, there is a certain symmetry in the structure of the book, so that the chapter that contains a focused discussion of freedom is in the middle, preceded by those that trace the reductionistic streak running through modernity, and followed by those that first show the scope for freedom under Islam in the past, and then the limitations on freedom attributable directly or indirectly to the prevalent interpretations and applications of Islam. All these chapters are framed by the first chapter, which deals with the vicious circle that results from the antagonism between a reductionistic modernity and a proportionate Islamic reaction (that also has a domestic component, rooted in movements across the Arab Muslim world to revitalize religious life perceived by reformers as decrepit by the eighteenth century); and the last chapter, which presents the elements of a hoped for synthesis between a modernity restored to its broad original scope and a revitalized Islam once again true to its multifaceted accomplishments, a synthesis that would provide the best setting for the realization of freedom.

What follows is a summary of all seven chapters. The summary gives away the general contents of my work, so some explanation for my decision is in order. The contemporary American reader of books that have an academic or scholarly flavor has been led to expect to be told, usually in so many words, exactly what is going on at every stage of the argument. Academic papers thus almost always open with a paragraph that includes statements such as "In this paper I shall do _____ or _____," with similar statements occurring in every main section. The practice has also become characteristic of longer academic works. This practice has been instituted for the sake of clarity, but like many other well-intentioned practices, it has become counterproductive. It now makes one expect to be spared the need to work out the contents and direction of an argument for oneself, and thus to diminish considerably the extent to which one becomes engaged in a work as a thinking reader.

Not only for aesthetic reasons do I recoil from that practice but also because I have an innate respect for the curiosity and intelligence of my readers. Moreover, because my work is written for an international audience, one must heed the fact that in Europe, for example, readers still prefer to find out for themselves where a book is leading them. I am confident that a great many Americans share that attitude. I shall therefore provide the summary that follows only to satisfy the informal professional requirement that one spell out what one is doing and to avoid having to do so repeatedly in the main body of the text. I also do this out of consideration for whoever may find this book difficult. In other words, those who want to know the "plot" in advance should keep referring to the summary. Those who prefer otherwise ought to ignore the next several pages and proceed to pages xxxvi–xli of this introduction, where I account for some of my other prejudices and procedural decisions.

In order then, chapter 1 presents the well-intentioned but shallow and improperly conceived modernization schemes pursued vigorously by the Ottoman and Egyptian authorities in the nineteenth century as a prologue to the more full-fledged schemes characteristic of the twentieth. This presentation is followed by the argument that those schemes run directly counter to local traditions and values and end by undermining the very societies they were meant to benefit. Islamic extremists then appear on the scene either to preempt the disintegration of society as they see it or to reverse already existing trends. But more often than not, they have neither an adequate understanding of modernity nor of Islam. Consequently, many in the Arab Muslim world find the domain of their freedom narrowed on both sides: neither (usually secular) modernizers nor their Islamic revolutionary adversaries have promised or delivered much freedom.

Because chapter 1 leaves us with the adverse effects of a vicious circle formed by the antagonism between powers acting on behalf of reductionistic views of both modernity and Islam, the most effective antidote is to overcome such reductionism on both sides. Freedom would then be immeasurably enhanced under a broad synthesis between Islam and modernity. Here we arrive by the end of the book. Chapter 2 lays some groundwork for a better understanding of modernity, by way of a focus on how it has been subjected to reductionism and later trivialized. Such an understanding is the first step toward bringing about the desired synthesis, particularly because modernity has been introduced into the Arab Muslim world almost exclusively in a reductionistic or trivialized vein. This makes it all the harder for people there to appreciate modernity's potential. Besides, one must not underestimate how difficult it has become to appreciate modernity's potential even in societies where it has advanced the most, for today the diminished view of modernity is confused everywhere with modernity as a historical development laden with possibility.

Specifically, chapter 2 exposes the dual myth of sovereign reason and its alleged singular contribution to scientific thought, a myth at the center of received views of modernity, the resultant reductionism, and the modernization programs derived therefrom. I argue there that reason is always guided by something else, be it our moral and social ends or, within science, by thematic preferences that scientists are the first to concede have an aesthetic or metaphysical basis. Such thematic preferences involve the choice, for instance, between finitude or infinity, between a steady state or an expanding universe, and between one with a beginning or one without it. These choices cannot be made scientifically, and yet entire physical and cosmological theories (and the technologies that they have made possible) depend on them. The aim of this argument is to show that there is no *theoretical* basis for modernization programs equated with rationalization, for even in science, certainly at the highest level, much more than just reason is involved. More important, at the practical level, the argument aims to show that just as science would be impoverished were it restricted to whatever "sovereign" reason may lead to, then how much more would individuals and societies have to lose were they to live within a thoroughly rationalized institutional framework. In that sense, to confine freedom strictly to the domain of "sovereign" reason would be to severely restrict it—for freedom would then be given to people otherwise forced by "rationalized" institutions and peer pressure to live within a narrow range of their humanity. In short, it would be a spurious freedom.

Chapter 3 is thus an overview of how freedom has been restricted to narrow domains because of dogmatic adherence to the primacy of "sovereign" reason. The chapter begins with a first impression of how we are to think of freedom (a more extended discussion follows in chapter 4). The Kantian view of freedom is taken as a model, but only to start with. The model is then modified because the distinction that Kant made between the spatiotemporal world and the transcendent realm is not as radical as once thought (we may think of the transcendent realm as meaning at the level of person or world when each is taken as a whole). The complexity of the world is such that it leaves much room for expression and maneuver. And personality is such that it eludes all attempts at complete analysis. Because, contrary to what Kant believed, it is not the case that everything in space and time can be known or predicted, freedom exists at both the spatiotemporal and transcendent levels. So Kant was mistaken in linking freedom exclusively with the transcendent realm. But freedom is intimately linked with the transcendent realm because freedom itself is a transcendence. No matter what we may be, we are always free to act as if motivated by a world that is ideal relative to the world as we usually know it. If we had no such motivation, morality would lose its foundation. Moreover, if we had no such motivation, we would gradually find that the world in which we are free is getting smaller and smaller, in the sense that there is less and less to be really free for.

Most of chapter 3 is therefore devoted to reflections on how the domain of freedom shrinks in the absence of transcendence. I begin with a general account of my own that I subsequently support with the perspectives of six authors. The first three (Berque, Habermas, and Broch) provide us with various elements of a general theory of how we have ended up with a more stifling world than we should have, the other three (Reich, Bellah, and Mardin) descriptions of such stiflement (Reich unwittingly). The idea that unifies those accounts is that a world exclusively composed of what can be supported through "sovereign" reason can only be a material world because everything else depends on other abilities that human beings have (such as intuition, imagination, aptitudes like those associated with the arts, and what has traditionally been called "intellection"). In such a rationalist environment, it comes as no surprise that what has flourished above all has been the drive to improve our material conditions to the greatest possible extent. The concatenation of systems and institutions now in place to support such an increasingly obsessive drive has therefore largely become the framework within which the freedom of individuals is exercised. In other words, we have arrived at a situation where human freedom is expressed (and human energy expended) overwhelmingly in the context of the drive to improve material conditions. This represents a serious deformation of human life and consequently a systematic and considerable restriction on freedom. Nevertheless, it is hoped that a better understanding of how the scope of modernity has been narrowed will help in the formation of a broader and deeper conception of modernity in the spirit of its Renaissance origins.

Chapter 4 makes an oblique contribution to the restoration of a more salutary conception of modernity by way of an extended elucidation of the different elements of freedom. Because this elucidation is entirely modern, it suggests how far modernity can diverge from how it has generally come across. The chapter begins with the assertion that the elements of freedom to be expounded upon are implicit in the many-sided critique that dominated chapter 3. For instance, that critique is consistently informed by the belief that freedom can be closely linked with the expansion of the realm of human existence to its furthest limits. Because a transcendent reality and the values associated with it have traditionally furnished boundless domains for the growth of the human intellect and soul, and for emotional expression, freedom may be associated with affinity for transcendence. And because this affinity has been *sometimes* made concrete and accessible in a community's ability to sustain a daily mode of life permeated with transcendence, then to be part of a *good, healthy* community takes up a significant portion of freedom in the aftermath of liberation (which, together with choice, is often what is on people's minds today when they think of freedom).

Liberation, I go on to argue in chapter 4, guarantees negative freedom for the parties concerned. So it is only a step on the way, to fail to look beyond which would deliver the liberated straight into the grinding mill of hyperconsumerism and frenetic technological progress. The fashionable tendency to nearly equate freedom with liberation is hence misguided.

An extended definition of negative and positive freedom is next given as a pivot for the movement from empty to meaningful choice. The positive freedom that must follow liberation is discussed first in terms of the community, for it often stresses the quality of the freedom to be exercised and the meaningfulness of the choices made. The role of the community is decisive in the attainment of freedom for three reasons:

1. Communities are partly forged by shared values and accumulated insights that over time amount to a moral and practical wisdom beyond what any individual can attain in a lifetime. Such wisdom helps orient the individual in a purposeful manner, thus turning the exercise of his freedom away from the forces that threaten it with dissipation.

2. A good community would regard individuals as persons, as whole human beings, irrespective of their social or economic function. A human being is then free to live as a whole and not disfigure his humanity by identifying his worth with one thing (such as his standing in a corporation or sport).

3. Such a community adds to the positive freedom of its members because it recognizes the transcendent source of its orientation. This enables the domain of purposeful activity to be expanded to one virtually without bounds.

Directed boundlessness is the central theme in the description of individual personal freedom that forms the last part of chapter 4. But this difficult theme is introduced gently, first by means of several examples of how the world as we experience it is far more open than it need be, as though to already invite the extension of our freedom. It is the freedom to which we are called by poets, architects, and musicians, by nature itself, our moral lives, and religion. Much of what we freely do appears as if in response to a transcendent world. The more we acknowledge this transcendence, the less elusive it seems. The discussion hence ends with the individual's encounter with transcendence and how, as the presence of transcendent reality assumes greater clarity and fullness in that individual's life, the occasion arises for the domain of freedom to turn infinite and yet retain its sense of directedness.

With chapter 5, we return to stay in applied philosophy. In particular, it is hoped that some of the difficulties in the discussion of freedom in chapter 4 will be alleviated once they are transposed to the Arab Muslim world, where the dimensions of positive freedom previously discussed in general will be shown in the flesh, so to speak. The two main dimensions of positive freedom can be recapitulated as follows:

1. The freedom within a community that gives individuals a social and moral identity, recognizes them as persons, and invites them to be open to a transcendent reality.

2. The freedom experienced by the individual who encounters the boundlessness of the world and what lay beyond it and yet experiences these as the meaningful domain of plenitude.

These will be respectively linked with the paradigm Muslim community and the mystical tradition in Islam (Sufism).

Much light is shed on the paradigm Muslim community through an overview of its genesis and the principles that gradually shaped it. These principles conform with the more mature definition of rationality developed by Habermas in a Kantian spirit. So chapter 5 begins with a brief presentation of rationality as understood by Kant and Habermas to give intellectual perspective to what is concretely known about the structure of Muslim communities. Islam can therefore be convincingly linked with an adequate conception of rationality, even while it retains the necessary direction for reason so that individuals may enjoy the positive freedom typical of vibrant communities. The considerable liberties associated with negative freedom that have been encoded in Muslim law will also be mentioned.

Chapter 5 then turns to the dark side of communal robustness in Islam, rooted in excessive preoccupation with the identity, unity, and strength of the community. Those who made such preoccupation their leading motive can be termed communal extremists. They have undermined freedom through their persistently rigid understanding of what the Muslim communal paradigm entails. The most eminent representative of communal extremism was Ibn Taymiyya, whose views will be summarized. But more space will be given to al-Ghazzali, who was able to articulate a middle ground between communal extremism and reclusive mysticism, a middle ground where positive freedom could flourish in both its communal and personal dimensions.

The way to a discussion of Islamic mysticism in connection with the personal dimension of positive freedom is then prepared through further illustrations of what is meant by "the directed turn to the infinite" discussed in chapter 4. These illustrations may help the reader appreciate the full extent of the freedom that is possible in the world of Islam. Then readings from the great Sufi author, Fakhruddin 'Iraqi, are quoted that exemplify the notion of a directed turn to the infinite and manifest the greatest positive freedom attainable by human beings. This is a prologue to the presentation of the relevant elements of Ibn 'Arabi's mystical philosophy, which enables us to systematize the discussion of positive freedom and place it in a metaphysical framework. In this framework, all the elements of positive freedom in Islam are brought together: the community, the individual, the world, and transcendence are defined such that they are tied together in an all-encompassing (but not pantheistic) unity, from which flows the meaning of Islamic scripture and laws, the life of Muslim communities, and the freedom of Muslim individuals.

Chapter 5 closes with a note on the origins and methods of Sufism, to show that for all the difficulty in expressing the content of mystical experience, Islamic mysticism has provided various definite disciplines to arrive at its goal. We shall see that to go beyond reason in Islam, reasoned ways have been developed.

While chapter 5 focuses on the considerable freedom traditionally available under Islam, chapter 6 explores how Islam can be fairly said to have undermined freedom. Secular intellectuals in the Arab Muslim world often blame Islam for many problems, none more passionately than the poets. The discussion thus opens with Adunis's attack in verse on al-Ghazzali and his legacy, interprets the poem, and then explores the actual conditions in medieval Muslim societies. It turns out that while conditions were poor for many, many Muslims, it was mainly because of political and economic developments that had little to do with Islam itself. On the contrary, the bulk of whatever consolation and edification there could be amid the general misery was due to the communal solidarity of Muslims and the solicitude of the Sufis. To the extent that these were embraced by al-Ghazzali, he could not be fairly reproached for the deterioration of conditions within Muslim-ruled domains.

However, it is different when we turn to the origins of Muslim quietism, something that helps explain the surprising lack of rebelliousness in the face of contemporary tyranny. Muslims originally accepted the extension of the Qur'anic injunction to obey their political and religious leaders (who were one and the same) to warlords and other despots to put an end to interminable conflicts among various factions and sects. It was assumed that Islamic values would be upheld by a religious leadership allowed to function more or less as it saw fit and expected to curb the rulers' excesses. This plan worked reasonably well at a time when the state was much weaker than today, but—as is argued in chapter 6—is disastrous given the power of the modern state and the disdain of many modern rulers for moral and spiritual concerns. Political unfreedom in the Arab Muslim world can therefore be *indirectly* attributed to a habit rooted in Islamic political culture.

The lack of intellectual freedom, for its part, was not the direct consequence of Islam itself, but of several factors that combined to pressure free thought almost to the point of suffocation. These factors include the triumph of Islamic orthodoxy, the influence of communal extremists, and a general aversion to dissent in the wake of invasions by the Mongols and the Crusaders, together with several revolts that were sometimes extremely violent. The rise of so-called Muslim fundamentalism will therefore be partly attributed to the long-term effects of intellectual stiflement; but it will also be linked with modernity, and especially with its perceived threat to Islamic values and its unwitting erosion of Islamic pluralism through the tendency of the communications revolution to engender uniformity.

The survey of unfreedom within the Arab Muslim world in chapter 6 concludes with an examination of the limitations on the freedom of women and Christians. Christians are singled out because of the historic and continued significance of the Christian-Muslim divide. The ambivalence of the Qur'an concerning Muslim-Christian relations is mentioned, but so is the remarkable humanity in the general treatment of non-Muslims throughout the Islamic domains until well into the nineteenth century (which point is made without applying anachronistic standards). The massacres that have periodically occurred in more recent times are therefore closely linked with how the domination of Islamic lands by the (at least nominally) Christian states of Europe has tipped the delicate and long-lasting balance in favor of fanatics and caused local non-Muslims, especially Christians, to bear the brunt of their wrath.

As for the exclusion of women from much that goes on in Muslim society, outwardly at any rate, this again can neither be directly attributed to the Qur'an nor to Islam as such. It is a result of a dubious interpretation of an ambiguous Qur'anic passage that was favored by social developments, and cultural attitudes that predated Islam. The ever-present influence of communal extremists did not help. And Muslim clerics, often more attuned to their secular traditions and prejudices than to their religious calling, did little to reverse the suppression of women, even when it conflicted with the teachings of the Qur'an.

After the extended discussion in chapter 6 of the relationship between Islam and the absence of freedom, chapter 7 begins with suggestions for the extension of freedom on sound Islamic grounds. These suggestions are informed by the need to acknowledge change, above all when historical developments have profoundly altered the import of key injunctions. For instance, "state" cannot possibly mean the same thing for the small community established by Muhammad at Medina in the seventh century and the contemporary Indonesian or Turkish state. This difference necessitates a new interpretation of the phrase "Islam is a religion and a state." Such interpretive analysis is among the possible constructive influences that modernity may have in the extension of freedom in the Arab Muslim world. Another is a novel understanding of pluralism, for which a strong case is made in chapter 7.

The discussion is then shifted to the situation on the ground, for many Muslims who take their faith seriously are already engaged in practices that depart from orthodoxy and do not seem the least bit troubled by that. This situation is most poignantly so in Iran and Saudi Arabia. Moreover, many Muslims have begun to express themselves with unprecedented freedom and openness about their political, cultural, and religious affairs, especially (but by no means exclusively) in exile. Among several Muslims with more than a perfunctory adherence to Islam, we already see signs of the freedom to come. These signs are presented informally and descriptively, in a manner befitting their subject.

The formalization of the movement toward freedom in the Arab Muslim world is elaborated by reference to the most constructive recent or contemporary work authored by Muslim intellectuals. This scholarly work is therefore the focus of the discussion in the third part of the chapter. The works discussed will contribute significantly toward the desired synthesis between Islam and modernity that this book affirms as the necessary context for freedom in the Arab Muslim world. This synthesis depends in large measure on how much of the shari'a may be regarded as divine and how much as the product of custom. The problem is then the determination of the principles according to which such demarcation of the shari'a can be effected whenever it is not obvious. Thus one way to distinguish between various Muslim intellectuals is in how they sift the customary from the divine in the shari'a, and in the principles they use to effect that demarcation. The views presented range across a broad spectrum, from conservative to middle of the road to radical. They belong to the following individuals: Seyyed Hossein Nasr, Ziya Gökalp, Muhammad 'Abduh, Fazlur Rahman, and Muhammad Arkoun.

But a synthesis that remains well grounded in Islam must ultimately be permeated with Muslim spirituality. This condition is certainly present in four of the five thinkers just mentioned. But the mystical contribution deserves to be the subject of a separate discussion. The thought of Sheikh Muhammad Iqbal and Bediüzzaman Said Nursi is highlighted in this connection. Iqbal was inspired both by Sufism and by the most brilliant Western philosophy of his day to show how the Qur'an could be read in a fresh spirit. Iqbal combines this reading with his philosophical views to make Islam as dynamic and modern as can be while remaining faithful to its identity and timelessness. Nursi offers a similar synthesis to Iqbal's, but his intellectual sources are more homegrown, rooted in the folk mysticism of Eastern Anatolia as well as synoptic works on contemporary Western science and thought. Nursi's synthesis is more explicitly inclined toward Islamic spirituality, and is more concretely directed toward individuals who would form a model community among themselves that could embody a novel interpretation of the Muslim communal paradigm. His work also incorporates an innovative reading of the Qur'an and attempts to help individuals regain the sense of enchantment in a world disenchanted by secular extremists.

The following path to freedom emerges from the final chapter:

Modernity has reached several saturation points, so that there is more room than ever for the reconsideration of its moral and spiritual failings. If modernity consequently begins to show a more mature and considerate face than it has of late, Islam is likely to relax its defensive posture, restored to confidence through the fact that its greatest offerings are concentrated in modernity's greatest failings. This condition would be the best possible one for the meeting ground between Islam and modernity. The fruit would be a dynamic synthesis, in which modern innovation and creativity are allowed to transform Islam while Islam helps return modernity to the high moral values and spiritual impulses that were present at its origins.

If such a synthesis were to work its way through the unavoidable encounter between Islam and modernity, then Islam will evolve to the satisfaction of Muslims, and the formal elements of the changes will be integrated into daily life. As we will have seen, there are already signs that many ordinary believing Muslims can express and enjoy certain liberties without any sense that they thereby compromise their faith. But these liberties stand to be deepened if they were rooted in the eternal dimension of Islam, and if Islam could fully recognize that freedom also pertains to the idiosyncratic expression of unique individuals and communities. For these changes to be effected from the Muslim side, besides the intellectual work involved, depends even more on the presence and activity of individuals who embody Islam's greatest virtues and manifest the highest realization of freedom. It is hoped that they can prevail in the tumult of the confrontation between heedless modernizers who trivialize modernity and Islamic zealots who trivialize Islam.

· · ·

What remains is the clarification of certain usages and preferences that stand out in this book. The expression "Arab Muslim world" has been chosen to refer to the domain to which the theoretical material presented in the second, third, and fourth chapters has been applied. A term is needed that at once refers to all countries with an influential or dominating Muslim presence without creating the misleading impression that it is the only presence in most such countries, for instance in the Arab world where there are millions of Christians. "Arab" should be taken to transcend religious differences. But "Arab Muslim world" is also used because of the obvious continuity between (secular) Arabic culture and the whole world of Islam, for Islam, as is very well known, was born in the Arabian peninsula and its holiest text has, according to Muslim belief, been revealed in the Arabic language. The Qur'an must always be recited, and preferably also understood, in the Arabic original.

The Arab peoples are so closely intertwined with Islam that it is difficult to think of one without the other. However, the two are far from identical, and the failure to distinguish between them while pointing out their affinity leads not only to serious error but also to grave political consequences. It is therefore necessary to repeatedly use a cumbersome expression such as "Arab Muslim world."

The word *modernity* presents a different problem. For in the context of arguments that dwell on how modernity has fallen short of the moral and spiritual standards present at its origin, "modernity" can seem to refer to an era that inherently falls short in that way. This is not the case. If modernity has been trivialized, it does not at all mean that modernity never had and still does not have the potential to far exceed the reductionisms that have steadily been imposed on it. Recent scholarship tends to differentiate between the modernity of the Renaissance and that of the start of the eighteenth century. The former appears laden with possibility, the latter reductionistic. It would be tedious to qualify all usages of "modernity," in the text or the footnotes, according to whether the Renaissance or eighteenth century or contemporary trivialized version is intended. The context should make this clear most of the time. The reader is occasionally reminded of these distinctions, lest anyone conclude that modernity is being identified with the reductionisms and trivializations that have distorted and deformed it.

Some critics and readers conditioned to certain expectations may notice that the bibliography in support of this book is somewhat "thin." Much could be said to preempt the negative judgment that automatically follows such observations, but here I shall limit myself to a brief statement.

This book is primarily a work of *thought*, and only secondarily historical, scholarly, or descriptive. I have naturally paid close attention to historical accuracy (to the extent that this is possible) and scholarly currency (constrained by my goal to complete this book in a finite number of years). However, for a book such as this, a limited, carefully chosen bibliography is preferable to the fashionable tendency to "read everything." I have tried to engage fully with a few works of the highest quality, written by authors considered the best in their respective fields. Such authors typically are not afraid to express their talents and personalities along with their erudition. It is their prerogative. And it invites, sometimes compels, the reader to think hard, which is how good ideas continue to circulate and grow. There is no substitute for trying to find the best books and read them as carefully as they may warrant, however slowly, however many years may have passed without their having been surpassed.

In their present frame of mind, some American and west European readers will notice that I *have* used gender-specific language throughout. Our cultural predicament is such that I must offer some justification for this. In the first place, "he or she" is an ugly expression. I shall not use it unless explicitly demanded by the context. Second, the complete avoidance of sentences that require gender-specific language is impossible in English without causing such constrictions on one's thought in so many different situations as to be tantamount to censorship. Third, the deliberate use of "she" instead of "he" represents an all too self-conscious (and petulant) attempt to keep score. Fourth, in any respectable dictionary of the English language, we are reminded that "he" also means "anyone" or "that person" (see, for example, the *Random House College Dictionary*, whose editors are certainly not averse to being "with the times").

I wonder how future historians will judge a culture that has allowed itself to become mired in such matters. A philosophical work should never be read with a political or pseudopolitical mind-set. Nevertheless, I have occasionally replaced *he* with *she* just to tell the reader who cares about such things that I am aware of the problem and do not mean for anyone to think "he" literally whenever I use it. Otherwise, I find it lamentable that there are so many people these days who dwell on such things and allow what is far more important to escape them.

Those who rightly admire the great philosophers of classical Islam, such as Alfarabi, Avicenna, and Averroes may wonder why they are not mentioned in a book that deals with freedom philosophically. There are two reasons:

1. Although it must remain open to the contributions of ancient and medieval thinkers, especially in view of the disappointments that have tarnished modernity, the philosophical conception of freedom that informs this book is modern. I intend to reflect on freedom generally and apply those reflections to the historical and contemporary situation in the Arab Muslim world in the light of recent creative thought, and as someone who is writing late in the twentieth century. There are timeless dimensions of freedom, to be sure, and they are what is most important about it. But these have more to do with psychological, moral, and spiritual content than with medieval theories. Besides, the transcendent nature of this content enables it to be illuminated through examples of a great variety, from among many groups of human beings in different times and places. The idea would then be to find a contemporary expression for freedom that includes its timeless dimensions. As it happens, apart from the individuals whose work is discussed in chapter 7, and a few others perhaps, not much has been forthcoming from the contemporary Arab Muslim world with respect to the *understanding* of freedom, rather than the *call* for freedom that dominates discussion of the subject. Thus a philosophical discussion of freedom will be found wanting without recourse to the spirit of modern Western thought and experience. So classical Islamic philosophy cannot be dwelled on here; but this must not obscure the fact that it is so rich as to still await adequate exposition for modern audiences, including those within the Arab Muslim milieu.

2. As far as the Arab Muslim world is concerned, I have chosen to focus on the most influential currents and judge how they have stood with regard to freedom. Even if an expert in Arabo-Islamic philosophy may find much that is useful in working out a contemporary or future synthesis, the fact is that the great philosophers of classical Islam have been far less influential than the scholars, jurists, theologians, and mystics. Certain intellectuals in the Arab Muslim world seek solace in the compatibility of philosophical ideas developed in medieval times with a modern conception of freedom. However, it is more important that such compatibility gain wide currency among Muslims, or at least their leadership. For this reason, it is essential to give priority to how a modern conception of freedom can be articulated by those whose Islamic credentials and wide following have never been in doubt. I therefore feel that it is best to combine the most encompassing notion of freedom, from a general and modern standpoint, with a discussion of how the three main currents in Islam—communal extremists, communal moderates (probably the most numerous), and mystics—may (or may not) embody it.

.   .   .

Another important group of thinkers were also excluded from this work. They are the Christian Arabs who have made tremendous contributions to intellectual life in the Near East ever since Lebanese Maronite clergymen embraced the Arabic language in the sixteenth century. This set the stage for the time when, three centuries later, Christians throughout the Near East would lead the Arab world to what is widely known as its Renaissance (an-Nahdah). They would fashion the language that became the medium for the Arab encounter with modernity. Their names are familiar to many educated Arabs: Ahmad Faris al-Shidyaq (1804–87, and originally a Maronite who converted to Islam), Butrus al-Bustani (1819–83), Shibli Shumayyil (1850–1917), Farah Antun (1874–1922), and others (Gibran Khalil Gibran, Mikhail Na'imy, Iliya Abu Madi, and Ilyas Abu Shabakeh were writers and poets who followed in their wake and would influence the literature of twentieth century Muslim authors). If their work suffered from an insufficient grasp of the implications of positivistic or other facile readings of modernity, this was made up for by their enthusiasm and the breadth of the cultural resources that they made available to every educated Arab.

A century so later, another generation of Christian thinkers has emerged, especially in Lebanon. They have learned from the mistakes of their predecessors and have assimilated the powerful critique of modernity wrought by several French and German philosophers. Freedom became a principal theme in their work. Charles Malik (1906–1987), René Habachi (1911-), and Khalil Ramez Sarkis (1921-) have been at the forefront of this movement. For the first time in the modern period, a genuine

Near Eastern Christian philosophy has been crafted that often has the depth and openness to be relevant to non-Christians (in contrast, prominent twentieth-century Christian intellectuals such as Constantine Zurayk did not depart substantially from Arab Renaissance thought). Why, then, were they not mentioned in my book?

In the first place, I deal with freedom, modernity, and Islam at the level of ideas. There is hence no attempt to include an intellectual history of, say, the encounter between Islam and modernity. Second, although it is true that contemporary Arab Christian thinkers have much to contribute to my argument, I could not make their work compatible with the dual perspective from which I deal with my thematic material, namely the Western, and that *internal* to Islam. Because Muslims are preponderant in the region to which the ideas in my book are applied, the outcome of their encounter with modernity (including their conception of freedom) mostly depends on how *they* come to terms with it, however well the Near Eastern Christian contribution may stand on its own merit. But the Western reader would do well to become aware of this body of work, especially what has appeared since the end of World War II and about which someone has yet to write a book in English.

The reader should also be alerted that there is an almost precise parallel for those developments on the Indian subcontinent, where Hindu writers would spearhead the intellectual encounter with modernity and would subsequently influence Muslim thought. Bengal was an especially rich terrain for that cultural exchange.

•　　•　　•

Among the habits that this book may disturb is that of ultraspecialization. The only foci for this book are freedom, its extension to the Arab Muslim world, and, in that context, modernity. The book is thematically unified, to be sure, as mentioned earlier. But no one field has all that is needed to address the chosen subject adequately. If philosophy is a necessary background for exploring freedom with some depth, then so are theology and literature. If history is essential in presenting the perspectives and realities of a world religion that takes pride in its continuity, then so are philosophy, theology, politics, and literature when these cannot be isolated, in the case of Islam, from its historical development. The study and critique of modernity, for their part, are distributed over several fields. And when government or corporate officials or "experts" presuppose a mythical scientific paradigm in a stubborn refusal to deal with social, historical, philosophical, or religious issues on their own terms, a knowledge of the sciences is necessary to expose that myth and show that science in the hands of the ignorant is a facade for what they seek to promote regardless of what science really is. Finally, because the assessment of how much freedom there is in the Arab Muslim world depends on our knowledge of the actual situation, an occasional reference to what good sociological or anthropological research and thinking have wrought is helpful, as is some native acquaintance with the geographical region in question.

. . .

In the last of his three Tanner lectures at Cambridge in February of 1989, the late Albert Hourani called for a multidisciplinary approach to the issues that weigh most heavily upon the Arab Muslim world. His words have been an inspiration, as have certain works to which he has led me, especially by Hodgson, Berque, and Mardin. There is illustrious precedent for approaching those issues from the perspective of as many fields as may illuminate them. If to live up to such works is not easy, then one does well to persist with them as models, for then one is sure to do better.

Freedom, Modernity, and Islam

1

The Assault on Freedom

Orthodoxy, Reform, and Reaction

Prologue

Freedom is deeply rooted in the human soul. There are limits to how much oppressive states, corrupt societies, and narrow civilizational horizons can deprive human beings of their freedom. Nevertheless, the realization of freedom depends on its outward expression, on the opportunities one is given to exercise the freedom that one inherently possesses. Only the truly exceptional can realize their freedom under the most adverse external conditions. The rest need a more congenial atmosphere.

Such congeniality has not graced the Arab Muslim world for a long time. Many attribute its absence to Islam. The real story, or the nearest one can get to it, is not so simple. If it were told, it would help us understand how freedom might be furthered in an area that needs it. But it would also help us understand freedom itself, and therefore whether the presence (or absence) of freedom anywhere has been judged according to the proper criteria.

The civilizational horizons for freedom in the Arab Muslim world have been narrowed as a result of a two-pronged assault. From one side, the assault came as follows: many areas from the thirteenth century onward have lived under regimes that had closed off the possibilities for doctrinal and sectarian pluralism. Almost all Muslims who are Sunni have been especially concerned with the unity and strength of their community, even if it were represented by a leadership that did not convincingly manifest Islamic virtues. The community was shaken by a series of foreign threats and victories, beginning with the Crusades and the Mongol invasions, continuing with the Reconquista and the ascent of imperial Russia, and ending with the long period of Western dominance that has yet to recede. This sustained offensive unfolded against a backdrop of internal strife within the Arab Muslim world, so that any stable political rule, even the most despotic, was preferred to continued disorder.

There was also residual awareness of the Muslim community's hetero-

1

dox roots. On the eve of the conquests by Muslim-led armies, there was a strong Nestorian presence in Aramaïc Iraq, the Mazdean religion in Iraq and western Iran, Buddhism in eastern Iran, Manicheans and Gnostics everywhere, and Armenian, Egyptian (Coptic), Ethiopian, and Syrian Monophysite Christians.[1] Such were the diverse origins of would-be Muslim multitudes. One can thus divine an urgent drive for unity, given that individuals do not forget their religious and cultural habits overnight. This drive could only favor orthodoxy—for pluralism would rapidly disinter the Muslim community's mosaiclike pre-Islamic composition.

We shall later come across two more factors that consolidated orthodoxy within the Arab Muslim world. One has to do with a group of Muslim zealots who first appeared when the Islamic empire and its rulers veered away from the moral and spiritual ideals of Islam. The other originates in precisely such rulers, who were therefore eager to demonstrate their Islamic credentials to gain legitimacy and popular support.

All the foregoing conspired to confine much of the Arab Muslim world to an orthodoxy far removed from the openness of Islam's first two centuries, when all aspects of Islam, including the status of the Qur'an, were vigorously debated. The last echoes of these debates died down with the Mongol sack of Baghdad in 1258.

A community may rest content with its orthodoxy while ignorant of other alternatives and may therefore fail to appreciate the freedom lost. If there was such contentment among Muslims, it was disturbed by the European economic and military invasions. In the Ottoman Empire and on the Indian subcontinent, Muslims were confronted with serious questions that it had been possible to avoid. Only now do we have an adequate grasp of what the attempts to answer those questions over two centuries have revealed: orthodoxy had undermined Islamic learning and spirituality through complacency. It had also left Muslims ill-prepared to grasp the foundations of European civilization, so they unknowingly reduced that civilization to some of its most highly visible signs, such as the various techniques associated with modern armies, administration, and engineering. Muslims who were averse to the consequences of orthodoxy, and were prepared to change their ways, thus fell—and still often fall—easy prey to positivism and a facile rationalism dominated by mechanism. In this, they were mostly encouraged by their European teachers, who themselves had lost touch with the full breadth of modernity's spiritual and intellectual roots, intoxicated as they were—and still often are—with their economic gains and military prowess.

This, then, is how the assault on freedom in the Arab Muslim world came from the other side: Muslims who had the courage and foresight to leave orthodoxy behind unwittingly espoused a shallow modernism that relfected modernity's increased shallowness in Europe and, now, the United States. This shallow modernism was a natural enemy to an orthodoxy that remained in place. A tragic vicious circle was thereby set in motion, the latest cycle of which has taken the form of the so-called Muslim fundamentalists. For a shallow Islam is the logical counterpart to a shallow modernism.

The vicious circle of narrow alternatives, both Islamic and modern, is the reason freedom has been so limited in the Arab Muslim world. The broad ground away from narrow alternatives, on the other hand, would constitute a congenial atmosphere for freedom. Because Islam and modernity have become irreversibly intertwined, we must deal with both main components of the broad ground, the Islamic and the modern, on the way to freedom. We must see how Islam and modernity, or developments rightly or wrongly attributed to them, have both undermined or favored freedom. And it will be argued here that it is precisely Muslims steeped in Islamic learning and spirituality who will be better able to grasp the foundations of modernity and forge the best original path between the two, a path whose originality will take it well beyond a mechanical combination. They can then set an example for the realization of freedom.

Toward Polarization and Reductionism
(the Ottoman Case)

In the middle of the last century, an Ottoman religious scholar was sent to France to study the natural sciences. The reform movement within the empire had become broad enough to create the need for a Westernized elite among the 'ulama. On his return to Istanbul in 1869, Hoca Tahsin Effendi was made dean of the recently inaugurated Ottoman University. One day soon thereafter, he wished to illustrate the idea of a vacuum by means of an experiment. He placed a pigeon underneath a glass bell. He then proceeded to draw air from the receptacle. The bird suffocated. Hoca Tahsin thought his audience would react in acknowledgment of the experimental demonstration they had just witnessed. Instead, he was accused of performing magic. "He was thus charged with being a heretic, had to discontinue his lectures, and was eventually dismissed."[2]

Innovation was less kindly received in the early part of the previous century. Sultan Ahmed III had sent an envoy to France in 1720, on the advice of his grand vizier, to report on governmental and educational methods with regard to what would be applicable to the Ottoman Empire. This was in the context of the growing realization that the fortunes of the empire in its confrontation with European powers would not improve unless the reform movement were Europeanized. The immediate consequence of Yirmi Sekiz Mehmed Çelebi's mission was the establishment of the first Ottoman printing press in 1726, with permission granted to print books on history, medicine, the philosophical sciences, astronomy, and geography, and the introduction of European methods into military training in 1727–28, with the attendant regulations written by one of the founders of the press. Tulips were grown and European manners were imitated during that period. All was not well, however. Mehmed Çelebi thought it wise not to display his knowledge of French. The press had to be justified to suspicious conservatives as "a new method to facilitate the training of doctors of Islamic law." Then the Janissaries revolted, as a result of which Sultan Ahmed III was forced to abdicate. The grand vizier who had been the architect of the controversial reforms "was executed and his body paraded through town."[3]

In 1577, an observatory was built in Istanbul. It was the only one in the Arab Muslim world and said to be as advanced as Tycho Brahe's. Astronomy and astrology had long been enthusiastically studied by learned Muslims, who had inherited and built upon those ancient Babylonian disciplines. A decade after the death of Suleiman the Magnificent, however, many leading Muslim clerics saw such studies as akin to magic and fortune-telling and judged them irreligious. When a plague broke out at the time, they were able to persuade the sultan that it was caused by "these bold efforts to penetrate God's secrets. In 1580 a group of Janissaries razed the observatory to the ground."[4]

One is tempted to blame clerics for the frustration of Ottoman reform and innovation. Yet the facts would not bear such blame out. The Ottoman religious establishment may have been beholden to fanatics late in the sixteenth century. However, from the eighteenth century onward, it began to show some grasp of what was needed for the empire to remain strong in the face of European gains. Thus certain religious officials supported the introduction of a printing press and bayonets for the artillery corps. Some went so far as to urge the government beyond its planned reforms in the military and economic domains, respectively toward the creation of a modern military and capitalism.[5] Imams in neighborhood mosques explained the reforms and argued for their legality to the general public. The first Turkish newspaper was established, edited, and proofread by religious scholars.[6] The chief physician of the Ottoman Empire, himself a mulla, broke Muslim taboos when he authored a work of modern medicine that displayed several illustrations of the human body.[7] Mystics of the Mevlevi order also favored innovation and are said to have persuaded learned clerics to support them.[8]

Opposition to change and innovation came mainly from lesser-ranking clerics and students at religious schools. They had come to resent the privileges granted to higher-ranking ʿulama, who came from aristocratic families and were often spared the long course of study and deprivation required of the rest.[9] The students were also worried that they would be out of work in the event of Europeanization, for their credentials would be limited to the traditional subjects of Muslim learning.[10] The Janissaries, who found themselves in the position of warriors for the opposition late in the eighteenth century, had also been suffering from difficulties within an overall economic decline. Their pay had become irregular. They could not see tulips and printing presses as an appropriate response to their problems and needs. The incongruity was magnified by the luxuriousness displayed by Westernized Ottoman officials. It was this, more than Westernization as such, to which they were strongly opposed.[11]

The following cleavage thus emerged among Muslim scholars and clerics within the Ottoman Empire:

1. Those whose fortunes were linked to the state, some through friendship and marriage, naturally supported reform. They were in a position to understand contemporary developments and felt that the empire had no choice. Their considerable privileges would also be thereby protected —or so they thought. Most 'ulama who held such views, however, had become distanced from the religious heart of their work. Many were stained with venality and corruption, while their excessive involvement in matters of state diminished their sensitivity to the moral and spiritual core of Muslim life, which had long ago first justified their office.[12]

2. On the other hand, the 'ulama who remained sincere in their devotion to Islamic values generally lacked social and political prestige and were out of touch with the realities of a changing world. They could garner the sympathy of the masses. But in the end they were unable to thwart a government determined to modernize and empowered by the early benefits of Europeanization.

Support for reforms designed to integrate Ottoman realms with modernity hence parted ways with genuine Islamic credentials. And it did not take the secular leaders of reform long to realize, once their initiative could no longer be turned back, that they could dispense with the hitherto obligatory Islamic veneer of justification. The propulsion of the Ottoman Empire, and later republican Turkey, toward modernity became more distant from Islam, more explicitly secular. Meanwhile, in the Ottoman heartland, those who genuinely adhered to Islam were left behind. For them, the possibility was lost to simultaneously forge and promote a workable future for the empire.

Even though the situation was quite different in other parts of the Arab Muslim world, for instance in Egypt as we shall see, by the middle of the twentieth century, we find the same pattern throughout most countries in question: the more outspoken representatives of the Muslim faithful are variously suppressed and, together with many of their followers, marginalized; and those attuned to both Islam and modernity are pushed aside in the relentless unfolding polarization.

Much of the Arab Muslim world in the latter part of our century has been in the grips of an ever more violent struggle between state-supported modernizers effectively distanced from Islam, and Muslims either hostile to modernity or who see it in profoundly different terms. Thus Muslim fundamentalists, who are often regarded as modernizers by contemporary scholars because of their means and methods, are in fact only interested in the technological and activist components of modernity. They quickly learn how to put the latest gadgets to use and how to mobilize their followers and campaign for their programs in the most up-to-date fashion. But their grasp of modernity's cultural foundation is poor. On the other hand, a state such as the Saudi, with a strong veneer of Islamic legitimacy, for all intents and purposes has the same demeanor toward modernity as the fundamentalists (which is not surprising when we recall that the Islamic sect in control there is rigidly literalist in its interpretation of sacred Muslim sources). So when a state appears to act on the side of the Muslim faithful while it modernizes, it is acknowledging modernity to a very limited degree. One still does not find an adequate simultaneous grasp of Islam and modernity, and initiatives taken in that light.[13]

Such polarization has not served the cause of freedom well in the Arab Muslim world. It seems that too many people are either unfree to express themselves as Muslims (not to mention non-Muslims, whose perfunctory religious expression is threatened by the Muslim backlash); or they are denied to partake of a culture that, while Western in origin, has acquired a definite indigenous aspect. That it has done so is not only a matter of course, for many in the Arab Muslim world are aware that this Western origin in turn had roots in the civilization wrought within a classical Islamic framework, a civilization largely built with the cultural residues of conquered lands, among them Greek philosophy, Indian mathematics, mysticism Christian and Buddhist, and several local legal customs and traditions.

•   •   •

Besides the limitations on freedom brought on by polarization, others are brought on by reductionism, so that one is not only forced to choose between Islam and modernity more often than not, but between a shallow Islam and an equally shallow modernity, all of which makes the domain for freedom in the Arab Muslim world unbearably small. For however alive individuals may feel within themselves, what can they be together in a world where they seem limited to one part of what ought to be a workable synthesis, and a truncated part at that? How much can individuals express and share within such a radically compartmentalized world of truncated parts? And we have not even mentioned what has so far been the most brutal (and obvious) restriction on freedom in the Arab Muslim world, namely, that effected by authoritarian states with modern means of suppression at their disposal (a scourge that will be analyzed in chapter 6 and linked both with past habits that have become self-undermining and the shallowness of what passes for "modernization").

The reductionism applied to both Islam and modernity, like many underlying currents in the Arab Muslim world, has roots in the distant past. It has to do with the perennial issue of how each of reason and revelation relates to the truth and to each other. Muslims, like other followers of revealed faiths, were quick to appreciate the great difference between reason and revelation. But for a long time, some of their luminaries believed that the two were in harmony, in the end yielding the same truth, or at least that if the truth given in revelation were superior, then at any rate it was still worth pursuing whatever truth can be established with the help of reason. After all, the Qur'an itself invited man to inquire into the world given him by his Creator. But we must note that the blanket term "reason" referred to an array of methods and faculties in the philosophies of Alfarabi, Ibn Sina (Avicenna), Ibn Rushd (Averroes), and Ibn Khaldun: a sophisticated logic, historical research, various methods of empirical investigation and verification, intuition and the imagination. If not all are present in each thinker mentioned, then several are. Meanwhile, on the side of revelation, the picture was no less subtle and variegated. Theology, jurisprudence, and mysticism all persistently showed the highest levels of thought.

By the thirteenth century, however, the rise of stronger Muslim states combined with serious external threats (above all from the Crusaders and the Mongols) to seal the victory for orthodoxy, which had always been powerful, but which had had to maintain much suppleness in the face of constant intellectual and spiritual challenges. The Ottomans were to repeat the cycle from an already diminished foundation: curious and broadly tolerant when they conquered Constantinople in 1453, they reverted to a sterile orthodoxy barely a century later when they became embroiled in a prolonged war with the Persians and self-conscious of their role as guardians of the Islamic domains. Under the regime of sterile orthodoxy, Islam eroded to hackneyed interpretations and studies of the sacred sources and laws,[14] while the repertory of inquisitive minds was reduced to its bare logical and empirical constituents. Whatever vitality remained was confined to esoteric sects and groups of mystics. Thus when the Ottomans became committed to reforms toward the modern in the nineteenth century, they found themselves encumbered with a faith that seemed static, and an esoterism that seemed out of place. On the other hand, their weakened intellectual traditions, confined to a skeletal logico-empirical framework, made them easy prey to the lures of mechanism and scientism.

Science was rediscovered in the Ottoman world by extrapolation from military and administrative reform, as a result of which cadets were sent to engineering schools, and government was run with the help of facts, figures, and the knowledge of foreign languages central to understanding the new techniques. As these became more efficacious and the science embedded within them began to surface, it was easy for those thereby impressed to make science the center of a new ideology, distanced as they had become from an exceedingly sterile faith or esoterism, ill prepared as they had been to grasp the breadth of the culture in which science had assumed an eminent place in Europe. It thus comes as no surprise that whatever passed for science among the Ottomans had a mechanical character. It either involved the use of mechanical devices or the streamlining of human organizations along mechanical lines. So science itself was not appreciated as a deeper discipline of which mechanism was merely the most obvious manifestation (not that this was as much appreciated by Europeans at the time as one might expect). Finally, when "rational" became an epithet for what is good and necessary, it was conflated with the scientific (which is to say mechanistic) methods and ideas on the rise. Late in the nineteenth century, among the Ottomans as among the Levantine intellectuals leading the Arab awakening from Egypt, "the rational" almost always meant "the scientific," and "the scientific" almost always meant "the mechanistic." Reason, science, and mechanism had unconsciously become one. To modernize was effectively to mechanize. And the Arab Muslim world has yet to extricate itself convincingly from the devastating effects of such reductionism, at the cultural as well as the existential level.

We shall soon turn to the Islamic counterpart of the foregoing reductionism, which contributed to its future enemy in more ways than one. But because the Islamic resurgence in the face of the failure of facile modernism is dominated by Muslim fundamentalists, and they most potently represent the effects of reductionism applied to Islam, the link between the two mutually antagonistic reductionisms might be better grasped if we were to illustrate with some poignancy how reductionistic modernism proved itself self-undermining in precisely the sort of way that a reductionistic Islam could most effectively exploit. Moreover, because Egypt has been one of the clearest settings for the unfolding of this vicious circle of antagonisms, it would be well for us to briefly review pertinent developments there over the past two centuries.

Reductionistic Modernism and the Secular Attack
on Traditional Islam (the Egyptian Case)

Just as we have arrived at the polarization and reductionism that have placed the Arab Muslim world at the mercy of a terrific struggle between truncated versions of both Islam and modernity by reference to developments in the Ottoman heartland, so can we deepen our comprehension of that struggle and some of its further turns by considering a wayward Ottoman province. It has already been mentioned that the pattern that now applies generally to the Arab Muslim world does not have the same history in different regions. What happened in Egypt is instructive not only with regard to how a similar result may be reached along a different path but also how the polarization intensifies.

Before Napoléon Bonaparte and his army arrived in 1798, Egypt had suffered wretched conditions, brought on by warring leaders who cared for nothing but their hold on the country. The less the country had to offer them, the more they taxed the people to finance their futile campaigns. Then came a series of poor harvests caused by drought in the regions of the upper Nile, and the famine was followed by epidemics. The Napoleonic interregnum was brief. No sooner were the French ousted by the Ottomans in 1801 than the respite ended and the all-round misery returned. But the Egyptian ʿulama noticed something during those three years. Under the French, who filled their administration with Egyptians, it transpired that the country could be much better run. So immediately upon the recrudescence of the wretchedness in 1801, the clerics set about to find a man who would rule Egypt in a novel manner and free it from want. Their search ended with Muhammad Ali Pasha. He was installed in 1805, triumphed over all domestic opposition by 1811, and remained in power until 1848. His descendants were to rule Egypt, albeit mostly constrained by the British, until 1952.

It is significant that the religious leadership in Egypt acted on behalf of the people and did so decisively in favor of the modern. We may recall that their Ottoman peers were mostly either faithful to Islam and close to their constituents or supportive of reform. With the kind of backing that he enjoyed, Muhammad Ali was able to change Egypt much more rapidly than the Ottomans from whom he had wrested autonomy. By 1831, the modernized Egyptian army was so strong that it defeated the Ottomans in Lebanon and Syria and threatened Istanbul before the Ottomans sued for peace. A second march into Anatolia was stopped only by the Europeans, who did not want a local "upstart" to control "their" market.[15]

We need not dwell on the subsequent subjugation of Egypt to Franco-British interests that culminated in the British occupation in 1881. These complex events are important here insofar as they contributed to what would later become the identification of modernization with hostile powers and the deliberate confinement of countries like Egypt to the economic periphery. For the British actions in Egypt, with consistent European support, left many Egyptians in no doubt as to the intent of foreigners and planted in them the seeds that would grow explosively, first with Saʿd Zaghlul Pasha, then with Nasser, and finally with the current Muslim fundamentalist insurgency.

However, two developments are most relevant here. In the first place, Muhammad Ali's military, administrative, educational, and agricultural reforms were to inadvertently mislead Egyptians about science and modernity in exactly the same way as in the Ottoman heartland; for Muhammad Ali was primarily interested in economic self-sufficiency and military strength. He initiated secular education only to the extent that this was germane to the mastery of the new technologies. All subsequent changes involved mechanical processes that came to be identified with science and reason. This is why the Egyptians were no less ready than the intelligentsia in Istanbul to embrace mechanism, scientism, and positivism—and conflate them. In the second place, however, because reform was much more rapid and decisive in Egypt than in the Ottoman heartland, and because it had the definite support of religious scholars who simultaneously remained faithful to the moral and spiritual core of Islam, it soon became possible for a new generation of Muslim scholars to endeavor a synthesis between Islam and modernity. This attempt peaked with Muhammad 'Abduh, who rose to the position of chief of Islamic law at al-Azhar between 1889 and 1905. He had been a student of the famous and controversial reformer Jamal al-Din al-Afghani (1838/9–97). Lapidus succinctly relates those ideas that concern us.

> For al-Afghani, Islam was quintessentially suited to serve as the basis of a modern society. Islam was a religion of reason and the free use of the mind. The Quran, he argued, should be interpreted by reason and was open to reinterpretation by individuals in every era of history. By stressing the rational interpretation of the Quran, al-Afghani believed that Islam could be made the basis of a modern scientific society, as it had once been the basis of a medieval society built upon faith.[16]

'Abduh did not go as far as his mentor, but he did introduce principles that were innovative enough to inspire religious scholars to this day.[17] For example, 'Abduh believed individuals could and should exercise their independent judgment *(ijtihad)* guided by reason whenever a matter is not directly addressed in the Qur'an and hadith reports. In particular, he thought that

> ijtihad was essential to regulate social relations which were governed [in scripture] only by very general rational ideas and human ethical considerations. In Islam he found general guidelines which had to be reinterpreted in each age, rather than an eternal blueprint for social and political organization. Thus, he denounced the slavish acceptance of past authority which, he held, had led Muslims to believe that the political and social arrangements of the past were a religious requirement for all ages.[18]

It is true that 'Abduh met with resistance from his fellow scholars at al-Azhar when he attempted to reform the venerable institution. Some of them probably saw him as a heretic.[19] But it is also true that 'Abduh eventually succeeded. From the turn of the century onward, a long series of changes culminated in the 1960s in the introduction of a school of engineering for the education of future technocrats who would maintain their religious bearings, and the founding of a women's college that has since grown into a university with a medical school of its own.[20] These concessions to modernity are more than what can be expected from the seat of Islamic orthodoxy. However, the overall effect was practically nullified by a subtle but steady growth in state control over al-Azhar. This control has resulted from a mutually beneficial relationship, one where the government helps al-Azhar promote religious programs in which the government has an interest while al-Azhar provides Islamic cover for sensitive policies. The most famous instance of such cover was the sanction given to the Camp David peace treaty with Israel in 1979. On the one hand, the attitude of the religious leadership could be seen as responsible, for there was no wanton or demagogical criticism of the government.[21] On the other hand, the acquiescence has severely eroded al-Azhar's traditional role as moral watchdog in the eyes of many. It has become possible to question the Islamic validity of the decisions made by top religious officials (for this is what they have become in all but name). The practice of routine support for the government at al-Azhar also dulls the consciences of those who are supposed to be better placed than any-one to reprimand or denounce the political leadership for whatever harm it may bring, say in the guise of a massive foreign debt.

We are back with the situation in the Ottoman heartland. Religious officials who supported government programs and policies (including those aimed at modernization) eventually became distanced from the people whose religious sentiments and interests they were respectively meant to exemplify and protect. Ironically, this happened despite the early support of clerics genuinely in touch with the people, for that sup-port eventually led to a state strong enough to co-opt the leading scholars at al-Azhar away from their calling.

Once the most powerful religious channels for protest were no longer available, Egyptians with an Islamic sensibility were pulled toward the fundamentalist alternative. Those who saw in Islam a hindrance for their own and their country's well-being turned to a rationalism that, as has been emphasized, was little more than a mechanistic scientism. The state has favored this course since 1952, although it has not been averse to manipulating Islamically fervent groups to consolidate its hold on power. Thus we observe polarization in the making, fed by reductionistic views of both Islam and modernity made mutually antagonistic through over-simplification.

Secular rationalism in Egypt, like in Turkey, was reinforced by a similar concern with weakness in the face of Western powers. The Egyptians felt this weakness with far greater immediacy because their country had had to submit to a Western power fairly drastically—the British ruled Egypt, directly or indirectly, from 1882 to 1952. The British withdrawal only pushed the Egyptians into a more intense confrontation with another serious problem they had been facing since at least 1948, when the state of Israel secured its independence by force. Israel was widely perceived by the Egyptians (and other Arabs) as a foreign (Western) power and still is, albeit less extremely. It exposed Arab and especially Egyptian weakness in an even more humiliating way than Britian, for the odds against it were thought to be immeasurably greater.[22] In that general climate, there was near unanimous acceptance of some form of rationalization toward the creation of a stronger nation. A crucial concession was granted. Freedom would be sacrificed so that the state's efforts to (rationally) mobilize the population unto victory would not be impeded. Freedom was furthermore perceived by the more leftist elements in the Egyptian socialist regime that had ruled since July of 1952 to depend on the condition of the Egyptian population as a whole, mainly with regard to the economic dimension. Unless the Egyptian population were freed from poverty and material inequity, freedom would not amount to much if it were granted in the liberal style. Freedom was thus suspended on two counts.

Victory over Israel appeared long in coming and then never came. There is a peace treaty now. Socialism has proven to be disastrous to the Egyptian economy (not that the piecemeal capitalism adopted since has fared much better). The rationale for the suspension of freedom withered away. Discontent with the lack of freedom has surely been compounded by the exponential growth in exposure to Western culture, mainly through television. Such exposure tends to wear away historical reserves of patience with authoritarianism in regions such as the Arab Muslim world. By now, no educated Egyptian can fail to conclude that he must be free as others are in many other countries, that all arguments for withholding freedom in Egypt are no longer valid.

The state must hence no longer be permitted to use reason as an instrument, otherwise it can take advantage of the greater power gained through the organized use of reason to further curtail freedom. Reason must become sovereign, and in its state of sovereignty, freedom is inevitably there for all. The cumulative effect will be to improve Egypt's standing—and that of similarly placed countries—vis-à-vis the Western powers. But this improvement is no longer the goal that enlists the services of reason. Reason is left alone, and what people together will do when they can freely use reason and thus act freely will lead, as a by-product, to a more salubrious country—or so the secular rationalists assert (whether any of this is true will be examined in the coming chapters).

A momentous shift in priorities has thus taken place. First, there was the argument that the state ought to modernize to protect the Islamic domains from the Europeans (the Ottoman rationale). Then came the drive to strengthen the state as such (Muhammad Ali), which inevitably led the state away from Islamic considerations. The same situation came about in Turkey simply because modernization, as understood by the Turkish intelligentsia and supported by clerics out of touch with their constituencies, distanced itself from its earlier Islamic justification. In both cases, the state gained power at Islam's expense. But in Egypt, the state's authoritarianism and its failure on the external front gave rise to the ideal of modernity—effectively mechanistic rationalism—for its own sake, together with the priority of freedom. In such a context, Hassan Hanafi, a leading Egyptian intellectual, could make the following pronouncement:

> Political authority has fed all irrational currents in our lives because reason resists and challenges authority, exposes illegitimacy, demands rights, calls for freedom, and [asserts] that there is no authority over man other than that of reason, and no argument acceptable except through demonstration and proof, for man does not admit the truth of anything that does not show itself to be true to reason. The sovereignty of reason amounts to the unveiling of counterfeit conditions and the recovery of rights, the unveiling of blemishes and the rattling of [political] systems. For reason is a revolution, since feudalism was eliminated thanks to the guidance of reason in the liberal systems that are its progeny. The sovereignty of reason makes dialogue possible between victor and vanquished, restores their original parity, and eliminates a relationship of dominance and subordination between the two parties.[23]

From his uncompromising espousal of the primacy of reason over all other sources of authority, it is natural that Hanafi should see a serious obstacle to that primacy in Islam as traditionally practiced and defined. Indeed, Islam is blamed for the absence of innovation, freedom and democracy:

> Rational life is necessarily accompanied by the discovery of nature and the affirmation of freedom and democracy, which is what happened during the Enlightenment, and the absence of reason for its part is necessarily accompanied by the sovereignty of the supernatural and the affirmation of dependence on and obedience to the forces that transcend nature.[24]

Hanafi then adds: "The impasse we have reached with freedom and democracy is the impasse of the last thousand years of our history."[25]

This is a dominant theme in his work. Hanafi is not content to let his analysis rest among the events of the last century. He perceives the long shadow of a cumulative mentality, an immovable attitude before which recent innovations seem like paper rockets brushing the walls of al-Azhar. The structure that lay deep within orthodoxy, however, may at least be unraveled in theory. To do so would lay bare the habits that continue to obstruct the sovereignty of reason and human freedom. Once that structure comes to be seen as the bane of the reformist drive, its hold on the minds of the people whom it has ensnared may diminish.[26]

Reason has suffered under orthodox rule because, according to Hanafi, it has mainly served the cause of apologetics. This involved the need to resolve all conflict, where such was encountered, between the evidence and what was given in the scriptures. The presupposed harmony of all rationally accessible things with divine revelation meant that they were not to be studied critically, and this included other historical or religious traditions as well as physical phenomena. They were studied with a view toward compromise. Least of all was the content of revelation to be subject to analysis. So the overriding concern was whether an object of reason agreed or disagreed with revelation, not how it stood on its own. In case there was disagreement, recourse to allegorical interpretation (at-ta'wil, sometimes also translated as "anagogical reasoning") was available. As a consequence, reason was denied the free movement between opposites that nourishes it. The function of reason was not to protest, but to adapt.[27]

Hanafi then turns to the man he holds to be at the heart of the bulwark against the free and healthy use of reason, al-Ghazzali (1058–1111). The great medieval thinker and mystic is believed to have systematically destroyed reason (Hanafi surely means a certain usage of reason, for it is hard to imagine reason itself being destroyed). This is because of al-Ghazzali's persistent attacks on the rational sciences, his forceful arguments against philosophers and philosophy, his "opposition to every rational civilizational tendency," his belief that the way of "the taste of the divine presence" (adh-dhowq) is superior to the way of theory and his criticism even of Islamic sciences such as theology and jurisprudence in favor of Sufism. A follower of al-Ghazzali would not seek learning through the rational analysis of nature, but through inspiration and the unveiling of a hidden reality.[28]

Hanafi's call to liberate the mind and then the person thus follows the curious course of a confrontation with al-Ghazzali's thought. Once this confrontation is resolved in Hanafi's favor, the ripples of the triumphant new critique would awaken a moribund orthodoxy to a modernist outlook that affirms the sovereignty of reason and personal or individual freedom.

For all the errors in Hanafi's argumentation and his historical presentation of al-Ghazzali's legacy that will become apparent near the end of this book, much is to be admired in his approach to a problem that almost everyone else addresses in contemporary and somewhat shallow terms. Wherever an institution such as the Sunni Muslim scholarly tradition is influential, complex, and immersed in centuries of historical continuity, to disregard it in analyzing the failure of new approaches to social and political life to gain the sympathy of the people for whom these are intended would surely make the analysis superficial. A well-established, supported, and argued orthodoxy can never be discarded, nor easily modified, especially when the corresponding parts of the modifying theory are no match for its adversary. The least that can be gained from a confrontation with orthodoxy is to propel the alternative toward the same standards. Much more is gained as it turns out. As orthodoxy, its context, and raison d'être are better understood, it is likely that some of its anti-modernist tenets will emerge as truths that complement, broaden, or otherwise improve the rival approach. It is even possible that the honest pursuit of such a confrontation, now that this has become a historical necessity, may lead to a hybrid outlook that leaves in place the broader outlines and unshakable truths around which orthodoxy is ultimately centered while making it more dynamic. Such is the spirit that animates Fazlur Rahman's *Islam and Modernity* and Mardin's *Religion and Social Change in Modern Turkey.*

Hanafi has chosen the correct method to assess the failure so far to attain modernist ideals still on the global ascendant and still well over the horizon in Arab Muslim life. He has chosen not to ignore a history that, when ignored, is prone to assert itself rather crudely, for instance, as fundamentalism. But even if he were right in supposing that for the past thousand years, reason has been incarcerated within apologetics, he is wrong to think that reason is thereby destroyed. The resourcefulness of reason is such that confined to just about anything, it finds subtle, elaborate, and ingenious expression. Dialectical reason is possible within apologetics, if only to cast aside the opposition. The Qur'an, hadith, and the edifice that has been continuously built on them are not exactly simple entities, nor is the vast totality of phenomena with which they allegedly have had to be uncritically harmonized. It requires genius to work out the harmony between two sides each of which has infinitely more to offer than one man's reason can absorb in a lifetime. And when the harmony is believed to have been worked out—witness the size and scope of al-Ghazzali's *Revivification of the Religious Sciences* (Ihya' 'Ulum ad-Din) and the duration of the tradition leading up to it—reason is not thenceforth in hibernation but, at worst, is sucked into the sublime handling of trivia, as in the commentaries and supercommentaries adduced by Rahman (and, for that matter, so evocative of much that goes on in Western philosophy and literary criticism today). Despite such pointless diversions, the avenues for allegorical interpretation, which requires the skillful combination of reason with the creative imagination, can never be exhausted in the case of texts whose meaning is as rich and open as many of the Qur'an's verses.

In fact, and to anticipate as we must at this stage, what we really find in Hanafi is not the concern that reason itself may be moribund through excessive orthodoxy, but that it may not be used in a certain way. This is the way of reason as defined by modernity and as enlisted to justify the historical changes imposed by modernity. In other words, it is not with the sovereign use of reason as a whole that Hanafi is really concerned, but with the use of reason to lighten the weight of orthodoxy and help bring about, from the bottom up, the social and political changes that he thinks are necessary. Now it so happens that these changes are also underpinned by the belief that they are the products precisely of sovereign reason. This is the effect of blind faith in modernity, for one then overlooks its relentless thrust, into which sovereign reason is helplessly drawn and its sovereign use no more than a claim with the appearance of a neutral principle. We are hence caught up in the metaphysical vicious circles typical of the confrontation between two world views. Reason is at once the (allegedly independent) ground for certain social and political changes, and the means for the critique that will soften attitudes and make those changes more acceptable to the people. To put it more clearly still: modernizers who already support certain changes because they have been won over by modernity believe that this decision is in agreement with sovereign reason, whereas in fact the decision has already been made and reason is subsequently used on its behalf. They then go on to promote those changes with the pretense that any rational individual would accept them, and thus they demoralize potential critics in a climate where no one wishes to seem irrational. On the other hand, there are those who have made a decision for Islamic orthodoxy and, at their best, can equally support their decision with reason. Reason by itself clearly cannot decide the issue between Islam and the kind of modernity that is trying to homogenize the world. Only after one has already decided for one side, on grounds too complicated to expound upon here,[29] but which certainly do not derive from the independent use of reason, can one harbor the illusion that the decision is in perfect agreement with sovereign reason. 'Abduh believed his Muslim faith to be every bit as rational as the ardent, logically astute secularist takes his worldview to be. So the appeal to use reason to move from one worldview to the other is really no more than the appeal to move from one worldview to the other. The person who believes he is using reason to make the move has in fact already made the move and then believed that this is where reason, left unobstructed, would lead anyway. Thus belief in reason to demonstrate that there is a historical calling to catch up and enter modernity is already the recognition and acceptance of that calling.[30]

The fallacy of sovereign reason, if this can be established, seriously undermines Hanafi's position. It would force us to call into question some of the claims of modernity that have become its own orthodoxy. It would emphasize the ease with which reason can serve the wrong master and stifle freedom. And it would show the wisdom of al-Ghazzali's concern over where reason may lead if left alone, especially on the moral plane, where the consequences for freedom are indirect but grave.

These concerns may have led al-Ghazzali to lay the foundation for a tradition that has impeded the penetration of modernity into the Arab Muslim world. But to say so without regard for his genuine and timely concerns, and without proper consideration for the philosophical context of his claims, is to do him an injustice. Furthermore, al-Ghazzali may offer something to those worried about the anomie and moral impasse that accompany extreme versions of modernity. If properly and imaginatively applied, his insights may help safeguard and enhance rather than undermine freedom.

Reductionistic Modernism as the Gateway to Fundamentalism

The General Case

In what follows, we shall have the occasion to examine how a decision for modernity's dominant global strain, especially if this be interpreted mechanistically, will set in motion a sequence of events that undermines the freedom of the modernized. By "freedom" one must mean not only the obvious freedoms typically enjoyed in many countries today but also the freedom to live in a society that one can identify with, a society in which one feels naturally rooted, acknowledged as a person, and surrounded with family and friends. These kinds of freedom are indispensable to the peoples of the Arab Muslim world, so much so that many are willing to overlook the sullen and rigid bent of Muslim fundamentalists who—genuinely or disingenuously—have cast themselves in the role of protectors of such freedom.[31]

We have already seen how the rapid institution of certain reforms has led the intelligentsia in the Arab Muslim world to an "upside-down" conception of science and modernity; for science came to them through limited versions of its applied forms, in administration, education, agriculture, and defense, and was extrapolated from these. Modernity itself did not encompass much more than those mechanisms of reform from which the modern Arab Muslim conception of science was extrapolated. Such reductionism was made possible by the earlier rise of orthodoxy and the subsequent discouragement of all intellectual curiosity and inventiveness that did not bear directly on narrowly circumscribed scriptural domains and obvious practical needs. There was no intellectual background against which modern reforms could be seen for what they were, namely, a partial manifestation of science, rationality, and modernity.

If such was the case in the nineteenth century, one can only imagine how the reductionism has been accelerated in ours. For the twentieth century dangles such a dizzying variety of goods—which, when not desirable in themselves, are made so through advertisement—that one has even less room to reflect on modernity and is more than ever tempted to confound it with those goods and the manner of their production or acquisition. Add to this the rapidly growing needs in agriculture, industry, and defense, against a backdrop of impoverishment, high unemployment, and blatant military weakness, and one can appreciate how difficult it is for the intelligentsia in the Arab Muslim world not to identify the technologies associated with the cure for these ills with modernity.

Finally, when authoritarianism is perceived as the gravest problem of all in the Arab Muslim world, and one accepts modernization for the creation of a democratic culture, then modernization becomes irresistible. At this point we can begin the presentation of a step-by-step process that shows how reforms undertaken with the best intentions profoundly disrupt and disorient the societies they are meant to benefit and create a potent agenda for extremists.

1. The first step, then, is more or less axiomatic: much of the Arab Muslim world is afflicted with poverty and authoritarianism. The need to overcome these has become so great and obvious that no one among the ruled free to speak out can even seem to oppose the measures necessary to alleviate them. All rulers, however authoritarian, must acknowledge the urgency of the struggle against poverty. And quite a number of them are now forced to pay lip service to the need to devolve their authority.

2. Now more than ever, the solutions to the problems of poverty and authoritarianism are respectively identified with state of the art technology and democracy.[32]

3. The appeal of democracy and the latest technology is so magnified by the urgency of the problems for which they are believed to offer rapid solutions that well-intentioned and intelligent reformers lose sight of the centuries of thought, work, and collective experience that have sustained Western technology and democracy.

4. Technology, and the organizational methods that go along with it (such as those involved in administrative streamlining), as well as the democratic process, when experienced and considered in isolation from their complex history, are no more than mechanisms. Given the foregoing, advocates of technological innovation and democratic principles in the Arab Muslim world are therefore highly likely to relate to them mechanistically. The West itself is not immune to such reductionism, historically distanced as it has become from the cultural attitudes and values that underlay its most famous accomplishments. For instance, we often notice Western political or intellectual leaders identifying democracy, especially when introduced abroad, with free elections and other mechanisms rather than with the budding of a genuinely democratic culture.

5. Modernity itself is thus also seen in mechanistic terms; for rather

than grasp its rational and scientific components in their variety and richness, not to mention the moral values underlying it, urgency and haste reduce modernity to its most visible aspects: technological and economic advancement and democracy, themselves reduced, as we have just seen, to mechanisms. So mechanism comes to dominate the Arab Muslim reformist spirit insofar as it strives toward revitalization along Western lines (regardless of whether this is accompanied with moral-religious conservatism or not).

6. Against a background of a modernity seen in mechanistic terms, composed mainly of mechanistic models for technical, administrative, and political change, it becomes possible to accept, tacitly or explicitly, a theory according to which society itself is a mechanism. The temptation to do so issues from the neat correspondence between the mechanical lines of revitalization and a mechanically comprehensible society in which that revitalization is supposed to take effect. For example, it would be most expedient to see society as composed of an aggregate of atomized, rational individuals, who accordingly choose their goals and work to realize them (in this process, rationality itself is also reduced to its mechanistic dimension). Once society is seen in terms of self-interested, unattached individuals, it becomes much easier to apply economic theories and marketing strategies.

7. Society thus comes to be treated as a mechanism in practice by the reformers and their reforms. With time, after the repeated application of plans and programs that presuppose a mechanically constituted society, it begins to reconstitute itself in the image of their presuppositions. If these entail self-interested and unattached individuals, then such individuals will be favored and the remainder forced to choose between emulating the former or being left behind.

8. However, a mere acquaintance with Arab Muslim society, let alone several years of native experience or fieldwork, shows it to be rather incompatible with the perception of its self-appointed reformers to the extent that the perception is primarily mechanistically informed. For Arab Muslim society is anything but a mechanism. It is held together by personal links that criss-cross and form elaborate networks. These links are usually natural. They are not subject to reflection. They have been affirmed by the Muslim code, or shari'a, from its earliest beginnings. In the parlance of social science, they are organic. And they strongly condemn self-interested behavior and urge individuals away from it (although the shari'a is realistic and accepts that there is a natural element of self-interest in human behavior; only it does not accept an environment that encourages this natural tendency to overpower all others). These organic links are not only found among tribal or putatively tribal groupings, the numbers of which in any case are fewer than is usually supposed, even in Arabia. One also finds them among the inhabitants of

the most Westernized neighborhood of the Arab Muslim world's most Westernized city, namely, the western tip of Beirut known as Ras Beirut. Between the limits of tribes and Ras Beirut lies a vast array of villages, towns, and cities, among whose inhabitants we invariably find personal networks originating in the extended family at their social core. The two Arab regimes that have most systematically undermined traditional social relations are themselves largely based on family and kinship, for all their modernist rhetoric.[33]

9. The modernist Arab Muslim drive hence adopts an outlook that at once is regarded as the harbinger of immensely popular reforms, and yet is in contradiction with Arab Muslim society. When that outlook unfolds in a series of practices that treat a largely personally interlinked society as a mechanism, these practices tear apart the very society that aspires to be revitalized and whose aspirations they are meant to fulfill. The pain and confusion may be such that the aspirations fulfilled pale before those thwarted. No one has manipulated that very real contradiction to greater effect than Ayatullah Khomeini. And no one continues to do so more successfully than the various groupings known in the West as Muslim fundamentalists, but who shall from here on be called "Islamic revolutionaries," at least in this study.[34] Those wary of the Islamic revolutionaries, both within the Arab Muslim world and in the West, must not let their wariness obscure the reality of the contradiction on which the revolutionaries thrive, nor imagine that the contradiction can be resolved by causing Arab Muslim society to lose its organic character.

The Particular Case

The foregoing sequence can be illustrated, albeit not with perfect correspondence to each of its nine stages, with the help of an interpretive reconstruction of certain passages in Şerif Mardin's *Religion and Social Change in Modern Turkey.*[35] While Mardin's work deals exclusively with Turkey, its range of applicability often extends well beyond Turkish frontiers.

By the middle of the nineteenth century, much of the Ottoman Turkish intelligentsia realized that their empire could not survive if the gap were not closed between itself and the European nation-states. However, the gap had become such that there simply was no time to emulate Europe's path to modernity, but only where that path had led. It was no longer possible to replicate Europe's slow evolutionary process at the everyday level, in which the outlook of Europeans and their socioeconomic setting had gradually changed and become substantial enough to broadly ground new political and legal directions. These new directions were the official consecration of what had already become part of European life and expectations. In Ottoman Turkey, those new directions were therefore sought, in both their theoretical and practical implications, without regard for their context and history.

The urgency with which Ottoman-Turkish reformers perceived the need to recover lost time combined with several other factors to radically secularize them:

1. They were exasperated with obscurantism and conservative backlashes, crude but understandable signs of a deeply rooted Ottoman-Turkish particularity on the defensive.

2. The progressive alienation of bureaucrats from the Islamic clergy and folk (both urban and rural) disrupted the continuity between high and low culture traditionally kept in place by Islam, unhinged high culture from its religious moorings, and thus freed it to drift into the secularist orbit.[36]

3. Secularism was reinforced by an abstraction based on what limited earlier reforms (within the bureaucracy and the military) had accomplished and speculation over the result of extending such reforms to all spheres of Ottoman life. Such speculation held optimistic visions before reformers in which all problems will have been solved. The conceptual framework that sustained such visions, namely secularism, was therefore thought superior to what seemed to hold Ottoman-Turkish society in the present and had let it bask in an eschatologically guaranteed universal harmony and order. It was thought superior to Islam.[37]

4. It is also possible that a disproportionate number of reformers were predisposed against the obligations that counterbalanced the security of family and community life.[38] They might have been the kind more inclined to an impersonal individualism both at work and in their choice of friends and associates than to a network of personally interlinked officials and submission to the authority of parents, uncles, and neighbors. Their inclination would have found secular thought congenial.

Secularism among several reform-minded Ottoman Turks quickly took on a mechanistic aspect for several reasons, all having to do with the lack of time for change to have followed its natural course. For example, there are limits to how much cultural history could in any event have been (or can ever be) accelerated. Although it is possible, say, for students from the Arab Muslim world to excel at advanced studies in every field, it is not possible for their intellectual or cultural history to be accelerated toward its Western counterpart.[39] The time factor is not the only obstacle, nor perhaps the overriding one. For there is also the fact of particularity. Whatever is particular to the West cannot wear the universalist cloak well for very long. This is sufficiently known by now. Conversely, whatever is particular to the Arab Muslim world, when we consider the full extent of its grounding, to the extent that it seems innate, will not yield to universalist pressures. Thus the only dimensions of the European reality that could be transplanted were those that had the dual quality of desirability (on account of their effectivess) and cultural neutrality. Just such a dual quality can be found in mechanism. Ottoman Turks had experienced its effectiveness over decades of military and administrative reforms.[40] They could then come to see it as an overall philosophy that would make their entire society more efficacious as such. Mechanism travels extremely well when the values that underlie it are invisible. Witness baccalaureate students from Cambodia to Lebanon to Senegal to Haiti solving the same mechanically designed problems of physics without feeling the least bit alienated.

The spread of secularist-mechanistic ideals, attitudes, and practice was spurred by bureaucrats who were able to leave their mark on the educational system. They convinced the younger generation that the new outlook was the only road to imperial salvation. Whatever stood in the way was ignorant or backward.[41] The new graduates were subsequently better positioned to take over top administrative posts in the new system and increase the number and power of secularists. This process has culminated in a unique cleavage that has appeared in modern Turkish society between higher education and government on the one hand and religious sentiment on the other.

The growing circle of secular reformers, whose orientation toward secularism grew more radical with the promise of a future utopia and frequent reminders of weakness through the military confrontations with Europe (besides what has already been mentioned), thus found itself intellectually and existentially prepared to see the society that needed to be mechanically reorganized as a machine, in the same way that the army and administration had come to be regarded as machines. The growing distance of those reformers from much of the society around them became such that they could no longer see that society for what it was and so, besides being prepared to think in social-mechanistic terms, they could act accordingly. They had cultivated an elaborate blindness to whatever begged to differ among those for whom the reforms were intended. The latter helped them along, for they no longer had the means to express their reserve effectively, not least because they could not see themselves as subverting imperial (or later Turkish republican) well-being. So the traditional sector of society had its heart and mind in different places. Even its heart became divided between the imperial/national good and the patterns of life thereby undermined. So long as those divisions remained unconscious, repressed (often voluntarily), or inarticulate, mechanistic reformers could see a clear road ahead.

So the reformers of Ottoman Turkey—with the complicity of many who could not countenance resistance to what would revitalize their realm, and who would become the victims of that revitalization—came to think of their society as an aggregate of individuals whose social behavior could be determined and output planned according to natural, mechanical laws as relentless and impersonal as the laws that had been discovered to govern planetary motion. The new social and political institutions would replicate that theoretical understanding.[42] Such a transition from physics to social and political thought, or from a physics of nature to a *social physics*,[43] was made easy by the growth in Europe of a "universal conceptual currency."[44] A logico-rational continuum grew along with European modernity and gave it intellectual support and flexibility. The same rules of reasoning were applied in various disciplines and the language in which they were expressed was unified. This language, in its crudest and simplest form, is a sequence of propositions each of which has a truth value.[45] This reduction of language, logic, and reason in all fields of inquiry allowed for mapping from one field to another through analogy. Thus the establishment of mechanism in physics allowed the postulation of a mechanistic frame of analysis in social science. (The use of "science" in "social science" is itself an example of mapping through analogy—if nature can be studied scientifically, then, by analogy, so can society, and human feelings for that matter, applying exactly the same rules.) There was neither the time nor the will to anticipate self-fulfilling theoretical prophecies, whereby prolonged theoretical practices in clear violation of their intended phenomena eventually made it seem as though the phenomena were pliable to those practices (usually at the cost of ignoring phenomena or aspects thereof that were obviously unyielding). In other words, a mechanistically inspired social science and practice fostered and sustained a sufficient degree of mechanically analyzable social relations, mechanisms, expectations, and actions that these seemed to constitute a social reality that vindicated the mechanistic approach. Meanwhile, all the social (and personal) phenomena that eluded the mechanistic net were theoretically forgotten and practically suppressed. To the extent that this practice ran contrary to an enduring individual and social reality, the potential for upheaval, violent if need be, was always there.

Mainstream Western thought and socio-politico-economic practice, which the Ottoman-Turkish reformers wished to emulate, had also been allowed to regard society mechanistically because the very use of the concept "society" indicated an abstraction from the individuals who formed it. The subdivisions of society were also abstractions. Social classes, the educational system, the government, and even the family could be described without any reference to the persons who were their members.[46] With the personal dimension out of the way, it became possible to construct theories and formulate policies according to the interplay between abstract entities. These touched on human nature rather coarsely, if at all. Such abstraction, once it had become habitual, made it possible to regard whatever resisted practical application as an aberration or atavism that time must be helped to erode.

But it so happens that human beings are the exact opposite of the fundamental forces of nature in that while the forces are everywhere the same, each human being has a unique personality.[47] At certain levels, this uniqueness makes the very enterprise of social theory impossible. It becomes possible only when human beings have practices in common, such as work, learning, or religion. Even these can be said to have a standardized or ritualized aspect and a personal aspect that varies with every individual. What is being stressed here, however, is a Western criticism of a Western tendency. The impersonalism of abstraction has led to the avowal of individual uniqueness. This is a well-known historical sequence. Less known is whatever counterpart the Arab Muslim situation provides.

Islam, which has traditionally abstracted neither society nor its subdivisions, did not give rise to romantic-existential protest either. In Islamic culture, society has always been composed of persons interlinked in personal ways: teacher to student, master craftsman to apprentice, mother to daughter, father to son, craftsmen to one another, the neighborhood community through their mosque and to their local scholar, judge (*qadi*) or saint, the lower-ranking bureaucrat to his family and locality, and so on, in a series of overlapping human networks so simple for those directly involved and so complicated and intractable for those who attempt to formulate them in abstract theoretical terms. The bonds cementing those networks are the antithesis of the legalism that governs contemporary social relations in the United States. They remain personal, as in "filial piety," "keeping one's engagements," "the sacredness of an oath," "establishing bonds of friendship," "fitting into the neighborhood," and "trying to establish a respectable status as a member of a (partly) religious community."[48] Such a culture is more likely to be appreciated and understood now that Western intellectual circles are more receptive to holism.

Imagine such a close-knit community, say, in eastern Anatolia, whose links with some government officials are also personal, perhaps to the point of officials genuinely belonging to it, suddenly forced to deal with officials who are foreign to the region and govern according to rules abstracted from the locality to the point of incomprehensibility. Imagine people accustomed to relate personally to one another, and this includes how they relate to the officials assigned to oversee some of their affairs, forced to interact according to a rigorously impersonal scheme defined by those abstracted rules. Imagine education and the application of the law subject to the same (perceived) abstraction. Imagine the consequences of the imposition of values entailed by compliance with the new rules in government, education, and the legal system, values so much at variance with their Islamic counterparts as to undermine the frame of reference that had given a social, moral, and religious anchor for the links that had held society together. Imagine how people accustomed to relate to the world through an allusive language full of symbolism might react when forced to live under a new system of relations between the individual and the world entirely expressed with the "universal conceptual currency" (defined above).[49] We have in all this the elements of a multilayered disorientation, certainly in regions away from the centers of the reformist Ottoman-Turkish drive. This has been the legacy of reforms abstracted from life in those areas. The effects of those abstractions were felt all over the Ottoman-Turkish domains. They can best be described as contradictory, for people were literally pushed to be what they emphatically were not—for how else does one describe a set of overlapping networks of persons linked in personal ways treated as a machine?

The Ottoman-Turkish experience is unique. But many of its elements are widely applicable within the limits set for this discussion. To illustrate the diversity of its relevance, let us turn to the Arab world. In the years of Ottoman decline, the Arab world had neither a sense of an empire to defend against Europe nor one of Islamic destiny and triumphalism. But the Arabs did experience the systematic exposure of their military, economic, and intellectual weakness vis-à-vis the West, no more so than when the state of Israel was created in 1948. Unlike the Turks, however, the idea that political and economic freedom would strengthen their states was not institutionalized for most Arabs. It largely remained the object of lip service and the dream of no more than a small majority among the intelligentsia (which otherwise endorsed, openly or tacitly, state policy). Instead, most states gained power at the expense of the people in the name of mobilization unto victory. But by now, Arab intellectuals widely believe in reforms enthusiastically taken up by Ottoman Turks more than a century ago. Overcoming poverty and authoritarianism, and regaining national pride, are popular objectives. Unfortunately, Arab intellectuals, between Ottoman decline, colonial intrigue, preoccupation with Israel, and widespread repression, are even less able to transcend the association of modernity (and freedom) with mechanism (and positivism) than their Turkish counterparts. When the door to reform is finally opened, serious criticism of its intellectual foundation is thus not very likely. If the Ottoman Turks believed they had little time to undertake reform at a more natural pace and with a proper cultural-historical grounding, the Arabs today believe they have even less time. Because no analytical method can be more rapidly appropriated and applied than mechanism, thanks to a simple logical structure that cuts easily across several boundaries, and because, as we have seen, the fruits of mechanism are more visible than ever, there is little chance that what Arab thinkers and reformers see as science, rationality, and modernity will be substantially more than mechanism.

On the other hand, what Mardin says about Turkish society extends to the whole Arab world and includes much of Arab *urban* life. Arab society is very much a matter of persons interlinked through overlapping networks in personal ways. Quite likely, the same persons who fully support the goals of impending reforms that promise wealth, political freedom, and a stronger bargaining position with the Israelis will witness the undermining of their social fabric through those reforms. To some extent, this has already happened in countries such as Syria, Iraq, and Algeria. Two of these have had, and one still has, Islamic revolutionary surges. The Arabs too will have to confront the problem of giving up the freedom to live within a holistic social structure, with the attendant purpose and meaning, for the freedom to be more affluent, vocal, and (materially) strong.

The Islamic Revolutionary Reaction and
Its Own Affliction with Reductionism

The material robustness and clockwork efficiency of the West as well as the threat it posed to local culture and values appeared simultaneously and dramatically in the Arab Muslim world. Once awareness of the gap between the two worlds set in, it grew rapidly into a sense of alarm; so did awareness of the dangers of closing the gap. With no time for the articulation of the same kind of broad-minded critical evaluation of modernity that many have undertaken in the West, there was frenzy on two fronts: the frenzy of zealots for whom the defacement of local culture was not too high a price for national or imperial strength and material well-being and that of other zealots who were willing to pay any price to preserve local culture. The second group could once afford to be obscurantist. They could follow the path of rejecting the West in toto. By now, however, the goals of reform are too popular and urgent to sustain any serious opposition. Yet the goal to continue to live under the social, moral, psychological, and spiritual aspects of the local worldview has not lost its appeal. How can the two sets of goals be gathered onto the same platform?

The key to the answer is in the word *platform*. All sorts of things can be gathered onto the same platform. It is a different story when a platform has to seep into the cultural and social reality. We can thus consider the new generation of fundamentalists, who, as was mentioned earlier, shall be referred to as *Islamic revolutionaries*.[50] They dominate engineering and medical schools at several universities in the Arab Muslim world. This may seem contradictory. But it can be argued that it is precisely in the applied sciences that revolutionary Islamic sentiment should grow. The Islamic revolutionary understands the reform imperative. He knows of the military, political, and economic weaknesses of which there are daily reminders. He sees in the study of engineering and medicine the *scientific* solution of these problems. He finds them relatively easy compared to the study of theoretical physics, mathematics, or molecular biology. Any intelligent student with a decent high school education can go on to study engineering or medicine. Advancement in the theoretical sciences is rather less automatic. The appeal of the applied sciences is heightened by the mechanical nature of how they are mostly presented to students. Because mechanism is culturally neutral, there is no danger that a potentially overzealous Muslim will find anything offensive or otherwise disturbing in those studies (whereas in physics or biology, for example, there are theories or even facts that a zealot may deem it better to deny to remain faithful to the Qur'an).

The study of the applied sciences allows the Islamic revolutionary to bypass the historical and cultural underpinnings of the theoretical sciences while assuring him that he has the intellectual and technological tools necessary for reform. On the other hand, because it is also in applied sciences such as medicine and engineering that he comes face-to-face with facts and methods that have engendered agnosticism and materialism, his aversion to modernity grows in the course of his study. So does his attachment to local culture. Because the Islamic revolutionary most probably knows students and professors who have gone on to conclude from what they have learned in the applied sciences either that God does not exist or, if He does, that He does not account for much, he feels still more embattled than he otherwise might. The study of the modern applied sciences out of their original European context cuts both ways. It either makes unprepared learners too willing to give up their traditional worldview or too frightened about the prospects of life without it.

The intolerance of Islamic revolutionaries is thus partly a result of hasty associations. They believe that the worldview behind the necessary reforms seems to naturally lend itself to godlessness and social fragmentation. Hence, if these reforms are to be adopted, there can be no compromises when it comes to religious and social practice. It is also worth noting the intolerance ingrained in modernity as another source of counterintolerance. The logic and language that have unified modern discourse have already been mentioned. In the hands equally of zealous Arab Muslim reformers and several Western intellectuals, this "universal conceptual currency" becomes the unique way for valid expression. Everything expressed through different means is either false, backward, vague, obscure, or otherwise worthy of dismissal. This includes whatever must be expressed through other means, as a result of which it became possible for Western thinkers and academics who spearheaded such intellectual and spiritual intolerance to profess the meaninglessness of religion, ethics, and art. In an important sense, the old Arab Muslim order was much more tolerant, because several studies respectively in different fields could go on simultaneously, which, if translated into the universal language, would appear contradictory or invalidate one another.[51] The trouble with this new language is that anything that does not lend itself to expression in its calculus must simply be left by the wayside. Thus, what has the appearance of truth and uniformity is in reality a partial view, among all that exists, of those aspects of existence that can be captured by such truth and uniformity. Hence the comedy of one European writer after another who, believing that they were explaining religion, were explaining it away.

The society and culture so dear to the hearts of Islamic revolutionaries is a reality that they and their ancestors have lived for a long time. Yet time and again, in the course of university life, they are confronted with a modernist discourse that at best has no room for the reality that grounded and gave meaning to their lives (and may deny it outright). On the other hand, they need to acquire the very intellectual tools that cannot be used to express their basic reality. This acquired inarticulacy makes it easier (and maybe necessary) to express that reality crudely. The sophisticated tools characteristic of the great centers of Islamic learning, ever capable of renewal, are far too removed from the simpler and more limited methods to which the revolutionaries have become accustomed for them to have any patience with the argumentative process essential to the refinement of their crude vision of Islam. In Turkey, this gap has been compounded by the republic's severance of all ties between Turks and the Arabic language. It is less extreme in the Arab world because the Arabic language is in use and remains a natural bridge to the traditional worldview. But the schism there exists at the level of conceptual tools, the modern among which are biased against tradition. Arab Islamic revolutionaries have a rich language to turn to, but lack the conceptual ability to avoid the need for blind adherence to (what they imagine to be) tradition in the face of undermining forces.

To appreciate the revolutionary Islamic symbiosis, let us recapitulate its origins. In the first place, there are two levels of intolerance.

First, the language that has become the dominant medium of modernity is structured along scientific lines, which in turn have been dominated, until this century, by a mechanical form of reasoning. To someone immersed in the use of this language and the attitude that supports it, what comes from the heart or the soul appears to be nonsense. A great diversity of subjects may be explored, but the exploration always erodes the nonmechanical aspects of each subject. This is not too great a loss when the subject deals with such matters as air-conditioning or which antibiotic to prescribe for a bacterial throat infection. The case is otherwise with family life, architecture, or religious experience. The power of modernity's reductionistic language lies in the assurance of certainty that it gives. One is always impressed by the correspondence between exact calculations in a design or medical diagnosis and the respective successful applications. The sense of certainty around which Muslim society had crystallized—the certainty that God exists, that Mohammad is His prophet, that the Qur'an is His word—is not of the sort that a calculus can confirm. The new certainty, under the illusion that its language is relevant to every sphere of human life, thus appears to make traditional Muslim certainty extremely doubtful. With neither the time nor the cultural-historical opportunity to consider the limitations of the discourse that appears to cast doubt over their traditional worldview—hence the inability to conclude that the principal language of modernity has little relevance to what it appears to undermine—the reaction can only be to restrict the use of that language to the applied sciences. However, there is no articulate case for viable alternatives, which pressures those wary of reductionistic language to turn to illusory media, comprising a language and symbols that have lost their contemporaneity. Thus, when the Islamic revolutionaries want to set aside the modern calculus and retreat into their spiritual abode, they express themselves archaically and—mechanically. The language and symbols of the past are alive for them only because these are what they desperately desire. They are not free to thougtfully seek repose in Islam.

Second, some in the Arab Muslim world take the reductionistic language of modernity to heart and conclude that what it cannot express must indeed have an inferior status. They consider the obvious results of the neomechanistic mentality, particularly the speed with which they have come about, and become very impatient with a more considered approach. They want roads built, armies strengthened, populations stabilized, telecommunications updated, and public health improved as quickly as possible. They see such goals as self-evident (which they are) and the mentality that accelerates their realization as superior (which it is only relative to what it realizes but may be inferior overall). They then deride the mentality that impedes the realization of self-evident material goals and wish it away. They look at the Arab Muslim world from the standpoint of certain indexes, see their world as far behind others, and associate the lag with traditional culture (or directly with Islam). Secular reformers in the Arab Muslim world thus find themselves inadvertently launching a frontal assault on the very society in which their lives have had their meaning. They unwittingly disorient, humiliate, and marginalize those who do not share the same alacrity in disowning their past. Such intolerance can be brazen and it can also be extremely subtle. Once again, the only reaction that does not make one the object of public scorn for standing in the way of modernity's promise is to affirm the promise while strictly denying the general cultural and metaphysical conclusions drawn from extending the modernist mentality to spheres of life where, so the Islamic revolutionaries believe, it has no business intruding.

Besides intolerance, various developments are rightly or wrongly associated with modernity when it is not just taken in the narrow sense, but in that of a basic change in one's worldview. Westerners can by now easily identify environmental despoliation, social fragmentation, purposelessness, moral torpor and religious slumber as consequences of modernity. Although awareness of these problems is growing in the West, the response oscillates between the extremes of progressivist arrogance and romantic nostalgia, with the effort to forge a more balanced and realistic course still to be properly wrought. For instance, a tendency has recently appeared within individualistic thought that shows it more mindful of social well-being. Meanwhile, the Arab Muslim world must still face the specter of social disintegration or godlessness as it ponders the outcome of reforms to the extent that these allow the worldview that sustains them to sweep in behind them. The specter becomes a nightmare when the modernist-Western drive for economic, strategic, and possibly cultural dominion over the world looms. Such a drive is not the only excess. On a smaller scale, there is the steady conversion of luxuries into necessities or the widespread expenditure of great energies at the workplace for what to others must seem trivial ends. Faced with all that, many Muslims find it an easy matter to divorce certain well-defined and obviously needed scientific and technical skills from the worldview that underpins them, which they then go on to reject. At least, their hope is to accede to the unavoidable on a limited scale and maintain, if not rejuvenate, their cultural, social, and existential bearings.

The foregoing associations and intolerances have contributed heavily to the symbiotic platform developed by Islamic revolutionaries.[52] They are eager to master modern technology and introduce the attendant benefits to their societies; so they flock to study the applied sciences. They also wish to protect their societies from any alien encroachments that they fear would deface their faith, morals, and mores; so they affirm these strictly. This symbiosis suggests a brilliant resolution of contradictory goals. The individual can be as mechanical and intellectually intolerant as he pleases in technology; but in social, political, and religious life, he affirms Islam with a vengeance. Under God's solicitous eye, he thus remains free from the laws of mechanism in what matters most.

The foregoing symbiosis, however, is untenable and has poor long-term prospects. If freedom is undermined when mechanism hijacks reason, so too is it undermined when mechanistic reason is wedded to religion shrunk to xenophobic or protectionist symbols. Although it is fair to say that Islamic revolutionaries have been driven to their intolerance, this does not detract from what is real and worrisome in their intolerance. Were they to rule, freedom would be lost on many planes. Intellectual freedom would be restricted by a narrow interpretation of what is godly and what ungodly. The closure of cinemas and the return of women inside an Islamic protective shield are likely signs of how cultural freedom would be limited. Only those who support the Islamic revolutionary platform are likely to feel politically free. Even religious freedom would be denied those among the traditionally minded clergy and the countless Muslims whose religious sentiments they express, for such clergy are perceived to have bowed to corrupt states.

These are the most obvious points that can be raised in criticism of the Islamic revolutionaries. But one can find serious weaknesses in the genesis and growth of their symbiosis, which is supposed to wed (a limited version of) modern science to religious tradition. It fails in both respects. An understanding of the applied sciences is far removed from the mastery of science, let alone the rational-critical outlook from which science steals the limelight. It is that more general critical outlook that underpins modernity and potentially protects it from reductionism, even if modernity in practice takes on a mechanistic aspect in most situations. The revolutionaries' view of their own religion is likewise reductionistic. The fear of alien encroachment has led to the exaggerated role of Islamic symbols that openly distinguish Islam from the West. Fazlur Rahman found a succinct expression for this vicious circle of reductionism and counterreductionism, with reformers who embrace a shallow Westernization (whom he calls "classical modernists") later opposed by their inevitable progeny, the "neorevivalists" (or "neofundamentalists," to distinguish them from eighteenth-century fundamentalists), who embrace a shallow Islam mainly sketched with its anti-Western markers.

The current postmodernist fundamentalism, in an important way, is novel because its basic élan is anti-Western (and, by implication of course, anti-Westernism). Hence its condemnation of classical modernism as a purely Westernizing force. Classical modernists were, of course, not all of a piece, and it is true that some of these modernists went to extremes in their espousal of Western thought, morality, society, and so on. Such phenomena are neither unexpected nor unnatural when rapid change occurs, particularly when it derives from a living source like the West. But just as the classical modernist had picked upon certain specific issues to be considered and modernist positions to be adopted thereupon—democracy, science, status of women, and such—so now the neofundamentalist, after . . . borrowing certain things from classical modernism [such as their attitude toward science], largely rejected its content and, in turn, picked upon certain specific issues as "Islamic" par excellence and accused the classical modernist of having succumbed to the West and having sold Islam cheaply there. The pet issues with the neofundamentalist are the ban on bank interest, the ban on family planning, the status of women (contra the modernist), collection of zakat, and so forth—things that will most *distinguish* Muslims from the West. Thus, while the modernist was engaged by the West through attraction, the neorevivalist is equally haunted by the West through repulsion.[53]

What further led the Islamic revolutionaries to an inadequate picture of their own religion was their alienation from the traditional representatives of religious orthodoxy. The process that culminated in alienation was long and complicated. It had to do with at least two factors: the gradual ossification over the centuries of the once vital exposition and instruction of Islam; and the image of the 'ulama as subservient to inefficient, corrupt, repressive, or anachronistic regimes. The revolutionaries were thus distanced from those who could potentially best steep them in their own religion. Without a proper religious grounding and without the intellectual background to come up with an equally profound alternative Islamic worldview, and driven by their anti-Western zeal, the Islamic revolutionaries have not been able to add constructively to Islam.

> [T]he greatest weakness of neorevivalism, and the greatest disservice it has done to Islam, is an almost total lack of positive effective Islamic thinking and scholarship within its ranks, its intellectual bankruptcy, and its substitution of cliché mongering for serious intellectual endeavor. It has often contended, with a real point, that the learning of the conservative traditional ulema, instead of turning Muslims toward the Qur'an, has turned them away from it. . . . The traditionalist ulema, if their education has suffered from a disorientation toward the purposes of the Qur'an, have nevertheless built up an imposing edifice of learning that invests their personalities with a certain depth; the neorevivalist is, by contrast, a shallow and superficial person—really rooted neither in the Qur'an nor in traditional intellectual culture, of which he knows practically nothing. Because he has no serious intellectual depth or breadth, his consolation and pride both are to chant ceaselessly the song that Islam is "very simple" and "straightforward," without knowing what these words mean.[54]

We are right back with the principal themes of the prologue to this chapter: the revolutionaries who agitate for their narrow vision of Islam are a much delayed consequence of the victory of orthodoxy sealed centuries ago. That victory, made in the face of repeated foreign threats to the Muslim community and by the demands of empire or state building, created a climate of conformism and spiritual sloth. When the power that rested on Western innovation and vitality was thrust into the Arab Muslim world, the intellectual resources were such that little more than mimicry of the West was possible, and spiritual conditions such that the inevitable awakening could hardly be tempered with equanimity. Individuals and their governments hastened to replicate the West's most visible goods mindless of the underlying traditions and values that supported their production, while those unwilling to deliver their lands to an alien culture and lifestyle have since found themselves unwittingly trapped in revolutionary activity on behalf of an inauspicious replica of Islam.

2

The Future of a New Illusion

Prologue

One of the basic ideas contained in the long passages that have been quoted from Fazlur Rahman's *Islam and Modernity* in the last chapter can also be found in the work of Jacques Berque. For what Berque expresses in such perceptive and vivid terms about the cleavage between the old and the new in contemporary Arab society applies in extremis to the Islamic revolutionaries. More intensely and explicitly than other groups, they seek to balance their submission to the modern imperative, especially in the guise of modern technology, with "a vengeful nostalgia . . . [for] the great classical past. . . . Thus they invoke invariance in certain domains to compensate for others' variations they have failed to master."[1]

The failure of the apparent Islamic revolutionary symbiosis revolves around two insights in the passage cited. There is the failure to absorb the nature and scope of the "variations" confronted (namely modernity); and the failure to forge an open, dynamic, and learned relationship with those revolutionaries' own Islamic heritage. This is exactly what we have seen in the previous chapter. But Berque also mentions the tendency "to adopt foreign methods in establishing facts and texts"[2] that help recover the allegedly invariant classical past. So the recovery of that past falls short not only because modernity, including those of its methods adopted to that end, has yet to be adequately grasped; but even if the supposedly relevant methods were adequately grasped, they would prove inappropriate in comparison with methods elaborated within the Islamic tradition toward its own development and sustenance. It is moreover questionable that an "invariant" classical past can be anything but a myth, for the past, however long it may endure, metamorphoses in ways that remain imperceptible precisely to those who believe—or want to believe—that it remains the same. Again, we are not talking here about technical or administrative methods, but about methods that pertain to the heart of Arab Muslim tradition—its texts, mores, rhythms, poetics, pathos, and sensibilities.

As a result of the twofold error, where modernity is first misunderstood and then its methods misappropriated, the old finds "its unhappy consciousness, or its distorting mirror" in the new.[3] The old sees itself in the wrong mirror, and sees the reflection through invisible blinders. At the same time, it is pressured to behold that distorted image as an ideal. But the old also wants to remain itself. Thus it can only be unhappy about itself, for it feels compelled to give up what it wants to remain to the extent that it wants to become the new, and compelled to refrain from the new to the extent that it wants to remain itself; and it is denied the new because it does not understand it well, and denied itself because its inadequate grasp of the new entails an inadequate grasp of itself.[4]

The prospects for freedom also suffer a twofold setback. A mechanical understanding of rationality, which is characteristic of the general misunderstanding of modernity, lets myriad mechanisms loose on a society more attuned to the emotional, collective, moral, and religious welfare of its members than to economic efficiency and unbridled technological advance.[5] A series of laws, regulations, rhythms, and violent dislocations, rooted in that misunderstanding of modernity, impinge on a more carefully paced, intimate and informally ordered lifestyle. As we now know, these are not laws, regulations and rhythms that bring out what is best in individuals from a moral or religious standpoint, but what most realizes a society's economic and technological potential. With every other human potential thereby obstructed, the domain of freedom shrinks. It becomes limited by economic and technological constraints. Islamic revolutionaries believe their vision of a Muslim society, which will be strictly enforced alongside modern economic and technological ways, will act to protect that domain from shrinkage. However, and here we turn to the second dimension of the setback that the prospects for freedom would suffer, the enforcement of that vision would only compound the obstruction of Muslim human potential, because it is rooted in a narrow view of Islam, truncated by the fear of modernity and distorted by the myth of an invariant past. Far from returning freedom to an openness worthy of human beings, it would restrict it to an unbearable degree. This would be particularly painful to the very Muslims in whose name revolutionary action might take place. For the carefully and sensitively articulated framework that is the centerpiece of their life world, and within which they have been able to express themselves adequately, would be endangered by a rash, coarse revolutionary temperament.

A crucial problem we are confronted with in the Arab Muslim world (and not only there), then, is the failure to understand modernity with sufficient breadth and depth, coupled with an analogous failure vis-à-vis local traditions and reality. This failure is in part a reaction to the other failure, in part its creation. We can see why this is the case if we first keep in mind that modernity everywhere has been accompanied by reductive tendencies, so that it is reduced in successive stages to rationality, scientific reason, and mechanism (the contemporary equivalent for the last is the tendency to reduce modernity to consumerism and market totalitarianism, of which more will be said later). Thus those who think within ever-narrower circles of reductionism, even when they reject modernity, will see all other alternatives, including that which they call "authenticity," in a similarly reductive spirit. Meanwhile, their rejection of modernity is deepened because of how they intuitively perceive a threat to what they cherish in their own lands. The rejection of modernity has been compounded by colonialism, neocolonialism (including colonization through technology, entertainment, communications, and information), and the widely perceived use of double standards by the powers of modernity. It has been further compounded by the high-handedness, arrogance, or corruption of many among those who stand for modernity in the Arab Muslim world. Such a climate of hostility stands in the way of a proper understanding of modernity. And so the vicious circle of reductionism, hostility, and narrowness continues and, in the Arab Muslim world, reaches its fiercest manifestation among certain Islamic revolutionaries. These revolutionaries are given further impetus by people in the old centers of modernity who are all too willing to make of Islam an enemy in the wake of communism's recent collapse. The old centers of modernity have usually been called "the West." The West, as many there are well aware, has itself often failed to adopt modernity in its broadest and deepest sense, especially in extending it to non-Western lands. And in this failure we must seek the Western contribution to the vicious circle.

Within the vicious circle created by all-round reductionism, suspicion, hostility, and narrow-mindedness, there can be no freedom. One of the crucial elements of freedom in the Arab Muslim world must therefore be a viable and properly worked out synthesis between the modern and the traditional. The most obvious approach toward that synthesis is a simple statement of what must be synthesized: an adequate understanding of modernity and an adequate understanding of tradition. Only then can a lasting meeting ground be found.

We shall seek that meeting ground in the last sections of this book. Until then, the relevant aspects of modernity must be treated first, followed by those that pertain to the Arab Muslim framework. Because modernity's first level of reductionism is brought about by more or less equating it with rationality, and because to that extent freedom is limited by what is rationally admissible, we must consider the place of rationality within modernity and see, in particular, how that relationship has affected the limits of freedom. But first, we must examine certain claims about rationality, claims that have been used to justify the expectations and actions of those who have placed rationality at the center of modernity.

Few actions have been more disruptive of traditional societies—and have in a serious sense undermined the freedom of those who live within them—than those inspired by the expectations that traditional societies can (and ought to) be recast in rational terms. The belief has come about that to rationalize a society is to liberate it and bring justice to individuals whom rationality would treat in complete disregard to their particularities. Hence the ambivalence of traditional societies toward a rationalist modernity. They hate the disruption but are drawn to the promise of freedom and fairness. They are averse to the impersonalism of rationalism, yet accept a concept of justice that requires the impersonal treatment of individuals in the name of perfect egalitarianism. But what if reason were not so independent and reliable an arbiter after all? What if reason itself were deeply connected with social and moral considerations?

In that case, both rationalist expectations and the actions that flow from them would be attenuated. The justification would no longer be there to bulldoze societies into rational schemes. The fear of the initial signs of impending devastation would subside. Freedom and justice would once again seem to have less to do with rationality and more to do with the persons and societies involved. A healthier cycle would replace the aforementioned vicious circle, so that modernity would move beyond rationality toward a more open and pluralistic outlook that had always lain within its compass, certainly if one were to take its Renaissance roots into consideration; and those who have felt threatened by modernity while at the same time attracted to it would find less to be threatened by and more to be attracted to as they begin to see their own traditions with equanimity and self-assurance.

The Link Between Rationality, Modernity, and Science

There is a good chance that Kant will continue to be seen as the greatest thinker to have worked within modernity. His later work, as those acquainted with it are well aware, is a creative synthesis of much that had gone on before it, while it has at the same time set the tone for much that has followed. Thus, though there is a strong rationalist flavor to Kant's writings, it is not possible to reduce Kant's thinking to a single lable such as "rationalism." Because of the richness of his thought, perhaps too rich for most to keep all of its strands in mind, one can learn much about the various reductionisms inflicted upon modernity from how his work has been read and taught over the last past two centuries or so. For instance, some have claimed to submit to no other authority than that of reason and take "reason" to mean the distillation of the way we think, say, when we engage in experimental science (itself a reductionism of scientific activity as such). Such people take reason, as they see it, to be neutral and the most reliable guarantor and supporter of freedom. Much as they may believe themselves followers of the Kantian philosophy, they pay no heed to Kant's clear assertion that there is no such thing as an independently operating theoretical reason. "Every interest," he wrote, "is ultimately practical, even that of speculative reason," which reaches perfection "only in practical use."[6]

What does Kant mean? First of all, we should keep in mind that "scientific reason," in our sense, refers only to part of what Kant calls "speculative reason." Kant's term includes rational inquiry into other fields, such as metaphysics, epistemology, and philosophical logic. Even that broader form of speculative reason, Kant insists, has an ultimately "practical" interest. For Kant, our practical interest revolves around the moral law, and of the need to obey it out of neither fear nor hope, but respect. The moral law matters for its own sake, not because of any ulterior motive to which we may enlist it. The moral law, in the Kantian philosophy, is the clearest sign that we are beings not only confined to the world of sense, but with a foothold in the world beyond it. As moral beings, we are attracted to the idea, however we may fall short of it in practice, of the promotion of the highest good. Even as scientists, our use of reason is in the end informed by our vision of the overall moral good.

Developments since Kant's death have shown us what happens when we operate under the illusion that reason, when put to theoretical use, can be separated from its moral and social consequences. We have seen examples of accountants who calculate that paying compensation to relatives of the dead costs less than saving lives through expensive improvements in safety and health standards, the invention of gas chambers as the result of the "scientific" determination of the cheapest way to put masses of people to death, and the development of nuclear, chemical, and biological weapons. Recently, it has come to light that the scientists working to produce an atomic bomb in the United States during World War II did not realize the consequences of their work, because they were trained in an intellectual environment where science and society were held strictly separate, and because the extent (and narrowness) of their specialization prevented them from communicating properly with one another when it came to matters of conscience.[7]

There are by now countless examples, not all as horrific as those mentioned, of the consequences of acting as though it were possible to separate rational thinking in science, business, industry, or government bureaucracy from the social and moral consequences of that thinking. Kant's position is stronger. It is not only that objectionable consequences compel us to keep an eye on the context in which we use our (otherwise independent) reason, but that our practical concerns ultimately direct all our uses of reason *as a matter of course*. Unfortunately, these concerns often hardly resemble the lofty goal that Kant ascribed to us. If some are motivated by the promotion of the highest good, many others are driven by the maximization of profit or power or even by a perverted notion of the highest good. Although Kant firmly believed that human beings, if truly attuned to their reason, would seek to promote the highest good, we have too many examples that show that reason—perhaps because "reason" is more limited for us than it was for Kant—goes astray if not guided by morally sound motives. Scientists and writers about science are finally beginning to acknowledge this.

> We are indebted to Descartes and Newton for fine examples of well-formulated theory, but humanity also needs people with a sense of how theory touches practice at points, and in ways, that we feel in our pulses. The current task, accordingly, is to find ways of moving from the received view of Modernity—which set the exact sciences and the humanities apart—to a reformed vision, which redeems philosophy and science, by reconnecting them to the humanist half of Modernity. In that task, the techniques of 17th-century rationalism will not be enough: from this point on, all the claims of theory—like those of nationhood—must prove their value by demonstrating their roots in human practice and experience.[8]

Stephen Toulmin has been writing and thinking about science for a long time. For forty years now, he has noticed the untenability of the received (and in his judgment distorted) view of modernity as entailing an outlook in which the exact sciences can be pursued apart from all other human considerations. By the time he wrote *Cosmopolis*, enough historical, sociological, and philosophical works had appeared to enable him to fashion a comprehensive account, not only in support of an argument against the separation of rationality from its social and moral context and consequences, but to demonstrate that such a separation is in fact impossible and can be sustained only as dogma. He delivers a powerful blow to that dogma by showing that even Descartes's theories, which have been most persistently regarded as the product of a disembodied mind, were closely tied to pivotal events in his life, above all the assassination of Henri of Navarre in 1610 and the Thirty Years' War (1618–48). Toulmin adds his voice to philosophers of science who have recently argued that we cannot divorce the ideas of a scientist from his personality or cultural milieu.

> Even at the core of 20th-century physics, idiosyncracies of persons and cultures can not be eliminated. The quirks and backgrounds of creative scientists are as relevant to our understanding of their ideas as they are to our understanding of the work of poets or architects. There are things about Einstein's general theory of relativity, for example, that are understood best if we learn that Einstein was a visual rather than a verbal thinker, and things about quantum mechanics that are best explained if we knew that Niels Bohr grew up in a household where Kierkegaard's ideas about "complementary" modes of thought were . . . discussed at Sunday dinner.[9]

Cosmopolis, with all the collective scholarship and thinking that it embodies, makes concrete what Kant had held at the height of modernity, namely, that there always is an overriding practical aspect to any theoretical use of reason.

A further reflection of the awareness that scientists have of the larger framework within which they pursue their professional activity can be found in the writing of Gerald Holton.

> Thus the anxious individual inquiry into the warrant for rationality has been replaced by discussions among some scientists of questions coming from another branch of philosophy, namely ethics. . . . The professional societies of scientists . . . have become notably involved in questions of ethics and human values, such as the access to science of previously disadvantaged groups; the rights of scientists to object to unethical practices; the human rights of colleagues in totalitarian systems; the desperate need for arms control, as well as for a sharing of scientific resources with Third World countries.
>
> To a degree unimaginable a few decades ago, scientists are discovering that there is a morality which the enterprise of science demands of itself— even if such concerns are as yet expressed by only a small fraction of the total community. Indeed, with about one-third of the world's scientists and engineers working directly or indirectly on military matters while the arms race proceeds unchecked, this transfer of attention from epistemological to ethical problems may be too little and too late. At this ominous junction of science and history, as we watch the growing reign of the irrational in world affairs, the debates of former times to give precision to scientific rationality seem curiously antiquated.[10]

What the discussion in this section points to is a series of convergent thoughts on the relationship between theoretical reason (including the rationality found in science) and the social and moral realms. For Kant, all uses of theoretical reason were ultimately informed by moral purpose. But the giddiness of material progress and increased power wherever it occurred, on top of a strong inclination to uphold the sovereignty and neutrality of theoretical reason (to which we shall turn later), made it easy to ignore that crucial link of which Kant was so aware. Two centuries later, we have ample evidence of what happens when we consistently separate—or pretend to separate—reason from the social or moral. This first awakened more thoughtful people to a negative form of reasoning, something along the following lines: "We must consider the social or moral repercussions of our rational activities, for the way things are going, we are headed for disaster." As this thought began to sink in, it became possible to rediscover what had been known since at least ancient times: that no rational activity is, in reality, isolated from the social-cultural-moral matrix in which it takes place. Now, however, this link can be portrayed in many ways. At the individual level, one can portray, for example, the complex interactions between a scientist's personality, his historical situation, and his scientific thought; and at the communal level, one can show how a number of pivotal events and concerns direct the way that a community sanctions the use of reason. One can also simply document how scientists are turning away from finding theoretical grounds to justify the methods with which they pursue their inquiries, and turning toward ethical problems connected with their research and its consequences.

Our theoretical work is always tied to the more concrete aspects of our lives. Kant believed that we ought to tie all our theoretical work with lofty moral aspirations. There is, however, no irrefutable argument to support his position, much as he sought one. The purpose that informs our rational activity is of many kinds. It may indeed be moral. But it may also be immoral or amoral. Evil is a fact of life. So are personal predilections and idiosyncrasies that do not directly lend themselves to good or evil.

Much of what is called rationality today is associated with the promotion of a complex. This complex includes a power structure that stretches beyond national boundaries, and which is sustained by a materialistic outlook on life. It has come to dominate the global economy and severely constrain culture and society. With a constantly expanding definition of what constitutes basic goods, people are more than ever turned from necessities to luxuries and drawn into a cycle of consumerism. The complex that marks our world today would collapse were people everywhere more thoughtful about what they need.

Several societies remain, in both hemispheres, where a balanced outlook on life that includes modest material expectations is the norm. In an important sense, to "rationalize" those societies is to incorporate them into the global power structure. It is to make the individuals that compose them more pliable to materialistic interests and concerns. From that limited perspective, such individuals would become more "rational" were they to identify their worth with their material assets and professional position instead of their dignity and sense of social and spiritual well-being. While such "rationalization" may empower certain societies economically, with noticeable improvements in infrastructure and essential services, as well as greater individual choice with regard to material life and possessions, both individual and collective freedom would be respectively constrained as follows: Individual freedom would be limited by the subtle suppression of whatever cannot be expressed in material terms, so that individual lives take on a more linear and strained character as they are channeled through a series of interrelated mechanisms (a problem that has long been known in the West); and collective freedom would be limited by the position that the group occupies within the hierarchy of the global power structure, usually a lowly one that entails more subtle forms of dependence (whereas a group that continues to encourage modest material expectations would not be so dependent on its position as defined by the prevalent complex, even if it were a lowly one, for it would have other criteria, which resonate among the people, for measuring its worth).

Unfortunately, far more likely through force of habit than evil intent, the accelerating worldwide promotion of democracy and freedom occurs largely within the context of the foregoing "rationalization." It is bringing down resistance to incorporation into the materialistically sustained global power structure. This is often the real, if not consciously intended, meaning of "democracy" and "freedom" when they are introduced to countries today.

Fortunately, however, with all that is now being said and written about our being on the threshold of a new era, and modernity apparently coming to an end, the climate has become favorable for highlighting the extrarational considerations that determine any rationalization. It is no longer possible to disguise the self-promotion of the global power structure and all of its attendant materialism as a rationalization that would be universally acceptable to all rational beings. Moral, social, and cultural conditions, which may differ greatly from one place to another, must be accepted everywhere as the context in which reason is put to use. These conditions, when it comes to the Arab Muslim world, have long been on the defensive relative to the ideal of modernization (previously "Westernization"). It thus comes as no surprise that their reassertion will be crude at first. The Islamism preached by the various groups of Islamic revolutionaries can be seen as one such crude reassertion of an alternative context, hitherto in retreat, for the use of reason. But once Muslims realize that modernity is gradually legitimizing a plurality of possible contexts for the use of reason, they will recognize that modernity does not entail the deformation of their environment and character—or that modernity has already moved beyond itself.

From External to Internal Constraints on Reason

The moral, social, and cultural considerations that one must take into account in the employment of reason may be termed *external* constraints on the use of reason. But there will be those who argue that apart from external constraints, which define the context and purpose of reason, reason itself is perfectly neutral. *Internally*, there are no constraints on reason other than the ways that the mind must limit it. Within itself reason is free to roam, limited only by simple rules that describe its use and basic concepts and relations, for instance, unity and causality, toward which the mind naturally inclines. The use of reason in science is often cited as a perfect example of free, impartial inquiry. Inspired by a series of great physical systems evolved over nearly three centuries, from Newton to Einstein, people have dreamed of a potentially transparent universal order and a social reflection thereof. But physics today is as interested in the phenomena of chaos, catastrophe, and complexity as in order, progress, and simplicity. The former are now acknowledged by physicists, who no longer attempt to reduce them respectively to the latter. The obstacles to a theory that reflects a postulated universal order have by now become formidable. And the social order presupposed by so many powerful institutions is further away than before, as can be seen by the worldwide problem of urban breakdown and the reassertion of increasingly particularized and narrowly defined identities. Thus the threat to personal freedom and the freedom that lives on within a given communal milieu, which comes from the drive to recast persons and communities in the image of a rationally conceived social order (irrespective of personal or communal uniqueness), has receded decisively to the extent that its theoretical underpinnings have all but faded. Yet the *practice* of herding unique individuals and communities toward an impersonal rationally conceived social order lives on in powerful institutions that shape human life everywhere. We might say that freedom, to the extent that it is linked (as we shall later see) to the personally and communally unique and to whatever lies beyond the scope of reason in any of its forms, continues to be threatened and compromised by the habits of highly influential institutions. It therefore remains crucial to point out not only the consequences of such institutional habits, which by themselves are sufficient to cause their leaders to rethink the bases of their activity, but also that they are—and have always been—theoretically untenable. With time, it will then become clearer to those averse to incorporation into an impersonal, rationally conceived social order that this order is both practically and theoretically impossible unless so radically modified as to become congenial to every enduring community as well as to the basic and broad potential of individual human life. Instead of the irrationalism of Islamic revolutionaries,[11] it will become possible to connect reason firmly and securely with ideals, ideas, and characteristic themes that live on in the various and far from identical Muslim communities spread over many parts of the world.

In laying out the internal constraints on reason, or those that prevent us from legitimately claiming that, say, reason is indeed sovereign in how it is employed in the physical sciences, we shall move from the general to the particular. Kant will once again provide us with much insight on the limitations to any idea that reason, in the sense that we understand the term (and indeed in a much broader sense too), is truly sovereign. Then we shall turn to Holton's reflections and observations regarding the natural sciences as a whole. Finally, we shall briefly examine the testimony of two prominent physicists themselves, before we return to consider the consequences for social theory and philosophy.

The Direction Given Reason by Ideas and Ideals

Kant recognized that our experience, when viewed as a totality, is understood and organized according to ideas, precepts, and principles that are beyond its reach. He placed himself in a line of thought that began with Plato, who had noted how the intellect naturally exalts itself to modes of knowledge well outside the bounds of experience, say, our knowledge of the just, good, or beautiful, which is the basis for our recognition of all particular instances of justice, goodness, or beauty.[12] In Kant's view, the knowledge beyond the scope of our (spatiotemporal) experience pertains to ideas of virtue, the greatest possible human freedom, and a Supreme Understanding. This knowledge is crucial. For without the idea of virtue, there can be no judgments as to moral worth or its opposite;[13] without the idea of the greatest possible human freedom, no laws or constitutions by which the freedom of each individual is made to be consistent with that of all the others;[14] and without a Supreme Understanding, no ideas that cause each thing as we know it to come to be and strive for what is most perfect in its kind.[15]

Kant has reworked the ideas that direct the human *understanding*, which is roughly equivalent to "reason" in our usage, into three: first, the absolute unity of the subject (which he terms a psychological idea); second, the absolute unity of the sum total of all phenomena (a cosmological idea); and third, the absolute unity of the being of all beings (a theological idea). From these, he respectively derived (1) a transcendental doctrine of the soul, (2) a transcendental science of the world, and (3) a transcendental knowledge of God.[16] These three transcendental ideas, and the doctrine, science, and knowledge to which they respectively give rise, can never be proved or disproved. Nevertheless, the unity of the subject, the world, and God determine how we employ the understanding (or "reason" for us) when we deal with experience in its totality.[17] They are the ultimate foundation for the unity of our knowledge and experience. Were we to pursue rational inquiry without these ideas, so that the unity of the inquirer as well as that of the world became doubtful, our outlook on experience would change drastically. With neither an idea of our own unity nor one of the world itself, our knowledge and experience turn dissolute. Now, according to Kant, the understanding, or "reason" in our contemporary sense, cannot prescribe a direction toward unity, even though it be so directed. It needs the help of *Reason* (with a capital *R*). Reason acts through the transcendental ideas. These ideas are not invented, but are imposed *by the very nature of Reason*.[18] Thanks to Reason we are given a canon for the extended and consistent employment of the understanding.[19] The inevitability of the three ideas that guide the understanding when it deals with the totality of experience, the inevitability that this totality converges toward the unity of the subject, the world, and God, is nothing but the inevitability of Reason's essential nature. Because we have Reason, our experience on the whole will be guided by the trinity of unities. If "reason" for us is equivalent to "the understanding" for Kant, then how might we interpret Kantian Reason?

It is best for us to think of "intellect" as used by ancient and medieval philosophers and theologians whenever we come across the Kantian term *Reason*. Because Kant includes everything that we ordinarily mean by "reason" in "the understanding," and he *still* has a notion of an intellectual faculty for which the unities of the subject, the world, and God are inevitable, then he is clearly crossing the boundary between the rational and what transcends it. It will presently become clear that Reason is not exactly the same as "intellect" in, say, Aristotle or Avicenna, but we lose its sense totally if we think of our usage of "reason," whereas we gain some idea of its scope when we substitute "intellect" for it. This is not the place to speculate on how or why Kant gave the intellect a rationalistic bent. But it is worth mentioning that the tenor of Kant's intellectual environment did not favor words evocative of an era with which the Enlightenment was at war, words laden with a sense of mystery that might reopen the door to theological and religious authoritarianism. If Kant was thinking of "intellect" as used in ancient and medieval thought, he would have naturally expressed it in terms more attuned to the spirit of his contemporaries. So he used Reason for something like "intellect," and tried to rationalize the intellect's nature, actions, and goals to his best abilities. He tried as hard as he could to give it the traits and form of a faculty that we can recognize as rational. Perhaps Hegel's response, in which Reason was transformed beyond any ordinary capacity for recognizing it as such—not to mention the responses of Fichte, Schelling, Kierkegaard, Schopenhauer, and others—is an oblique commentary on where the emphasis in Kantian Reason lay.

Be that as it may, what matters to us is the affirmation, whatever our understanding of Kantian Reason, that reason as we know it wanders aimlessly without the transcendental ideas. It drifts or is usurped by the forces that be. We may take issue with Kant's belief in their inevitability, for the Reason that naturally provides the transcendental ideas is nothing like reason as we know and understand it. The inevitability of which Kant speaks is certainly not the same as that we run into when we invoke the principle of contradiction or the transitivity of equality. It is an inevitability that can only be confirmed, if at all possible, through something like a mystical illumination. For our purposes, we are left with the more general claim that reason without the transcendental ideas has no direction and thus spreads itself chaotically and aimlessly over the myriad experiences offered it. But we can hardly call someone who rejects the unity of the subject, believes in a world fundamentally irreducible to a single nature (widespread in physical science after Niels Bohr), and denies the existence of God, whatever else we may wish to call that person, *irrational*. So there are two levels where Kant implies there is only one. Reason has its own thematic ideas or postulates given it by the intellect. But these are not inevitable. Just as a physicist may equally guide his work by the hypothesis of continuity or discontinuity, so can the philosopher guide his by theism, atheism, or agnosticism.

The transcendental ideas that guide the understanding may be thought of as the locus of ultimate convergence for our *knowledge*. Kant's *Critique of Pure Reason* is a work with so much to say about knowledge that those who have lived since then and are primarily concerned with the theory of knowledge have given the impression that Kant's most famous work deals with nothing else. Yet it does. Kant did not end with knowledge in *any* of his critical works. If he knew that the understanding ("reason" for us) found its direction in ideas such as the unity of the subject, the world, and God, he also knew that our lives taken as a whole needed analogous direction, otherwise they too might go astray. Thus even Reason, more like the intellect in ancient and medieval thought than reason today, and more fundamental than reason today because it furnishes the ideas that direct reason, itself needs direction. Although Kant doggedly maintains that the direction of Reason is provided by itself,[20] he can no longer make inevitability claims about it. The evidence he first adduces is psychological: Reason's desire to find a firm footing beyond the limits of experience; or the presentiment that Reason has of "objects" that possess a "great interest" for it.[21] These objects are Reason's goal. Kant again presents the goal for which Reason strives in trinitarian form: the freedom of the will, the immortality of the soul, and the existence of God.[22] Kant reminds the reader that these are not necessary for knowledge, but that they are "recommended" to us by our Reason for practical reasons.[23] They are there not at the level of theory, but at that of life itself. Our lives are ultimately centered in the problem of what we ought to do and whether the will is free, whether there is a hereafter, and whether God exists.[24] To affirm freedom, the hereafter, and the existence of God is to provide a firm footing for reason beyond the limits of experience and to clarify the nature of that primal presence of which we are sometimes vaguely aware and yet has time and again, through various periods and places, been revealed or divined as the center of our being.

What bearing does that trinitarian goal for which reason strives have on our everyday lives? Although Kant does not think that there is a solid theoretical path from the level of, say, the freedom of the will to that of the sensible world, in that the effect of one on the other and their interrelationship are not logically derivable,[25] he nevertheless believes that the ideal world can influence the sensible world. The moral world is only an idea, for instance, when it is defined as how the world can be as a result of free will and how it ought to be as a result of moral necessity. Yet the moral world shapes the actual world around us to the extent that we act to make the actual world conform with the moral world. The objective reality of the idea is seen in its actual employment by Reason in its practical affairs to bring about certain changes in the concrete world.[26] That we act and sometimes make great sacrifices to further our moral ideas gives them a reality that is otherwise hard to demonstrate. The reality of our moral ideas becomes manifest through those actions and (sometimes) institutions in which they take on a living presence.

Our moral ideas, for their part, spring from our desire for worthiness in the world of grace. They relate to God and our hope in an afterlife. We cannot act purposefully without them.[27] Were we all to act purposefully in that manner, Kant further maintains, our action would be effective, for the world itself is arranged to accommodate the systematic fulfillment of such collective moral action. From this, he concludes that the world must through and through be founded on the idea of the supreme good. This is the ultimate unity that pervades the world from within and so creates the ground for every unity we can attain. The supreme good accounts equally for the unity of knowledge, the purposefulness of our moral action, and the potential to realize our moral ideas in the world. The priority of the supreme good is so clear in Kant's mind that he finally sees the expansion of knowledge through Reason, beyond all experience, as not the cause, but the *effect* of the purposiveness instilled in us by the practical side of Reason with the supreme good in its view. We can expand our knowledge beyond what is ordinarily given us in space and time because, inspired by the presence of the supreme good that pervades and unites the world, we act with moral purpose. Our knowledge is lifted out of the confines within which we ordinarily must seek it by our sense of a divine presence and our moral response to it. Thus, the everyday knowledge that we are able to demonstrate is transformed. We come to see it in an entirely different light. We shall eventually see how there is a corresponding way for the expansion of our freedom; for we have a similar ability, if we are up to it, to live freely at a level well beyond the scope of our common conception of freedom. After all, the boundaries of the world in which we exercise our freedom are at least as important as the fact of being free. One is not all that free if the world in which one is granted freedom be small and limited in its possibilities.

Kant never gave up on the possibility of expanding knowledge without being able to firmly derive the expansion from any possible experience. In the end, he makes it clear that the source of such transcendent expansion is transcendence itself. We are made in a way that enables us to respond to transcendence, and as part of our response, our knowledge grows in ways unwarranted by experience. The supreme good also guarantees the unity of our knowledge, and the interconnectedness of all things in accordance with universal and necessary laws. And it defines our action.[28]

In the Kantian philosophy, then, reason as we know it is twice removed from sovereignty. Reason ("the understanding" for Kant) is regent for the intellect (Reason for Kant), which provides reason with the ideas that give it direction. And the intellect is regent for the Supreme Being whose goodness gives it (and reason) direction. Hence reason, which Kantians and neo-Kantians invoke in all parts of the world (especially those parts deemed more at the mercy of the irrational), is merely viceregent in the view of the man whose work they all look up to. Any hopes placed in reason's sovereignty are therefore tragically misplaced. This can be affirmed regardless of whether one accepts Kant's idea of the supreme good, regardless of whether one believes in God and the hereafter. For whatever one believes in, any human being in full possession of his faculties consciously or unconsciously has a life plan centered in certain values, principles, ideals, or goals. These form the widest determinations for his life. Once they are formed, and as a secondary process, the person, whatever he does, makes certain decisions about which thematic choices to make in the everyday employment of reason. A physicist must decide, when the evidence points more than one way as it often does (and some argue *always must*), whether, say, he prefers a symmetrical or an asymmetrical theory, or whether he regards the world as a continuum or a collection of discrete events. And as a human being, he must decide, say, whether there is a beyond, and whether to be moral or just self-interested. These decisions inform all his uses of reason, whether in his scientific work or in his life as such. There is no escape from the acknowledgment of reason's viceregency. So transparent a fiction as the sovereignty of reason can persist only through habit, powerful motives and interests, or blind faith and dogmatism.

It is ironic, and a sign of the bias since then, that so many followers of Kant have been oblivious to the hierarchy in which he unequivocally placed the faculty that they have called reason. The ancient and medieval residue in Kant's philosophy runs far deeper than many have bothered to underline. But Kant himself, in a heroic attempt to reconcile irreconcilables, paved the way for those who have subsequently misread him. He sought to reconcile the intellect, free and open to be suffused with transcendence, with a rationality understood more and more in calculative or elementary logical terms. He wanted the qualities by which the intellect might recognize the being that pervades the world, let alone the world's unity and supreme goodness, to be rationally recognizable. He wanted to rationally account for the eschatological. He wanted it to require no more than for us to be rational to affirm the afterlife, the existence of God, and the unity and goodness that guarantee our proper theoretical and moral direction. He thus differed from the ancients and medievals. His concept of the intellect was not quite like theirs, for they had recognized the transcendent dimension of the intellect for what it is. But Kant also differed from Descartes, Leibniz, and Spinoza because what he called Reason was broader than allowed by their rationalism. Unfortunately, these differences, underlain by the attempt to reconcile irreconcilables, could only engender, as we now know so well that they did, two groups of thinkers whose separation eventually made them unable to communicate. The German idealists and their successors took to using "reason" as a name for what sounded exceedingly irrational (or they disdained reason). On the other hand, those who took "reason" for something uncontroversially rational ended up with a terribly narrow view of the world, as was the case with the radical empiricists and logical positivists. In this light, perhaps, we may see those who once clearly differentiated between the rational and spiritual dimensions of the intellect and acknowledged each for what it is more favorably. Medieval Islamic thinkers, for example, were highly rational in their science, logic, and argumentation on behalf of their theological or legal views. In these, they celebrated rationality. But they also remained in touch with the spiritual anchor for their work and cultivated various disciplines to that end, mystical, illuminationist, pietist, or otherwise. Meanwhile, various Muslim thinkers over a long time worked to bring the rational and the spiritual together. For the shari'a and hadith scholarship combined rigorous and painstakingly rational methods of inquiry and argumentation with the awareness that they were suffused with the spiritual reality that ultimately grounded them. Islam has strongly favored the coexistence of the rational with the spiritual, where the rational is frankly set in a spiritual climate and the spiritual is wrought to the limits of human reason in concrete forms while retaining its identity. The idea was to bring the rational and the spiritual together by seeing each in its proper place, and recognizing that one complements the other. Islam has therefore been equally wary of a rationalism that appears threatened with drift and a spirituality that is available only to a select few.

Kant knew the intellect better than any among his contemporaries and immediate predecessors whose work is available to us. But he tried so persistently and expicitly to give it a rational character that the gradual tilt in favor of the rational at the expense of the spiritual was hastened and willed along by those who did all they could to institute that tilt. This has the gravest implications, for if reason has its direction in the ideals that define a life plan, which, if not spiritual, are certainly either moral or involve some conception of human nature, aspirations, and so on; and because these ideals are by definition not rational, then to allege that reason is sovereign is in effect to put it at the mercy of the most influential forces. These forces may act openly or secretly.

The submergence of the spiritual by the rational has been accompanied by a twofold shrinkage: reason itself gradually collapses into mere calculation, for it loses the drive to transcend itself (a drive clearly and passionately affirmed by Kant); and the domain in which freedom may be exercised narrows accordingly, above all amid the pervasive pressure to rationalize. These important developments will be treated in the next chapter.

Before we take temporary leave from Kant, we should perhaps reflect on the unity of his philosophy rather than the tension that plagues it. So far as reason is concerned, we find, in the Kantian philosophy, that it is integrated into a whole ultimately shaped by an ethico-religious vision. We began with what may be termed "internal" constraints on reason, or those constraints that have nothing to do with moral, social, and cultural factors external to its use. These internal constraints ultimately take the form of transcendental ideas that direct the general use of reason, ideas that pertain to the unity of the fundamental poles in our tripolar existence: subject, world, and final source (regarded by Kant as divinity). But we have also seen how those internal constraints are given by what Kant calls Reason, which itself is immersed in the transcendent reality of which it has a "presentiment." This transcendent reality grounds the moral purpose with which our lives are imbued as well as the unity of our knowledge. So in the end, our (rational) pursuit of knowledge and our moral lives become united in the source of all that exists. Reason is hence integrally tied to our moral ideas and spiritual being. The constraints that by now seem external to reason, such is our habit of separating its use from social, moral, and cultural consequences, are really part of the correct employment of reason. For Kant, to reason correctly is to act so that the moral good is promoted as well as to expand knowledge and seek the systematic unity of all things. A scientist who reasons as he should cannot fail to promote the good.

The Constraints on the Use of Reason in the Natural Sciences

We now turn to the (internal) constraints on the use of reason in science —for many continue to uphold scientific reason as a paragon of sovereign reason. They assert that people everywhere, provided that they be rational, will reach the same conclusion given the same experimental procedure. "Let us forget about transcendental ideas, moral purpose, supreme beings, and all that," they say, "and concentrate instead on how scientists reason. For while we can never agree on the same moral or religious outlook, or even whether there is a transcendent reality—and we remind you that endless wars have resulted from such disagreements *when they mattered*—we have seen the emergence of a worldwide scientific community where agreement comes easily. For science is based on a universal form of reason. Perhaps we can then extract this scientific reason, which we may call the 'scientific method,' and transpose it to social thought. For human beings and societies are part of nature, and there is no reason why we cannot treat them as scientifically as other parts of nature. We may then have the key to move decisively and enduringly toward social order and peace all over the world."

Although this outlook is now widely regarded as a fantasy in Western intellectual circles, it continues to live on in the popular imagination and in the habits of certain powerful institutions that help perpetuate that fantasy. It also enjoys a wide appeal in non-Western countries among members of the intelligentsia who see reason as the liberator from traditions that they have come to regard as a hindrance. It will thus come as a shock to many when they are forced to confront evidence that draws a picture of science other than that suggested by the rationalist conception of scientific method. Such evidence was harder to come by in the heyday of Newtonian mechanics, but with the advent of electromagnetic theory, the life sciences, relativity, and quantum mechanics (not to mention the emergent chaos and complexity theories), it has become hard to ignore.

In the foregoing section, in an illustration of Kant's ideas about the constraints on the employment of reason, it was mentioned that the scientist faced with evidence that points more than one way (which some believe to be the case for all evidence) must decide on certain preferences as he develops a hypothesis or theory based on the evidence. Gerald Holton has studied this feature of scientific work for a long time. He has documented its pervasiveness sufficiently for us to affirm that those who *contribute* to science—as opposed to those who are functionaries in the public institutions built around the work of the contributors—must at some point direct their theories in ways uncalled for by the evidence and the analytical methods at their disposal. Holton calls the foci of these necessary directions "thematic hypotheses," "which are unverifiable and unfalsifiable and yet not quite arbitrary."[29] They are small in number. They arise from certain ambiguities surrounding nature, which is either regulated by a unified fundamental law or is a plurality that cannot be integrated into a single regulatory framework, finite or infinite, eternal or created, purposeless or purposeful, completely empty in some areas or throughout filled with physical substance, continuous or discontinuous, and can be described quantitatively or requires a qualitative account. The full list is not much longer. Sometimes a thematic hypothesis becomes more persuasive after the alternatives have consistently failed.[30] For instance, the evidence in recent decades favors a discontinuous universe that has a beginning over one continuous without beginning or end. However, the history of science provides several examples of such situations that have endured for centuries, only for the alternative thematic hypothesis to return with aplomb. This happened with the long dormant atomic theory.

The best testimony for the inevitability of thematic hypotheses is Newton's suppression of a fifth rule of reason he had originally intended to include. The rule would have required that what was not derivable from the things themselves, nor demonstrable from the phenomena, be discarded. Newton knew that he had to depend precisely on what he would thereby have discarded in his theory of planetary motion. He could find no medium, nor conceive one, through which gravity might be communicated. He believed it to be caused by God.[31] Without gravity, the theories that propelled physics to the extent of inspiring the idea of universal mechanism in many intelligent and learned people in the eighteenth century would have foundered. Gravity was "a bridge built over the gap of ignorance."[32] Although gravity today is a concept that works impeccably in the applied sciences, we are still uncertain about how to conceptualize or describe the effects to which it has given a name.

In our century, scientists found three radically different alternatives when faced with the same evidence. Once wave-particle duality became known, and it looked like the energy states of electrons in orbit around the atomic nucleus were discontinuous, Einstein and Schrödinger were not prepared to give up on continuity. They applied themselves to a wave-mechanical explanation that would reimpose their vision on the evidence. Heisenberg, in contrast, embraced discontinuity and went after an algebraic solution that emphasized it. Niels Bohr came up with the brilliant suggestion that electrons considered as particles were discontinuous with respect to their possible energy states whereas as waves they obeyed the hypothesis of continuity. He also took this dual existence for an irreducible fact. Holton describes the criteria for scientific choice faced with the same experimental data as "aesthetic."[33] This was echoed some years later by Hawking, when he makes it clear that all scientific theories at a certain level have aesthetic or metaphysical motives.[34]

The criteria for choosing among various thematic hypotheses are aesthetic or metaphysical. This accounts for where battle lines are drawn and how deeply the commitment runs. Nowhere is the commitment more manifest than when faced with overwhelming evidence. Einstein, incensed with the irrepressible rise of the Uncertainty Principle, finally exclaimed: "God does not play dice!"

The overall flashpoints between classical and quantum physics occur along the line separating the following pairs of opposite thematic hypotheses or *themata*: causality versus indeterminacy; statistical description or probabilistic distribution; a sharp subject/object separation versus the impossibility of such separation; the definability of closed systems versus the inseparability of the system under observation from the agency or devices that observe it; and the negligibility of the observer's effect on the experiment versus the observer's or experimental apparatus's influence on every state of the system under experimental control.[35] Note how a certain state of mind favors one side over the other. For instance, the impulse to control favors a sharp subject/object separation together with the definability of closed systems.[36] A subject completely detached from his object is free to manipulate the object. If the object is furthermore defined as a closed system, then it is at least in theory completely comprehensible and thus completely manipulable. Engineering works approximate this condition very well, for buildings and the materials that compose them give every appearance of closed systems utterly apart from their builders (this appearance deceives too, because buildings are subject to environmental influence and do reflect the attitudes and purposes of their builders). Closed systems detached from their observers, in theory perfectly knowable and manipulable, conjure images of the realization of certain visions and dreams. On the other hand, the interdependence between subject and object, together with systems that reflect the nature and actions of their observers as well as how they are observed, and which are assumed to interact with their surroundings, favor empathic types attuned to what they study and prepared to accept surprises.[37] Whatever one's temperament or preferences, the controlling impulse is foiled by a reality wrongly assumed to be totally controllable. Highly accurate measurements can be made, but what one measures is otherwise pretty much in flux.

Similarly, those who view or study a culture or religion as a closed system detached from themselves are more likely than not to belong to a milieu where control of culture or religion is paramount. Control need not mean foreign domination. It is more likely to be domestic, say, the ideological use of religion or the commercial use of culture. As it happens, when culture or religion are viewed in this way, still more is missed than in physical science. For culture and religion can hardly be known when one is as distanced from them as one is from colliding billiard balls.

Science turns out to be (at least) a three-dimensional activity disguised as one with two dimensions. Its more obvious two dimensions are empirical fact and analytical ratiocination. The standard account presents science as the rational gathering of empirical facts into compact theories. These two dimensions themselves, however, are not quite what they seem.[38] Empirical facts are no longer simply observed, but are determined by observation and the apparatus used in the process. They are not constant either. Facts that today are important were unknown or neglected in the past and vice versa. We are always surrounded by far more phenomena than we can examine experimentally. A number of factors already predispose us to select from among them, and to regard those that we do select in some ways rather than others. When it comes to the analytical systems that are available to us, and within which we perform the calculations that concern the empirical facts under consideration, we must also make choices, from among those systems as well as in how we use what we choose. The choice has been greatly increased with the discovery of non-Euclidean geometry, algebra in imaginary spaces, and other highly abstract mathematical fields.

If we were to look at the standard two-dimensional presentation of scientific activity unproblematically, we find another limitation. Even if empirical fact and analytical ratiocination were what many believe them to be, they do not by themselves amount to all that much; for empirical fact now boils down to meter readings, and ratiocination to tautologous logical and mathematical propositions.[39] Science surely involves more.

The third dimension, within which the themata featured in this section exist, is one where we also encounter the fundamental presuppositions, notions, terms, methodological judgments, and decisions that cannot be resolved into empirical fact or analytical ratiocination.[40] Many themata have been pointed out so far. Others are the theme of an active or potent principle (within which the discussion of forces takes place), the theme of conservation (say, of energy or momentum) that is held even when observation makes this very difficult, and the faith in laws that concisely express discoverable natural regularities.[41] The aesthetic or metaphysical motives for the selection of and commitment to certain themata have already been mentioned. More can be said about the minutae that must accompany the scientist's overall vision, which guides him through various empirical and mathematical possibilities. The minutae on the one hand involve intuitions and judgments that must be made and for which no algorithm is possible, and on the other issue from the humanity of the scientist, whose aptitudes, errors, prodigality, ingenuity, and passions shape his theories. Thus it is somewhat inappropriate to describe what is indispensable to science outside of fact and ratiocination as just another "dimension." What transcends the standard two dimensions appears to consitute a multifarious realm, too complex, unpredictable, and opaque for a satisfactory account, but certainly present. It is there in judgments that must be made, intuitions without which theory bogs down, and themata that direct the overall project, all of which are a partial manifestation of the realm that Holton terms the "third dimension." This multifarious realm, in which the metaphysical or aesthetic criteria for the selection of themata have their origin, defines the extent to which reason in science is more dependent than we knew or wanted to know as recently as a generation ago. Now, we do know that reason by itself, faced only with empirical fact, has nowhere to go without help from many sources (all of which, to repeat, lie outside of it). In science, these sources account for the intuitions, judgments, and themata indispensable to scientific progress. If a scientist makes no conscious effort to delineate the thematic emphasis of his work, and falters whenever he must rely on his own intuitions and judgment, he is but a technician who operates mechanically after the direction of his work has been chosen for him. Such are the limits of reason in science.

In human affairs at large, what lies beyond the scope of reason has been emphasized within a Western critical tradition that traces itself to the problematic opened up by Kant's efforts to delimit reason. More often than not, however, this tradition either distanced itself from science, which it only grudgingly acknowledged, or was openly hostile to it. Opposition to that tradition and intellectual orthodoxy meanwhile increasingly took the form of modeling all human affairs on the activity of science. Both positions are no longer tenable given the discovery that science, at bottom, is itself propelled by the nonrational. The elements of this discovery have been latent. Only recently has the latency become realized in a strong philosophical position.

It turns out that physical science differs from psychology, sociology, history, and other fields only because of the greater prominence it can give to facts and ratiocination, and the relative ease with which the indispensable nonrational factors have been concealed. The myth of physical science as the rational activity par excellence demanded the concealment of the nonrational that pervades its direction and countless points along which it unfolds. But even the most exact sciences are now known to be impotent without themata the criteria for whose selection are aesthetic or metaphysical. Hence there is no longer the need to emphasize the nonrational in opposition to science; nor is there any justification for diverting other fields toward the path taken by physical science on the grounds that it is an unalloyed mix of fact and reason.

As for the claim that certain current policies aim at the rationalization of a given society or economy, it is sheer nonsense. Not even physics can be rationalized. To rationalize a society or economy means to reform it according to objectives, ideals, and criteria that are influential for reasons that have nothing to do with reason and remain hidden from those critically (or otherwise) unprepared to investigate the reforms and the motives behind them. Given a certain dogma, for instance, that human beings are primarily creatures who seek to maximize their material desires, and a certain goal, for instance, the extension of the market for a number of corporations, or a combination of such motives, an economy or society is pressured accordingly and the process glorified as "rationalization." This is not to say that such processes are unnecessary or undesirable in toto. The theoretical refutation of rationalization claims should rather help obstruct their ruthless application and unmask the misrepresentations, falsehoods, and fantasies that accompany economism or market totalitarianism.

The Testimony of Two Leading Contemporary Physicists

For those who remain skeptical despite the cogency of Holton's work, and for those who wish to see the foregoing illustrated at some length, it is necessary to turn to what eminent contemporary scientists have written about their field. Because physics continues to be upheld as the "hardest" among the "hard" sciences, then surely if physicists themselves have acknowledged the account given by Holton, the acknowledgment could be extended to the other natural sciences and, easier yet, to the social sciences. Stephen Hawking and Paul Davies have been chosen because they are recognized authorities in physics and popular expositors of contemporary physical theory.

Our brief overview of contemporary physics will include the following:

1. A sketch of the structure and shape of the world as revealed by contemporary physics.

2. Where contemporary physics stands with regard to the ideal of the scientific method.

3. Where contemporary physics stands with regard to the ideal of a rational worldview.

The reader for whom a summary of the following overview will suffice may wish only to read the italicized passages that recapitulate the various points made. These recapitulations will be repeated in the following section, where they are matched with the analogous implications for social thought and reform. The general reader, however, may be happy to learn that this is the only chapter where I have felt it necessary to present the issues in a manner that, while common in some academic writing, may demand more than those unaccustomed to it are (quite understandably) able or willing to give.

Readers who are satisfied with what has been said so far, or who do not wish to be diverted from the general run of the argument, ought to proceed to page 74, where they will find the concluding remarks for what they have read in this chapter. Those remarks will not have been substantially changed by what is said about contemporary physics and its implications for social thought in the intervening pages, but merely reinforced.

As for readers who are relatively ignorant of the contemporary sciences but will read on because they would like to know more or see how I am going to support an argument that they already feel uncomfortable with, let them rest assured that what follows has been submitted or presented to a number of professional scientists (including two physicists), who have judged its contents to conform with what they know. In truth, far from being controversial, what is revealed here is but an inkling of the dramatically different landscape that continues to emerge from the natural sciences.

The Structure and Shape of the World
Studied in Contemporary Physics

The physical world is composed of elementary particles. Its shape is determined by how the particles are related, which includes the forces that act upon them. It has traditionally been conceived within a spatiotemporal framework. And an overall reality is thereby constituted: unimaginably large numbers of elementary particles causally related through fundamental forces in a spatiotemporal frame of reference. Although this picture suggests compatibility with Newtonian mechanics, we shall presently see how radically the structure and shape of the world have been altered by contemporary physics.

The elementary particles. Since the days of the ancient Greeks, a tradition in the study of nature views it as made up entirely of very small particles. These particles are held to be few in kind. The astounding variety of the macrophenomena that we experience is due to different combinations of huge numbers of those elementary particles. The image that has often accompanied atomism is that of building blocks in various combinations. However tiny the particles may be, they must be discrete entities that, when combined in sufficiently large numbers, become distinct objects for us.

The definition of a physical thing has changed, however. Physics no longer deals with matter that can be easily visualized in terms of building blocks and what is thus built. It no longer even deals with matter itself exclusively. The world now studied by physics is one with matter, energy, and things such as black holes (the points predicted by relativity theory where all known physical laws break down) and gravity waves that are nonmaterial by definition.[42] For "hard" matter, it makes sense to presuppose building blocks; for energy, black holes, and gravity waves, it does not. In fact, energy, black holes, and gravity waves are beyond the pale of common sense.

Matter itself, the sole component that intuitively lends itself to mechanical analysis, is now interpreted as "locked up" energy. If matter is unlocked, it becomes energy. If great amounts of energy are concentrated, they become matter. What Einstein captured in his famous and ingeniously simple formula has since been experimentally verified.[43]

To the extent that matter is analyzed as matter in the traditional sense, that is to say, as "made up" of elementary particles, the set of particles that physicists have so far established has several strange members. Along with the triad of major subatomic particles, the electron, the proton, and the neutron, the positron, antiproton and antineutron have been predicted and then discovered.[44] If the pairs are respectively combined, we are left with radiation. A collision between an electron and a positron, or a proton and an antiproton, means annihilation. Thus the name "antimatter" has been coined to describe the parts of the universe where there are positrons, antiprotons, and antineutrons.

What about electrons and other positively charged material particles? Can we not at least pin them down as such and still regard them as building blocks? No, for two reasons. First, no subatomic particle can be pinned down to a specific motion; it inhabits a world "full of murkiness and chaos."[45] Second, the wave/particle duality has been admitted since the early part of the century as a result of Niels Bohr's insights, so that an electron is a particle or a wave depending on the point of view from which it is considered. Moreover, the wave is not a wave *of* a particle (the particle does not itself undulate). Rather, it is a form of information about the particle. A particle spreads information as a wave that enables us to know, say, its position or energy levels.[46] It is experimentally an indifferent matter whether a particle exists as such in the absolute sense or whether assuming its existence leads to the correct results under specific conditions. Otherwise, all that is encountered is information. The universe, for all we know, may be a sea of information that is concentrated in certain ways at certain points (we shall see this more clearly at the end of this overview).

Furthermore, physicists discovered that the groups of elementary particles matched mathematical symmetries. When they were emboldened to postulate an underlying symmetry, they discovered still more elementary particles, such as the quark. Quarks are so tiny that they may be better described as a mathematically successful way for measuring matter than as matter's building blocks.[47]

In general, contemporary physicists regard the question of whether they are dealing with physical or mathematical entities as experimentally equivalent.

The framework for elementary particles. Although the notion of an absolute space has been questioned by Leibniz in the seventeenth century (for he believed that space exists only insofar as there are different things that exist simultaneously[48]), and that of an absolute time by Saint Augustine in the fifth (for he pointed out that temporality must be a feature of the created world in contrast with the eternity of the heavens[49]), only recently have we reached the stage where physics itself could go no further were its framework absolute space and time. Today, galaxies are no longer thought of as moving apart through space, but as "stretching" it.[50] Space is an elastic medium. It is created according to the movement and energy of the objects creating it (which vindicates Leibniz). It is thought to have arisen from an infinitely shrunken, unbounded state from which the universe exploded.[51] Furthermore, the shape into which this elastic medium is wrought is not spherical nor anything similar, but one that allows it to connect up to itself in various ways. Such a shape is called a "hypersphere." In a sphere, we may move from one end to another across its diameter. In a hypersphere, the analogous "ends" may meet at the same point. Finally, there is the abstract suggestion that space and time are components of a more primordial geometry, and that our relatively coherent and organized universe emerged from a correspondingly more primordial state described by that geometry.[52]

Fanciful though this last excursion may be, it no longer makes sense to uphold the notion of physical things *in* space, because physical things *determine* the shape of space. The argument is easily extended to time, for time has been combined with space to form a four-dimensional spacetime continuum, which Einstein and his successors have held to be the framework for physical things.

Classical ideas about where things are and how they succeed one another no longer hold up to current experimental procedures in physics. It is no longer possible to imagine physical things as entities that can be analyzed into a few components in space and time. The Cartesian system of coordinates, in the physical world, is an idealization.

The relations between elementary particles. Our tendency to describe relations between phenomena in causal terms is so natural that Kant included causality among the categories of the understanding that precede and determine the shape of all experience.[53] Kant argued that we necessarily relate phenomena causally (and in two other ways that need not be pointed out here). Our notion of one thing causing another is usually temporal or, if the cause and effect are simultaneous, they express a clear relation of dependence (such as the dependence of our lives on breathing). In quantum theory, however, individual particles may appear unpredictably relative to space and time. Given sufficient curvature of space, where gravity gains in intensity, the creation of particles becomes probable (no other account has been found for experimentally encountered particles).[54] The unpredictable appearance of particles not only occurs at the more warped regions of space but also where space itself fades into the singularity points (black holes) predicted by relativity theory. These singularities are defined as points where all knowable physical laws break down, for those points happen to be the boundaries of the spacetime continuum. As physics admits the existence of what lies beyond space and time, it must admit the emergence of particles from that beyond without causation, unpredictably. It must admit the possibility that *anything* might emerge unpredictably from those singularities.[55] This possibility constitutes a more serious breakdown of conventional causality.

Likewise, the understanding of the *influence* between particles must outgrow the association between influence and simple causality. Collisions between electrons had been viewed analogously to those between rigid bodies, say, billiard balls. By now, the process is understood in more detail. Each electron travels with a complex web of short-lived ("virtual") particles buzzing around it. As two electrons approach each other, some of these particles are transferred from one to the other, which causes a momentumlike disturbance. This constitutes not only the influence that approaching electrons have on one another, but a description of the way forces operate between them (the abstract mathematical terms used to compute these subatomic processes lead to very accurate results).[56] Thus forces in quantum theory are generally modeled on exchanges of particles, which may or may not carry mass. Instead of the old notions of gravitational pull and the nuclear "glue," tiny particles flitting back and forth are postulated.

With various levels of unpredictability and the replacement of the notion of active forces with that of exchanges of particles, it seems unlikely that a standard concept of causation can be sustained as the manner in which physical entities are fundamentally related.

The contemporary view of the overall physical reality. Whereas the characteristic feature of mechanism is the analysis of physical reality into its components, which are then found to constitute the whole according to simple natural laws, physics has been obliged by quantum theory to regard the whole *as such.* The experimental demonstration of a theorem put forward by John Bell in the 1960s to settle an argument between Bohr and Einstein showed two particles (photons or electrons) moving apart from a common source in the following way. However apart they may be, the measurement of one determines the definite qualities of the other. This influence between them cannot occur in any normal fashion, for because it is simultaneous, it would involve travel at an infinite speed. No physical theory or experimental evidence admits a speed greater than that of light, let alone infinite. The only way to account for this influence is to treat the two particles as a single totality, or an indivisible whole.[57] Any analysis would mean either denial of the evidence or the violation of self-evident physical truth (that speed cannot be infinite). The success to which reductionism has carried physics must now give way to holism.

Holism treats wholes as more than just aggregates of discrete parts. Examples of what must be treated holistically are the relationship between a newspaper photograph and the dots that "make it up," a jigsaw puzzle and its pieces, an advertising display and the circuitry that makes it visible, and a symphony and the individual musical contents of the score. In each of these pairs, the first is more than the sum of the second. For example, the picture revealed by a completed jigsaw puzzle is a whole beyond the mere fact that it is composed of several little pieces. Life and the soul must be similarly seen in relation to the "matter" in which they occur.[58] Life is there whenever well-organized arrangements of physical substances reach such levels of complexity as to make the probability of their spontaneous assembly zero.[59] One encounters life only when an incredibly complex arrangement of atoms and molecules act as a whole. Holism does not refute reductionism, but complements it. Parts taken as an aggregate exist *at a level different* from their existence as a whole. The soul, mind, or self thus belong to a category different from firing neurons.[60]

Besides the consideration of reality from two complementary points of view, namely, that which admits of division into parts and that which requires its treatment as a whole—and it is noteworthy that the analysis into hitherto unimaginably small parts has led to the reality that must be regarded holistically—contemporary physics is quite explicit about the observer's role in *shaping* reality. This runs contrary to the venerable tradition of the ideal observer who conducts his experiments in perfect detachment and reports results that pertain to things as God might see them. In the well-known two-slit experiment, the ambiguity between wave and particle is resolved by the actions of the observer.[61] The direction of the deflection of a particle after it hits a target is likewise suspended until the observer decides whether it is left or right.[62] In general, quantum theory faces a hybrid world of simultaneous possibilities that only an observer collapses into a concrete reality. To know what state certain particles are in is to collapse the various possibilities presented into a single one. The very definition of reality thus changes radically in quantum theory: It is not something out there to be known, but something to be decided from among the various possibilities by the observer who conducts the experiment.

Physical reality has two complementary aspects: one that is analyzable into component parts and another that must be regarded as a whole. Moreover, it is not experimentally treated as independently existing, but as comprising simultaneous possiblities that can be resolved only by the observer's intervention.

Contemporary Physics and the Ideal of the Scientific Method

Academics and laypersons who idolize and idealize science, if they are consistent with their own criteria, must accept the surprises sprung by physics in its search for reality. They must accept a reality that in every way—its elementary constituents, its fundamental framework, the relations and influences (forces) between the constituents, and the reality thereby formed—undermines the structure of reality built by mechanism. This structure was dominated by the idea that one could start out either with point masses or rigid bodies, discover and name a handful of forces operative in their rest and motion, and describe their operation entirely in mathematical terms.

A reality fraught with ambiguity, where the elements can be resolved into matter or its opposite, particles or information about them, where the formation and form of space depends on its physical constituents; and where the elements interact through exchanges of messenger particles, relate in terms more subtle than any hitherto imagined, form integral wholes even when they are far apart, change according to the decisions of the observer, and appear or disappear unpredictably—such is not the world that the heralds of peace and prosperity for all mankind envisaged when they extended the crystalline structure of a mechanically viewed universe and its simple, clockwork dynamics to the realm of social change. Physical reality now comes across as strangely evocative of the domains of art, literature, magic, mythology, and mysticism.

As bizarre as physical reality may seem to those who believe they find their bearings and justification in ideas about science and the scientific method inspired by the success of modern physics, they may still uphold their ideal of a fair, universal method, by whose dictates the phenomena are observed, gathered, and related without prejudice, save for the basic concepts, categories, and relations universally employed by reason (which are believed to be few). They also believe that this process can be repeated with identical results given identical experimental conditions and competence.

Such an ideal is already problematical in three respects based on the foregoing survey.

1. The observer, as we have seen, participates in decisions as basic as whether something is a particle or a wave. The nature of reality depends on how he sets up the apparatus. The observer does not always interfere so drastically with the phenomena under observation, but the ideal of detached observation can no longer be consistently upheld.

2. For experiments to be at all possible, reality must be analyzable into parts whose relations are then discovered. But given reality's dual aspect, one susceptible to reductionism and the other holistic, reality in its holistic aspect cannot be subject to any analytical or experimental process. It simply manifests itself at certain levels, or one is led to it perforce lacking any other explanation for experimentally encountered events. It is absurd to speak of the observation and analysis of integral wholes. The source of holism in physics may be obscure, but it is clear that life relates to specific collections of atoms and molecules or the mind to the brain in the same way that an integral whole relates to the parts that are there whenever the whole is there (but are *not* therefore parts *of* the whole). From the outset, the scientific method, whatever it turns out to be, has reality in view only to the extent that reality is susceptible to reductionism. In other words, before it even gets going, it has a prejudiced view of reality.

3. The so-called basic concepts, categories, and relations universally employed by reason, an always controversial idea, are more clearly than ever neither as changeless and metaphysically demonstrable nor as sim-

ple as Kant had thought (it is interesting to note that Aristotle was more flexible regarding both the finality and number of basic concepts, categories, and relations). If relating phenomena and events causally comes naturally to human beings, the causality required by contemporary physics is so subtle and unusual as to make one wonder whether it can be meaningfully called "causality." If the concept is retained nevertheless, then reason itself is more obviously subject to change than previously thought, and claims that begin with "Any rational human being would———" become more suspect than they have always been. In particular, the elements of the rationality that oversees the scientific process themselves become open to question.

The observer actively intervenes in the experimental procedure. The scientific method, understood in the usual idealized manner, can deal only with the analyzable aspect of the physical world (and not with its holistic aspect). And the characteristic causal mentality traditionally associated with the scientific method is no longer compatible with physical reality.

Besides those three difficulties, we can find serious disparities between every quality attributed to the scientific method and scientific activity itself:

1. It is claimed that scientists relate the phenomena without prejudice. These phenomena are supposedly brought together by reason, objectively, so that scrutiny would yield no logical objection given the data. Unfortunately, physicists today do not have recourse to such luxury. When they attempt the prediction of the heat left shortly after the universe emerged, as a result of collisions between enormous numbers of matter and antimatter particles, and make up appropriate measurements in the universe to judge the accuracy of their prediction, they are faced with calculations so large as to dramatically increase the possibility of error. Instead, they hope "agreement can be achieved with very plausible models."[63] The criteria of plausibility are often left conveniently flexible. In dealing with the physics of the universe, the following pattern seems to hold. Either the calculations entailed by the hypothesis relative to the phenomena are too large to guarantee accuracy or calculations must be given up and replaced with models that can never be as objective as logical or mathematical operations. Some eminent physicists go further. For instance, in the name of a goal such as the unification of the fundamental forces of nature, they put forward a hypothetical particle that (1) they know in advance not to match observed particles and (2) involves calculations of such magnitude that they can practically never be completed.[64]

2. The impartial gathering of the phenomena is likewise an ideal that is inconsistent with scientific practice. Basic phenomena change de-

pending on the theoretical limitations set for them. When Aristotle studied motion, he dealt with any change from matter to form, and from potentiality to actuality. When Galileo studied motion, he restricted himself to motion as change in position rather than one in form or being. Whereas Aristotle would study the motion of a person from childhood to adulthood or ignorance to knowledge, Galileo would study it only as movement from one position in space to another. Galileo's restrictions allow for mathematical generalizations universally applicable to bodies in motion. But they leave out many kinds of qualitative motion taken by Aristotle to be part of physics. Just as what we consider a "body in motion" changes, so do other conceptual changes determine what we include among the phenomena to be studied and what we leave out. Furthermore, when conceptual stability is achieved, several more phenomena are still left out. Galileo's physics ignored heat and sound. The physical sciences generally exclude "most types of single-event occurrences that do not promise experimental control or repetition."[65] So the phenomena subject to experimental research, and amenable to the repeatability much admired outside of science, are carefully chosen to allow close experimental study that can be repeated indifferently among diverse observers. But is repeatability itself correctly attributed to experimental science?

3. Several factors make crucial experiments in contemporary physics practically unrepeatable. Some of the phenomena encountered are far too ephemeral to realistically allow their repeated observation. The life span of certain particles is so short that one wonders whether they exist at all or are merely the haphazard movements of sensors on extremely sensitive instruments. Other phenomena occur so rarely that the repetition of experiments that depend on their occurrence simply takes too long. How often can one go through thousands of cubic meters of water in an abandoned mine in search of an event that might occur in a single proton among the countless present? Even simple experiments, as any student of laboratory science can attest, require careful and deliberate adjustments to set up the identical conditions necessary to confirm an earlier result.

Besides what inheres in the phenomena under investigation, the cost and complexity of experiments, and that they involve teams of scientists working simultaneously, perhaps in different countries, have also become problems.[66] To raise the necessary money a second time, ensure that the experiment is set up to produce the identical initial conditions when it is highly complex, and bring together an international team of experts to this end is no longer a matter of rolling a miniature automobile down a wooden incline.

4. In tandem with repeatability is the attribute of falsifiability, made popular by Popper. The truth of science, so the argument goes, lies in the

falsifiability of its hypotheses—they can be convincingly and comprehensively refuted. But for something to be falsifiable, it must be possible to express it in the language of the logical system that forms the basis for our judgment. It turns out that the language of quantum or relativity theory cannot be formalized in that way and hence cannot be falsified in a manner as conclusive as some would like.[67] Moreover, a new scientific theory is sometimes accepted not because it falsifies the old, but through the sheer collective weight of the arguments put forward in its support. This is how the atomic theory was kept alive long before the instruments that permitted the detection of atoms were built. This is also how Newton's gravitational theory gained currency.[68] Throughout the history of science, no one has been able to falsify theories based on either the plenum or the vacuum for the simple reason that it is impossible to measure the vacuum (the very act of measurement means the emission of tiny particles that would occupy the space supposedly empty). Among the theories that take physical space to be a plenum (and similarly for the vacuum), one can supersede the other. But one cannot cross from one basic presupposition to the other. The plenum versus vacuum controversy is as intractable as those in ethics and metaphysics. We have come across the general case of such scientific controversies in the foregoing discussion of thematic hypotheses as treated by Holton.

It is a curious thing when a method supposedly culled from a prestigious and successful discipline, and enforced as a yardstick for the validity of claims made in other fields, is persistently ignored by the same discipline's luminaries. Contributors to science pay scant heed to the scientific method. In his remarks on common notions about the scientific method, Henry Harris, Regius Professor of Medicine at Oxford, mentions that scientists deliberately introduce changes into experiments so that they may obtain more information (which makes talk about repeatability moot), and scientific problems are "kicked around" rather than methodically investigated (because methodological openness has proved productive in research). He denies that there is any "logic of scientific discovery."[69] The value of hypotheses is determined after the fact by an evolutionary, ad hoc procedure.[70]

The physical sciences have made spectacular advances since the end of World War II in an atmosphere of methodological skepticism, free invention, theoretical boldness, dissent encouraged even among junior members of the community, and metaphorical language.[71] Lest one imagine that this is only recent, one quick look at the past reveals the prevalence of regard for openness, innovation, pluralism, personality, and freedom from philosophical constraint. Ernst Mach called for young scientists to study the work of the masters and use it as a playground for their imagination.[72] Bohr underscored the impossiblity of canvasing new fields of experience with principles that worked in the old. Boltzmann advocated a pluralistic approach in which the older principles are retained for the domain where they are useful and new principles invented for new domains. Duhem believed that science is best served when each intellect is allowed to freely realize itself according to its own disposition. And Einstein declared flatly that epistemological concerns are a hindrance for scientists.[73]

The facts gathered by contemporary physicists often cannot be related through precise calculations. Models, approximations, and hypothetical entities are put forward instead. Nor are the facts themselves selected without prejudice, for they are (and have been throughout the modern period) limited to the kind that favors experimental control or repetition. Nor does a prejudiced choice of facts guarantee repeatable experiments, either because the facts themselves have an elusive quality or because the cost and complexity of the experiment prohibit repetition. Nor are the hypotheses that emerge from scientific experiments accepted because prior hypotheses are refuted, for scientific hypotheses are not founded on universally accepted presuppositions, but are chosen from among competing pairs of themata, and today can no longer rest on mathematical support because of the vague nature of the phenomena dealt with. Finally, contributors to science, as in all other human activities, reflect their intuitions, prodigality, ingenuity, aptitudes, errors, and passions.

Physics and the Ideal of a Rational Worldview

However fluid and complex the phenomena within the scope of science are, however the method by which they are related to one another is as notable for its inscrutability as for its logic, and however observation involves the observer and reduces neutrality to an abstraction, some people may nevertheless uphold a rationalist view of science based on their faith that the scientist brings no beliefs unwarranted by reason into science. Let us see whether an eminent physicist's account of his work and his field justifies such faith.

Stephen Hawking is considered by some the successor of Galileo, Newton, and Einstein. He occupies the same post at Cambridge University once held by Newton, that of Lucasian Professor of Mathematics. His brilliance and eminence, perhaps a little exaggerated by his enthusiasts, are beyond doubt. So is his wish to leave nothing to God in the history and operation of the universe. Hawking would therefore be more motivated than anyone to ensure that a universe divorced from God is not instead wedded to the whims and wishes of secular-minded scientists.

To nonspecialists who follow their field, the two most compelling questions faced by physicists pertain to the origin of the universe and the interrelationship between the four fundamental forces of nature with a view to their unity. Here we must limit ourselves to the first so that this overview not become too long. However, the reader may rest assured that a similar argument can be constructed based on the same sources were he to turn to the second question.

As a result of highly advanced methods of measurement combined with a much-enhanced computational capacity, physicists now believe they possess data about the universe near its origin. Some of this data gives much cause for perplexity.

1. All regions of the universe must have started out at the same temperature. If this were not so, information would have had to travel across the universe at a speed greater than light.

2. Had the universe expanded at a rate smaller by one part in a hundred thousand million million, it would have recollapsed before it ever reached its present size. Had the rate been larger by a similarly unimaginably small amount, the expansion would have been too rapid for the formation of heavenly bodies.

3. Had there not been tiny differences in density in the early universe, no local irregularities would be possible. This means there would be no galaxies, stars, or planets.[74]

The second feature, for instance, may be highlighted as follows. The force at the origin of the universe would need to be extremely delicately balanced, just strong enough to allow the universe to expand, and just weak enough to allow the formation of galaxies, stars, and planets rather than the rapid dispersion of the cosmic material. The margin of error in this equilibrium is estimated at one part in ten raised to the sixtieth power (one with sixty zeros behind it).[75] In practical terms, this means no margin at all.

All this naturally implies an astonishing degree of order. To appreciate this, consider the probability for the selection of such a high degree of order. If each model for the universe were the size of a pinhead, the creator would have to scan a sheet of paper as large as the entire observable universe with a pin to select our universe. Considered not a deliberate act of creation but the spontaneous emergence of order from a wider state of universal chaos, our universe would (a) take an infinitely long time to emerge and (b) would originate from a state that we cannot observe in principle.[76]

Hawking recognizes what the accumulating evidence near the origin of the universe means.[77] He finds the pull toward a divine creator enhanced by evidence ironically sought with a view toward the elimination or great reduction of divine intervention and purpose in the universe.

Because Hawking admits that the initial conditions that his work helped establish are the kind that can only be chosen very, very carefully, the only alternative is to demonstrate that our universe could result from other initial conditions.[78] Immediately, we notice wild speculation taking the place of what methodical calculations and measurements commonsensically suggest because the physicist does not like the implications of the suggestion.

Hawking is led at first to what is called the "inflationary model." The basis for his choice does not lie in the evidence, but in his wish to secure a universe independent from God. This model assumes a universe that expanded at a mind-boggling rate in its early phase and then acquired the uniform and balanced conditions of our own universe after a slow or fast (depending on the model in question) cooling and transformation. Hawking himself eventually realizes that such models fail.[79]

Because Hawking cannot change the model for evidence that suggests more purposiveness than he is comfortable with, the only recourse left is to get rid of the evidence! Hawking suggests that the universe need have no initial conditions at all. What does he propose instead? That the universe would "just be," finite and with no boundary. If this is not a dogmatic assertion faced with "unpalatable" evidence, then it is hard to come up with one. It is also a nonsensical assertion, for no physicist can give meaning to the proposition "the universe has no boundary." To do so would mean that the physicist can also assert that there is nothing into which the universe might extend. Such assertions are *in principle* beyond the reach of science. Hawking notices the impasse into which the facts have driven him. His response is candid.

> I'd like to emphasize that this idea that time and space should be finite without boundary is just a *proposal:* It cannot be deduced from some other principle. Like any other scientific theory, it may initially be put forward for aesthetic or metaphysical reasons, but the real test is whether it makes predictions that agree with observation. This, however, is difficult to determine in the case of quantum gravity, for two reasons. First . . . we are not yet sure exactly which theory successfully combines general relativity and quantum mechanics, though we know quite a lot about the form such a theory must have. Second, any model that described the whole universe in detail would be much too complicated mathematically for us to be able to calculate exact predictions. One therefore has to make simplifying assumptions and approximations—and even then, the problem of extracting predictions remains a formidable one.[80]

Hawking graciously makes it clear to all who care to notice that his theories, designed to overcome evidence that suggests divine purpose and intervention, share their openly extrascientific and nonrational motives ("aesthetic or metaphysical reasons") with *any* other scientific theory. Moreover, unlike other theories that become established owing to their predictive accuracy, Hawking's theories deal with a domain so vast that exact predictions can never be calculated. This is so despite the manipulations ("simplifying assumptions and approximations") to which scientists routinely help themselves, and which do not conform with our image of how they derive and establish mathematical models that express relations between the phenomena.

Hawking's treatment of the origin of the universe tells the story of evidence accidentally arrived at by a process of thought intended to secure man's hold over nature once and for all through knowledge that pertains to the entire universe. The supernatural implications of that evidence then gave rise to unabashed attempts to change it. In the end, we were left with a model mainly supported by the assumption that the universe must be without a creator and without divinely given purpose.[81] At every point, the enterprise was driven by a motive that belongs neither to science nor to reason, but to aesthetics or metaphysics: a Godless universe. When the universe hinted that it had been ordered by God after all, in the very evidence gathered through advances made in the enthusiasm to drive Him out of it, the universe was brazenly redrawn to exclude Him. Only this time, the possibility of any scientific demonstration that it is indeed so with the universe has also been excluded.[82] Similarly, to unify the four fundamental forces of nature, when faced with the intractability of gravity, physicists have introduced entities that have never been observed, have physically impossible qualities, and force flagrant violations of the rules of mathematical analysis or do not lend themselves to it at all. The unification of the other three (electromagnetic, weak, and strong nuclear) forces has already required considerable departures from the possibility of mathematical and experimental unanimity.[83]

We are thus back with Holton and Kant. For we can clearly see, in how Hawking and others deal with basic physical questions, that a metaphysical orientation is necessary as part of the procedure of dealing with those questions. And though no particular metaphysical orientation suggests itself on purely rational grounds, we can observe how strained the argument becomes when an idea such as that of a purposeless universe that "just is" is upheld against the flow of the evidence and in defiance of thinking that can reasonably be regarded as mathematical. Ideas about the character of the universe—whether it is a created, purposive unity or some opposite or variant of these—are thematic hypotheses on a grand scale, on a par with Kant's second transcendental idea for the direction of reason, namely, the absolute unity of the sum total of all phenomena (or the unity of the cosmos).

Scientists bring ideas into their overall picture of physical reality that, by their own admission, have no basis in science (or reason), but reflect metaphysical or aesthetic preferences. These ideas are necessary to give scientific research direction. Thus is an idea such as unity introduced. So is it with the competing ideas of a purposive universe that has a creator, and an uncreated universe without purpose. And these ideas are adhered to even when faced with insurmountable evidence or major computational obstacles.

The Implications for Social Thought and Reform

*Specific Implications Derived by Analogy from
Contemporary Thought and Research in Physics*

The belief that social thought must reflect the structure and method of scientific thought as culled from the procedure followed primarily by physicists, chemists, and, more recently, biologists has always been tendentious. It has never enjoyed the luxury of solid justification. Yet it has acquired the status of article of faith because of the preeminent position gained by the natural sciences throughout late modernity, the (pious) hopes of reformers, and vested commercial and political interests. For to order a society properly, an ordered analysis and approach are needed, as is a reality that sustains them—and late modernity's aversion to religious authority has ensured a secular rationalist sense for "order."

With time, the origin of the link between science and society will be clarified, and each will be seen precisely for what it is. The term *social science* may either be dropped altogether, or the word *science* will be enriched in its meaning and be made equivalent to the German word *Wissenschaft*. The complexity of human individuals and collectivities is already acknowledged to a far greater extent than a few decades ago (as is the complexity of nature). It will eventually be recognized that it is impossible to study human phenomena adequately along standard scientific lines. Meanwhile, it may be useful to point out that the emergent picture of the physical world, and the procedure followed to construct it, no longer justify the mentality that still preponderates in social thought and analysis. For a careful look at physics itself makes it hard to stand by the following argument proposed by so much social thought and even more social planning and reform.

One often begins with a single, anonymous individual. This individual, regardless of all conceivable particularities (such as cultural background or ethnic identity), and assumed only to have reason or common sense, is then held to have a few fundamental motives. These typically are the maximization of profit, protection against violent death, the eradication of disease, the possession of various consumer goods, and so on. All motives are tied to the general instinct to seek pleasure and avoid pain (the sole basis for most utilitarian moral philosophy as well). Effectiveness of the response to those motives is then tied with quantifiable fields, such as management and marketing methods, availability and distribution of resources and goods, statistical research and censuses that cover a given population, and so on. The social reality of a given group of individuals is then measured according to the effectiveness of the response to their motives. If the numerical threshold for an effective response is passed, then the society concerned is said to be in order.

This no doubt will look like a caricature to many readers. Nevertheless, despite how far it may depart from social reality as it is encountered in experience, and social theory that tries to match the complexity of that experience, it is worth noting to what extent it pervades government institutions and international agencies that wield much influence over daily life everywhere. And it is also worth noting its reverberations in social thought as well. As easy as it may be to dismiss the foregoing argument as a caricature, it remains entrenched in social and economic theory and practice, and thus deserves to be exposed as crude even if it were the true analogue of its counterparts in physics. Conversely, even if social thinkers were (without justification) to restrict themselves to the analogues of contemporary methods in physical science, and heeded the reality yielded by these methods, they would approach their study with greater adequacy and sophistication than has recently been the case.

To highlight what social scientists can learn from contemporary physicists, let us repeat, one by one, the italicized recapitulations of the last section and follow each with the relevant analogue or implication for social thought.

In general, contemporary physicists regard the question of whether they are dealing with physical or mathematical entities as experimentally equivalent.

If "crude" matter has become ambiguous with regard to whether it is fundamentally physical or mathematical, how must it be with human beings, whom even materialists affirm as the highest known form of "matter"? It is surely no longer *scientifically* justified for any thought or practice to start out with an atomistic conception of human beings, whereby they are seen as impersonal point-individuals ("particles") having a few fundamental motives.

Classical ideas about where things are and how they succeed one another no longer hold up to current experimental procedures in physics. It is no longer possible to imagine physical things as entities that can be analyzed into a few components in space and time. The Cartesian system of coordinates, in the physical world, is an idealization.

An elastic physical space-time continuum determined by the movement and nature of things in it invites more serious consideration of the many elastic and elusive aspects within the space and time available to human experience, for example, Marcel Proust's highly empirical and phenomenally rich investigations of lived time. In general, the idea of an absolute frame of reference with a few dimensions allowing the easy breakdown of any entity into fixed components proves to be a very limited construct. This must be noted by social scientists, especially economists. For the scientific ground for limiting the analysis of human motivation to a short list with a materialistic bias is no longer there. The "components" of human life surely are at least as complex as those for "crude" matter.

With various levels of unpredictability and the replacement of the notion of active forces with that of exchanges of particles, it seems unlikely that a standard concept of causation can be sustained as the manner in which physical entities are fundamentally related.

No doubt at a coarse level, human beings can be related in simple causal terms under the influence of a few well-defined forces. The unpredictability of human beings has in the meantime always been acknowledged. But modernity has viewed unpredictability as an unfortunate irrational proclivity to be subdued. However, if the "dumbest" particles in our world have unpredictability built into their movement and their very emergence, how must it be with the "smartest"? There is a scientific basis for a more positive attitude to the unpredictable in human affairs. There is equally a basis for no longer viewing the forces and influences that govern human life and relations in simple causal terms. If the course of elementary particles is influenced by the exchange of information among them, one can only imagine how limited any theory must be as to what influences the course of human life. One can also appreciate the almost cruel extent of the inadequacy in the administration of human affairs according to schema such as utility curves.

Physical reality has two complementary aspects: one that is analyzable into component parts and another that must be regarded as a whole. Moreover, it is not experimentally treated as independently existing, but as comprising simultaneous possiblities that can be resolved only by the observer's intervention.

If physicists accept that physical reality must sometimes be analyzed and sometimes treated as a whole, then how must it be for the social field, given that the integral wholeness that grounds social cohesion is much easier to observe than that which links elementary particles? And what about the individual's ability to view himself as a whole, and individual action and practice that presuppose such wholeness? The analytical model used in much social thought would fall short for elementary particles, let alone human beings. If it were put remorselessly into practice, it would cause great suffering for individuals to the extent that their wholeness is violated and their social context jeopardized (and destabilized) through the steady erosion of its holistic aspect.

As for the acknowledgment by physicists that reality depends on the observer's interventions, this is amply demonstrated in social thought. Thus the Arab Muslim world, a reality that probably eludes any written account, is collapsed into a mere part of itself according to whether one is a Marxist, an empiricist, a positivist, a rationalist, a Muslim 'alim or something else. The Marxist will reduce Islam to a class phenomenon;

the empiricist will consider only the diverse phenomena of Islam as he encounters them directly or through the work of others, without committing himself to any transcendence of the phenomena and with the implication that they are tentative; the positivist will insist that they are tentative and must give way to others that exemplify a more "advanced" state; the rationalist will exclude, dismiss, or seek to overcome whatever eludes his reason; and the Muslim religious scholar will regard Islam as the permanent earthly embodiment and governance of an absolute reality. Quantum physics suggests a reality that must be collapsed into one of its possibilities for the theoretical and experimental process to continue. It is indifferent to the possibility of a reality "out there," because it is experimentally impossible to deal with it at the quantum level in any event. But a reality like the Arab Muslim world, more substantial, varied, and concrete than the world of elementary particles and fundamental natural forces, cannot be a matter of indifference just because it happens to elude a limited choice of theoretical and experimental perspectives. For one thing, we know it is there. For another, it does give rise to studies such as those undertaken by Hodgson, Hourani, and Berque, who combine various disciplines and theoretical approaches with depth and feeling to produce work that does immeasurably more justice to the reality they face than when it is collapsed to fit into the range of a single philosophy such as rationalism or empiricism.

The observer actively intervenes in the experimental procedure. The scientific method, understood in the usual idealized manner, can deal only with the analyzable aspect of the physical world (and not with its holistic aspect). And the characteristic causal mentality traditionally associated with the scientific method is no longer compatible with physical reality.

If physicists are free to depart from an idealized scientific method that they never completely respected and routinely disregard, then so are social thinkers free to develop the methodological sophistication demanded by their field. There is no need at all to follow elementary analytical procedures and for theories based on a naive idea of causality.

The facts gathered by contemporary physicists often cannot be related through precise calculations. Models, approximations, and hypothetical entities are put forward instead. Nor are the facts themselves selected without prejudice, for they are (and have been throughout the modern period) limited to the kind that favors experimental control or repetition. Nor does a prejudiced choice of facts guarantee repeatable experiments, either because the facts themselves have an elusive quality or because the cost and complexity of the experiment prohibit repetition. Nor are the hypotheses that emerge from scientific experiments accepted because prior hypotheses are refuted, for scientific hypotheses are not founded on universally accepted presuppositions, but are chosen from among competing pairs of themata, and today can no longer rest on mathematical support because of the vague nature of the phenomena dealt with. Finally, contributors to science, as in all other human activities, reflect their intuitions, prodigality, ingenuity, aptitudes, errors, and passions.

The analogy here is quite direct. Surely when we hear that physicists do not deal with facts that can be related through precise calculations, there is no need for social thinkers to restrict themselves to such facts. Indeed, it is atrocious to reduce the social field to what is quantitatively manageable for any other than purely statistical purposes. All facts relevant to human life can be "legitimately" (still taking "hard" science as a yardstick for legitimacy) considered by social thinkers and reformers, whether they lend themselves to precise analysis or not. Social thinkers are also freed by the example of physics to put forward models, explanations, and even ad hoc descriptions that are compatible with the complexity and variegation of their field. They are scientifically free to contrive whatever approach is necessary to deal adequately with the phenomena at hand. And their approach, however it may fail to yield to generalization, will be judged scientific or not according to how well it fits the phenomena (which, incidentally, has always been the case with science, all the way back to ancient Greek times. For science, in the end, is the attempt to find the best fit with the phenomena or, as some ancient Greeks used to say, "save the phenomena").

Thus, for instance, instead of leaving out the aspect of Arab Muslim society that owes its existence to informal networks of interlinked persons, because social thinkers cannot deal with it "theoretically," they ought, on purely scientific grounds, to discard their "theories" and deal with what is there before them. Similarly for how self-worth is connected with the local cultural reality and is operative as a powerful motive. Moreover, social thinkers need no longer be concerned if their findings are not repeatable by others, for physicists too must sometimes give up on that ideal. So if, say, religious experience is "unrepeatable," so much the worse for those who demand repeatability as though to hold up an ideal that deliberately excludes certain dimensions of individual and social life—for to have the most rudimentary understanding of religious experience is to know that the very attempt to observe it, with a view to repeating the experience and verifying the claims based upon it, the very idea of a neutral and independent gaze at such experience, destroys the conditions under which it might occur. Thus to insist on repeatability for the experience of transcendence and the validation of metaphysical and religious claims already implies a hostility that mocks the impartiality professed by those who raise the objections.[84]

It seems, in retrospect, that the "scientific method" culled by social thinkers can be accounted for more by their hopes, dreams, prejudices, and penchant for reductionism than by what goes on in the physical sciences themselves. Finally, social thinkers and reformers need not suffer the futility of the attempt to sacrifice the personal factors that invariably enter good scientific work for the sake of the ideal of impersonal research that is not even characteristic of contributors to physics. Hodgson's work, which is a remarkable contribution to the study of the Arab Muslim world, is also intensely personal and idiosyncratic, and perhaps is one because it is the other.

Scientists bring ideas into their overall picture of physical reality that, by their own admission, have no basis in science (or reason), but reflect metaphysical or aesthetic preferences. These ideas are necessary to give scientific research direction. Thus is an idea such as unity introduced. So is it with the competing ideas of a purposive universe that has a creator, and an uncreated universe without purpose. And these ideas are adhered to even when faced with insurmountable evidence or major computational obstacles.

Social thinkers are also free, even if they worry about whether their approach is "scientific," to introduce their overall metaphysical or aesthetic preferences into their work. Indeed, they must. To pretend otherwise is to attempt the concealment of ulterior motives. Thus, an allegedly impartial account of individual or social phenomena will, on examination, be found laden with metaphysical or aesthetic ideas and ideals—for instance, the idea that rationality is more advanced than irrationality and so, for instance, all myth must be replaced with "hard fact." But note that affinity for the mythopoetic is, at the very least (from a scientific point of view), on a par with contempt for it. And the failure to acknowledge it is, among other things, unscientific.

General Implications for Social Thought and Reform

The discussion throughout this chapter leads us to conclude that reason cannot itself serve as the agent for the desired synthesis between tradition and modernity. Reason, as used in science as well as in other fields or activities, is centered in and guided by thematic hypotheses, ideas, or ideals. This seems in doubt only when one is unaware of how one's use of reason is directed. But aware or not, one's reason is directed whenever it enters an activity more substantial than the performance of trivial calculations that have no real bearing on human life or knowledge. To disregard this crucial dimension in our use of reason is to subject human life or knowledge to a hidden agenda that might or might not be congenial thereto.

It is hence important to unveil the direction of the use of reason when it remains unclear, and especially when the pretense of its sovereign use is proclaimed. For if it turns out, for instance, that the thrust of a social reform program that appears rational is guided by the idea that human beings are primarily motivated by a self-centered materialism, and it turns out that such an idea is harmful to human life—say, because it engenders social breakdown or because its intended beneficiaries have a profoundly different vision of human priority—then that reform program can be objected to on many grounds, among them that it is irrational. Reform programs often disguise motives that, if exposed, may prove disagreeable to their intended beneficiaries. At this level, what we are really confronted with is a struggle between different visions of human priority, different sets of ideas, ideals, or thematic hypotheses.

Sovereign reason, then, is inadequate for forging the necessary synthesis between tradition and modernity, because in reality there is no such thing as sovereign reason in all of its nontrivial uses, and because to overlook this is to impose other ideas and motives concealed by the claim that reason is sovereign and that social programs based on this claim must therefore be accepted on rational grounds. Such imposition may cause much harm. What, then, is a more dependable agency for the synthesis? In the first place, it was mentioned near the beginning of this chapter that a deeper understanding of modernity is an essential component of bringing that synthesis about. One of the elements of that deeper understanding is to elucidate the true relationship between science and reason, and the nature of reason itself. Reason and science have been the preeminent symbols of modernity, for in science reason is believed to have had its purest use. But it turns out that a thorough exposition of the *activity* of science reveals an activity as complex, variegated, and elusive to "pure" rationalization as any other. If science has long rested comfortably behind a veneer of rationalism, it is because this veneer has more glitter in science than in other fields. Much that goes on in science accords with the popular conception of rationality, enough for a cursory view of the sciences to give the impression that rationality pervades scientific thought and research through and through. The imposition of a rational mode of thought at the forefront of education and public discourse has also contributed to the concealment of the nonrational aspects that are necessary in every nontrivial use of reason.

There is hence no need to fear modernity because of the belief that it entails reductionism to rationalism (in the narrow sense) or the scientific method or any related mentality. On the contrary, modernity has within itself the critical resources to expose the serious limitations of rationalism and the idealized scientific method that accompanies it. Modernity allows a broader and more amorphous or pluralistic approach for the sake of compatibility with the phenomena, whether in theory or in practice. It has already allowed the integration of rationality into an ethico-religious vision in the work of Kant, modernity's greatest exponent. If others do not find Kant's unifying vision agreeable, modernity in any event provides for the recognition of various ideas, ideals, and thematic hypotheses having a social, moral, cultural, political, or religious character, and which shape the lives of individuals and communities and integrate their use of reason. Some thinkers, such as Habermas, as we shall see just before this study returns explicitly to the Arab Muslim context, redefine rationality to incorporate such openness. Contemporary rationalists, then, have recourse to a richer and more elastic conception of reason. Social thinkers and reformers, for their part, are free, even if they continue to feel pressured to look over their shoulders at the physicists, to consider that broader and deeper framework for the use of reason (or a broader and deeper rationality, which almost amounts to the same thing). They are free to consider individuals and societies in as sophisticated and sensitive a manner as is merited by the reality at hand. They are free, and moreover required, to treat individuals and societies with full regard for what fundamentally moves and animates them: their particularity, their motives, the interrelationship between motives and how individuals or societies *as a whole* relate to them, the personal component of social cohesion and vitality, the transcendent factor in personal and social life, integral wholeness as an aspect of individual and social life, and so on.

The implications for freedom are enormous. Social thought and practice that submit individuals and societies to a narrowly based rationality, one centered in an idealized scientific method that contributors to science violate at every turn, will steadily tear away at whatever it is about individuals or societies that does not fit a narrow rationalist mold. If the institutions that bear persistently on our lives operate, say, according to the premise that rational beings are basically self-centered materialists, then it will nurture all that makes us tend toward that premise and will disenfranchise those who see human life in different terms. The more radical the difference, the greater the disenfranchisement. But if it can be argued that the greater part of freedom does not lie in the choice of material opportunities (centered in the choices available for making and spending money), but in the diverse factors partially listed at the end of the foregoing paragraph, then institutions that operate on the premise of self-centered materialism will severely restrict human freedom.

Freedom, as we shall see by the end of the following two chapters, is not nearly so much a matter of almost unlimited choice within a narrowly defined domain as an extension of our being into successively more encompassing realms. Our humanity is far more constituted and realized by cultural particularity, social vibrancy and intimacy, and transcendence than the possession of certain goods or the occupation of a given position within a moneycentric corporate array. To treat humanity as though some of its more limited dimensions had priority is to considerably limit human freedom. Thus the transition from a narrowly rationalist social theory and practice to one that truly appreciates the human phenomena at hand parallels a greater realization of human freedom. Needless to say, the former is not a necessary condition for the latter. The endless resourcefulness of human beings is such that some individuals have been able to realize their deepest freedoms even under tyranny. What will rather change through institutional openness is the *opportunity* provided for the realization of deeper freedoms than are nowadays characteristic, so much so that the common conception of freedom reflects an impoverished outlook.

The next chapter, then, deals with how freedom has been impoverished. Like the rest of the book, it reflects a tension concerning an important question: Is it modernity itself that is prone to reductionism, because of the very way that it has emerged and asserted itself, or has modernity always had it within itself to broadly encompass individual and social life? Such a question cannot be settled in this book, for it is still being vigorously debated by historians who are providing us with increasingly sophisticated accounts of modernity's genesis. Whether modernity itself is profoundly reductionistic depends in part on how it is defined and dated. The more closely associated it is with rationality, and the further its date is moved forward from the Renaissance, the more it seems it can be fairly judged to entail various reductionisms. Conversely, the more modernity is rooted in the Renaissance, the more open it will be seen to have been to the nonrational and the transcendent, and the less plausible the claim that reductionism has issued from it. This tension between openness and reductionism can be found in Kant's work as well. For our purposes here, what matters is that we have indeed, especially in this century, been subjected to a many-layered reductionism centered in a narrow conception of reason believed to have been exemplified in an idealized scientific method. Others can settle the issue of whether modernity caused such reductionism or whether it has been diverted from a nobler and broader compass that truly belongs to it. If modernity is judged to have been inherently reductionistic, then it can also be safely affirmed that we now live in a new era whose bent has yet to become unveiled. On the other hand, if it turns out that modernity has been hijacked, then we continue to live within modernity and have moved toward a more authentic phase that has always lain within its possibilities. Either way, we seem on the threshold of an era that allows greater fulfillment for human freedom, even while various disintegrative forces loom everywhere. These too may be a sign of significant civilizational change. In any event, for those who are not yet fully part of it, there is less reason than before to fear modernity.

3

The Fate of Freedom
under the Rule of Reason

A Preliminary Sketch of Freedom

Our sketch of freedom will be formed by way of certain Kantian distinctions and how they may be critically modified in the light of what we have come to know in the past two centuries. According to Kant, everything that occurs in our ordinary experience can in theory at least be accounted for. This is because all ordinary experience is spatiotemporal and so can be fitted into an intricate web of causally linked phenomena and events. Whatever can be so fitted is deprived of freedom, for if we know its causal antecedents, we can in principle predict what follows. Freedom, to the extent that it exists, must therefore be attributable to something that does not occur in space and time. Freedom is transcendent.

On the other hand, we know that freedom is attributable to human beings. Kant himself made freedom the cornerstone of his moral philosophy and metaphysics. But we cannot attribute freedom to human beings to the degree that they are spatiotemporal entities, because we began with the assumption that all such entities are causally determined, and their causal determinations are theoretically knowable. Now, Kant made the important distinction between the spatiotemporal aspect of human beings and their nonspatiotemporal, or transcendent, aspect. The first he called the *appearance*, or *phenomenon*, the second the *thing-in-itself*, or *noumenon*. All phenomena belong to the phenomenal world of appearances, while the noumena belong to the noumenal world of things-in-themselves. The phenomenal world is in theory entirely knowable by science, while the noumenal world is inherently opaque to it. Our freedom belongs to the noumenal world, and is attributable to human beings not as appearances, but as transcendent things-in-themselves. Were we to ascribe freedom to our phenomenal aspect, we would create a contradiction, for phenomena can be entirely accounted for and do not in principle admit freedom.[1]

Our psychological conception of freedom, one in which we feel ourselves free to choose, is thus illusory if we assume that psychology deals exclusively with phenomena in space and time. It is illusory because our observations of psychological phenomena belong to the theoretically knowable world, and the choices that we make at that level only appear free because the causal chain into which they can be theoretically fitted is as yet unknown to us. Similarly, any perception of freedom that belongs to the world of sense yields an illusory freedom, for all that is accessible to our sense perception lies in space and time and is therefore causally determined. If we are really free, it must be because we can transcend the world of sense and all that we experience in our immediate sensory surroundings.

For Kant, the clearest expression of our transcendence, and therefore of our freedom, is our moral being. That we care to be moral at all is a transcendence of what the world of sense experience suggests we ought to care about. For as moral beings, we often go against our material (or sensory) interests, sometimes to the point of risking our lives or sacrificing them altogether. We act as if moved by ideals that nothing in our everyday concrete sensory experience suggests. These ideals, and our affinity thereto, constitute a world beyond the world of sense experience, a transcendent, noumenal world. And the moral law is how we regulate the daily consequences of that affinity, for instance, to do unto others as we would have them do unto us. That is why the moral law in the Kantian philosophy is so intimately tied to freedom. The moral law is the symbol of our affinity to a transcendent world, or to a world that inherently escapes all causal attempts to determine it. Despite the apparent bondage that results from our duty toward the moral law, the moral law liberates us from a level of existence where freedom is (theoretically) impossible.

Notice that a similar argument can be constructed for the artistic and religious dimensions of life. For art and religion similarly suggest affinity with ideals that belong to a transcendent world. But our worldview has changed considerably since Kant developed his critical philosophy. We no longer believe, certainly not in any simple sense, that whatever lies within the scope of science is part of a causally determined world. For science itself, as we have seen, does not necessarily advance through causal reasoning. The complexity of scientific thought suggests much freedom *internal* to science. A physicist is free to choose between, say, a created, purposeful, bounded world or one without creator, purpose, or boundary. Nothing causally determines one choice or the other. He is also free to choose how the theories informed by his view of the cosmos are tested. An aesthetically attractive mathematical symmetry could be just as apposite as a theory that requires precise calculations. And the scientist's personality colors his work at every stage. All this was mentioned in the last chapter. So was the striking discovery that the physical world itself is not completely submissive to the dictates of causality. One might also add examinations of our experience from other fields, such as those given in depth psychology or cultural anthropology. The picture of our empirical world has become the domain of various disciplines with multilayered methodologies. Does this fundamentally affect Kant's conception of freedom?

It does. For the sensory world turns out to be far more open, variegated, and complex than anyone beholden to the Newtonian outlook on the physical world could conceive. The sensory world itself suggests freedom. It is only partly causally determined. Otherwise, it opens up to layers successively more encompassing. One need not wait for the verdict of the "hard" sciences to know this. Anyone who has encountered nature in its beautiful, awesome, or spacious aspect can attest to how we seem called to a boundless world. And the experience of boundlessness is associated with the freedom that one seeks in nature.

Rather than think of freedom as strictly belonging to a trancendent world, we may think of it as spread all over the different levels of experience that are possible for us. We may think of freedom as mere choice within a fairly narrow domain; or as expansiveness in a boundless world full of meaning; or everything in between. We moreoever need no longer separate the sensory and transcendent worlds as radically as Kant did, for the sensory world, whether in how it teases scientists into ever-greater departures from methodological orthodoxy or in how it calls us further, opens up paths to transcendence. The problem arises for freedom when we deliberately close off the sensory world to the possibility of transcendence, and when freedom itself is thereby eventually incarcerated within the narrow domain of trivial choice.

Freedom is ultimately a transcendence, to be sure. For however well we may understand ourselves and our world, we are always free to transcend what lies within our understanding. We are free to make a mockery of any analysis of ourselves, free to assert our being in a manner that easily cuts through all that we may be told through depth psychology, behavioral studies, history, sociology, or anthropology. One need think only of supposedly "primitive" tribes who, when aware of an impending visit by anthropologists or ethnographers, hastily hide their modern trappings, wear their "traditional" dress, and put on a "primitive" display (a folk dance or ritual) for the benefit of scientific research. To paraphrase Wittgenstein, we give meaning to all the disciplines through which we study ourselves. We fashion their canons and set their direction. This "we" always lies beyond their scope because it delimits their scope. There is something about our personality (now paraphrasing Berdyaev) that is more fundamental than any conceivable set of statements made about it, even when these are organized into a scientific or pseudoscientific discipline.

Such ideas complement the traditional approach to freedom and transcendence. Although the affinity with transcendence, and the freedom to expand our lives meaningfully into boundless realms, are exemplified in art, morality, and religion, a more amorphous exemplification may be encountered in the simple fact that any attempt to set strict boundaries on our being or personality, especially if it be analytical or causal, is more easily made a mockery of than formulated. There is a "raw," residual sense in which we are considerably more than is granted in our discursive explorations of ourselves. We can be made aware of this eternal remainder owing to the depth of human being or personality. And this remainder, this forever unknown and unknowable aspect of ourselves makes our freedom truly interesting.

Kant roots freedom firmly in transcendence because he is not content to rest with the raw awareness that one is free in all sorts of ways. He wants to affirm the true ground for freedom, which finally involves the transcendence of all that can ever be said, delineated, or accounted for. No demonstration can be given for that affirmation, for all demonstrations belong to a realm in which, by definition, transcendence is impossible. But the various kinds of experience widely available to individuals that have been mentioned so far make a strong case for the transcendent root of freedom. Another method would be indirect appeal: We look at what happens when transcendence is denied. Throughout much of modernity, transcendence has been denied, because of the association of transcendence with religion and the legacy of religious authoritarianism and religious wars, and because the scientific worldview that gave modernity a strong impulse appeared to dispense with transcendence. The better we can show that such denial has resulted in narrower and narrower domains for freedom, the stronger the appeal to recognize once more the transcendent root of freedom. This line of thought occupies the present chapter.

The next chapter turns to freedom itself in some detail. There we shall learn more about the transcendent aspect of freedom, as well as the difference between freedom as mere choice within a narrow domain and freedom as meaningful expansiveness in boundless realms. For we may, after Kant and Isaiah Berlin, think of freedom in both negative and positive terms. The negative sense of freedom is that in which we emphasize our freedom to choose, whether among trivial or serious matters, and the opportunity we are given to do so through lack of interference from the authorities. The positive sense of freedom is that in which we emphasize the quality of our choice and what we do with the opportunity we are given, the transcendent root of freedom, and freedom itself as meaningful expansiveness in a boundless world. However, we must not be misled by the dualism "negative/positive." For as our choices grow more and more consequential for our being, we become more able to exercise our freedom in vaster and richer worlds. It is not true to say that freedom either involves choice or a transcendent sense of fulfillment, for the plunge into transcendence is itself a choice, although one in which no government has the power to interfere, and which is not as easy to retract as the choice of salad dressing.

> In regard to time, the import of the resolution is that once I have made a choice I will unconditionally *stick to it*. I cannot give it up again; there is no other I behind what I am as myself. If I do give it up just the same, canceling what I was in it, I destroy myself at the same time. The existence on which I have entered in my original resolution is the font I live by, the font that animates everything new. My resolution starts the *movement* that can give my life a self-based continuity in the diffusion of my existence.[2]

Karl Jaspers in this passage is not talking about any kind of resolution or choice, but about formative or constitutive choices, or choices as a result of which one is what one is in a sense so deep that to change one's mind (which one is free to do) would leave one faced with an unbearable emptiness. So the freedom to choose moves from a narrow to wider and wider domains.

A Brief History of Shrinkage

In the previous chapter, we came upon the problem of finding an authentic synthesis between tradition and modernity as the required context for freedom. Because such a synthesis demands a proper understanding of modernity, and because certain claims have been made about rationality on behalf of modernity, those claims were examined. We found that rationality always depended on a nonrational grounding, in the ideals that motivate people, the ideas and thematic hypotheses they might have in mind, or the various motives interwoven with one's cultural background. This finding has grave consequences for any claims or plans for social reform that are based on the idea of sovereign reason. For such claims and plans, besides being based on a myth (because the "sovereign" reason on which they rest is not even found in physics), willingly or unwittingly disguise a tendentious process as universally acceptable to "rational" beings.

Despite the theoretical untenability of rationalism, there is no doubt that it has been put into practice throughout much of modernity. Whether modernity itself is prone to such practice or whether it has been hijacked by it cannot be decided here. What matters is the reality of the practice and its relentless refusal to face the possibility of transcendence. What also matters is the steady demarcation of a narrow domain for freedom, where the narrowness is compensated for by the allure of countless trivial choices to be made, busyness, and pecuniary opportunity. This narrowness, the surprise outcome of an age loudly marked by liberation, will be the main focus of this chapter. But let us begin with a historical sketch of the general tendency toward shrinkage that has prevented modernity from fulfilling its promise. The use of "shrinkage" is meant to highlight the contraction in the spheres of human activity that are favored by modernity, or the direction that modernity has taken. Relative to the potential fullness of human beings, what is practically favored represents shrinkage.

A token of the shrinkage characteristic of modern practice (and quite a bit of modern theory) is the shrunken domain of reason itself. We shall see that this is the ironic consequence of the insistence that reason must be sovereign, and above all separated from transcendence. Because much individual action and social evolution have already been urged toward rationality, so that choices, thoughts, and acts thought to be rational have been favored over others, shrinkage in the domain of reason means further shrinkage in the domain of freedom. For the marginalization of the nonrational already involved a shrinkage in the domain of freedom; and further restrictions in the meaning of "rational" could only mean more shrinkage in the domain of freedom.

Our best measure for the shrinkage of the domain of reason is to compare what it was at the dawn of modernity with what it usually is now. The domain of reason once extended all the way to the mind of God. It is now frequently reduced to calculations that machines perform far more swiftly and accurately than human beings.[3] It used to be embedded in cultures taken as a whole. It is now transferred to the operations of systems such as those we find at the administrative and economic levels. How did this transformation come about?

In the previous chapter, we have encountered the various ways that reason depends on what lies beyond its scope. These ways followed directions given by themata, ideas, or ideals (we have seen how this is an intrinsic fact to physics). If anything was an ideal that would guide the use of reason at the outset of modernity, surely it was the insistence on the independent judgment of the individual. For the tenor of modernity has been set by the individual turning his back on authority, mainly the authority of the Church to define his life, but also other kinds of social constraint. The individual's decision to exercise independent judgment became a symbol of individual freedom.

Once individuals greatly enhanced their freedom to exercise their own judgment, as scientists, tradesmen, philosophers, and adventurers, they still had to contend with the need to confirm the soundness of their judgment. It was also crucial to find the means for agreement, on the soundness of judgments as well as other potential areas of dispute, in the wake of the Thirty Years' War (1618–48) that devastated many areas of

Europe, especially in and around Germany, and was a result of the failure to agree on religious dogma (religious war was another reason individuals turned their backs on religious authority). But with the rejection of tradition came the loss of its function as a personalized authenticating body for individual judgment. Thus the only available means to guarantee the public acknowledgement of sound judgment and general public agreement were logic, experimental verification, documentary evidence, or whatever else might be confirmed independently of the individuals confirming them. From the beginning, then, a great paradox set in: individuals who wished to judge matters independently had to judge matters in ways independent of themselves to have any public assurance of soundness and agreement. In other words, an individual who exercised his independent judgment and sought public agreement with the outcome (a natural desire) unwittingly narrowed the domain of his judgment to whatever lends itself to independent confirmation. In a sense, the individual no longer really judged for himself. He had to judge independently of himself. The world gradually shrank to whatever could be demonstrated logically, verified experimentally, recorded in unimpeachable chronicles and testimony, and so on. This is not to say that the rest of the world ceased to exist. But it came to be regarded as elusive, as perhaps the origin of claims by high priests that they knew better and ought therefore be followed by their flock, as the realm of theological disputes that gave rise to religious wars, as subjective or unreliable, as something no reasonable person would take too seriously.

Modernity thus steadily limited reason to activities that more readily lent themselves to independent confirmation. The more reason was diverted from the mind of God toward calculation, the better it performed its designated task. The more reason became the distillation of systematic analysis, experimentation, administration, design, production, and distribution, the more independent it was of the individuals who used it and the more obvious and independently ascertainable the results of this use.

Reason, thus delimited to what was essentially calculation, became the symbol of an ideal's triumph. It symbolized the success of individuals who exercised their independent judgment in having the soundness of their judgment publicly, and in theory universally, confirmed—and applauded. For the devices and transformations thereby wrought were awesome. And the public that accepted such a delimited rationality attained the consensus and stability it had sought after the Thirty Years' War. There were, to be sure, other factors besides the revolt against the oppressiveness of the Church and the need for agreement and stability that favored a particular delimitation for reason as well as for the domain of individual judgment: the miserable material conditions in much of Europe;[4] a simultaneous rise in commercial and quasi-industrial activity, with a corresponding growth in trade networks; and growing intellectual curiosity combined with the new cosmology and a sense of adventure. If this last factor, the revolt against the Church, and the need for agreement and stability gave form and impetus to the ideal of individual judgment, then the combination of material deprivation and commercial-industrial growth gave it much of its content. It was obvious that many people needed and wanted to be better off. It was equally obvious that the means for bringing this about were already in place. All that remained was for there to be the will to devote enough human energies for a sufficiently long time to that end.

An unforeseen process, given the choices made in the early stages of modernity, contributed further to its concentration around the material. It so happens that the closer one remains to the surface of the world, the more one can have one's observations and hypotheses independently confirmed.[5] This surface includes all brute sensory data, all that is easily perceived by the senses or easily handled. At the same time, distance from the Church and everything that paralleled its authority also meant distance from the traditional ways that the world beyond its surface had been made accessible. However, as is clear in Kant's philosophy, human beings were not yet ready to turn their backs on transcendence. But the transcendent world moved away from the purview of modernity's vanguard because once the traditional means to make it accessible had been rejected, there was no other way to publicly share it. Transcendence being what it is, there are as many approaches to it as there are individuals. It is intractable to independent attempts to confirm one's experience with it. In a culture that depended more than ever on independent confirmation, the transcendent could only recede. Bitter memories of the use of transcendence to oppress Europeans and the disputes and wars that had arisen from disagreement over its content could not have helped either. The combination of all the foregoing developments—the natural range for successful independent confirmation, and the natural exclusion of the transcendent from this range (urged on by antipathy toward transcendence)—when we also recall the very real impulses that were there, helped materialism gain primacy at the practical level.

So individual judgment, independent confirmation of judgment, and the phenomena that lent themselves to the independent confirmation of individual judgment all converged toward the improvement of the material conditions of life.[6] Now, not everything that can be measured (or otherwise independently confirmed) necessarily relates to material conditions. But under the impulse of great material deprivation and restless commercial and industrial activity, the convergence did occur. The ideal of independent individual judgment was not meanwhile forgotten. It remained a symbol of individual freedom. But its other expressions were increasingly marginalized, consigned to abstract realms, public rhetoric, private conversations, and small associations. Whenever the ideal was invoked in a public movement, the eventual outcome was more equitable participation in the ongoing process of material improvement.

The contemporary global economy, the sometimes huge bureaucracies intertwined with it, and the technologies that preserve and enhance them are the progeny of that drive to improve material conditions. This drive has by now far exceeded even inflated criteria for material comfort in areas of the world where modernity has most set in. It has taken on the character of self-perpetuation, out of touch with the real conditions that had motivated it. Nevertheless, such is the pervasiveness of the economy, bureaucracy, and technology that reason has been increasingly defined in their terms. This is so whether one speaks in terms of systems or elaborate machines that help in their management. So reason as the common denominator between individuals exercising their independent judgment has in practice largely shrunk to the distillation of the operations necessary to sustain contemporary material conditions and expectations.

For those caught up in that global process, it is easy for reason, which is drastically narrowed when viewed as the distillation of the operations necessary to sustain that process, to seem sovereign. An individual sufficiently immersed in the sustenance and improvement of material conditions will regard the ideals and assumptions that philosophically sustain this as self-evident, and will therefore see no unwarranted tilt in the subsequent delimitation of reason. Reason will seem as directed as any rational individual would. The sovereignty of (an actually much delimited) reason continues to be an article of faith that is much emphasized. This emphasis is heightened under the influence of the extension of the right to public independent judgment to as many individuals as possible all over the world (which is the effective meaning of the global human rights campaign). For if public independent judgments are to be meaningful, there must be a faculty that allows them to be made, and which itself is not subject to any other authority. This faculty is reason, in practice delimited by the global process that has just been mentioned. But there are almost insurmountable psychological barriers to the acknowledgment of the truth surrounding the current practical delimitation of reason, deeply embedded as it has become in its economic, bureaucratic, and technological activity. For modernity is marked and sustained by the belief that human beings have acted and continue to act freely and independently in furthering its cause. Hence, to acknowledge the loss of such freedom and independence through subservience to the operations necessary to sustain contemporary material conditions and expectations is to feel deprived of the original meaningfulness of the whole enterprise that we call "modernity."

Given the foregoing overview, what then is generally the current practical range of freedom? The central concern with freedom in the modern era has doubtless been sincere. But from the beginning, freedom, which is absolute only in theory, was pushed firmly in two convergent directions: freedom from traditional authority, above all the Church, and freedom to improve material conditions. Individuals in time became freer than ever to dissent from authority and to pursue their material ambitions. This pursuit became increasingly remorseless the further the world mediated by tradition receded. As the world's material aspect came to dominate what one saw of the world, the pursuit of material ambitions seemed more and more natural. And freedom, which in itself is unfathomable and certainly extends to persons at many levels of their existence, material and transcendent, practical and moral, profane and sacred, came to be largely exercised in the domain defined by the complex activities built around the global drive for the improvement of material conditions. To be free means evermore to have unprecedented access to the accumulation of wealth, an endless variety of goods, and dominion over the earth. The freedom gained *from* material need is turned steadily *toward* material pursuits.

A crucial distinction must therefore be made between the ideals espoused by modernity, the adherence to which remains sincere in many quarters, and the actual situation when it comes to freedom. The political, social, and legal allowances for freedom are greater than ever before in many places. But this freedom, won over centuries and at great cost, is almost immediately and usually imperceptibly translated to free choice within a domain defined by the global drive to improve material conditions. This choice may be direct or indirect. An example of indirect choice is the growing number of elections that really revolve around economic decisions. Furthermore, the rhythms of life and the architecture at the heart of modernity emphasize the material aspect of the world to such an extent that the absence of the remainder is less likely to be noticed than before. If people's homes, workplaces, and public meeting areas have nothing in them to suggest anything beyond brute function, if shopping centers are built to impress and inspire the awe once reserved for the dwellings of monarchs and demigods, then the world in which one is free looks more and more like a world restricted to whatever bears on one's material existence.

The shrinkage of the domains of freedom and reason are neither universal nor irreversible developments. Their convergence at materialism is rather the clear direction at present, a direction that appears difficult to reverse in the immediate future and whose theoretical terminus[7] appears far more plausible than it was at the turn of the century. Part of the problem is time lag: We live in a time when the struggle for freedom, understood in its ideal sense, is still far more perceptible than what freedom for the many who have successfully struggled for it amounts or may soon amount to. It is still possible to present the history of modernity as a protracted struggle to universalize the ideals that had originally inspired it. Universal suffrage took centuries to become a reality. So did many other laws, statutes, and state-sponsored programs (such as public education) that enhanced freedom. These were far more visible than possible future convergences that would ensnare freely acting individuals within extremely complex systems. Because only recently have we been able to elucidate the extent to which the struggle for freedom has become shaped and constrained by materialism, freedom as an ideal remains a credible credo for modernity. This is all the more so in countries, among them much of the Arab Muslim world, where more freedom is widely desired. It is thus nearly impossible to grasp how severely limited freedom might become very soon after it is won, given the current global situation.

An accidental convergence has occurred that has imparted a cruel irony to modernity, whereby an ideal is virtually condemned to be usurped by other powerful concerns because of the manner of its definition and application; for such has been the fate of freedom when it was mostly seen in terms of independent choices and judgments made according to reason, and when reason, presumed sovereign, was steadily drawn into the orbit of economism, bureaucratism, and scientism. But if we have met such an accident of history, then the tremendous appeal of the ideal most vulnerable to that accident—and the memory or urgency of what respectively has been or must be done in its name—make it very difficult to develop a clear view of that accident.

Further Reflections on Shrinkage:
Berque, Habermas, and Broch

Berque and the Shrinkage of History

Toward the end of his book *Cultural Expression in Arab Society Today,* Jacques Berque reflects on history itself to further expound upon its character in the region that concerns him most.[8] His bold sketch not only captures for us a historical shrinkage that parallels the developments outlined in the foregoing overview but also suggests the broad context necessary for the restoration of the lost equilibrium.

The temptation is always there to identify the movement of history with actual choices or forces that happen to be on the ascendant. We often come across accounts that see history as a "train of civilization" that moves relentlessly forward, passing through different civilizations along the way—and then leaving them behind. This "train" has lately been identified with material progress, science and technology being its preeminent symbols. Berque proposes that we instead consider history *a reservoir of multidimensional possibilities.* At any given historical moment, there are several directions that history can take, because several different outlooks and tendencies coexist. The depth of certain among those outlooks and tendencies is such that even if one were to overwhelm the others, these never become extinct, but lie in wait for a more favorable historical moment. So they remain latent when apparently absent. Their apparent absence is due to the much greater visibility and brute force of the dominant possibility. For when a historical choice is consciously embraced, the repression of others follows—not for too long, perhaps, for they remain alive, ready for opportune reactivation. For instance, a civilization driven by the presupposition that human beings are primarily self-centered individuals whose interests are material may give way to one that aspires for communal health and harmony or high cultural and moral standards. Ideals such as the improvement of material conditions, communal well-being, cultural excellence, and moral rectitude are always around, however the balance between them may shift.[9]

If Berque is right in his vision of history, then the paradigmatic society is one that pays heed at least to some among the many historical possibilities that must be accommodated in pairs if great tension is to be avoided. Foremost among these pairs are the transcendent and the immanent, and the eternal and the everyday, for human beings have shown time and again that they care about both what goes on in their immediate environment and the (transcendent) source of meaning in their lives. Where the transcendent and the immanent, the eternal and the everyday constantly intersect, the paradigmatic society lives a historical simultaneity. This "intersection of a temporal series and the regularities transcending it" will later define for us the direction along which shrinkage may be reversed and the domains of freedom, reason, and history consequently broadened and deepened. For we can also understand the shrinkage brought on by modernity along the course it has largely taken as a temporal series cut off from whatever transcends it, and then falling back into itself like a star deprived of the centrifugal forces holding it together. Once the temporal series is reopened to the regularities transcending it, so that there is a region where the two interact ("intersect" if we wish to maintain Berque's geometric metaphor), the potential for the former's range and meaning is once again well realized. Nothing can drive time more forcefully and further away from the ever-narrower channels into which it is pressured than eternity. People engaged in the everyday, as long as a genuine sense remains of a transcendence that they occasionally turn to, however ephemerally, develop an innate resistance to becoming enslaved by what must preoccupy them.

Berque then contrasts two different worlds according to his sketch. For the Arabs, the regularities that transcend the temporal series are references to God, the unchanging relationship between the Arabs and their ecology, and their continuous attitudes on the secular plane. These transcendent regularities define a historical balance and continuity that, from a different perspective, have a price: the necessary sacrifices for advancement (which roughly means "material advancement") are not made. On the other hand, the societies where modernity has advanced the most, "obsessed" with their advancement, have had to suppress other historical possibilities to the extreme.[10] This suppression has caused great tension in their historical condition. But the narrowness of history's domain in their case is overcome through a carnival-like "revolutionary stimulus," in which the credo of modernity is repeatedly reaffirmed and renewed. That history has been driven along a fixed track is compensated for by the vertigo of the materially productive possibilities thereby unleashed, every great leap of which takes on the form of a radical change in human life ("the communications revolution"). It is unlikely that Berque here implies history must either be balanced, broad and static or frenetic, narrow and dynamic; rather, if a static historical condition filled with meaning is stifling from the viewpoint of the desire to advance, then a dynamic one in which advancement becomes for its own sake, and therefore meaningless, is stifling in its own way. Moreover, the contrast is not as clear as Berque suggests. For it can be argued that many Arabs are now besotten with a coarse notion of advancement, while many who live in the centers of modernity are having second thoughts and beginning to strive for a more balanced historical movement. Within the assumptions made here, the most productive encounter will be between those having second thoughts and those in the Arab Muslim world who have a lively awareness of their age-old virtues. Through such an encounter the synthesis between modernity and tradition required as the proper context for freedom will be forged.

At the very end of his book, Berque connects his thoughts on the relationship between historical balance and the intersection of the transcendent and the immanent with the problem of meaninglessness.[11] He perceives modernity as soaring paradigms unable to reconcile themselves with the "old song" of tradition (once more, the temporal series cut off from the regularities that transcend it). The loss of meaning that ensues is illustrated by formal structures without reference, for example, institutions that function oblivious to their original purpose and have acquired a life of their own. We can see this clearly in the case of the legal system in the United States, originally steeped in a shared moral outlook and designed to protect individual rights, including the right to a fair trial, but now routinely used by lawyers to openly perpetrate various injustices simply because they argue cleverly within a law eerily detached from its initial ethical moorings. The law has effectively become a playground for profiteering (or the promotion of increasingly narrow group interests). The incredible number of lawyers in the United States testifies primarily to the complexity of the game and the size of the pay. For the "old song of tradition" to return to the legal system means for it to steep itself once more in the positive morality that alone justifies it.[12] Another example of a formal structure without reference is when originally and exclusively human concepts take on a detached academic existence and (absurdly) wind up being defined without reference to their human dimension. Berque adduces the definition of information in biological and chemical terms, as whatever moves mass and resists entropy, with nothing said about *what* information is, where it comes from, and where it is going. Texts and a host of other things have met a similar fate. To seal them from their natural openness to what defies formal and detached structure is one of the consequences of the suppression of all historical possibilities that lie outside the immanent and everyday.

In such an environment of suppression and the structural, discursive, and conceptual limitations that follow, discord and dissent are also stifled. Dissent must increasingly take on the aspect of appealing to an altogether different world (for within the world delineated by modernity, there is no room for real dissent, only permutations and variations on given themes); and the world itself rapidly approaches the monolithic where modernity has advanced the most (and awaits a similar outcome where it has not), helped on by communications that relentlessly unify the planet and suppress the historical chasms between its different regions through the superficial acceleration of the developments that close them (which Berque believes constitutes an undercutting of historical movement). These two developments have increasingly squeezed opposition into irony and intellectual demolition on the one hand, and violence on the other.[13] Thus the deconstructionist and the terrorist become the most unlikely bedfellows. So do the football hooligan and the Islamic revolutionary who writes with conviction about a global "Zionist-Crusader campaign and conspiracy against Islam." In the absence of the kind of balance that survives in the Arab Muslim world, modernity seems to be driving humanity toward a meaningless uniformity (in itself a severe distortion of an always potentially multidimensional history), and gives such an impression that to oppose its drive is intellectual or practical lunacy as for these to have frequently become a self-fulfilling prophecy. This, at any rate, is the darkest shade of Berque's prognosis.

The actual course that modernity has been taking may not be as uniformly meaningless or monolithic as Berque feared nearly two decades ago. It is true that detaching institutions from their original moral impulses continues unabated. Similarly, a discourse that had its life in concrete human references is abstracted to a ridiculous degree in several intellectual circles. Universalist economism, helped by the communications revolution, overlooks the plurality of outlooks on life that people have and the plurality of dimensions in each individual's life that transcend economics. It then creates a global constituency in its image. But modernity was not predicated on thorough decontextualization until well into the seventeenth century.[14] If we were to date the origin of modernity in the Renaissance, then we find within it the resources for the restoration of a balance in danger of being lost. As has been mentioned, we need not settle the issue here of whether modernity is inherently reductionistic (Toulmin appears to think that it is, if we date it from the seventeenth century). But works by Toulmin and Berque themselves, as well as several other authors, tell us that there is awareness and concern that modernity is headed toward more severe impositions of reductionisms that impoverish human life and threaten it with the explosive reaction of those least able to endure such impoverishment. It is the antireductionistic current within modernity, or, if one prefers a more futuristic appellation, the antireductionistic creative impulse of postmodernity, that is of greatest interest to the constructive course for the encounter between tradition and (post) modernity.

Habermas and Subjectivity as an Agent of Shrinkage

We find in Habermas a powerful advocate of the antireductionistic current mentioned in the foregoing discussion. In *The Philosophical Discourse of Modernity*,[15] he offers us many fruitful reflections on the direction modernity has taken. Habermas himself believes in modernity's credo, which makes his attempts to uncover the sources of its failed promise all the more credible. His main aim is to remind modernity's critics that they must not confuse the conceptualizations, forces, and misguided associations that have led to shrinkage with the (for him) laudable ideal of a rationally expressed freedom or liberation that has thereby been shrunk, held as it is within a narrow domain. He points out such confusion in his discussion of thinkers from Hegel to Foucault, which also contains one of the historical strands that runs through the shrinkage. Habermas is clearly among those who see modernity (and rationality) as inherently full of promise, but sadly hijacked from several directions toward narrowness and reductionism.

If, as we have seen, the domains of freedom and reason have largely been shaped by revolt against the Church (later extended to the rejection of transcendence), combined with a drive to improve material conditions and a yearning for a method of agreement that would never again degenerate into religious war or some other serious conflict, and if these can alternately be seen as a lopsided historical condition where vast regions of historical possibility are cordoned off, then these developments have been reinforced with the help of the principle of subjectivity. If individuals expressed their freedom in judgments independent of traditional authority, if instead these judgments had to be confirmed by the individuals themselves, and in ways that other individuals could identically repeat for the confirmation to be public, then the individual had to see himself as subject relating to objects. He stood as far apart as he could from the realm of his knowledge or action, believing that only thus would his vision be clear and distinct. In fact, he stood as far apart as he could from himself as well, for only thus could he know himself satisfactorily according to the new criteria. In this position of detached subjectivity, the individual had access to certainty or, at any rate, what was invariably experienced as certainty. Descartes's *cogito*, the apogee of existential minimalism in which the doubter initially holds everything but his own bare mental existence in doubt, required the greatest possible distance between subject and object. If the certainty experienced in that cogito could be more widely gained, then the price had to be the retention of the position from which it was inseparable, namely, that of unequivocal subjectivity. Subjects distanced as far as possible from the objects of knowledge, with the ideal of perfect detachment in the background, could agree solidly on their knowledge. Such agreement would not degenerate into violent conflict and could only be overturned through argumentation irresistible to reason.

Thus subjectivity became the key feature of modernity's physiognomy.[16] It became deeply linked with individualism (the subject in action apart from the world), freedom (in the forms of the right to criticism and the autonomy of action), and idealistic philosophy (where individuals felt sufficiently detached from the world to attempt to shape it entirely according to their subjective visions). The principle of subjectivity became established by the Reformation, the Enlightenment, and the French Revolution at the levels of faith, state, and society, and of science, morals, and art.[17] It became embodied in the structures of modernity. Habermas defines the principle of subjectivity as including the self-relating, self-knowing subject bending back upon himself as object and the installation of reason as the supreme seat of judgment before which anything that made a claim to validity had to be justified.[18] This entails a separation of the subject from himself and the rest of the world; otherwise objectivity would not be possible. The ideal of solid agreement meant that subjects would view everything in objective terms, that is, according to reason, even themselves when they turned inward. And the accounts of individuals and the world that were wrought in this spirit reflected that separation, as did individuals themselves and their (urban) environment to the extent that those accounts held sway. Individuals without emotions and block buildings without ornament would be reflections of the requirement for rational agreement.

The separation of the subject from himself and the rest of the world taken as object—the condition under which reason functions best as the supreme seat of judgment—is the origin of the well-known problem of alienation first discussed by Hegel. In the context of our problematic, this separation does much to restrict the domains of reason and freedom, for to be intellectually habituated to the consideration of otherness (other individuals, society, other cultures, the world) in complete detachment from oneself itself involves a drastic reduction in what is present and in how one thinks about it. The subjective gaze may yield clear, distinct, and universally confirmable accounts over which no wars may be fought. But such accounts inherently lack what can only be known interactively. Metaphysically, the world is reduced to the shape it assumes when beheld in complete detachment, and further reduced by the limited rational form given that shape. Sociologically, personal networks are collapsed into aggregates of atomized individuals. The irony here is that the very principle of subjectivity that intellectually underpins individual freedom does not yield, within its compass, much to be free about. Detachment can be experienced as a kind of freedom, but once it sets in, the spaces won for freedom start to look strangely empty. This problem was recognized by Hegel. Nevertheless, the thrust of his philosophy was to recover the lost potential of Reason,[19] which, as Habermas narrates it, he had seen plunged by the principle of subjectivity into a devisive and alienating state.[20] This, for us, is yet another reminder of reason's remove from sovereignty.[21] Under such conditions, Hegel gave a harsh verdict: the Europeans were no freer than the Mongols! The only difference is that the Mongol owed allegiance to a lord outside himself, whereas the modern Europeans are in bondage to an internal lord that only admits whatever is universally accessible to reason subjectively employed and dismisses everything else as "impulses, inclinations, pathological love, sensuous experience," and so on.[22]

Habermas himself explicitly diagnoses the problem of the shrinkage of reason's domain, and the consequent limitations on the movement of modernity, in terms of the usurpation of rationality by subject-centered reason.[23] This cognitive and instrumental moment of reason was favored because at the outset of modernity, reason and the imperatives of economic-bureaucratic subsystems were simultaneously freed. People were free to think for themselves and judge independently, but this freedom coincided with the need for strong centralized states in the aftermath of the Thirty Years' War and with the aspiration for prosperity after the deprivations of the seventeenth century. Thus other moments of reason were suppressed. One incongruity that has helped clarify these events is the attempt to canvas the whole domain of reason exclusively by subject-centered reason, which was doomed to failure. For example, it is by now well known that we bring all sorts of background assumptions, many of them cultural, to our use of subject-centered reason. Without these assumptions, which are taken for granted, subject-centered reason cannot be put to use. How, then, can it uncover the very thing that makes it possible? The cultural background of the use of subject-centered reason is therefore one area on which it cannot shed any light. As those other areas that Habermas believes lie within the domain of reason resist the intrusions of subject-centered reason more insistently, the limitations of subject-centered reason become better known. The question remains, however, whether rationality in whatever form is immune to usurpation. If Habermas thinks it is, then the evidence does not support him well.

As the subjective stance, a stance of utter detachment, gains universality, it becomes dismissive of whatever is particular (besides whatever is only interactively accessible). If it seems the quintessence of freedom to stand alone over and against the world as one studies it or plans one's life, then the world is also gradually and necessarily converted into a monotonous landscape. For a universally known and knowable world must everywhere look and be the same. The principle of subjectivity, if ever rigorously practiced, would entail the destruction of all that is local, particular, idiosyncratic, genuinely communal, and ineffable in human life, and all that is transcendent. We are quite far from such devastation. But many of our institutions are built around the principle of subjectivity (as witnessed by the prestige of the epithet "objective"). Perhaps this overly geometric view of freedom, which sees it embodied in point-individuals pulled out of their context and free in their thought and action over and against it, can be replaced with a fuller conception of freedom, one more compelling than its geometric counterpart: a strongly expressed particularity. For a person constrained by his personality is far more meaningfully free than the hypothetical being who is perfectly detached, "liberated" from his personality—in short, a nonperson.

The principle of subjectivity also restricts freedom more directly. Once a culture is immersed in the ideal of reason's unassailability and the practice of subjects who regard as much as they can in objective terms, an objective realm of study and action subject to rationality begins to take on a reality, validity, and vastness that makes it easier to exclude all other approaches. Dissent takes place officially within the sphere of acceptance of the principle of subjectivity. Arguments are then over different ideas about the same world approached in the same way. More serious dissent, that which questions the principle itself, drifts further from sight. The outward success in the reduction of the world to the objective, in scientific discovery, medical cures, a (materially) much higher standard of living, and the sheer power of modern states, contributes to this marginalization. What Habermas stresses in the course of introducing post-Hegelian thought is how the crossing of a threshold in modernity's reverence for the principle of subjectivity effectively made that principle immune to criticism and its domination invisible.[24] From then on, according to Habermas, modernity's major problem has been the constant resistance of life and the world *as they really are* to the expectation that they must be within the reach of the principle of subjectivity. In effect, this expectation, a result of the extrapolations made from great early strides, has severely restricted the world in which individuals could now be free. It has even diminished individuals internally, inasmuch as it also regarded the self, now taken as object, as transparent to objective study. This led to a two-fold distortion: what is not really objective was made to appear so; and what could not be given even the appearance of objectivity vanished. Individuals were trapped in an intellectual framework thoroughly incompatible with their concrete existence (their selves, personalities, emotions, beliefs, and values). And for a long time, the human sciences, which were always potentially a massive act of intellectual redress, were in fact ruthlessly furthering the illusion of objectivity and pushing that incompatibility to its breaking point. They were founded to extend the territories conquered by the principle of subjectivity.

Habermas himself takes the view that there is nothing inherently wrong with what he calls the normative content of modernity. He depicts the problem instead as an unfortunate entry by "rational forms of life . . . into a deceptive symbiosis with the technological mastery of nature and the ruthless mobilization of social power. This equation of happiness and emancipation with power and production has been a source of irritation for the self-understanding of modernity from the start."[25]

Under these conditions, ever-more complex systems were evolved to consolidate the freedom gained. As has already been mentioned, freedom then became seriously constrained by what those systems demanded for their sustenance. Habermas recognizes this development. But the difficulty with his view resides in his uncritical acceptance of modernity's normative content, the thrust of which is encapsuled by its interpretation of the concepts of self-consciousness, self-determination, and self-realization.[26] Habermas believes modernity at the outset might have had a healthy understanding of these concepts. But Habermas overlooks the attitudes and motives that shaped modernity's interpretation of its pivotal concepts and, as we have seen, brought on the unfortunate symbiosis between reason and the complex systems evolved under the banner of the "technological mastery over nature and the ruthless mobilization of social power." The materialization of the domain that individuals investigated following the model of self-conscious reasoning, and in which they determined and realized themselves, was all too likely (granted that it was unintentional), given the combination of factors pointed out on several occasions. Once that materialization came to the fore, human energies and intelligence hitherto spread over several spheres became concentrated around material pursuits to explosive effect, so that the contemporary rate of change is astounding and way ahead of conceivable need or what common sense suggests. The complexity of the systems evolved, which many believe are the instruments of freedom, but have in fact become the instruments for its limitation, is the outcome of too much expended on too little.

It is not just that self-consciousness, self-determination, and self-realization were given an unfortunate interpretation from the outset, as Habermas suggests. Rather, the attitudes and motives that sustained the very presence of these concepts at the moral and intellectual heart of modernity made their lopsided interpretation and application only a matter of time. Self-determination, for instance, never exists in a vacuum, but is always relative to what one experiences as opposition to one's struggle to determine oneself. The mere mention of self-determination entails knowledge of the opposition, and the goals from which one is being impeded. This already defines its shape and direction. Furthermore, "self-determination" may also carry the nuance of an individual declaring his independence from society. It certainly did so at a time when individuals were struggling to declare their independence from social authority (and authoritarianism). The historical dimension of concepts such as self-determination cannot be disregarded. Thus, when an issue may be equally considered from an individual or social point of view, emphasis on self-determination under certain historical conditions will repeatedly favor the individual viewpoint and will eventually create a society in its image. This becomes likelier still when self-determination (understood as the determination of the *individual* self) combines with self-consciousness. Self-consciousness, to a certain degree a natural human trait, can pathologically separate human beings from their surroundings if given too much emphasis. A civilization that *defines* itself partly through the self-conscious individuals who participate in it can hardly be expected to wind up with societies that are anything but an aggregate of individuals, each profoundly distanced from the other. Self-consciousness as a self-consciously declared civilizational norm is heavily partial to the principle of subjectivity that Habermas and Hegel both realize has usurped reason —and modernity. It is the epitome of self-consciousness for individuals to detach themselves from themselves, take a cool, studied, and curious look at themselves, and then at everyone and everything around them. There is a natural affinity between self-consciousness (viewed normatively and not as just another human tendency) and the principle of subjectivity. Hence the seeds of shrinkage are there in the readiness of self-consciousness in combination with self-determination (and self-realization) to latch onto the principle of subjectivity, which must in turn rely on the increasingly narrow employment of reason. The normative content of modernity may itself have nudged reason into a "deceptive symbiosis." The *historical* content of modernity made that nudge all but inevitable.

Broch and Shrinkage in the Absence of Plausibility Points

The philosophical passages that are clearly marked off in the third novel of Hermann Broch's trilogy *The Sleepwalkers* [27] contain a remarkable sequence of ideas that deepen our grasp of the reductionistic sweep assumed by modernity. They express Broch's insight that there is a deep connection between the functional style that has invaded architecture since the turn of the century, singleness of purpose in human action, and the recession of any ultimate point on which the plausibility of chains of reasoning rests (and the implied loss of a source for the meaning of life).

Broch first tries to articulate the relationship between truth, style, thought, action, and logic.[28] Each epoch is governed by a style, "style" here understood in its broadest sense. Just as architecture and the plastic arts reveal an epochal style's visible aspects, thought, loosely speaking, reveals its laws. The aim of thought is truth. What is judged to be true is thus true in accordance with the laws that intellectually describe the prevailing style. To say that something is true is to say that it is supported by laws that characterize an epochal style. To search for the truth given these laws is to find whatever can be validated within that style. And truth itself becomes a value that encapsulates the validity of the prevailing style; for when a style prevails, truth is not declared relative to it, but is felt as real truth. Thus truth, given the prevalence of the style whose laws support it, itself appears to validate that style. The prevalence of style means precisely that one can no longer fathom its presence and must experience what is true within it as really true (and its laws as universal laws).

We may reverse the logical order of these assertions to clarify the order that Broch is after. In our thought, we strive after truth along lines of reasoning and judgment that are acceptable to us. Whether these are in reality universally valid or mere convention is immaterial so long as we do not question their regulatory function in our thought. In either case, they constitute a method of thought that is an expression of the style prevalent in our epoch. Whatever truth is arrived at by this method is hence nothing but the encapsulation of that style's validity. We are evidently not dealing with the sort of validity that results from independent verification, but from sheer prevalence (through various motives, attitudes, upbringing, education, related historical developments, and perhaps also a kind of metaphysical order that limits and defines the nature and interrelationship of these).

The prevailing style can be abbreviated when we abstract from thought and project it into logical space. "Logic" here must also be understood in its broadest sense. It is more elaborate and deeper even than grammar. A historical era, modernity, for instance, can be said to have its (internal) logic; or how the balance shifts between the eternal and the everyday, given human nature and social and historical reality, also has its logic. In such a broad sense of "logic," a logic can be found that abbreviates each epochal style. Different epochs will reveal different logics that distill their inner workings. The character of such a logic will tell us something about the character of an epochal style. One way we can evaluate such a logic is to examine how it stands with respect to several pairs of opposites. One pair that preoccupies Broch is the ornamental and the functional. The less ornamented the logic that abbreviates a style, the more functional it is. If the overall logic is devoid of ornament, it becomes revealed in, say, corresponding actions and visual styles. These respectively are singleness of purpose and a purely functional architecture. Broch, surrounded with buildings designed according to minimal criteria for sheltering humans (heedless, for instance, of how congenial dwellings are on the psychological plane or whether their inhabitants may wish to make an emotional investment in them and see them as *homes*), and people who ruthlessly submit everything to a singleness of purpose, deduced an overall logic that he took to be the abbreviation of an overall governing style. This logic seemed to him devoid of ornament, completely functional. Given an underlying metaphysical reality that takes the abbreviated form of a logic without ornament, then for an action to be valid (or justified) is for it to be carried out with a singleness of purpose; and for architecture to be accepted, everything must be suppressed in the name of function. When such a style prevails, all that is lively, colorful, and distinguishing about human action and dwelling, indeed about everything human, is dismissed as superfluous, as mere ornament. So ornament for Broch becomes a metaphysical symbol for what makes us far more than automata living in boxes, a symbol that extends to traditional architecture as well as the heart of human personality and action. The expurgation of ornament thus "involves nothingness, involves death, and a monstrous dissolution is concealed behind it in which our age is crumbling away." [29]

But how have functionalism and singleness of purpose gained the upper hand? Like all other historical possibilities, they are latent. But there must have been a deterrent to their preponderance and the "monstrous dissolution" that follows when functionalism and singleness of purpose become civilizational norms. Broch traces the recession of the deterrent to dissolution to the time when God was pushed so far into the abstract realm that human action practically ceased to refer to Him.[30] Broch thinks that both the primitive worldview and monotheism provide such reference. This has to do with both having end points for what he terms "lines of inquiry." In primitive society, because each thing is inhabited by its own demon, the lines of inquiry may be as short as a single step. Very short chains of reasoning can relate to objects in such a world. The plausibility of everything is quickly arrived at. Monotheism, in contrast, involves very long chains of reasoning. But the lines of inquiry all converge at God, to whom everything is ultimately attributed. God makes all things plausible. The difference between the primitive worldview and monotheism is that whereas the primitive worldview has infinitely many plausibility points, Monotheism has only one. Either way, lines of inquiry and chains of reasoning have a definite end point. The meaning of all things is known.

Today, these lines no longer converge, but run parallel to one another. There is no point at which inquiry can stop or meaning can rest. Behind every logic, there is a metalogic. All solutions are temporary. All meaning is doubtful. Thus, whereas logic in the primitive worldview and monotheism has a distinct shape, the one with short lines ending at the infinitely many demonized objects, the other with very long lines converging at God, it is shapeless in the modern era. Logical shapelessness is reflected in a general lack of meaning.

It is not just lines of inquiry that run parallel, according to a shapeless logic with no ultimate plausibility point, but lines of action as well. Whereas war, business, art, and politics would have to be centered in God in the monotheistic worldview (or regulated by custom and myth in a primitive setting), the withdrawal of God enables each to unfold according to its own logic, without regard for other fields or for any overall reference they might have in common.[31] The declaration of the sovereignty of reason signaled the recession of the monotheistic plausibility point. But it also signaled the sovereignty of war, business, art, and politics. It is no accident that the phenomena of total war, ruthless competition, l'art, pour l'art, and a singularly compunctionless politics have found fertile ground under that regime. As Broch writes,

> the logic of the army demands in general that all military resources shall be exploited with the utmost rigour and severity, resulting, if necessary, in the extermination of peoples, the demolition of cathedrals, the bombardment of hospitals and operating-theatres:
> the logic of the business man demands that all commercial resources shall be exploited with the utmost rigour and efficiency to bring about the destruction of all competition and the sole domination of his own business, whether that be a trading house or a factory or a company or other economic body:
> the logic of the painter demands that the principles of painting shall be followed to their conclusions with the utmost rigour and thoroughness, at the peril of producing pictures which are completely esoteric, and comprehensible only by those who produce them:[32]

and so on. It is noteworthy that Broch wrote this before Stalin and Hitler came to power. Now more than ever, the demands of that logic can be met. The recession of plausibility points opens the field for singleness of purpose and obsessive functionalism; and the will to functionalism pushes plausibility points ever deeper into their withdrawal. So what appears like a style full of dynamic possibilities—for this at face value is a style whose lines have nowhere to converge—becomes a faceless style, because whatever ornaments it falls by the wayside with nothing to genuinely sustain it—or turns into ornament in its most trivial sense (a sky-scraper built in the shape of a jukebox).

The condition we are left with is only temporarily one of autonomy for war, business, art, politics, and the rest. For

> woe to the others, if in this conflict of systems that precariously maintain an equilibrium one should gain the preponderance and overtop all the rest, as the military system does in war, or as the economic system is now doing, a system to which even war is subordinate,—woe to the others! For the triumphant system will embrace the whole of the world, it will overwhelm all other values and exterminate them as a cloud of locusts lays waste a field.[33]

Broch sees the regime of economism as metaphysically preordained by the sovereignty of reason; for what is the sovereignty of reason other than the attempt to banish plausibility points? Under that regime, man

> no matter how romantically and sentimentally he may yearn to return to the fold of faith . . . is helplessly caught in the mechanism of the autonomous value-systems, and can do nothing but submit himself to the particular value that has become his profession, he can do nothing but become a function of that value—a specialist, eaten up by the radical logic of the value into whose jaws he has fallen.[34]

Broch depicts a strong current within modernity, one that he fears may overwhelm it, that imposes a faceless functionalism the world over. Liberated by the absence of accountablity to any transcendent authority, human beings have been able to pursue profane activities without any hindrance except for what others might do to curtail their progress. After the horrors of World War II, there has been an emergent consensus to transpose singlemindedness into the economic and commercial spheres. This consensus was spontaneous, inspired by the hope that prosperity and material preoccupation would divert humanity from violence. Its legacy is complex and extremely powerful overlapping systems that, as a price for maintaining widespread affluence, demand the functionalism and singleness of purpose that constitute a faceless culture. The constitutional guarantees of freedom in many countries work themselves out, in practice, for all too many individuals, as an elaborate form of enslavement. For the machinery of widespread affluence nowadays depends not only on more individuals directly putting in longer hours of work than a few decades ago, but on their having the mental pliancy to accept and internalize the attitudes required by that machinery's smooth operation. We are quite familiar with such developments, but Broch locates them precisely within a crystalline historical-theological-philosophical framework.

However, one must not be misled by Broch's taut scheme to forget the crimes of those who claimed to act in the name of transcendent authority in western Europe in the late Middle Ages. These include not only the Inquisition but, to mention two more, the extermination of the Cathars in Provence and the sack of Constantinople in 1204. The problem of transposing transcendence into what are essentially large-scale turf wars cannot be ignored, nor can one belittle the merits of ensuring that the dignity of transcendence be saved from political degradation through some enforced separation of the two. The dilemma faced by modernity is harsh: the recession of transcendence gradually and steadily sucks human endeavor into materialism; while the official introduction of transcendence into the public sphere invites the criminal use of its aura in an all-too-profane power play. In the spirit of Kant's attitude, one might rather stress respect and affinity for transcendence as such, without which there will be degradation whether transcendence is publicly in the foreground or tucked away from our daily pursuits.

An Assessment of the Contributions of Berque, Habermas, and Broch

Berque, Habermas, and Broch have provided us with various perspectives on how modernity has failed to fulfill its promise and the consequent limitations on our freedom. For Berque, the failure is expressed through historical reductionism: the multidimensional possibilities found at any time in the reservoir of history have apparently been reduced to the single dimension of material advancement. The balance between the eternal and the everyday has been undermined to the detriment of freedom. For in the presence of the eternal, the everyday becomes meaningful with the infinite vistas that lay open before it. And in relation to the everyday, the eternal is constantly turned toward its concrete, accessible aspect. The everyday without the eternal eventually wallows in materialism and turns meaningless. And the eternal becomes cold, obscure, and oppressive when heedless to the everyday. Thus Broch links both kinds of imbalance: historically, meaningless, materialistic everydayness has been preceded by an infinitely remote and abstracted eternity. The symbol for an everydayness without meaning is the shapeless logic that encapsulates an epochal, cultural, or civilizational style characterized by functionalism and singleness of purpose within narrow domains. This dramatically reveals how time, when it unfolds within well-defined constraints such as the withdrawal of the eternal, eventually mocks the ideal of freedom so central to modernity. And Habermas ascribes the failure of modernity to a habit that has stifled the domains of knowledge and action, the habit otherwise known as the principle of subjectivity. For under the pressure to forge an unimpeachable consensus, every aspect of knowledge and action that cannot be evaluated by a universalistic form of reason gradually fell away. The ideal of subjects anonymously making sense of the world and planning their action, in complete disregard to any particularity such as their personality, beliefs, or cultural identity, has brought an appropriately senseless world and sphere of action to the foreground of modern civilization.

However, we must not regard those reflections as amounting to a final verdict on modernity. Habermas, Broch, and Berque are, after all, modern thinkers who directly or indirectly espouse modernity and have thoroughly imbibed it. Their work, like that of several other profound critics, renews our hope in the dimensions of modernity that have been silenced. If they underline a tendency so powerful within modernity that it seems at times to overwhelm it, they also offer broad views that do much justice to the full potential of human life and freedom. It seems within modernity's sweep to fashion the following:

1. A vivid intersection between the eternal and the everyday that steers history from its runaway advance along a material path toward a more balanced, multifarious movement (Berque).

2. A richer conception of reason more attuned to our layered existence and surroundings (Habermas).

3. A brilliant narrative that, even as it depicts the functionalism and singleness of purpose into which modernity is judged to have fallen, encompasses various personal, moral, cultural, and historical possibilities (Broch).[35]

The way to freedom, then, is reopened through the affirmation of positive transcendent values on condition that they remain close to the everyday and, in that setting, to allow the expansion of reason along a more fruitful and appropriate course and encourage the expression of character and particularity, away from the suffocation of functionalism and singleness of purpose. Such a way to freedom is the collective contribution of three modern thinkers. It helps restore our appreciation of the potential for freedom within modernity as one more step in the understanding of modernity necessary for the synthesis between it and tradition. This, as has often been said, is the only viable context for freedom in the Arab Muslim world and, indeed, wherever tradition resonates or can inspire modernity toward an exit from the forces that have stifled it.

Illustrations of Shrinkage:
Reich, Bellah, and Mardin

Let us now return to the negative tendency highlighted in the foregoing discussion and bring it somewhat closer to our present reality. For if modernity could well be otherwise, one must nevertheless face what it has largely become in many quarters.

We know, and modernity surely acknowledges, that human being is broader, deeper, more energetic, and more intelligent than to be contained by materialism. But the drive to improve material conditions has become so powerful and autonomous as to draw human being as extensively as possible into its orbit. As a result, human being has been channeled into technological and productive excellence, for the sustenance and further advancement of which systems of great complexity have been evolved. This evolution is not normal, but accelerates wildly because of the gross incongruity between the (human) potential expended on the process and the process's capacity to absorb that potential. For when a person works with great energy in a domain much too narrow for him, his mastery of the activities within that domain will advance to an incredible degree. This is why several products are made obsolete even before we become accustomed to them, and well before it is necessary to replace them.

There now are systems in place, then, that support the astonishing standards attained in the quality and variety of goods, and the expansion of market opportunities beyond what was imaginable a few decades ago. These systems also depend on a very high degree of specialization. Hence modernity, with so much promise for human freedom at the outset, to the extent that it has become beholden to those systems, inadvertently and relentlessly transposes freedom from the full possibility of human being to choice among the available specializations. These specializations have taken on a more abstract character—which may be up to human energies and intelligence (if not to breadth and depth)—but their economic function remains concrete. They in turn become more complex as their half-life grows shorter, so that not only do they require a commitment that rapidly approaches the unbearable, but one must be prepared to reeducate oneself in order not to be left behind when one group of specializations is supplanted by another. We shall presently have the occasion to see, in the words of an economist and a sociologist, both contemporary, both eminent, illustrations of a reality that dispels any doubt over whether Broch overreacted to what he had seen earlier this century.

Robert Reich and the New Economic Reality

There are three components to the new economic reality according to Robert Reich: specialized products and services for specialized markets that are traceable around the globe; constant improvements in the quality of mass-produced items (mainly to keep up with the competition, not because these items need to be that good); and the infrastructure necessary for these. Because the first two are a direct function of the competence of the workforce, national economic strength is thus defined in terms of the workforce and the infrastructure provided.[36]

What does the first component involve? Again, three things: the identification of marketing opportunities for a specialized product; the design and assembly of such products in a way uniquely tailored to the opportunity; and brokers who are sufficiently attuned to both ends of the process to gather the right team for each under their financial auspices.[37] Thus, marketing analysts, with the help of ever-more elaborate and comprehensive data bases, swoop down on the distinct groups indicated in search of perfect fits between specialized needs and specialized products. Whatever item is fancied by a small group of people, if it lies within the limits of current technology, is more likely than ever to be made and reach them. Conversely, a small group of people (at least) can be made to fancy virtually any existent or contemplated item. A vortex of supply and demand is thereby generated: people are free to desire any conceivably makeable thing, which they will sooner or later get, and marketing analysts will sooner or later find customers for anything they have (or have in mind). All are pulled into a market that constantly grows in variation, intricacy, and subtlety. Markets are successfully found for products attractive to those committed to certain ideas or movements—environmentalists, romantics, feminists, and fundamentalists, for instance. These movements are trivialized, if they are not trivial to begin with, and converted to market forces. For the people who voice opposition to the spread of the market's tentacles, a market is found as well. This is what modernity seems busiest with today, perhaps enduringly symbolized by the popular comparison of the erstwhile two Germanies just before reunification: food lines in the East, supermarkets in the West; Trabants in the East, superbly engineered luxury automobiles in the West; and so on. The paucity of references to the political and spiritual freedom supposedly won by the East is indicative and ominous.

As for what it takes to maintain an infrastructure compatible with an exponential rise in the activity of the market, the Germans are already transforming a road network that any visitor will attest is more than adequate "into 'smart' superhighways that can regulate traffic flow by computer," while "Japan is building a $250 billion fiber-optic network that by the year 2000 will carry video, voice, and data around the nation up to 1000 times faster than existing networks can."[38]

And what will all those energies and expenditures yield? The routinization of the following scenario that Reich dreams up with good cheer:

> A London department-store buyer of high-fashion apparel orders a line of dresses devised by a New York fashion designer. Within an hour of the order the designer sends via satellite the drawings and specifications for making the dresses to a fiber-optic link in Hong Kong, where they appear

on a high-resolution computer monitor, ready for a manufacturing engineer to transform them into prototype garments. The prototypes are then reproduced in a Chinese factory. The designer, the engineer, and the factory supervisor conduct a video teleconference to work out details, and the finished garments arrive in London less than six weeks after the order was placed.[39]

Robert Bellah and Market Totalitarianism

To the different perspectives so far presented on the conditions that threaten to exhaust modernity with the demands of a global, multifarious, labyrinthine, and partly abstract marketplace whose rate of advancement will soon outpace the human capacity to sustain it, Robert Bellah adds the misconceptions that have surrounded the ideal of individual autonomy. The first misconception is to regard "institutions . . . as objective mechanisms that are essentially separate from the lives of the individuals that inhabit them." This is rooted in the (mis)understanding of individual autonomy as an escape from institutions rather than "as dependent on a particular kind of institutional structure and community." The second misconception views individual autonomy as entailing a world in which individuals are autonomous from institutions *as well as from each other*. When a world is built in the image of these two misconceptions, with the attendant detached, mechanistic view of institutions and the demotion of virtues such as care and resposibility, when, in short, individual autonomy is elevated to the position of "almost the only good," it becomes "an empty form without substance."[40]

These assertions can be developed into a full argument supported by the various accounts we have come across of the steady shrinkage in the domain of freedom delimited by modernity. Here, we merely illustrate the consequences of modernity's direction, as Bellah depicts them. At the theoretical level, an atomistic interpretation of the idea of individual autonomy allows theorists initially to define human motives above all in terms of self-interest,[41] and with time exclusively so. Thus the influential school of economic thought headed by Milton Friedman starts out with the assumption that human beings are nothing but self-interested maximizers. Because Friedman also takes money to be the primary measure of self-interest, then what the self-interested seek to maximize is their wealth; and economics, the science that deals with money, becomes a total science. Because economics today is dominated by "rational choice theory,"[42] this theory also finds its way into sociology and has pretensions to become the new moral philosophy.[43]

At the practical level, we witness various recent conquests for the market. Government safety experts, when confronted with the argument that the value of human lives saved cannot be compared with the cost of the relevant safety devices on the grounds that human lives are priceless, respond: "We have no data on that."[44] Private homes are flooded with commercials and commercially minded entertainment.[45] A church guarantees money back for contributors who feel, after ninety days, that God has not kept His promises and given them a blessing.[46] The university, no longer a center for the disinterested pursuit of truth in most cases, but a response to the needs of a growing economy and state, is seen by a high-ranking Stanford official as one more element in the market system, delivering a *product* according to certain public expectations.[47] He matter-of-factly equates a *past* interest in the classics with the contemporary interest in money (!), and states flatly that the education *industry* must be responsive to market demand.[48] Successful corporations that in their own way have constituted communities for many employees who have long served them are commodified. They are eyed as commodities to be bought, stripped of their assets, and "reorganized" for immediate profit.[49]

Bellah is a sociologist who has headed an extensive amount of team fieldwork. He is as well positioned as one may be to depict the effects of the market's ascendancy. Perhaps his examples most eloquently portray the shape of the world for which so much has been sacrificed and illustrate how far modernity has strayed from its original promise and given in to markets that have become its legacy. Market totalitarianism, an expression apparently coined by Bellah himself, is the inheritance of a liberation lopsidedly driven by need and greed and cut off from any transcendent restraint.

Şerif Mardin and the Shrinkage of Freedom's Domain in Turkey

Turkey is unique in the Arab Muslim world in its enthusiastic and almost unquestioned embrace of modernity. Even if this has not penetrated as widely among the Turkish population, especially in rural areas, as the elite had hoped, modernity is present in the institutions at the republic's core. Moreover, the Turkish intelligentsia are so thoroughly secularized that there is a most peculiar barrier between higher education and religious belief. To be modern in Turkey has more or less come to mean to leave the past completely behind, including Islam in all but name. Thus the shrunk domain of freedom has a unique topography in Turkey.

Because many in Turkey, possibly a great majority, continue to relate to their society along communal lines, a state ideology that treats society otherwise will seriously constrain their freedom as social beings. The communal view of society takes it to be a network of personal relationships, "interlinked with ties of personal obligation," in the context of which persons evaluate themselves.[50] Whatever an individual may strive and struggle for within himself must "be tested against the conceptions that others hold of oneself."[51] If, instead, society is taken for a machine, with a structure utterly indifferent to the personality of its occupiers provided they meet certain impersonal criteria, those whose expectation it is that society be communal lose not only the means for evaluating themselves, but all that they may be and express as persons integrated into personal networks. These losses are not absolute, but relative to a Turk's involvement in the modern institutions that compose Turkish republican society. This involvement may be considerable, and it may be marginal. However, the pressure is definitely to become more rather than less involved. Prestige and the new ideal of self-worth in republican Turkey are in proportion to one's standing in its institutions and their affiliates.

In theory, individuals who make the transition to modern Turkish society are forced to relate to one another in functional terms (that is, relative to the functions they perform in a structure such as a state institution or private corporation) rather than in personal terms, and are treated as such by state officials. The form takes precedence over the person who fills it. This shift of emphasis from person to function means that whatever is personal, but does not pertain to the function at hand, is left out of social interaction. This remainder is as vast as the difference between persons and functions. The freedom lost, then, is the freedom to be persons in society over and above the functions performed. Turkey today covers a very wide social spectrum, from large impersonal institutions to traditional communities. So the freedom to be persons in society has by no means been lost. But with modernity favoring the impersonal institutions, and the state ideology sanctioning a mechanistic view of society, the social dimension of freedom has been much reduced and continues to be threatened.

Equally far-reaching has been the assault on the widely shared idiom of folk Islam, which

> is pervasive in the sense that it covers all aspects of life in society and that it is shared more equally by upper and lower classes than its equivalents are in the West. Daily life-strategies are framed by the use of religious idiom, and the fund of *Qur'anic* symbols on which it is based has a widespread popular usage. This sharing of an idiom to structure life strategies may be the foundation of what observers of Islam see as its "democratic" or "populistic" aspects.[52]

Here, we are in the intermediate zone between the social and the individual. The life-strategies are framed by individuals, but they are drawn from a fund shared by society and are therefore approved in advance. Turkey's headlong rush into modernity has ravaged that religious idiom. Not only have Islamic institutions that publicly affirm the idiom been undermined, but the mentality that relates to the idiom and dwells within it has been derided and dismissed. Above all, the idiom of folk Islam escapes the net of the universal currency that has become modernity's language. It cannot be validated by modernity.[53] It cannot be adequately understood by "sovereign" reason nor studied "scientifically." It is not designed to make way for the advances of the singleminded drive to improve material conditions, certainly not when it comes to sacrificing everything for the organization and mobilization necessary to attain the highest productivity given the available resources. The idiom of folk Islam is, from (the preponderant version of) modernity's standpoint, either an obstacle or a nuisance. The Turkish intelligentsia have largely adopted this attitude. And the freedom their countrymen once had to act within the framework of their religious idiom has been restricted. The restrictions go so far as to indoctrinate the Turkish population by means of an educational system that (officially) leaves them without the symbols that shape their approach to God.[54] The loss of the traditional context for freedom of action is not nearly compensated by the freedom delimited by late modernity. For we have seen at length how modernity has advanced along a path so narrow as to severely shrink the domain of freedom.

For the modernized and modernizing Turks, their freedom is restricted by the turn modernity has taken; and in their constant assaults on the domain of freedom for other Turks, they restrict other Turks' freedom too. Ironically, the freedom enjoyed by modernized and modernizing Turks owes much to the extent to which modernity has *not* overtaken their land (so that in a tentative and tenuous sense, they enjoy the best of both worlds as is vividly illustrated in the fact that their elections and political debates still have more than economic meaning); and the freedom of the other Turks lies mostly within the unofficial and often considerable residue of its traditional domain.

Shrinkage Old and New of Freedom's Domain in the Arab Muslim World

No other Arab or non-Arab Muslim state has embraced modernity quite as radically, explicitly, and enduringly as Turkey. The three exceptions that come to mind, the old South Yemen, Algeria, and Afghanistan, have recently undergone fundamental changes. The Marxist regime that controlled South Yemen has lost out in the reunification with the North to a government that claims to be more in tune with its Islamic heritage. The socialist system in Algeria has given way to military rule, which is under such pressure that it can no longer restrict the sustenance of Muslim institutions to private initiatives lest these become entirely dependent on and controlled by Muslim revolutionaries, whose power directly or indirectly influences official policy. And recent Communist rule in Afghanistan, which never really won over the population at large, was from the outset an aberration for which Soviet power alone was responsible.

Modernity, however, has advanced, often deeply, into every society in the Arab Muslim world. All governments acknowledge it in varying degrees. For instance, the state in each of Indonesia, Malaysia, Lebanon, Egypt, and Tunisia is strongly committed to modernity. Even the revolutionary Islamic regime in Iran, which had set itself apart from the present state of modernity as a matter of ideology (albeit unable to act consistently with that ideology at all times), has recently officially accepted the free market and expressed the desire for much improved relations with the West. All governments pay tribute to modernity in their rhetoric and initiate policies or adopt projects that further its advances. Unofficially, modernity advances even further in corporate practice, industry, trade, business, the professions based on the applied sciences, the military, the classroom, and the work and discourse of large sectors of the intelligentsia.

The question today is: Will the advances of modernity in the Arab Muslim world gradually and inexorably restrict freedom to choices *within* ever-more complex systems evolved in the course of a great and across-the-board rise in material standards? Is this what will follow the political liberalization that is bound to occur given the present and foreseeable global situation, so that freedom, at present restricted politically and incarcerated in a tradition that has yet to profoundly and authentically revitalize itself, will once again be restricted, more subtly and intricately than before? Will the limits placed on public debate be replaced with the limits of a ubiquitous language and logic that underlie modernity's present direction, limits that are so hard to see for those who live within them that the *identification* of the opposition, let alone that of the best course of action, itself becomes a problem? Will genuine and lively public debate, as we now see in Turkey and have seen in Lebanon until 1975, sooner or later give way to cold calculations about the most efficacious economic permutation, with real dissent banished to the dwindling margins of the worldwide process (as variously portrayed by Mardin, Berque, and Habermas)?

Only if those who will lead the way see tradition as an obstacle to modernity instead of a source of enrichment, and so share Hassan Hanafi's belief that the authority of sovereign reason is the best alternative to political and traditional-religious authoritarianism. Those who suffer the yoke of repressive regimes have such a clearly defined goal that they understandably fail to see the full consequences of whatever ideals they invoke in their quest. To those surrounded with highly visible forms of authority, reason beckons as the way to freedom. The struggle for liberation from visible authoritarianism can be so involved and protracted that a potentially more insidious authoritarianism remains invisible to it, as it is to many for whom the struggle has long been over. Hanafi in Egypt, although he is rather harsh in his judgment of a comparatively tolerant state (and a more tolerant society), sees the promise of reason almost as Kant did. Almost. For Kant did not quite see reason as sovereign, certainly not from ideals such as freedom of the will, the immortality of the soul, and the existence of God. Besides, a philosopher such as Hanafi surely has access to a critique of the failed promise of sovereign reason, now two hundred years old. That reason is never sovereign, and must submit to some authority or other, can only escape those conditioned by a most unusual historical or personal situation, from which they seek liberation. And for those who, consciously or unconsciously, equate freedom with liberation from that situation, the only freedom left—if they persist with the fiction of sovereign reason—will be that to attain enviable material standards and choose among the endless individual roads that lead thither.

The Arab Muslim world has not yet declared itself willing to submit solely to the authority of sovereign reason. It is at a crossroads. Modernity will definitely advance further into it, at an accelerated pace now that the politico-military obstacles are crumbling. But the traditions and institutions that can mediate the advancement of modernity and influence its direction are still highly resonant throughout the Arab Muslim world. These come in a great variety, some dating earlier than any known monotheistic creed. They have neither been as oppressive as the Church in medieval Europe, nor are they regarded by the people of the Arab Muslim world with anything like the hostility and bitterness felt by Europeans at the dawn of modernity (at least if one takes at face value the stigma modernity has attached to the medieval period, in recent decades under serious revision in Europe and the United States). Those traditions and institutions are frequently and substantially incorporated into Islam, certainly in the guise of life-forms that we have come to identify as Islamic. Thus Islam is a focus for the potential enrichment of the direction of modernity, and for this direction to be once more compatible with human being and the freedom commensurate with it (the same is true for Near Eastern Christianity). But the role of Islam can be constructive only if its institutions manage to escape the struggle between parochial traditionalists and singleminded revivalists. In the final chapter, we shall come across the relevant aspects of how Islam may find itself healthy and dynamic and thus provide its share of the synthesis between tradition and modernity that is the required synthesis for lasting freedom; and naturally, we shall see that traditionalists are not all parochial, nor are the revivalists all extremists.

Some compare the present situation in the Arab Muslim world with that of Europe in the early Renaissance and try to set guidelines for change based on subsequent European history. However, the Arab Muslim world has never been, nor is it now, directly comparable with Western Europe at the dawn of modernity. Then, it was more advanced than Western Europe in most senses of the word. Today, it is a balance between modernity, itself still in hybrid form in that part of the world, part "Western," part local, and resonant traditions that more often than not have their moorings in or have been incorporated into religion. The global power of the present direction of (Western) modernity threatens to upset this balance. On the other hand, a resolute defense and reinforcement of this balance may arrest the spread of either a monolithic modernism or an extremist Islamism. If the most immediate outcome of this struggle is the delineation of the future domain of freedom for the Arab Muslim world, a further effect may be experienced beyond its boundaries. All resistance to modern disequilibrium will become interconnected given access to current technology and each local hue of that resistance may be colored by its counterpart elsewhere.

As a general question, the character that modernity is to assume in the Arab Muslim world has been discussed for more than a hundred years. All along, the debate between traditionalism, modernism, and hybrid views has been lively. What is new here is the discussion of this question from the standpoint of freedom, and in the light of many important developments since the question first surfaced. Among them: the clarity that writers and critics in Europe and the Americas have recently attained about the history and direction of modernity; the more visible materialistic turn modernity has taken; the significant increase in its power; the much more sophisticated and encompassing study of the Arab Muslim world; and the more comprehensive understanding of freedom now that it has been officially secured in many places. With a deeper understanding of both modernity and tradition, a far more viable, dynamic, and original synthesis between the two has become possible, which makes earlier views shallow and facile when anachronistically transposed to the present. If the form of the general question remains the same, it has changed radically in both style and substance.

4

The Recovery of Freedom

Prologue

The elements for the recovery of freedom have already been given in the previous chapter. The reader may recall that it began with an account of the Kantian linkage between freedom, transcendence, and the moral law. We saw that Kant denied the possibility of freedom in the sensory world because he took it to be entirely causally determined. But the sensory world turns out to be far more complex and layered than Kant and his mechanistically minded contemporaries had believed. It is causally determined only to a limited degree. Otherwise it suggests and invites openness. This openness suggests freedom and transcendence. We shall explore the everyday manner in which we are called to a transcendent freedom in the latter part of this chapter.

Nevertheless, the Kantian linkage between freedom, transcendence, and morality has a profound validity, for our freedom is most truly characterized by the continuous potential to expand our being for all the sensory limitations imposed on it. We can always be far more than we would be if our sole purpose were to survive as the dominant species on earth or to advance materially. Much of this "excess" is stored in what might be termed a communal outlook. This living shared inheritance, which includes morality, is a partial embodiment of our affinity for a transcendent realm. There is a communal anchor for our freedom to the extent that freedom is a transcendence and communities are partly constituted by how the human affinity for transcendence has been regulated and codified. Vibrant communities offer their members daily reminders of freedom's vast domain. The middle part of this chapter will deal with the communal dimension of freedom.

In the previous chapter, some clues have also been extracted from the critiques offered by Berque, Habermas, and Broch as to how conditions might come about *from within modernity* that would favor the realization of freedom. Berque left us with the thought of the need to reaffirm positive, transcendent values on condition that they remain close to the everyday. Habermas, implicitly according to what we have seen so far and explicitly as we shall see in the next chapter, advocates a conception of

113

reason more compatible with the full scope of individual and collective human life than the narrow rationalism characteristic of the principle of subjectivity. And Broch passionately calls us away from functionalism and singleness of purpose toward the expression of character and particularity in a world filled with meaning by its trancendent aspect.

If the modern world were to be recast in the image of those three thinkers, transcendent presences would return to intermingle with daily life and orient it, rational activity would encompass the greatest range of human life that makes itself communicable, and meaningful creativity would flourish, be it in art, worship, or cultural style. These are not exhaustive images of freedom, but signposts away from a course that threatens to stifle it.

Unfortunately, one of the most visible images of freedom in contemporary culture is that of a diminished liberation. Freedom, it seems, is largely reduced to the liberation of this or that group from this or that authority or constraint. The liberated groups may be national or ethnic, minorities or pseudominorities. Pseudominorities impose themselves as "political" minorities only in an already apathetic and confused moral environment, whose further dissolution they then help bring about.

Freedom has become largely reduced to the desire of individuals whose being is dominated by a national, ethnic, racial, or issue-oriented focus to express what that focus entails. Although one must never belittle the extent to which, say, the Algerians were denied their freedom by the French or North American blacks by their white overlords, and therefore the extent of the freedom won by their respective liberation, it is of even greater concern what the freedom of such groups becomes once they have achieved liberation. What is the *quality* of the freedom of someone who is "free at last"? To ignore this question is portentous for freedom, for a person "free at last" may then find little real freedom left to fight for or exercise. Freedom ultimately does not pertain to human beings as Algerians, South Ossitians, blacks, or opponents or proponents of euthanasia, but to human beings *as such*. If one must not belittle the achievements of certain (but not all) liberation movements, one must not condone the preoccupation with liberation belittling the horizons of human being to the extent of reducing it to its national, ethnic, racial, or issue-oriented component. For this would bring on a tragic diminution of freedom in the wake of liberation. It would prepare the ground for the diversion of freedom to the frills and thrills of the marketplace.

The liberation that has most preoccupied the Arab Muslim world in recent years is at the national level. We shall therefore begin with a few reflections on national liberation and its aftermath in the context of our discussion of freedom. Similar reflections can be fashioned for the hypothetical time, perhaps nearer than is often assumed, when the Arab Muslim world will achieve widespread liberation from overtly authoritarian rule.

From National Liberation to Empty Choice?

National Liberation and Its Aftermath

Modernity has advanced the most where national liberation is no longer an issue. Northern and western Europeans have moved so far from the fear for their national freedom that they may be on the verge of ceding it for the sake of a unity that promises to consolidate their accomplishments and open new vistas for modernity's advancement. They are among the minority of human beings who are free to reflect on the freedom that they are constitutionally and in practice guaranteed. Such reflection already comprises an intellectual-spiritual tradition all its own. We thus chance upon a striking simultaneity when we turn to the Arab Muslim world. Although its struggle for national liberation has yet to end, those who live there have increased access to well-established critical thought centered in what awaits them well into the next century.

National liberation has mostly been only formally secured in the Arab Muslim world. Except for the Palestinians, whose quest for self-determination we may assume resolved because this will change nothing in what follows, independence is formally there. That independence has yet to become substantial in the region. This is not only due to "neocolonialism," as it has been called, or the demands of the global market. These have no doubt dampened the early joys of national liberation. But other limitations on freedom in formally independent Arab Muslim countries are more elusive and consequential. As Berque points out, decolonization also frees the decolonized to come face-to-face with their other problems: poverty, malnutrition, illiteracy, and the lack of meaning by which to orient themselves.[1] If the means to address the first three are fairly clear, this is not the case for the fourth, the most decisive for freedom. Suppose for a moment that all people in the Arab Muslim world were brought out of their economic and political[2] misery, well fed and educated—what then? What would they be as free beings?

These problems are present together and must therefore be confronted simultaneously. Thus, alongside the effort to improve material conditions and education, we witness societies in a general state of groping. Their quest for meaning is nascent and hence prone to false starts.[3] The nascence of their quest contributes to the limitations on individual freedom of choice and expression (which those with an inadequate understanding of the region attribute exclusively to repressive regimes and institutions, as if these operated in a vacuum and were not themselves part of the general groping). Whatever emerges from this quest will be decisive for the extent of the freedom enjoyed once it is constitutionally and practically guaranteed. It will define the identity that anchors the ability to choose and follow through one's choices meaningfully (a notion to be elucidated in the course of this chapter).

Despite the partial lag between the Arab Muslim world and places where modernity has advanced more substantially (a lag that can be measured only relative to modernity's own chronology and is relevant only to the extent that modernity is inevitable), they have in common, respectively as a future prospect and a present concern—with modernity's global components uniting present and future—the problem of how or whether, given freedom of choice, freedom may be meaningfully exercised. If the meaningful exercise of freedom requires a distinct identity, so that individuals and societies do not wander amid endless choices unto self-enervation, then it is a requirement for both the Arab Muslim world and places where modernity has advanced more substantially. It may well be that for one (the Arab Muslim world), an age-old identity has but to be transposed in modern-day terms[4] without killing its spirit, whereas for the other, a new identity has to be forged, perhaps in part through the recovery of the residue of the old. This recovery may be inspired by the example of what is already there in the Arab Muslim world, albeit in need of revival, so that the call to transpose an age-old identity in modern terms is reciprocated with a call for modernity to revitalize itself through what is age-old but still vibrant. One already notices admiration in certain modern quarters for the civilizational depth that gives the Chinese and, possibly to a lesser extent, the Indians such confidence about their identity. Fernand Braudel's *The Identity of France* is a clear indication of the renewed dynamism with which identity is being addressed in Europe (far removed from the ludicrous folklore encouraged by coarse nationalism). On the other hand, Japan is a unique case of a society whose identity has been almost unscathed amid a vertiginous plunge into modernity.

The Two Tyrannies

Liberal thinkers such as Isaiah Berlin are reluctant to push beyond the state where individuals are guaranteed as much freedom of choice as minimal social coherence and order allow. They fear that the recognition of any public appeal to move beyond that state leads to an authoritarian or tyrannical body legitimized by that appeal. If, for instance, we were to admit that the Church knows what is best for us, the Church may before long regain control over our lives; or if "true freedom" were impossible without a certain social order, then we may in the end delegate absolute power to those dedicated to its establishment. An identity that anchors the ability to choose and follow through one's choice meaningfully thus elicits similar fears among liberals. It evokes memories of conformism and parochialism. Yet it must be possible to partake of a collective identity that enhances rather than limits individual scope, just as we have witnessed the similarly paradoxical (or *apparently* paradoxical) possibility of the *absence* of an official collective identity at many levels in the United States leading to a remarkable degree of voluntary conformism. This does not depend, it seems, on whether a collective sense of identity thrives or not.

On the other hand, pervasive silence as to how one might exercise the freedom one is guaranteed, originally to fend off tyranny, encourages, as we have seen in different accounts, another kind of tyranny. There is no escape from the fact that modernity has definite origins and motives and that from these, a direction must emerge. Ordinarily, it would merge with other directions along a balanced path. But the other directions, it so happens, issue from sources more vulnerable to the accusation that their expositors or messengers explicitly tell people how they must live.[5] The tendency is to brush those sources aside. Individuals are then supposed to be able to make their choices unmolested.[6] Instead, the realm of their choices is steadily and ruthlessly circumscribed by unofficial forces. The drive to improve material conditions, and all the elaborate systems it has bequeathed, has a harmlessly neutral appearance. This appearance is its danger. For with all other drives under pressure or marginalized because they appear not to be neutral, the drive to improve material conditions has become dominant in a way that no one could foresee.

The tendency to brush aside whatever does not contribute to material prosperity, and the security and stability that support it, has been exasperated by Europe's travails in this century. For in the aftermath of two world wars, the first fought largely in Europe and the second no less intensely there, whose toll is too well known for repetition, and the threat of a nuclear conflagration that followed almost immediately, nineteenth-century ideas about the need to advance society to a level where prosperity and security were not precariously maintained, but issued smoothly from solid social foundations, acquired great urgency. It became much easier to imagine, yearn for, and actively seek a new phase in human experience, in which people live well and peacefully because whatever there is within them that runs contrary to these goals has been overcome, suppressed or—best of all—"outgrown." In 1949 Berlin could therefore correctly characterize the new policy as one that diminished "strife and misery by the atrophy of the faculties capable of causing them."[7] If one could assume such atrophy, then it was possible to think of human problems as belonging to the realm of technical analysis, instead of being related to instincts, emotions, and tendencies that are closely tied to human nature. All issues could be reduced "to technical problems of lesser or greater complexity."[8] We see this reflected in postwar European public affairs, where emphasis has gradually shifted "away from disagreement about political principles (and from party struggles which at least in part sprang from genuine differences of outlook) towards disagreements, ultimately technical, about methods—about the best ways of achieving that degree of minimum economic or social stability."[9]

The vivid memory of long periods of violence and devastation in Europe had made security, stability, and prosperity so desirable that many were willing, openly or tacitly, to cede control of "vast tracts of life" to

> persons who, whether consciously or not, act systematically to narrow the horizon of human activity to manageable proportions, to train human beings into more easily combinable parts—interchangeable, almost prefabricated—of a total pattern. In the face of such a strong desire to stabilize, if need be, at the lowest level—upon the floor from which you cannot fall, which cannot betray you, let you down—all the ancient political principles begin to vanish, feeble symbols of creeds no longer relevant to the new realities.[10]

These words ring far truer today than when written. It may come as a surprise that the United States now seems more prone than any other part of the world to the changes discerned by Berlin. However, while the United States has largely escaped the horrors visited upon Europeans, it is filled with immigrants who want nothing more than peace and prosperity. Because it also happens that the bulk of the population where modernity has advanced furthest shares the outlook of the United States' immigrant population, namely, peace and prosperity before all else, the following has come about quite voluntarily:

> The words of St.-Simon's prophecy [have] finally come true—words which once seemed so brave and optimistic: "The government of man will be replaced by the administration of things." The cosmic forces are conceived as omnipotent and indestructible. Hopes, fears, prayers cannot wish them out of existence; but the *élite* of experts can canalize them and control them to some extent. The task of these experts is to adjust human beings to these forces and to develop in them an unshakeable faith in the new order, and unquestioning loyalty to it, which will anchor it securely and for ever. Consequently the technical disciplines which direct natural forces and adjust men to the new order must take primacy over humane pursuits— philosophical, historical, artistic. Such pursuits, at most, will serve only to prop up and embellish the new establishment.[11]

All these developments suggest strict neutrality with regard to how freedom is to be exercised so long as prosperity, security, and stability not be undermined. Yet it is clear that this constraint is severe on the domain within which the freedom to choose is to be exercised, hostile as it implicitly is to any strong position on the exercise of freedom other than that entailed by the constraint. It emerges in the passages just cited from

Berlin's work that human life compatible with that constraint is truncated indeed, herded as it appears into the technical (and now also consumerist) dimension.

Strict neutrality thus weakens and lessens the possibilities for the exercise of freedom. It delivers the realm of choice into the hands of those forces and interests that officially (and only officially) have no say in how one is to exercise one's freedom, but also officially promote the advancement of security, prosperity, and stability at all costs. In short, strict neutrality is a sham. It conceals the forces and interests that officially embrace freedom of choice and in reality channel individual choices into ever-more complex paths that crisscross the domain over which those forces and interests hold sway. This domain and its language are today so familiar and pervasive that to stand outside of them, if at all conceivable, automatically gives one an irrational mien. As Berque, Habermas, and Mardin have told us, never before has *real* dissent been so difficult. Hitherto, those who dissented feared for their bodies or souls. But dissenting *thoughts* were easy to come by, an ease possibly connected with the bodily or spiritual cruelty inflicted as punishment respectively by men or God. The absence of Hell from the present consciousness and the vastly improved bodily treatment of human beings under modernity's auspices (mainly with respect to the court and prison systems, not necessarily in how people treat one another's bodies in more modern lands, or the bodies of other people in less modern lands) may have something to do with the much-reduced possibility for real dissent. If in the past people were afraid to *express* their dissent, today it is much more difficult to *think* dissenting thoughts given the intricacy of the systems that ensnare modern life. To be sure, ceaseless twaddle passes for dissent, but it is mostly a show that enhances what it is meant to criticize. Very rarely do we find dissent today that compares with a heresy in olden times. One is deterred and thwarted by the sheer complexity of what one must see through to make a radical departure that is analogous to heresy. University students who may start out with the elements of true dissent are typically overwhelmed by the time they graduate—or are secure in their work.

A context congenial to the meaningful exercise of freedom must therefore be found between the two tyrannies, the one explicitly telling people what they must do at every turn to be "truly free," the other refusing to tell them anything at all and in the process delivering them over to the forces and interests that be. Because this situation describes modernity today, a considered approach to freedom beyond choice is to note some kinds of discontent with the current state of modernity in places such as the United States, but also in the Arab Muslim world. Afterward, the construction of a loose framework for freedom may be ventured, building on genuine popular sentiments that frequently exhibit themselves these days. In the absence of any such exercise and any practice that manifests the underlying awareness, national liberation and democratization may not lead to freedom, but to submission to a subtle form of tyranny.

Resistance to Shrinkage

The United States is arguably the locus of modernity's furthest advance at present. Historians and others have adduced different factors that have contributed to this advance. Of special interest to us is the United States' unique character. It is a nation that openly regards itself as *invented,* and as permanently amenable to creative change and reinvention, originally along with a divinely ordained destiny. The United States is thus radically unhinged from the ordinary sense of identity and tradition. These are literally open-ended and self-consciously man-made, so much that the virtues of open-endedness and *man*-ufacture often take precedence over content. Thus the United States is a singularly fertile ground for the advance of a modernity whose direction has become profoundly indifferent to any positive notion of identity, indeed destructive thereof. As the perceived divine element in the United States' invention receded, the combination of reason and elementary empiricism became the only way to maintain consensus. We have seen what happens when reason gains ascendancy (mistaken for sovereignty) in an environment where individuals believe they must judge for themselves independently. We have seen how relentlessly the ideals of sovereign reason and independent judgment have led modernity, given its specific origin and history, toward preoccupation with the drive to improve material conditions, so that freedom has become threatened with restriction to the unprecedented opportunities and choices within the systems thereby propelled.

If there is any natural resistance to such dissipation of human possibility, one can hardly find a better place to observe than the United States. Officially without a positive definition of its identity, for such is the case when identity is exclusively defined in terms of principles and ideals, the search for a positive identity has if anything intensified. It is a search at times farcical, excessively self-conscious, or hopelessly romantic, but these too are signs that positive identity is naturally constitutive of human being. All over the United States, many different kinds of small communities are emerging, not all of which are cultic or fundamentalist. The decline of small towns and rural life is much lamented. Thinkers at major intellectual centers have begun to articulate serious communitarian thought and have documented a nationwide yearning for its realization. Most of the communities in question are not meant to be ethnically or racially homogeneous, even if many in fact are. What they all have in common is ideals believed to have a trancendent source, usually religious, usually Christian.

Moreover, if the rhetoric of modernity be taken at face value, human beings are supposed to outgrow superstition and scoff at institutions such as the office of confession. And yet people in the United States are highly superstitious and confessional. Astrology, palm reading, autobiography, and psychoanalysis are all popular. As frivolous as these often are, they bespeak recognition of the beyond and a deep sense of moral accountability, which respectively ground the furthest reaches of personal freedom and freedom within the enabling community. These are the two kinds of freedom the consideration of which will help us canvas positive freedom without the risk of abuse by those who can only tyrannize others toward the alleged fulfillment of their freedom.

If the United States is a fruitful field for the study of the spontaneous rejection of the limited realms that modernity has imposed in its later development on the exercise of freedom, so is Europe in an altogether different way. Modernity originated there. And no sooner had some people begun to realize that much greater freedom from arbitrary state action, social barriers, poverty, ignorance, and religious authority would unleash systems so complex as to ensnare life within them to a previously unthinkable degree than they raised their voices, first in alarm, then in sustained and rigorous protest. The deeply moving, often brilliant, and sometimes prophetic works of Schiller, Kierkegaard, the young Hegel, Romantic writers and poets, Schopenhauer, and Nietzsche are testimony to resistance to the newly elaborate herding of human life and thought, a resistance so natural that the herding is anticipated with a view toward its preemption, if only for the sake of posterity. If the sentiments echoed in that continuous testimony were usurped by fascists earlier in our century, this should deter from neither their truth nor their value. Meanwhile, Church authorities, largely discredited and demoted in the public eye, struggled to define new avenues to gather communities around the age-old values and ideals at their heart.

In the Arab Muslim world, as is well known and much discussed nowadays, various Islamic movements, revolutionary, revivalist, traditionalist, progressive, mystical, or otherwise, express among other things resistance to the prospect of denying them the means for the articulation of their spiritual being at both communal and individual levels. Secular intellectuals and groups are unfortunately too caught up in the struggle for the constitutional and practical guarantee of freedom of expression, association, and so on, to reflect on the actual content of freedom afterward. Although, as has been mentioned, the Arab Muslim world is still in a hybrid situation, where modernity's penetration not only is partial but also still conducive to substantial transformation at the hands of local culture, the signs that the promise of greater freedom is accompanied by the unannounced possibility that it may become limited in more subtle or insidious ways are there. Exposure to the work of European and American authors adds markedly to the extrapolating tendencies, so that in some sense the future is seen in the present without the need for prophetic endowment. Those who resist shrinkage in the Arab Muslim world may not expicitly espouse the cause of freedom in the sense that it will presently be discussed. But just that freedom is unmistakably at stake.

The spontaneous resistance to the shrinkage of freedom's domain has, in the examples just cited, either a populistic or an individual-idiosyncratic quality. As the attempt is made to congeal these around a more ordered approach to freedom, they will respectively relate to the communal and personal dimensions of the positive exercise of freedom. The two must be taken together; for it is persons who shake communities out of the ossification to which they are vulnerable, and communities that protect free self-expression from the descent to solitary, narcissistic, irrelevant screams.

From Empty Choice to Freedom
Through the Enabling Community

Negative and Positive Freedom

The most common notion of freedom today is to do or be whatever one wishes without interference, at least over a substantial range of action. This notion is negative, for it does not stress what one does or is, but limits itself to the assurance that there be no outside intervention in what one does or is (or as little of it as possible). The appellation "negative freedom" is therefore sensible. However, given negative freedom, one may find oneself unable to make any of the many available choices. One may find a good argument for several conflicting decisions, whether they pertain to a single action or a life plan. One may become indifferent to all available options lacking any other motivation. Finally, one's will may become so weak, or one's mind so lost in the confusion and relativism, that one effectively no longer makes one's own choices and is simply led around by the prevalent influences. This condition is no doubt hypothetical, the more so the more it is taken to its logical extremes. But it sheds light on the need, given negative freedom, for the ability to go ahead, make choices, and follow them through. The more significant the choices, the more they require from the person who seeks to follow them through. At the level of a life plan, the execution of a choice demands commitment, an impossibility if one is confused or chronically weak-willed. There is, then, a sense in which a person must be able to bring something into the area of choice, the more so the more significant the choice, if one is ever to move past the preliminary state of the availability of choice. A person who is incapable of this transition is profoundly unfree, at best a permanent and benumbed spectator. One can earnestly claim that the availablity of choice in such a state is only formal. It is effectively as though one had no choice at all. The notion of a person's capacity for the transition beyond the brute state of choice is positive. The freedom to make choices, in the sense of the capacity for the actual selection from among them and commitment to their demands, entails a positive notion, for which the appellation "positive freedom" is appropriate.[12]

If freedom is not only noninterference by others, but *how* one goes about one's choices, then a paradox arises. For if we care about what we and others choose, then we take a stand on one another's choices. Our positive freedom entails a limit on our negative freedom. If it matters that we exercise the available (negative) freedom meaningfully, then we instinctively interfere, if only a little bit, to ensure that others do too, at least by implication, at least when it comes to those closest to ourselves. But modernity has been so repelled by the extensive external (social) direction of individual life that it fears any direction of it at all. It has thus naturally and heavily favored the reduction of freedom to its negative (brute individual) component. To free individuals from social pressures, it has pressured society to loosen the links traditionally set up between its members to the point of fragmentation or near disintegration. Consequently, and quite unexpectedly, it has eaten away at the (partly inherited) capacity for positive freedom.

Modernity has set inordinately more choice than hitherto before individuals who are less able to make them, particularly when the choices are crucial. The choice of toothpaste flavors or the color of one's underwear is not difficult (although the gross superfluity of goods prolongs the purchase and increases the means for dispersing one's freedom), the choice of a car or house somewhat more demanding. But the choice of a spouse or friends demands rather more, as does the choice to live in accordance with aesthetic, moral, and religious ideals. In a corrupt customs department or law firm, it takes far more than good intentions to maintain moral propriety. Very few individuals can do so entirely on their own. Precisely because the consequences of important choices are so demanding, one usually needs the support of others who share a similar outlook. These others may be a loose grouping of close relatives, friends, or associates; or large communities. One is far more liable to go astray or lose the will to persist without any such support. This support vanishes when the solidarity between human beings is eroded. But such is precisely the outcome in a society that emphasizes negative freedom obsessively and causes the fragmentation of the communities within it, no more so than when the prevalent assumption is that human beings are self-interested, profit-maximizing individuals. Too much emphasis on positive freedom is also undesirable, for though positive freedom naturally leads to an interpersonal or communal solidarity, which facilitates the persistence that is almost always necessary to follow through one's crucial choices, there is a danger that the line between much-needed support for a person's positive freedom and heavy-handedness may be crossed.

Charles Taylor and the Careful Advance
Toward Positive Freedom

The contrast between positive and negative freedom warrants further elucidation as we seek to clarify the basis for our judgments about whether we are really free. In Taylor's words,

> Doctrines of positive freedom are concerned with a view of freedom which involves essentially the exercising of control over one's life. On this view, one is free only to the extent that one has effectively determined oneself and the shape of one's life. The concept of freedom here is an exercise-concept.
>
> By contrast, negative theories can rely simply on an opportunity-concept, where being free is simply a matter of what we can do, whether or not we do anything to exercise these options. . . . Freedom consists just in there being no obstacle. It is a sufficient condition of one's being free that nothing stand in the way.[13]
>
> [But i]f we are free in the exercise of certain capacities, then we are not free, or less free, when these capacities are in some way unfulfilled or blocked. But the obstacles can be internal as well as external. And this must be so, for the capacities relevant to freedom must involve some self-awareness, self-understanding, moral discrimination and self-control, otherwise their exercise could not amount to freedom in the sense of self-direction . . . where, for example, we are quite self-deceived, or utterly fail to discriminate properly the ends we seek, or have lost self-control, we can quite easily be doing what we want in the sense of what we can identify as our wants, without being free; indeed, we can be further entrenching our unfreedom.[14]

The key elements of the transition to positive freedom are self-understanding, self-control, and moral discrimination. The hypothetical extreme of unfreedom would then be for one to have no idea who one is, no control over one's actions, and no sense of moral right or wrong, good or bad. Note that the guarantee of negative freedom does not preclude living in that hypothetical state. It is quite possible to imagine a highly productive society populated with such beings (as it has indeed been imagined), prevented from mutual infringements through strict enforcement of the law. The exclusive public recognition of negative freedom does not necessarily lead to that hypothetical state. But nothing that helps prevent it would be publicly sanctioned.

That people are meaningfully free even where resistance to the public recognition of (positive) freedom is highest is due to an imperishable feature of human life: as much as we may desire to be free from as many sorts of interference as possible, we do distinguish among our wants and goals. We have minimally a rough idea of the relative significance of these. Some are subject to what are termed "weak evaluations," others to "strong evaluations."[15] Weak evaluations pertain to things such as the quality of hotel service and umbrellas. When, however, we evaluate a moral action according to whether it is noble or base, a work of art to whether it is significant or trivial, a life to whether it is integrated or fragmented, and a character to whether it is good or bad, our evaluations are strong.[16]

We can also differentiate between weak and strong evaluations when we contrast their relationship with what is good. If I want an umbrella or a hotel to stay in, then what I want is good simply because I want it.[17] But if I want to act nobly or rid my character of its vices, then what I want is not good because I want it, but because it is itself good.[18] In general, the objects of weak evaluations are good or bad depending on whether one wants them; whereas those of strong evaluations are themselves good or bad (Taylor is noncommittal on whether they are good or bad *in themselves* or because they were *made* to be so, say, by divine decree).

Taylor then opens a window to our strong evaluations: we know what matters to us through how we feel about some of our experiences. Over time, we may notice how some of our actions have led us to self-contempt or self-reproach. We may notice how we were ashamed to have done something. Shame, like wonder, outrage, and joy, is a way that something matters to us. It is how something is relevant or important to us. It defines our image of ourselves, our aspirations, purposes, desires, and sentiments as moral beings. It is what Taylor calls an *import*.[19]

Whenever we feel something such as remorse, we show an intuitive understanding of right and wrong. The imports involved are revealed to us. From a collection of such experiences, we can form a "moral map" of ourselves.[20] We begin to grasp the shape of our aspirations, our vision of the good life, what we are all about, and what really matters to us. The clearer this all is, the more we can evaluate strongly, and control and know ourselves. These, as we may recall, are the key elements of the transition to positive freedom.

Any individual who wishes to ascertain the presence of strong evaluations in his life need do no more than remember occasions when he felt remorse, wonder, outrage, shame, or joy and uncover his moral identity from these.[21] For they do give insight into the life that one seeks to live as a moral being, and thus the strongest basis for the discriminations necessary to proceed meaningfully in an environment where there is so much freedom of choice.

Choice, Freedom, and the Enabling Community

Choice is not relevant to freedom at every level. We do speak of choice when it comes to material goods, services, homes, and even a spouse or friends. But it would be absurd to say that someone chooses to feel outrage, joy, or shame. We do not choose how our moral identity is revealed to us. Nor is that moral identity itself subject to choice although it can be transformed to varying extents because of conscious decisions. The option is always there for a person to reform himself in accordance with what is better. Even then, however, there is still a sense in which a person does not choose to acknowledge the goal of his personal reform as better, but simply recognizes it as such. Such recognition is an ability. Communities that have traditionally recognized certain personal goals as better than others bestow this ability upon those who belong to them. Another avenue for the bestowal of such ability is through what religious thinkers have called "grace." Intuitionist philosophers have attributed that ability to the intuition of the individual. The most accessible of these is the community that enables individuals to discriminate in moral, aesthetic, and religious affairs.

The relationship between choice and positive freedom is thus complex. A person should have the right to leave his community and choose to belong to any other or, if he thinks it desirable and possible, none at all. But a person who stays with this choice and does not advance to the point where he is deeply embedded within a community or well along a solitary path toward fulfillment—and both are points where the choice to change course exists more in theory than in practice; such a person will barely be able to exercise his freedom when it comes to strong evaluations. He will freeze at the threshold of ways along one of which he must proceed with conviction (for without conviction, the choice is meaningless and may just as well be a result of manipulation). The less choice a person has to depart from a course on which he has embarked, the more positive his freedom.[22] The assumption here is that choice is at the level of a reasonably healthy outlook on life as a whole, not a choice like that made by criminally minded persons who get caught in a vicious circle of violence that finally closes in on them. A person so committed to a course that provides him with a healthy outlook on life that he almost loses the choice to leave it can for that very reason act as a free person. For from such an outlook issue the strong evaluations that enable one to proceed meaningfully through a world filled with options. The community is decisive in ensuring that the outlook in question deals with life as a whole and is indeed healthy. Individuals must at least depend on the wisdom embedded in communal traditions for some of what they forge on their own if they are not to lead themselves (and other) astray.[23] This does not mean that communities which bestow upon their members the ability to be positively free ought to impose severe (external) constraints on those who wish to leave. Whether one embarks on a course that one is deeply committed to and thereby enjoys greater positive freedom should be a personal matter. If one is to flow freely along the roads cleared by communal effort, one ought to belong freely as well. One ought to feel the commitment and the freedom deep within oneself.

To associate freedom too much with choice therefore narrows freedom's domain. The ability to act, think, and live freely depends not only on the absence of external obstacles, but also on one's internal state of readiness. However we may remove the external obstacles in the path of a person whose inner life is parched, that person would not be free whenever faced with the need to make a strong evaluation. But much of what constitutes one's inner life, including one's moral identity, is not subject to choice. One does not and cannot choose much of what enables one to be positively free.

Individuals do not usually confront the situations in which strong moral evaluations are called for in isolation. They do so in the company of others. Over time, a corpus might emerge of collectively shared strong moral evaluations, based on the intuitive or natural understanding of what is right or wrong, good or bad, noble or base, higher or lower, and so on. A collective moral outlook thus emerges, a moral vision. This vision defines the moral tradition of a community. It constitutes the moral fiber that holds a given community together. The community, like the individual, does not choose its moral vision casually. That such moral vision often withstands great historical upheavals and sometimes transcends space and time suggests transcendent origins. Many communities believe that their moral visions have transcendent origins and believe this to be the basis for their moral endurance. If one were to examine the facts, one most likely cannot assemble them in a manner that suggests the fabrication of transcendence, made possible by the passage of time and urged on by the need to legitimize shared outlooks through an appropriate mythology. The anatomy of the more remarkable examples of the persistence of shared moral visions, sometimes against terrible odds, will at several points pose serious problems to those who believe that their transcendent origins were a fabrication. To suppose transcendent origins for this kind of moral vision may even at the theoretical level provide a better and more comprehensive explanation for its power and persistence.

What has just been said about a community's moral vision extends to its overall vision, including its positions on art and religion. Such a community may identify itself with a given religion and draw the subsidiary elements of its overall vision from this. Whatever the case, an individual who belongs to such a community at a later stage will inherit its accumulated knowledge and wisdom regarding how to go about the strong evaluations that one must make several times in life. He will inherit, while he belongs to a community that constrains him, a vision that will enable him to exercise the opportunity to be free. Paradoxically, an individual who is constrained by his community (but freely committed to it) can act more independently than one who is not constrained by any, unless he happens to be that rare individual with mystical or quasi-mystical tendencies, or an extraordinary resilience and resourcefulness in forging his solitary path toward greater positive freedom. An individual unconstrained by any community and without the resources to forge his own way is not independent, but ripe for manipulation. Only when a community's practices become perfunctory and the form of whose vision turns stale and stifles its content do the constraints compromise the freedom of its members. As it happens, the rare individuals who can stand outside their communities and nevertheless be positively free are often those who revitalize them.

Further Remarks on the Enabling Community

It is useful at this point to distinguish between the two related terms *community* and *society*. As contrasted by John Macmurray,[24] society tends to be organized around a common purpose, whereas common purpose flows from a community. A society, whether a debating society, a professional association, or a modern nation-state, tends to regard its members relative to their function within it. The common end defined by such a society transcends the personal ends of its members. In a community, on the other hand, each member is regarded as an integral whole. The ends of a community are a reflection of the ends of autonomous persons, and if anything, it thus enhances the self-expression of its members. The contrast between society and community is put this way by Macmurray.

> Society demands from its members a devotion to a common end which transcends all "private" ends, and a loyalty which is ready to sacrifice both oneself and one's neighbor to accomplish it. But from the standpoint of community, such a demand is absurd and blasphemous. For its values lie within, not beyond, the nexus of relationship; and all cooperation is a means of expressing the common life. Persons, not purposes, are absolute.[25]

A person who is treated as an integral whole is more free than one who is treated relative to his function. At best, whatever within a person transcends his function is ignored by society. At worst, it is consistently diminished until the person identifies as closely as is humanly possible with his function. Very few functions have the potential to occupy the full-fledged being of humans, and even then, it would be odd to think of them as functions. Mystics, artists, missionaries, social workers, or political leaders may reach the heights of involvement that enable them to identify strongly with what they do. But this is inadequately expressed by the word *function*. Words such as *vocation* or *calling* come to mind, already a sign that as we approach the being of a whole person, we leave functions behind as a rather limited part of human life. A person who can express his being as a whole has immeasurably more freedom than one whose expression is restricted to the domain of his function.

While Macmurray makes a useful and valid distinction between two different approaches and attitudes toward human collectivities, which we may call the "functionalist" and the "personalist," his identification of these respectively with society and community may be questionable. Sociologists have long contrasted functionalist with personalist societies. Personalist societies certainly are more authentic communities than functionalist ones. But if personalist societies are identifiable with communities or communal outlooks, then "society" can no longer be distinguished from "community" according to whether the collectivity under consideration is functionalist or personalist. Rather, a collectivity that is merely a society may be based on the functions of the persons it joins. It may even encourage a functionalist attitude. But a society can also join its members as full-fledged persons. For that, we can say, a society must have a communal aspect.

A community, then, enables the individual to exercise greater positive freedom because it treats him as a person, beyond any function he may have within it. This is in addition to placing the person firmly within a framework where strong evaluations can be made with ease. Thus, as we approach the direct consideration of freedom in the Arab Muslim world, the thoughts of Mardin on the freedom that has been lost in modern Turkey can be better appreciated. The Muslim community, whatever its special traits (some of which will be highlighted later), has given its members the distinct identity without which they can not be positively free, and has emphatically treated them as integral persons so that it is taken for granted that the Muslim must be able to express his whole being, no matter how encompassing this may be, within the framework laid out by the community. Islam has been particularly solicitous about the rigorous construction of a framework commensurate with the breadth and depth of its individual adherents. Furthermore, through acceptance of the divine revelation at its origin, as explicit an acknowledgment as there can be of a transcendent ground for a community, it has allowed "human nature and nature in general . . . [to] flow with more intensity," with only "quite moderate prohibitions" as the price.[26] Mardin introduces the Jungian notion of archetypes in support of the extent to which the acceptance of transcendence expands the horizons in which the self is formed. For the self, according to Jung, evokes transcendent ("numinous") archetypes at the subconscious level of its formation. These parallel a culturally determined conception of deities, which in a Muslim context would be God as revealed in the Qur'an. A process is then triggered that allows the self to come into its fullness.[27] We shall return to these themes presently.

Meanwhile, we have gained a third dimension of the enabling community in the event that it explicitly acknowledges transcendence at the heart of its vision. Once it has given the person a solid point of departure to overcome the hurdles that must be faced in the exercise of freedom, once it habitually treats him as a whole so that no dimension of his personhood may be ignored by it, it opens up unlimited realms for that person's development and unfolding, positing as it does a living and caring infinity before him that draws him as far as he may be drawn toward it. However the responses of different individuals to this invitation may vary, that it should exist is testimony to the unfathomable terminus of positive freedom. If few venture so far, many more experience themselves, be it ever so vaguely, near the infinite, so that the limits of their being are always consiously experienced as beyond their present position. This is the epitome of expansiveness. This kind of expansiveness represents the most flowing state for human beings, hence the quotation from Berque in the last paragraph: "Human nature and nature in general . . . flow with more intensity." As for nature itself, in Islam, and certainly not only in Islam, if nature too were regarded as rooted in transcendence, and as responsive to its origin, then it would be cared for such that it too might flow rather than writhe and choke as disenchanted moderns abuse and refashion it.

The Enabling Community, Morality, and Positive Freedom

We often view communities from a modern perspective with regard to how they constrain our freedom. But many communal constraints are there either to ensure communal solidarity, without which the community would have no more than a perfunctory existence, or to direct individuals toward the freedom and fulfillment of which they are capable. To the degree that communal solidarity is ensured and individual direction provided the constraints are largely justified. A community that truly serves the freedom of those who belong to it needs and *deserves* solidarity.

What follows applies only to healthy communities. The modern perspective makes us well aware of the consequences of providing no individual protection against communal excesses that in the past have been oppressive in various ways. There is no justification for communal practices that, say, sanction the inhuman treatment of women or suppress creativity through some spurious ideal whereby a paradigmatic person is believed to have thought on behalf of a community once and for all. The modern standards by which such communities are deemed unhealthy appear irreversible. A healthy community, however, provides its members with an identity, treats them as persons, and reminds them daily of the transcendence that throws their freedom (and creativity) wide open. It also acts as an effective buffer to the steady encroachment on the domain of freedom of the intertwined systems created and supported by the global drive to improve material conditions, and it encourages the temperate introduction of those systems only as needed and not for the sake of blind competition.

A person cannot act freely in a way that matters without knowing who he is. Although personality always transcends communal archetypes and stereotypes, much of a person's indentity can be given him by his community. This does not refer to tribal or neotribal affiliation, but to the aesthetic, moral, and religious levels of existence. For instance, the moral map of which Charles Taylor speaks, which reveals the moral identity of an individual, can largely take shape through the moral vision bequeathed by a community. A community enables an individual to find his way around the moral realm. It urges him toward a clear sense of moral discrimination and direction.

Furthermore, as we have seen in the Kantian philosophy, morality involves a transcendence. For morality involves an aspect of our being beyond what brings us pleasure or what we may be inclined to do in a specific mood. It involves the human aspiration to live up to ideals that seem to belong to another world, an aspiration that strangely fills and animates the lives of those who realize it. The moral code so routinely seen in its conformist, suffocating aspect is therefore also a symbol of the human affinity with transcendence. If one understands morality not as an arbitrary list of injunctions and prohibitions, but as a call to the transcendence to which human beings are naturally open, then one may see it as a vehicle for freedom to the extent that it transports the life of the moral person from a limited realm to one that is infinite. In the deepest sense of the word, morality is a means of liberation (despite the bad name given morality by glum, dour, cruel, or even hypocritical moralists).

Another way that the world in which individuals live grows roomier is by recognizing them as persons, over and above whatever social functions they may have. To limit the recognition of individuals to their function is to imprison them within what may be extremely narrow confines of their being. When a community recognizes the individuals who belong to it as persons, it once again liberates them from the cells within which they perform their functions. And morality enshrines the treatment of individuals as persons.

Although morality seems central to the threefold manner in which the community is a boon to freedom—for it flows through one's identity, sense of personhood, and affinity with transcendence—it by no means holds a monopoly over how a community furthers the freedom of those who belong to it. When it comes to daily reminders of transcendent presences, for instance, a community offers shrines and narratives that place an individual very close to a world into which he can never exhaust the possibilities for extending his being and fulfilling his existence, and which puts all that ensnares him materially in perspective. A community may also offer public spaces and cultivate rhythms of life that shield individuals from the demands of their functions and steer their lives away from functional confinement toward a more balanced state imbued with real variety. Such offerings—shrines, narratives, public spaces, and rhythms of life—extend and deepen the identity that lies within the province of morality. One thus knows better who one is, has a personal rather than merely functional existence safeguarded by several hidden but intimate threads woven into the communal fabric, and lives in an environment teeming with transcendent presences nearer and warmer than the stern divinity sometimes suggested by scriptures. One is more free.

The Personal Dimension and the Limit of Positive Freedom

Introduction

The idea behind the exploration of the personal dimension of positive freedom that follows is quite simple despite the conceptual difficulties involved in giving it a clear and convincing articulation. This idea is centered in a spatial metaphor, one that ties freedom with how much "room" a person has for his being. In earlier discussions, there was much criticism of the restriction of freedom to an unprecedented number and variety of choices *within* the domain delimited by the intertwined global systems now in place after a sustained drive to improve material conditions. Here we turn to the possibility of freedom extended to an unlimited domain, far away from any relevant notion of choice. However those global systems may restrict our freedom, indeed even if it be restricted through other more obviously negative realities, such as tyranny or economic hardship, one may nevertheless recognize the signs of a realm that allows one to be truly free.[28] The signs in question are not necessarily divine, at least not directly, but envelop us at different levels, in both nature and artifacts. These signs, as the partial phenomenology to follow will indicate, call us to broader and deeper realms, at great remove from the narrow confines to which several apparently unavoidable historical developments threaten to herd us. Our positive response to those signs and our immersion in the world that they suggest constitute a substantial realization of our freedom.

Presently, we shall therefore reflect in this spirit on what language, music, nature, architecture, ethics, and religion reveal. The reflections will be brief and very general, for the aim here is to underline just how common are the signs that point at a deeper level of freedom. Slightly more attention will be given language, for some of the ways that language suggests transcendence can be brought to light only philosophically. Collectively, those general phenomenological reflections will serve as a bridge toward the transcendence that infinitizes the possibilities we enjoy as free beings.

Meanwhile, a few preliminaries are in order, beginning with how we may connect the communal and the personal dimensions of freedom. This connection is most obvious in the founders and revivers of communities whose members have been able to exercise their freedom soundly and substantially, for such founders have surely known that positive freedom fully exercised flows into the unfathomable. If such a community should continue to enable its members to exercise their freedom positively, as has been pointed out in the previous section, then it would have to remain open to whatever it is that draws us to positive freedom. It would have to remain open to what each person can experience for himself, if only to a limited degree, as the source of his positive freedom. Such personal experience has reached its peaks and received its best documentation in the lives of mystics, saints, and religiously or metaphysically motivated artists, writers, and thinkers. The openness of a community to the sources of positive freedom and its congeniality to great personal expression thereof represents another connection between the communal and personal dimensions of freedom.

Next, we must disabuse ourselves of a misleading image that has often been associated with freedom and the underlying attitude that forces us to take a radically disengaged view of the world. In the earlier discussion of how the domain for freedom has been steadily, and for the most part unwittingly, shrunk by modernity, it was suggested that freedom itself had been associated with an inappropriate image: point-individuals distanced from their context (and the world in general), who therefore think and act over and against it. Freedom is then seen in terms of the untrammeled movement of thought and action. Such a geometrical-mechanical model of freedom presents an insurmountable hurdle if one is to make the initial steps toward positive freedom, as accessible as they otherwise may be. Those who remain attached to it must recall its dead-end history in the ideal observer approach to science and philosophy and the failure of that approach to provide a successful standard even for much of contemporary physics. That image of negative freedom parallels the representational model where, in a hypothetical state of detachment from the world, we represent it to ourselves. The resulting representation is supposed to be universally valid to the extent that it is the product of universally shared faculties and their uniform application. The world is therefore limited, as an object of knowledge, to disengaged and uniform examination. What it also is practically does not matter in that frame of mind. When we habitually view the world in such a disengaged frame of mind, it makes sense to concentrate on freedom as choice, whereby we imagine ourselves as point-individuals set apart from the world, ready to act to further our plans and satisfy our desires.

Negative freedom was from the beginning intertwined with a disengaged view of the world, where the freedom to choose was more important than the immersion of oneself in a world of significance. Note that negative freedom, as a state where one is free to choose in the absolute, *requires* disengagement. But it can only moderately imply disengagement, for disengagement taken to its logical extremes is recognized as pathological. It is natural to be somewhat engaged. But we only become positively free, making the requisite strong evaluations, developing our personality, and flowing in our being, in a strong state of engagement, if not with the community that enables us to be positively free, then with whatever calls us to our positive freedom. So the states that accompany negative and positive freedom are contradictory. A person who habitually regards the world with a disengaged attitude cannot properly appreciate the positive dimension of freedom. And a people obsessed with their negative freedom will impede the conditions necessary for its positive realization, including those required for the sustenance of vibrant communities. Their laws and mores will reflect this and hence favor atomized individualism. Against the background of actual modern history (as we have seen in chapter 3), this means delivering individual freedom over to the domain delimited by the systems that have come to embody the global drive to improve material conditions.

The Empirico-phenomenological Approach to Positive Freedom

The calling to personal positive freedom is spread over the whole range of the phenomena that we encounter, from ordinary occurrences in nature to the recurrent quests among individuals to immerse themselves in the universal transcendence that makes everything more than it seems. The realm of our positive freedom is most immediately suggested by natural phenomena already well beyond what nature need be and might have been, and ends with the realization that the individual's whole being is open to transformation by an immensity that at once draws and eludes it.

We begin our brief phenomenological survey of the daily calling to transcendence with language. It may have been better to immediately cite the literary and poetic usages that emphatically deny a materialistic theory of language. Poets, after all, have a knack for using words that throw open wide vistas in an otherwise opaque infinity, as though the words themselves were formed by the peals of a mysterium to which poets alone are attuned. In their hands, we are tempted to see language not as a tool whose biological success has been astounding, but as a medium suspended between earth and heaven. The song and meaning of poetic language are present in all cultures, high and low. They are an omnipresent, daily reminder that the world we are given as free beings is far greater and nearer than we are often told. Nevertheless, there are also some structural features about language and how we use it that manifest the true scope of the world in which we may realize our freedom if we so choose. There the survey makes its first step. (Again, the reader must bear in mind that the sole purpose of the survey is to affirm the commonality of the calling to transcendence that lies at the heart of our positive freedom. This calling will be repeatedly associated with the many important respects in which our world stretches far beyond the limits that would suffice for a certain number of functional necessities such as survival to be met.)

Language. We find immediate access to the realm of positive freedom in our language. So many different concepts, phrases, and usages tell us that the domain of our being transcends its apparent limits. This is true even when we use language in a way that appears to impose strict limits on our being. Consider, for instance, those same assertions through which transcendence (and freedom) are *denied,* such as "Everything is (necessarily) the result of processes and forces" or "There are things, processes, and forces (and nothing else)." Whoever makes these assertions fails to notice what the existence of concepts such as "things," "results," "processes," "forces," and "necessity" signifies. To be able to speak of necessity, deliberately, consciously, perhaps even imaginatively amid a lively argument, is a transcendence of necessity. As soon as a range of phenomena is delimited by the notion of necessity, even if one insists that this comprises the whole range, another range ungoverned by necessity is outlined, however unintentionally or negatively. Only the urge to govern all that exists with necessity can blind one to the other sphere of existence subtly announced as one utters those deterministic pronouncements. It is the sphere of the capacity for conception, argumentation, differentiation, and the urge to insist that necessity governs all things. Similarly for the other concepts used in the expressions cited: they too imply a transcendence of thing-ness, forces, processes, and whatever is a result of the last two.[29] For example, as soon as we begin to use a concept such as "thing" or "force," we delimit the world in a way that implies the existence of other ranges for which a concept such as "thing" or "force" cannot be used. We may also argue in the same spirit that statements such as "Everything is matter" are either false or say practically nothing. For if "matter" is a well-defined limitation on the phenomena, then we are attributing something limited to an unlimited realm. If, on the other hand, "matter" is a fluid term that never rests in a definition with clear limits, then to say "Everything is matter" does not reveal very much. In the first case, we always imply the existence of something that transcends matter, while in the second, we push matter further toward a transcendent meaning as we get to know the phenomena better and so edge closer toward a tautology—or nonsense. For what use is "matter" if it must eventually signify transcendence?

Wittgenstein came to a similar conclusion along another path. He was concerned with how the misconstrual of transcendence (of which the personal experience he dwells on is an example) as something to be contrasted with immanence as, say, we contrast earth and sky, helps the cause of dialectical materialists who propose that the spirit is merely matter in a highly evolved state. Instead, he stressed the qualitative difference between transcendent and material phenomena so that it makes as little sense to speak of transcendent phenomena arising from material phenomena as of numbers having colors. Wittgenstein's recognition of the profound difference between transcendent and material phenomena, a difference that makes it impossible to intelligibly compare or contrast the two, is more mindful of the true nature of transcendence than the old celestial metaphors now that astrophysics has materialized the heavens. It forces consideration of transcendence *on its own terms*. Once this has been established, the reverse of the dialectical materialist's position can be affirmed: the only reason why it makes sense to speak of material phenomena, such as physical, chemical, and physiological processes, is the unbridgeable gap between them and ourselves. At least in certain ways, we must, as indeed we do, stand outside, exist outside the material processes that we demarcate with such ease. The very act of thinking about them manifests this transcendence. Here is how Wittgenstein puts it.

> It seems to us sometimes as though the phenomena of personal experience were in a way phenomena in the upper strata of the atmosphere as opposed to the material phenomena which happen on the ground. There are views according to which these phenomena in the upper strata arise when the material phenomena reach a certain degree of complexity. E.g., that the mental phenomena, sense experience, volition, etc., emerge when a type of animal body of a certain complexity has been evolved. There seems to be some obvious truth in this, for the amoeba certainly doesn't speak or write or discuss, whereas we do. On the other hand the problem here arises which could be expressed by the question: "Is it possible for a machine to think?" . . . And the trouble which is expressed in this question is not really that we don't yet know a machine which could do the job. The question is not analogous to that which someone might have asked a hundred years ago: "Can a machine liquefy a gas?" The trouble is rather that the sentence, "A machine thinks (perceives, wishes)": seems somehow nonsensical. It is

as though someone had asked "Has the number 3 a colour?" . . . For in one aspect of the matter, personal experience, far from being the *product* of physical, chemical, physiological processes, seems to be the very *basis* of all that we say with any sense about such processes.[30]

The last two decades of his life saw Wittgenstein reflect on various ways that language transcends mechanical formulation. He considered words that shifted meaning in different contexts, expressions that cannot be explained away functionally, and several grammatical intricacies. If those who mastered their languages had long known their way through the phenomena featured in Wittgenstein's later work, he nevertheless brought out their philosophical significance at a time when language had been treated as just another field to be disciplined. So it is not news that we find words such as *comedy, tragedy, serendipity, ecstasy, crime, mystery, character, soul, honor, disdain, exquisite, theorem, good, evil, compassion,* and *harmony* in our language. They have been around for a while. However, not enough has been said about what their presence tells us. Many words in our language indicate that human being dwells in an open environment, open especially to what lies beyond the material and functional limits of daily life. This openness has been with us for millennia, even though we may have been distanced from it by habituation to the terms, expressions, and activities that pertain to it. But the immediacy of this multifaceted openness is always available to our experience. What follows presently are a number of such empirical passages to transcendence.

Where certain sentiments and aptitudes have been dulled, language becomes a vast archaeological site for the recovery of myriad devices that echo transcendence with varying intensity. Moreover, language taken as a whole is a symbol of the beings who have dwelled within it. Our principal expressive medium is quasi-mechanical only at its core. The further we move from this core, the less rulebound we are. No complete set of rules can account for the mastery of language, but only for its functional use. We are beings, it seems, who need an expressive medium that is far more elastic and open-ended than our survival and even affluence demand. Elasticity and open-endedness, to be sure, make room for jest and play. These, however, are but the companions of what has driven language to its limits. When we look at how language has been used when mastered, we find it replete with turns toward transcendence.

The contrast between the functional and literary uses of language can serve as a token for the contrast between unfreedom and freedom. If we dwell within the functional, we restrict ourselves to what, according to our linguistic heritage, is a narrow domain. In contrast, we need not deny the functions imposed on us when we transcend them. Just as a good writer respects the rulebound core of his language, so can the person who recognizes and experiences transcendence honor his many mundane obligations. Mundane obligations themselves may have a transcendent dimension. Human life is such that the rulebound core can never be closed off from what transcends it.

To be negatively free is to marvel at our language in the many expressive choices it offers us. Nothing yet is said about where some of these choices might lead. To be positively free, however, is first to appreciate the extensive record our language has kept of beings who have dwelled, spontaneously or in response to an explicit calling, well beyond the confines of their ordinary functions and material surroundings, and recognize such transcendence as the true domain of freedom. Here positive freedom begins. And it grows with the ability to experience the transcendence that has made language elastic and open.

The contrast between the functional and literary uses of language is like that between a machine and a human being. A machine can perform certain functions, often better than humans. But humans can invent machines and use them to compose music or listen to the background noise radiated by the origin of our universe. The trouble with negative freedom is its indifference to this contrast. Positive freedom, on the other hand, is an affirmation of the true domain for our freedom. It means the extension of our freedom from a mechanical domain to one that more nearly approximates the transcendence toward which we have repeatedly ventured, certainly as our language so often shows.

Music. Most of us recognize a melody when we hear one. Here we must also consider what it means for there to be melodies at all. It is quite possible that natural sounds, birdsongs above all, suggested melodies to human beings. Suppose this were so. The difference between all other sounds and melodies is as great as that between the functional and literary uses of language. The emergence of a melody from the possibilities of sound is a leap into transcendence. So might one understand the transcendent: it stands out as a melody would in an otherwise cacophonous world. And we have yet to advance to folk songs, harmony, or sonatas. Positive freedom belongs to a realm as far removed from our functions as music is from (random) cacophony. At the level of negative freedom, we survey different sounds in the world without commitment. At the level of positive freedom, we become sensitive to the musical among them and perhaps make music too. We are beings whose freedom extends into a world like that called up by music. An exclusive emphasis on negative freedom, like the failure to insist that sonatas sound better than jackhammers, may bring on a world in which jackhammers set the tone.

Nature. Contemporary wisdom has it that all birds have evolved from dinosaurs. Maybe so. Wherever they came from, it is astonishing for there to be creatures such as birds, let alone ones who sing with the sonority of a cardinal, the mellifluousness of a purple finch, or the repertory of a mockingbird. If birds, in their color, variety, and song, are an extravagance, it is all the more so when we think of dinosaurs as their ancestry. That phenomena such as birds should appear in nature, that their voices, motion, and plumage should be what they often are, show nature herself suggesting realms well beyond the functional and material. The freedom provided by this beyondness rests not only in the variety of nature's species but also in their quality. It is one thing for nature to produce countless phenomena that we might indifferently classify, quite another for some of them to enthrall and delight us. This extends to inanimate nature as well. We can imagine a world in which snow is dark gray and has a foul odor, a world that otherwise functions like ours. The perfect composition of snow crystals, the peculiar silence with which it falls, and its beautification of urban or suburban landscapes do not seem meant to be ignored, dismissed, or reduced to the flimsy causalities of meteorology. Almost every human being almost every day can encounter a natural phenomenon that, if it does not demonstrate transcendence, at any rate evokes it. Our world itself offers us a more substantial domain than is initially apparent, one with song and dance and meditative silence, which may mirror the extent of our freedom.

Architecture. Every culture, however humbly, has sheltered people with a touch of ornament. If modern architecture has failed spectacularly, it is because it disregarded the nonfunctional aspects of homes. When the poor of Saharan towns see it fit to embellish their adobe hovels with decorative patterns or pictures usually in white, or the rugs inside central Asian yurts are brilliantly colored, we understand how pervasively human beings express themselves in nonfunctional terms. As much as shelter, they need intimations of other worlds, or, at any rate, one more animated than their own brute surroundings. Architecture in its very existence is a manifestation of freedom at a most basic level—in one of the fundamental ways that we are bound to a material reality (the need for shelter), we nevertheless try to meet that need in a manner that shelters our being as a whole. Whether the art that reflects our expanded sense of dwelling is high or low, we know we must somehow dwell within its reaches.

Ethics. In how we treat each other as well, we exist considerably beyond the exigencies of survival and social cohesion. For this, to be civil is more than enough. At this otherwise unsatisfactory level of human interaction, there is transcendence already. In fact, the more rudimentary the civility, the more inhuman the society. Courtesy is the ethical analogue of ornament. Even functional interactions have traditionally been adorned. The functional attitude dismisses courtesy as superfluous. It does not realize that what is superfluous to the function at hand may not be superfluous as a token of human interaction. Beyond courtesy, there is no limit to our transcendence of the functional. The innumerable examples of charity, compassion, love, fidelity, courage, generosity, and magnanimity in the lives of ordinary human beings, which sometimes rise to supererogatory peaks, are perhaps the most potent display of our transcendent character. We hardly recognize those for whom such moral qualities are alien as fully human, nor can we fulfill our humanity without the sustained effort to cultivate them. Freedom is only a shadow of itself in the absence of the moral, suffocated by the congested channels through which human being must otherwise flow, if not altogether thwarted in the contest for material prizes. This should all be so familiar as to sound like the reiteration of second nature. Yet reiterate it we must to highlight positive freedom still more intensely. If negative freedom is a state in which moralities are studied and compared, or perhaps where the whole moral enterprise is put into question on "rational" grounds, positive freedom affirms morality as a sublime expression of our transcendence, a domain for the expansion and edification of our interaction as well as our individual lives.

Religion. The difference between negative and positive freedom is like that between the bemused classification of sound and the enjoyment of music, or a businesslike attitude and friendship, or a shelter and a home. Negatively free, we affirm various phenomena and choices in every sphere of our lives without discrimination. Positively free, we affirm the transcendence of the world in which we have managed to dwell, the depth of its possibilities, and pronounce that as the direction for the fulfillment of our freedom.

Reflection on the ubiquity of transcendence, and its intersection with revelatory historical moments, has led to the idea that transcendence is rooted in a unitary source. All the world's major religions share this idea. Muslim, Christian, Taoist, or otherwise, religion at its best and most authentic overflows with people who have embodied the ascent toward transcendence and with it at times lifted whole communities out of their wretchedness. Religious experience, properly considered, is the orientation to transcendence as a whole and for its own sake. It is therefore not a turn toward transcendence through a specific contemplation, action, or composition, but a whole person's orientation toward transcendence as such with attention on its unitary souce.

Religion therefore has it within itself, albeit a potential that it often fails to attain, to be the most comprehensive affirmation of transcendence possible and to encompass therewith all the particular encounters with transcendence that have been illustrated. It has it within itself to be the ultimate domain for the positive freedom of its followers. Because religion is shared by a community, the religious community could become the enabling community par excellence as well as the repository of avenues for *individuals* to exercise their freedom most positively (and perhaps, though by no means always because conformist pressures often lead to ostracism, offer the fruit of their solitary ascent to their communities in revitalization).

For our purposes here, the prevalence of religion shows how widespread the response is to the idea of an overarching source for positive freedom. It is therefore all the more painful that zealotry, corruption, and a bureaucratic mindset frequently stifle the very freedom that religion could express and support so well.

An additional reflection. Kant believed that the principles of morality, for which we have an affinity expressed through our ideals, establish our grounding in the transcendent world, which Kant called the "noumenal," or "intelligible," world. Although Kant appeared to be making a formal assertion, there is substance to it. For if we meditate on the significance of what we expect and aspire for, in terms of our own character and that of others, we certainly seem to be responding to an order different from that which immediately presents itself to our senses. This order transcends all that is demonstrably known to us. But it is nevertheless concrete. For when we acknowledge this apparently virtual order relative to which much of our moral behavior makes sense, it gradually comes to manifest itself as a more fitting realm for our being and freedom.

We need not ascertain the existence of that transcendent realm through morality alone. Artists, for example, submit themselves to standards totally uncalled for by their immediate context. So do craftsmen and inventors, mystics and teachers. As the foregoing partial list tells us, many are the signs of this apparently virtual realm, which becomes emphatically concrete when it is acknowledged, then recognized, as a legitimate domain in its own right, one in which we experience ourselves coming into our own as free beings. The signs are too many to ignore. At the very least, they leave us with the sense of an unbounded world for our freedom and compel us to consider the possibility that behind such bounty lay a significance variously uncovered by sages, prophets, and saints.

One such sage is the Iberian-born Arab thinker and mystic Muhyiddin Ibn 'Arabi (1165–1240). In his inspired metaphysical outlook, he beheld the entirety of existence suspended between the divine light of pure being and the shadow of nothingness. All things exist to the extent that they are oriented toward the light, and do not exist to the extent that they fall into the shadow.[31] As one immerses oneself a little more in the vision that unfurled in a corpus of enormous scope, the implications of the light/shadow metaphor solidify into an ontological root for the distinction that has been made in this reflection. We either turn toward realms where our being becomes fuller and our freedom more substantial or we enclose ourselves within patterns that dry up our being and truncate our freedom. The historical developments that have detracted from the promise of modernity and distorted its direction are an instance of the latter. For Ibn 'Arabi, it is always necessary to find the ultimate resting place of our orientation. In the end, every turn we make is one toward being (light) or nothingness (shadow). Everything takes its measure from the manner of its suspension between pure being (or light) and nothingness. The more illuminated the realm in which we dwell, the fuller is our being and the more unbounded the domain of our freedom. How free we are therefore depends on how far we are in our grasp of the illuminative aspect of our existence. For the mystical sage like Ibn 'Arabi, freedom is a function of the individual's nearness to God.

In modern philosophy, existential thinkers have paid special attention to the distinction between realms in which our being is trivial and those in which it is more fulfilled. The work of Kierkegaard, Nietzsche, Jaspers, and Heidegger, taken together, enables us to distinguish the outlines of limited freedom and unbounded freedom both from the standpoint of the individual concerned and from that of the world in which the individual finds himself. The more trivially the world is defined, the more trivialized the being and freedom of the individuals bound to it. All but Nietzsche tried to establish that distinction ontologically, as Kant once did not so long before them when he declared freedom to be noumenal, and Ibn 'Arabi longer ago still when he traced the fundamental openness of the world and all within it to the divine presence that suffuses them with its light.[32]

Further Reflections on Positive Freedom

The elements of positive freedom can also be found in the character of human consciousness. A human being is always free to shape himself in certain respects, to have a vision of himself ahead of where he now is. He can direct himself toward that vision as he strives to embody it more genuinely. Similarly, human beings can reflect on their condition and critically assess where they stand. Either way, each human being has the ability to stand back from himself, to look at himself as though from a distance. He can also look ahead of himself or look back. This distance, in both its spatial and temporal aspects, maligned as it often is because it stands as a barrier between human beings and the world, is also the inner arena for the exercise of freedom. The distance at which a person can situate himself from himself not only allows choices between all sorts of plans, values, ideas, or ideals, but makes it possible for substantial changes to take place, changes that human beings are free to undergo. This inner distance defines the being of humans as fundamentally dynamic. A personality is always in the making, however fixed it may be in its broad outlines. Human beings are not only free to set aspirations for their personalities before themselves, but free in their being to eventually assume the shape of the ideals of their personal longing. (Likewise, the distance between a human being and the world gives him much leeway in affecting the shape of the world.)[33]

A token of such personal freedom is style. Every illustration given in the foregoing phenomenology corresponds with a style. Each person uses language, relates to art and nature, makes his home, and develops his moral and religious outlook in a certain style. The word *style* does not even make sense without freedom. It presupposes the freedom to forge one's path through various open-ended realms according to one's own personality. The blander the style, the less we feel a human presence. Human existence without style is unthinkable. It so happens that where style becomes markedly qualitative, it reflects the transcendent dimension of each realm. Without transcendence, style would vary only quantitatively. It would be a matter of this combination rather than that—and in language, for example, there is no end to the combinations one can produce. On the other hand, a style wrought in the encounter with transcendence exhibits stylistic choices given by the encounter itself and infused with the vitality of transcendence. This constitutes the life running through language, home, and personality. It is hardly an imposition on style for it to be permeated with transcendence, for the attempt to embody a transcendent reach in language, music, or moral character can be far more varied than is required for each human being to be uniquely associated with it. There are far more ways to embody a transcendent reach than there are human beings. Each attempt at embodiment can easily be unique for each human being and be mirrored in a unique style. The reason for this is that immersion in transcendence is finally unfathomable and can therefore be expressed in an infinity of ways. To immerse oneself in transcendence in fact guarantees a singular uniqueness.

A concept related to style, and also a token of the free inner structure of consciousness, is "personality." If one's linguistic or moral style marks the freedom to forge a unique path through open-ended realms, then personality marks the freedom to throw one's whole being into open-endedness viewed as a totality. A personality can thus either manifest dissipation or purposiveness. It can bear the imprint of either narrow realms or transcendence. But in all cases, in part because of the constant distance of the self from itself, it is open-endedness plunged into open-endedness. That is how free we are to begin with. But it is a freedom that may end in slavery if personality simply fades into a meaningless world. Transcendence is meaning at the level of person and world. A personality forged through immersion in the transcendent, like the analogous styles, will not lose uniqueness for the sake of clarity. On the contrary—transcendence has the peculiar feature of shaping style and personality while offering them an inexhaustible realm to further shape themselves, in ways unique to each person.

Now, if transcendence is experienced as having a unitary source, a source alternately within reach and out of reach, but always beyond the furthest human reach, then personal immersion in transcendence has definite shape, a definiteness that increases over time and which defines

personality and style. Yet for all its definiteness, for all the manifest purposiveness, the directed experience of transcendence remains one of free
movement within an infinity. With such an outlook, one effortlessly finds
one's way through the ordinary transcendence in which human beings
dwell. .

•   •   •

We are at the limit of positive freedom. The dissipation of personality,
in contrast, marks the absence of positive freedom. In between lies the
ordinary domain of positive freedom, in which style and personality
have already taken shape. They become the outer standard for how well
freedom is exercised, and signs of the inner capacity for positive freedom.
We thus read the extent of the positive freedom attained by individuals
in their style and personality.

An unaided encounter with transcendence, given the sheer vastness of
the open-endedness into which our being may extend itself, and the
greater and greater obscurity of expression in the struggle to pinpoint
one's position as one makes further transcendent strides, may bring about
personal dissipation. Even without transcendence, the open-endedness
of our surroundings can absorb the scatterings of the most multifarious
and energetic personalities. The obscurity of the advance into transcendence, relative to rational or commonsensical communicative criteria,
should one be bound by these, easily lends itself to the renunciation of
transcendence in despair. Most individuals thus need genuine guidance
and encouragement when faced with the elusiveness of the domain
where positive freedom blossoms. Different fragments of that domain
encountered by different individuals can be shared. Generations of such
sharing accumulates to build storehouses of lore and wisdom. These help
others on their way. The storehouses have historically been dramatically
expanded and deepened by moments popularly regarded as religious
revelations. In monotheistic religions, God is the source of transcendence,
of beings capable of transcendence, and the terminus of their positive
freedom. The outlines and sometimes the details of personal cultivation
toward that end are also given.

Religious communities, when they are as flexible as their potential
allows, set the tone and clear the avenues for the domain where the
persons who compose them become positively free. Those more in need
for guidance and encouragement find it readily. Those who can proceed
alone find themselves in any case headed toward the same limit, but
experience their ascent more inwardly. Those who lose themselves in the
open-endedness, even when they renounce transcendence in despair, are
tolerated or even treated with compassion or respect so long as they do
not present a serious threat to the well-being of the community.

From a modern point of view, the key is how rigidly and comprehensively a religion defines the community gathered around it, and how liberally it sets the criteria for what constitutes a threat to its well-being. Even when a religious community furnishes much detail for how individuals must cultivate themselves within it and treats those who lose themselves severely, it cannot be categorically condemned, for it still provides positive freedom both as an enabling community and as one that cherishes the edifice that culminates in the terminus of positive freedom, which individuals are free to attain inwardly and by themselves if they are so able.

If Christianity has defined the communities it has gathered around Jesus Christ rather loosely and has reached a stage in its history where it tolerates even those who lose themselves in open-endedness in bizarre or perverse ways, Islam has defined its communities in great detail and is not so willing to allow them to be threatened by the open renunciation of transcendence, let alone wayward consequences that may follow.[34] If one is to assess where Islam stands with regard to freedom, one must not be carried away by the severe manner in which some of the wayward are judged and occasionally treated (for Islam has historically tolerated much waywardness and heterodoxy). It is our own modern prejudice to grant the (morally and religiously) wayward unprecedented leeway, although to what extent this has been made possible by the rise of economism to modernity's fore is yet to be decided.[35] After all, the market and the systems evolved by late modernity are morally and religiously inert, ready and willing to draft everyone if possible. Islam may nevertheless gain from its confrontation with modernity by relaxing its positions on those who follow other paths, especially if these be religious or decidedly spiritual, if only for its own vitality. One must not forget that its marvelous synthesis grew in plularistic fields, where a lively confrontation took place with other religious, cultural, and intellectual possibilities. As we shall see in the last chapter, this process already unfolds fruitfully. But one must not expect, much less demand, that Islam cease to be the focus of some of the most effective enabling communities and transcendent quests ever witnessed. Islam remains a vital repository of the two paths to positive freedom that have just been sketched, the communal and the personal. Viewed thus, it becomes a powerful antidote to the shrinkage of the domain of freedom under the regime of modernity brought about by the inadvertent conjunction of the various historical and ideological forces mentioned in the previous chapter. On this basis we ought to judge the work of thinkers such as al-Ghazzali and to examine the status and prospects for freedom in the Arab Muslim world.

Our discussion of freedom in the Arab Muslim world will revolve around our understanding of human freedom in the light of what has been laid out at this juncture. What is decisive for freedom is its positive aspect. Positive freedom is to live and be acknowledged as a whole person, to be able to move with purpose across a transcendent domain, and (almost always) to be part of a community built around personal ties and the collective recognition of that purposive movement (which includes the values, methods, principles, ideals, and relevant evocations for personal cultivation to that end, and almost always includes affirmation of the source of transcendence, under whose gaze personal cultivation and communal well-being are brought into clear focus). Within these broad strokes of positive freedom lies the capacity for strong evaluations and the forging of a distinctive style and personality that are also associated with positive freedom.

5

The Islamic Transposition of Positive Freedom

Prologue

As the Islamic components of the synthesis that would join Islam authentically with modernity will presently be elucidated, so that a viable context for freedom is brought forth, let us review the principal themes that have emerged regarding modernity. In the first place, modernity cannot be said to enhance or inhibit freedom by itself. Several roads were cleared by modernity. Some lead to freedom, others to traps so elaborate as to defy clarification. These traps are set by the accidental conjunction of a limited form of rationality with a popular desire for material prosperity, political security, and individual autonomy. However, modernity also harbors fields where positive freedom may link up with transcendent presences and propel human life to boundless realms filled with meaning. No encounter with modernity is complete without a grasp of that dual aspect. Within modernity's own inner regions, to see it the first way and not the second is to drastically reduce its scope and break its promise.

Modernity's openness saves it from its propensity to head into blind alleys. The storehouse of modernity contains the elements for a comprehensive liberation from the restrictions imposed by a simplistic rationality. That such rationality came to be seen as simplistic, as inadequate even to account for the making and acceptance of the theories that have most contributed to the advancement of science, is a reminder of modernity's openness. It is further a sign of maturity that the result is not necessarily the summary dismissal of reason, but the restoration of its dynamism and broadness. Even then, as Kant always accepted, reason has its limits. But at least it may go far beyond the domains circumscribed by elementary logic. A fluid, expansive conception of reason then serves as a nearer springboard for transcendence.

We shall find such a novel conception of rationality in the work of Habermas. It will underline how the Islamic framework for positive freedom may be judged to have unfolded along rational lines (and will implicitly discourage the temptation to identify modernity with simplistic

147

rationality any more than with materialism). The intention is not to apologetically present Islam in a rationalist light, but to see how well Habermas's conception of reason travels within the Islamic worldview, especially with regard to those of its elements that bear most on our problematic. Then we can move on to consider the relative congeniality of the ideas articulated by exemplary Islamic figures to positive freedom as it has been portrayed at the end of the previous chapter. In the meantime, we shall also see how the rationale that pervades the Islamic worldview concretely and spontaneously embodies awareness of the sources that ultimately give direction to reason, an awareness always present in the work of Kant. We have seen that without such awareness, reason steadily falls into a caricature of itself and herds those who proclaim its sovereignty into the clutches of the forces unleashed by the simultaneous desire for material prosperity, political stability, and individual autonomy (defined as independence from authority embedded in the community to which one belongs). Those forces, we may recall, delimit a domain that is too narrow for human beings and severely constrains the expression and realization of their freedom.

The Reevaluation of Reason and Its Context

Contrary to the impression given by many of those whose thought he has inspired, Kant, as has been emphasized earlier, was entirely open to the transcendence without which freedom cannot be positive. His openness was such that he defined freedom in terms of transcendence. It was not just a personal openness, but one that he attempted to universalize. At the ordinary level, for instance, when reason is used to make moral judgments or draft democratic constitutions, Kant believed that reason is directed by three overall ideas: the absolute unity of the subject; that of the world; and that of the being of all beings.[1] Moreover, the higher level of reason, which furnishes those three ideas, itself takes a "great interest," as Kant put it, in three ideals: the freedom of the will; the immortality of the soul; and the existence of God.[2] These ideals are operative at the level of life itself, taken as a whole.

Kant maintained that the ideals of reason are provided by itself.[3] Reason has strong intimations of what it strives for. However, no matter how broad our concept of rationality, if it still reasonably pertains to reason, then Kant's expectations were too high. Whatever one may hold against polytheists, those who insist that the world is fragmented and relish it, and writers whose newfangled works reflect personal disintegration and dissolution—let alone atheists or determinists, whose presence is pervasive in Western intellectual circles—one cannot accuse them of irrationality; for they can all provide rational arguments in their favor if they so choose. Else why have atheism and determinism not been refuted once for all?

In Kant's time, there remained at least residual commitment to the ideas and ideals that respectively are essential for the unity (and general health) of inquiry and life. Take them away, and what we are left with is detached rationality at the everyday level. This, as many have eloquently and articulately shown, is *not* the independent use of reason. For the misguided equation of independence with detachment from overall ideas and ideals that reflect the resonance of a transcendent vision has led to attachment to far more pedestrian and (unexpectedly) constricting extraneous influences. The illusion of the independent use of reason has been unmasked as reason surreptitiously in the service of an accidental convergence of historical forces that now appear centered in technological or material advancement. These, if anything, have pressed on with greater energy and ferocity once they held the reins of reason. With no counterveiling extraneous influence, the unities that Kant included in a rational framework could be dissolved at will. Some were seen as unnecessary, others as obstacles to further progress. The unity of the subject, for instance, is laden with overtones of moral agency and responsibility. Because many modern developments have favored behavior generally seen as inimical or destructive by the perennial moral sensibility, some intellectuals have found themselves questioning the reality of moral agency and agency as such. If the agent is a fiction, then so is the basis on which he is held to be morally accountable.

These more radical views, as far as they may have spread among the population at large, above all in the United States, have not succeeded in overturning the sensibility that Kant could still count on when he confidently let reason embrace the ideas and ideals that direct it toward the highest good, from which the best expression of our freedom would follow. But the long misuse of the Kantian philosophy and, more important, the unpalatable social and personal consequences of a cavalier faith in reason's autonomy and adequacy have led those still authentically in dialogue with the Enlightenment to rethink the nature, limits, and extraneous grounding of reason. Reason is now acknowledged to be embedded in a general outlook on life and several social practices. These ensure resistance to its usurpation by forces that relentlessly narrow the realms of human existence and freedom. But, as we shall see, what in the West is a reevaluation of the relation between reason and its context in the light of the failings attributable to reason's dogmatic detachment from any context is, in the Arab Muslim world, knowledge that has been there for centuries and has never really been forgotten. What for Habermas are new principles, albeit at some points dependent on enduring aspirations and practices, are in the Arab Muslim world a way of life for which the norms have been continuously transmitted over nearly a millennium and a half.

The most articulate, concise, and revealing statement about reason in Habermas's *The Philosophical Discourse of Modernity* appears in the course of a long footnote.

> Reason is valid neither as something ready-made, as an objective teleology that is manifested in nature or history, nor as a mere subjective faculty. Instead, the patterns looked for in historical events yield encoded indications of unfinished, interrupted, and misguided processes of self-formation that transcend the subjective consciousness of the individual. As subjects relate to internal and external nature, the social and cultural life-context in which they exist is reproduced through them. The reproduction of life forms and life histories leaves behind inpressions in the soft medium of history which, under the strained gaze of those seeking clues, solidify into indicators or structures. This specifically modern gaze is guided by an interest in self-assurance. Constantly irritated by the risk of deception and self-deception, it snatches nonetheless at configurations and structures from which it deciphers formative processes in which both learning and mislearning are entwined.[4]

Two centuries of criticism since Kant, some of it constructive and some of it modish, have refined his conception of reason to the point where it can no longer be defined independently of all human particularity. Certainly, a few laws and theorems of elementary logic seem universal (but arguably so, for the most fundamental laws of logic, such as those pertaining to contradiction and identity, have been respectively shown by philosophers since Heraclitus and Leibniz to be far from simple, or valid in their simple form under all conditions); and many arithmetic operations and geometric theorems are universally valid. But the further the reach of the rationality under consideration, the more it is tied to historical developments. These, at moments frozen in time, yield patterns whose structure can be schematized. A portrait of a culturebound or civilizationbound rationale can be painstakingly drawn. But, just as the rationale transcends the whims of individual subjects and is truly collective, under no circumstances does it match the crystalline, ahistorical rationality for which Kant believed he had adduced metaphysical grounds. Reason, within the limits prescribed for it by Kant, and taken as a whole, is not a permanent edifice, but a series of patterns in flux. The flux is shaped by the slow transformations that a certain way of life undergoes in replicating itself—a process filled with groping, discovery, trial, and error. And the rationale is distilled from the elements in a life-form that seem most pervasive and enduring. Only under pressure from the modern desire for certainty is what is pervasive and enduring singled out so obsessively that it appears eternal and universally valid. Perhaps this is rooted in the realization that knowledge henceforth could be validated only by human beings with reference to their own capacities and not, for instance, through the authority of tradition or the presence of the known.

In a quite different way from what we have been able to conclude from the relationship between reason and physical science, we thus notice that it is no longer possible to dismiss *any* life-form as irrational (whatever our other motives for dismissal) and still be consistent with the criteria implicit in the foregoing quotation from Habermas. Least of all is this possible when we consider a civilization as developed, sophisticated, and continuous as the Islamicate. We can, if we wish, categorize different forms of life based on their technical accomplishments or their amenability to the assimilation of modern technology. But we can no longer call this categorization rational according to a substantial concept of rationality. For the more substantial our concept, the more it becomes intertwined with cultural or civilizational patterning.[5] On the other hand, if we insist on reason's independence from any cultural or civilizational patterning, then reason does not extend far beyond things such as syllogisms and engineering methods.

When Habermas emphasizes the stable aspect of reason, he relates it to consensus formation in a "communication community."[6] Without consensus, the cooperation and mutual understanding characteristic of communities that have evolved languages such as ours (hence "communication community") would not be possible. Reason can thus be studied through the elements of that consensus. We need not be astute observers to notice that those elements, even in the most pedestrian conversations, involve more than the rules of elementary logic. For instance, when I am driving in Italy and stop to ask an Italian for directions in English, she must make several assumptions not logically derivable from a sentence such as "How do I get to Rapallo?," among them that I wish to drive there, that I want the most direct way to get there, and that I do not speak Italian.[7] These constitute an understanding between human beings without which the simplest communication would never get off the ground. It begins at this level. And one can only imagine how much more complex and profound that understanding becomes as the compass of the conversation expands.

The totality of such understandings within a given community, which forms the backdrop for all conversation and collective action, is alternately referred to by the expressions "the background" or "the life world." The life world is the context in which reason works its way. It is the store of things from which, whenever consensual interpretations are needed, they can be drawn.[8] These collective interpretive patterns, which distinguish the community that makes them, constitute a large segment of its rationality. More simply put, a community's rationality is intimately connected with the way its members see things. How people see things differs from one community to the next. These differences show variations in reason across space and time.

The solidarities of groups also rest in the life world; for these "are integrated by values and culturally ingrained background assumptions."[9] To underline the integral ties between reason and the life world, Habermas coins the term "communicative reason."[10] When we reason communicatively, as we must when we speak to someone other than ourselves, the criterion for truth is no longer correct assertions about objects or the successful execution of plans, but whether claims are redeemed after the argumentative procedures set by the communication community.[11] Habermas might have extended his lush scheme to include procedures in which assertions are accepted other than argumentatively, and criteria of acceptability that incorporate a broader notion of validity than just truth. For the rationale of a community embraces, for instance, a *style* of recognizing the reasonableness of a statement. It is not always a matter of arguing that an assertion is true, but perhaps recognizing that what someone says makes sense. This we also do as rational beings.

Habermas admits that no rational reconstruction of the life world or background is possible.[12] The argument for this is superficially circular, but when contemplated with more subtlety, it has great intuitive force. The life world is the ground on which reason rests. In fact, reason, now seen in terms of successful communication within a community, is embedded in a life world, intertwined with it. For there to be a rational reconstruction of the life world, reason would have to detach itself from its own ground.[13] But then it ceases to function altogether. We can confirm this in how we first learn a language or in how dictionaries are put together. However close we get to an ultimate first step, there remains a set of presuppositions, impossible to spell out at the limit, without which that step can never be made. To learn, we must already know. To reason, we must already have an understanding. And just as we can never learn what we must know to start learning, so can we never reason about the understanding we must have to reason.

From this point on, reason, if we are to make any use of it at all, must be seen in its context, the life world in which it is embedded. If the consensus that evolves in each life world has features unique to it, then these usually pertain to what in any case cannot be universalized. Even if it can, one need not worry unduly that different people go about the same thing differently. The traffic flows in Britain and Japan although people there drive on the "wrong" side.

Reason and Its Context in the Arab Muslim World

A stark contrast between recent intellectual developments within modernity and the prevalent outlook in the Arab Muslim world is their inverse order. Habermas came to realize that reason is firmly embedded in its context, the life world, after a long and sustained criticism of the idea that the one might be detached from the other, a criticism amplified by the dire social and personal consequences of a rationality believed (with initial celebration that still reverberates) to have lost its transcendent moorings. But Habermas's intellectual ancestry forces him to refrain from a more explicit discussion of the life world than he has come up with. Although we can never clarify what enables us to begin learning a language or everything that must be assumed for the sake of successful communication, much can be said about the "values and culturally ingrained background assumptions" that solidify a group so that communication is successful at deeper levels, levels at which, incidentally, persons are free to be treated as such, find guidance in their seach for meaning, and advance beyond the moral dilemmas and emotional or psychological difficulties they are bound to face. Much can be said about the formation of communities (and their rationale), not only in a manner entirely consistent with the new more realistic and workable standards for rationality but also with regard to how they form persons who, while constrained by the communities to which they belong, are paradoxically freed to realize their personhood.

If a reading of Habermas suggests that modernity is working its way back to the context from which it had attempted to detach reason, and that from the debris of stampeded life worlds we are about to witness a resurrection, the Arab Muslim world is witnessing a moving—if occasionally vulgar and self-defeating—resistance to the insistence that the same error be made there. Wherever Habermas has arrived with regard to the life world as a masterful critic with the rich inheritance of Kant behind him, the Arab Muslim world has been for a long time. Marshall Hodgson's study complements Habermas's critical work, for the fruits of Habermas's theoretical endeavors are reflected in Hodgson's vast and magnificently interwoven tapestry, with as much documentary substantiation as one dare hope for. Right before our eyes, vividly, we experience the formation of Muslim communities and the edifice that embodies the paradigm against which they are measured. Hodgson presents us with a comprehensive picture of communities, and persons within them, expressing and articulating themselves over centuries in accordance with various loosely linked interpretations of the Islamic vision. Within that expression-articulation, reason has remained embedded and much freedom has been possible. Berque, in flashes of his own, has highlighted the peculiar animi that define the Arab Muslim world's enduring ability to stretch its life well beyond the small and tepid compartments formed by a rationality willed in modern times toward detachment.

When we turn to the Arab Muslim world, we no longer need to discuss ideas and ideals abstractly, as Kant did. Nor do we need to remain overly vague when we discuss the life world, as Habermas does. For there we find, clearly spelled out, resonant ideas and ideals, themselves part of an integrated outlook; and we find a *historical and empirical* path toward layer upon layer of the Arab Muslim life world. If this life world cannot become transparent to us, we can know much about it, for much has been recorded about its formation, much of it remains alive, and much of the rest can be gleaned from the outlook and attitudes of peoples among whom Berque, for one, has lived, worked, and traveled most of his life.

When someone with as much firsthand knowledge of particular Arab peoples and regions under particular conditions as Berque generalizes, we can trust that the generalization rests on a solid empirical foundation. Among the characteristics that transcend the many differences between Arabs is how they relate to God. This relationship, direct and pervasive, can and must be included when the overall orientation of Arab peoples is involved. As for how we may do so, the following passage from Berque is apt. Because it includes the Arabic word *wijdan,* however, it is necessary to stress the difficulty of translating it into English. "Conscience" might be kept in mind, but only if one is able to mix in a notion of sentiments, feelings or emotions. *Wijdan* in the context below is best thought of as a prevaling (popular) sentiment that also encompasses primordial conscience, or conscience before its resolution into specific ideas of right and wrong:

> The Arab *wijdan* relates the immediacies of life to the presence of a fundamental. . . . It is true . . . that the fundamental is habitually transcendental, and that contemporary history interprets return to basics in a different way. It nevertheless remains true that the presence of basics (whether defined theologically or naturalistically) and their emergence in personal and collective life characterize the Arabs' behavior in persistent fashion. They endow it, at the very time the Arabs are entering the industrial world, with an enviable ability to draw upon resources and even to begin from scratch. . . .
>
> [It is not] inconsequential that . . . the depths of the fundamental . . . are felt by the Arabs . . . as less adverse than by us. This might, in the end, be their surest weapon in their struggle for progress, and their most precious contribution to a world civilization.[14]

Berque does not obscure the presence of God in Arab life through the use of "fundamental." In the passage just cited, he merely wants to describe the presence in a more diffuse manner. Elsewhere, he leaves us with no doubt where those fundamentals converge. When he speaks of various regularities that transcend the temporal, first he mentions, now turning specifically to Muslims, "references . . . to God as established in the Koran and as the postulate of much of [Arab] conduct."[15] A few pages later, he underlines God's presence more poetically. There are two gazes that the Arabs feel directed upon themselves. The first, alienating, but also transforming, emanates from the West.[16] The second, which they have always been able to oppose to the first, and which comes "from an infinitely more remote and deeper source," is the gaze of God.

This gaze has been focused on one's life for fourteen centuries, which meant virtually since eternity began. Palpable at the best-preserved levels of the population, penetrating the collective subconscious to depths no other testimony had reached, or doubtless will ever reach, it ensured that the Arab was never alone and lent him a triumphal attribute equal to all his misfortunes.[17]

That, Berque believes, is the gaze that prevents the existence of Arabs from "be[ing] reduced to impotent banality." "That," he continues,

is the gaze which makes a destiny of an act. Rilke said it along [sic] ago:
   "What is called destiny is this: to be face to face,
   Nothing other than that, and always to be face to face."
For to be "face to face" with something is also to face up to it.[18]

The Arab Muslim world feels itself constantly called to "face up" to God. Whoever ignores or underplays this gaze fails to properly address that world. Such has been the fate of much radical or "enlightened" thought. When Sadiq al-ʿAzm, one of the region's boldest and most learned and intelligent critics, seeks to excise the unknowable (al-ghayb) from Arab life,[19] he does not realize that this amounts to the renunciation of the ground of its foremost convergence. For the unknowable is seen as the province of God alone, Himself fundamentally unknowable, and so is related intimately to the essence of the transcendent gaze the Arabs feel directed upon them and on which the meaning of their lives rests. It is not so much the unknowable that impedes the Arab Muslim world as the failure to separate the knowable from the unknowable, give each its due, and pursue the knowable vigorously with the assurance that it cannot wrest from the unknowable what belongs to this alone. As is well known, the Arab Muslim world has embraced the knowable most when it felt at the height of its immersion in the unknowable.

Ghali Shukri, another prominent critic, makes the same mistake as al-ʿAzm. He envisages an Arab society no longer influenced by the unknowable. Berque refutes this.

The formidable power of attitudes related to the *ghayb* in the societies under examination transforms the objective of its condemners into a pious hope, since the liquidations judged to be desirable have not yet been carried out by European societies themselves (including the eastern European), however unquestioningly these latter are taken as champions of reality![20]

> Radicalism must . . . take account of [Islamic] belief, if only because it is
> virtually unanimous and because the masses would not brook a direct
> attack upon it.[21]

Thus Michel 'Aflaq, the Orthodox Christian who founded what has so
far been the Arab world's most successful (and notorious) party of the
left, had to pay homage to Islam, in Berque's words, as "the vital stirring
which, in the Arab homeland, enlivens . . . internals, potentialities, to use
our terms."[22]

It would be futile, then, to separate the ideals in which Arab Muslim
life is centered from it, or to describe the Arab Muslim life world in vague
terms as an instantiation of the life world whose principal features were
adumbrated by Habermas. What we encounter instead is a concrete divine presence, which informs attitudes and actions, an overarching
swathe of meaning thoroughly interwoven with the everyday. This presence, to be sure, easily satisfies the conditions under which Kant thought
reason must be put to use. God is hardly less, in Arab Muslim eyes, than
the "being of all beings," in whose existence "reason takes an interest."
The many mundane reflections of God's gaze in Arab Muslim life form a
large segment of the background for communal consensus and argumentative or other discursive procedures. It cannot be stressed enough, however, that what we may theoretically describe as an ideal presence or root
of background formation is in fact a concrete reality through and through.
Reasoning and many other activities take place in a divinely infused
context as a matter of course. For anyone to actively promote the dogma
of detached reason, never mind its recent discrediting by reputable persons within modernity, is for him to will the Arab Muslim personality to
disintegration.

What makes the divine gaze or presence more potent and pervasive
still is that, from the Arab Muslim point of view, it has been clarified. It
has historically and ever since been revealed as an example to be emu-
lated for all time, not just for individuals, but for society as a whole. The
direct origin of the paradigm that is the reference for patterns of social
and communal relations is Mohammad's Medinan society. It has been
preserved in the chronicles of the Prophet and his companions. From
these, schema have been drawn that circumscribe Arab Muslim life and
inspire it. But the Arab Muslim conquests have also led to an encounter
with other ancient civilizations. They stirred up "a whirlwind of ideas
and things" and made myriad experiences possible. Theology, law, grammar, and poetry were reordered in that environment congenial to the
mind and spirit. Both the Qur'anic revelation and pre-Islamic culture
served as sources. These hybrid developments were influential in the
social paradigm that emerged. Nevertheless, it was always held to be a
direct reflection of the Medinan model. The rules elicited from that model

constitute what Berque terms "a prosody of existence," analogous to the rules governing poetic composition. They defined modes of conduct characterized "(a) by the strength of the relationship they maintain with what we have, very approximately, called paradigms, models, and invariances; and (b) by the palpable, even sensual, richness of this relationship: qualities for which the entire Arab tradition is indebted to the origins, and feels as immediacy."[23]

The divine presence has realized and continues to realize itself as a communal paradigm, embodied in rules that at certain points are prosaic and quite specific. These are mitigated by the divine gaze that, if proper attention is paid to it, casts the prosaic and the specific in its own light, as it is believed to have had from the outset. The rules symbolize the community that potentially enables Muslims to overcome the (moral, psychological, and other) hurdles that must be faced in the exercise of freedom, treats them as persons (so that each individual's full humanity is taken into account, and not just his social function), and reminds them of the gaze that expands individual personal horizons as far as they may go. Muslims already live in a milieu with a shared experience of enablement, patterned around the recognition of persons as such, and open at every corner to transcendence. They live, in other words, provided that they live through the full implications of their own communal symbols, in positive freedom (how and to what extent that positive freedom may be limited, for them as well as for others, will be taken up later). Positive freedom, as discussed in the previous chapter, has a personal and communal aspect. These we find combined in the life of Muslim communities, at the frontiers of which there have nevertheless been astonishing quests for personal freedom.

Because the paradigm that defines the context and possibilities for Arab Muslim positive freedom has existed continuously for almost fourteen centuries, and so its origins not only reverberate but are experienced as immediately present, a recapitulation of the historical formation of the paradigm will improve our understanding of freedom in the *contemporary* Arab Muslim world and the rationale that has evolved. And we shall see that the rules that symbolize the mundane expression of the paradigm are none other than the shari'a, which must therefore be seen more in its symbolic role than in the mundaneness of many among its rules.[24]

The Paradigm for Muslim Communities:
Origin, Principles, and Rules

The prophet Muhammad founded the first Muslim community at Medina in the early part of the seventh century. Because Muslims believe he was also the recipient of the revelations that were later collected in the Qur'an, he was directly in touch with the sources that inspired and legitimated his community. His contemporaries also needed no intermediaries, for they listened to Muhammad's recitations of the revelations as they came to him. The community built by Muhammad and his associates flowed from the revelations and his personal leadership. Among the several features that distinguished it were the following:[25]

> —Equality before the law.
> —Legal and financial protection for the weak against the strong (Muhammad gave himself the right to dispense with one fifth of the booty as he pleased, and he used that right for charitable purposes).
> —Strengthening families and protecting them from clans.
> —Greater dignity and economic independence for women.[26]

As specific and mundane as some communal practices might be (as indeed they must), the Qur'an juxtaposes the profane with the sacred. It encourages the everyday to remain in the neighborhood of transcendence just as it brings transcendence toward the everyday. The act of worship is never far from even the most prosaic passages in the Qur'an.[27] And so is it supposed to be in the community. People worship while living the good life to which their book calls them. Their daily existence, attuned to the new spirit of justice, equality, fairness, and uncluttered, unequivocal faith, is meant to be infused with transcendence. It is meant, however confined by worldly constraint, to extend into the infinite—always, in Islam, referred to the only and utterly transcendent God.

That kind of communal existence was not so much a paradigm as a pursued collective endeavor in Muhammad's lifetime. Time—and drastically different worlds into which conquering Muslim armies repeatedly ran—distanced Muslims from a past thenceforth turned into a paradigm. As memories of the founders faded and accounts of their deeds no longer always agreed, and as the need increased to make the paradigm compatible with the peoples now within the Islamic dominions, principles and rules that would at once perpetuate the paradigm yet make it flexible enough to gain acceptance among a wide variety of peoples had to be devised.

Among the changes since Muhammad's death in 632, some of which were already pressing within a few decades on those who sought the good of the community, the following are noteworthy:

1. As early as the time of Muhammad's second successor, 'Umar Ibn al-Khattab (ruled 634–644), the formation of an imperium had encouraged the separation of personal piety from raison d'état. This, another three successors later, under the rule of Mu'awiya Ibn Abi Sifyan, became the blatant official identification of the unity (and the good) of the community with communal interest and military power rather than close association with the Prophet.[28] Nothing symbolized this more than the

shift of the center of power from Medina to the new centers of military (and commercial) power, first Damascus, then Baghdad, and finally wherever a warlord could impose himself. The transformation of the Muslim community into an empire made it impossible to maintain the Medinan paradigm at every level. The rule of an empire favored expediency and power plays. Ideally, it should have remained suffused with transcendence. In practice, the political community and its moral and religious symbols had to drift apart. (This development will be pivotal in the next chapter, where I shall underline the necessity to distinguish, with regard to the root of unfreedom, between Islam and practices that resulted from the expediency that accompanied and followed its expansion into an imperium.)

2. Whereas in a small community entirely personally interlinked it is possible to sustain moral enthusiasm, the opportunities abound for moral indifference in an empire. The complexity of administration also makes greater demands on competence than uprightness. These changes created the need for a clearly spelled out moral orthodoxy—and a body to enforce it, if the empire were to remain meaningfully Islamic at all. Under such an imperative, the Qur'an was standardized already in 'Uthman Ibn 'Affan's time (ruled 644–656). No longer could reciters with fabled memories transmit its contents to the people.

Meanwhile in Medina, piety-minded Muslims, faced with those changes, began to see themselves as the true custodians of Islamic ideals. Their work, begun during the rule of 'Uthman, confirmed the rift between the political and religious aspects of Islam.[29] They were further inspired by the example of those, like Hasan al-Basri (d. 728), who were moved by an "intense sense of the divine challenge in their personal lives."[30] Islamic personal ideals thus began to take form and a critique of the worldliness and excesses of the imperium was developed. Faced with the terror of Marwanid rule[31] and the absolute 'Abbasid monarchy,[32] the community had to be protected and edified through other than political means.

The piety-minded attempted to work out the social implications of Islam as purely as they could. If this meant a return to the spirit (and, as much as possible, the letter) of the Medinan paradigm, it also meant, faced with the potential confusion of cultural and religious diversity within the empire, minimal recourse to pre-Islamic traditions. As the identity of Islam emerged, so did its exclusivism. In the attempt to free Islam from adverse imperial effects, the seeds for much intolerance were planted. (This too must be highlighted when the problem of unfreedom in its Islamic context is addressed in the next chapter.)

Among the specific positions taken by the piety-minded in Medina were:[33]

1. The declaration of the centralized monarchy to be an (illegitimate)

innovation. (Innovation, or *bid‘a,* thenceforth referred to any departure from the paradigm, and hence entailed illegitimacy.)

2. The condemnation of moral laxity and luxuriousness. This included the mistrust of displays of urban luxury, thus the demotion of the visual arts, and social distinction, out of egalitarian considerations. A cult of the ordinary or even mediocre was promoted.

3. At a time when Arabs were still favored over other Muslims, tribal values of personal liberty and dignity were extended to all Muslims. No Muslim was forced to obey without his assent.

4. Priority was attached to being Muslim over being Arab, also to end discrimination.

5. Knowledge *(‘ilm)* was identified with (a) Qur’anic recitation and explanation, (b) chronicles of the sayings and deeds of the Prophet known as the hadith reports, and (c) the guidelines set for personal and social action based on those reports and the precise legal rules derived from the example of Muhammad and his early associates.

A sign of the ascendence of the piety-minded was their influence in the choice of a major caliph, ‘Umar II (ruled 717–720). After 750, in ‘Abbasid times, they could influence the choice of *qadis* (special judges in the Islamic courts).

The piety-minded generally did whatever they could, as the Islamic dominion expanded, to maintain a community patterned on the Medinan paradigm, imbued with transcendence. A code gradually emerged that regulated personal and social life. The code was grounded in the following three principles:[34]

1. For something to be approved, it had to be either done by Muhammad or by his contemporaries without his objection.

2. All duties were to be understood in personal rather than official terms. Once it was decided that a person had certain responsibilities, he could not transfer them to others. (This set the tone for the personalism characteristic of Muslim communities. The concept of associating a duty with an office rather than a person was alien—and still often is.) This principle presupposes personal relations between all Muslims.

3. The mission of the community was to extend its rule over all infidels, to ensure that God's true ways obtained everywhere.

However, even the principles in which the Islamic code was grounded changed as the community grew from a small Arab community at Medina to a minority Arab ruling class in a vast empire. They were respectively transformed to:[35]

1. The orientation of all action toward the Qur’an (which by then had been standardized, and which was a more reliable way to determine whether something should be approved or disapproved than memory of what the Prophet and his contemporaries had done).

2. Personal relations between all Muslims of repute (which could be

sustained given the Islamic empire's open borders and which replaced the now impracticable ideal of personal relations between all Muslims).

3. Consensus of the community (a subtle demotion of proselytization in the wake of great conquests that diminished the need for universal conversion. Muslims quickly felt secure about the long-term prospects for their faith).

These transformations themselves soon were not enough. In 'Abbasid times, many non-Arabs had become members of the ruling class. The Qur'an was not specific enough for the derivation of legal rulings needed for an increasingly variegated and complex society. There were too many Muslims of repute for them all to be personally interlinked. And the consensus could no longer be based on agreement between Arabs, nor could the overwhelmingly Arab character of norms prevail. Thus, at the end of the second transformation, the principles respectively became: [36]

1. Orientation toward the Qur'an and hadith reports (the chronicles that recaptured Medinan life in more detail and therefore increased the legal options to meet the needs of a wider community).

2. Personal relations between all Muslim scholars, or 'ulama.

3. Consensus of the community based on the chronicles of Muhammad's Medinan community and Islam rather than Arabism as a norm for communal life.

The code grounded in those principles is known as the shari'a. Nowadays, the shari'a has a reputation for inflexibility among non-Muslims, who then go on to suppose it inherently inflexible. This is a mistake not only at the level of specific rules but, as we have seen, even at the level of the broad principles in which the shari'a is grounded. We shall return to this fact when we later consider the shari'a and its possible transformations in our time. Meanwhile, let us return to one of the problems in the derivation of the shari'a, that which pertains to the authority of the chronicles or reports on which it depends.

A report could be accepted only if it were transmitted through an unbroken chain of reputable and reliable men leading all the way back to Muhammad. These criteria, according to which reports became authoritative, are known as isnad. Now, it so happened that very few reports could be supported with the proper isnad. As these would not have been enough for the derivation of the necessary rules,

some of the pious had little hesitancy at simply inventing isnads—and in fact hadith reports themselves as well—in a good cause; for they assumed (quite explicitly) that whatever was true and of value to Muhammad's community must have been said by Muhammad, as an agent of Providence, whether it was actually recalled by anyone or not—or even whether it had actually passed from his lips. (We have hadith reports ascribed to Muhammad making Muhammad assert just this!) Accordingly, a considerable body of hadith was soon available with the required isnad documentation going back to Muhammad.[37]

Once again we notice flexibility and ingenuity where we are least led to find it: in what Muslims regard as a sacred body. Muslims will rarely acknowledge that invented hadiths or isnads have found their way, whatever the motives, however pure and noble, into the hadith corpus. On the other hand, hadiths and isnads cannot be invented at will, any more than papal edicts or principles that issue from Vatican councils. They can be only the product of those most competent to deal with the good of the community. In Islam, they can be done only with utmost consistency with the spirit of the Prophet's and his contemporaries' sayings and actions. And here too, we find the seeds for as much contemporary reform as Muslims aspire for. If most Muslims see it fit to listen to music and go to the cinema, and do not see these as harmful to their community (which for the most part they need not be), then the shari'a will in the end reflect this.

Muslim history telescopes. In a discussion of the genesis and evolution of the Muslim communal paradigm and the rules that symbolize it, we will notice many points that are continuous with the present and from which we can take up the issue of change. This should come as no surprise, for Muslims do not see their communal history as a discontinuous sequence, but as an enduring paradigm, or *qudwa*. So we cannot neatly set apart the discussion of the Muslim past from that of its present within the problematic of this book, but only shift emphasis from one to the other.

Once the principles stabilized and order was established in the authority of the hadith reports, it was possible to derive the rules gathered into the shari'a more consistently. In broad outline, here is some of what the shari'a decreed:

1. The greatest possible protection of individual rights short of the infringement of the rights of others.

2. Emphasis on personal dignity.

3. Protection of the weak against the strong. Thus interest was banned because it was seen as a form of usury, and contracts were valid only if they involved real exchanges between the two parties. (The personal guarantee of a contract by an honorable man was deemed more valuable than the fact that it was written.)[38]

4. Prescriptions in the performance of prayer and pilgrimage (some of which must be understood in the context of the belief that true reverence of God demands effort and exertion, and not just easy words).[39]

5. A mild criminal law (by premodern standards, so that caliphs in practice had to be *stricter* than the shari'a decreed to enforce public order).[40]

6. Equal rights for all women and children linked to a man (as opposed to no rights for mistresses and their children in pre-Muslim times).[41]

7. Women to keep property brought with them into a marriage.[42]

8. The guarantee of inheritance for all children, and equality between sons.[43]

If the reader were to review the features that distinguished Muhammad's Medinan community listed at the beginning of this section, compared them with the positions taken by the piety-minded at Medina once they were faced with the imperial reality, and then with the shar'i decrees just highlighted; and if he further noted the evolution of the three main principles in which the shari'a had been grounded through two transformations, he would find an evident continuity. This continuity must be kept in mind. It is essential to Islamic life. The reader would also find the elements of change, perhaps not as smooth as in the presentation of a brilliant historian, but change nevertheless. Therein lies the key to Islamic life in modern times: change that somehow leaves it attuned to its enduring spirit. And in the obverse lies the key to whatever stagnation and constriction have afflicted Islamic life in several areas of the Arab Muslim world. When the forms that embodied its spirit were themselves seen as unchanging, they drifted toward disembodiment. If the demotion of the visual arts once had its rationale in the desire to curb urban luxury and lassitude, then to extend such demotion to other arts, with no regard for the creative and uplifting potential of art, is to petulantly favor demotion over the rationale that once justified it and may now be shown to be in competition with a different rationale. Similarly, as we shall see, the veil is rooted in custom, not religion, and may be said to defeat the original Islamic goal of improving the lot of women if thoughtlessly transposed into the present. To see the shari'a as a disembodied form is to suffocate Islam, whereas the liberation of Islam seems to traverse the shari'a's spirit.

To identify Islam with veils, ill-humor, the extension of iconoclasm to music, film, and theater, and hatred of the civilization that threatens it (instead of a more mature confrontation), as many Islamic revolutionaries do, is to defile it—and to fancifully reconstruct it. It is Islam reduced to the mirror image of modernity's narrowness, rather than the transcendence of that narrowness, of which Islam is so abundantly capable. It is Islam made in the image of a nemesis that it can easily overcome. For Islam never banned humor to my knowledge, nor would one think it inclined to do so; it originally gave women a better life; the theater has long been popular among Islamic folk; and Islam was once enormously successful in its encounter with other civilizations for which, far from hatred, it showed a self-assured curiosity, respect, or admiration.

Reason, Freedom, and the Muslim Paradigm

Both the extended and short characterizations of reason given by Habermas and quoted earlier imply criteria that are easily met by the methods according to which the shari'a has been drawn. If Habermas understands reason as consensus formation in a "communication community," [44] then the shari'a is eminently rational, for it explicitly aims, through one of the three fundamental principles from which it is drawn, at the consensus of a very large community indeed. It has symbolized that consensus for more than a millennium. For all the legal competition it has recently run into, it persists as a popular token of Muslim consensus.

When we consider the more extended characterization of reason, as an abbreviation of "patterns looked for in historical events [that] yield encoded indications of unfinished, interrupted, and misguided processes of self-formation that transcend the subjective consciousness of the individual," [45] then what better example do we have than the distillation of three principles from a historical community (and paradigm) that have been allowed to remain consistent with imperial Islamic actuality and from which rules in harmony with the paradigm have been regularly derived? Reason in Islam is a reality at times remarkably complex and sophisticated. How else do we account for the ingenuity with which rules were successfully referred to the paradigm, however temporally remote the paradigm had become? How else to explain the dual nature of Islamic history, with the paradigm at great temporal remove, yet lived and related to as though in the present?

There is another explanation for the last question. The paradigm has been lived or related to as a present experience, despite its great temporal remove, because it has a status analogous to Kantian ideals. If Kant singled out, as we have twice seen, three eternal ideals in which "reason takes an interest," the Islamic outlook turns, over and above discrete ideals, to a paradigmatic *totality*, in which reason continuously takes an interest and within which it finds its bearings (as Kant thought it must). The difference between Islam and the Kantian philosophy, however, is enormous on one crucial point: Kant did not ascribe a revelatory status to the ideals of reason. He maintained that reason provided them, and otherwise had a presentiment thereof. The paradigm that encompasses reason in the Islamic life world, in contrast, issues directly from revelation. That Islamic ideals have endured with such force whereas Kantian ideals have been a subject of contention almost since their enunciation and have largely been forgotten by most of Kant's intellectual progeny alerts us to at least two reflections: the ideals of reason cannot be given by reason itself; and the correlation between acknowledging them (or their equivalent) as revealed and their remarkable endurance is worth pondering.

The shariʿa is hence rational by contemporary measure. Rationalists in the Arab Muslim world who question this are evidently still committed to the view of reason that detaches it from its context, and they seek to promote such detachment and demote whatever stands in its way. But this is most unlikely because Islam is essentially tied to the paradigm that orients the use of reason within it. Such a destiny cannot be understood in rational terms, any more than the attempt to disengage reason from its context. Both are at a level beyond the scope of reason. Besides, there is mounting evidence, much of it gathered with the assumption that sovereign reason is realizable, that sovereign reason is an illusion. If so, the call to disengage reason from its actual context, and declare that only thus is rationality realized, disguises the will to substitute one context for another, for instance, economism for Islam.

Reason in Islam can thus be observed partly in the derivation of a code intended to perpetuate the communal paradigm or *qudwa*. It is as rigorous and logical as any other we may look up to as an instance of good thinking. Because the context for reason is well defined in Islam (which is better than to pretend it does not exist now that we know it is always there), the possibility for logical sequences in the history of Islamic thought is continuously there. And Hodgson has seized on that possibility to beautiful effect. We have seen an illustration of this in the last section.

When it comes to freedom, we must first remember that freedom was not an issue at the time of the articulation and first two transformations of the three principles from which the shariʿa was gradually derived— not in the explicit sense in which it is an issue today. But the shariʿa did reflect the life of a community that had made deep inroads toward positive freedom on every front. The shariʿa always recognized individual Muslims as persons, and as such, dealt with relations between persons. In Islamic courts, a person could never be reduced to his function—and the greater implication was that individuals ought always be regarded as persons. Not only were individuals (at least in principle) always free to live as persons, but their specific liberties were safeguarded. From the time that the piety-minded in Medina declared the monarchy to be an (illegitimate) innovation, or *bidʿa*, there has been a tendency to protect the community from the excesses of the state. If the state had grown too large and complex to remain true to Islamic ideals, then it would be prevented from turning the community away from them. Still more specifically, personal freedom was enhanced through emphasis on rights, dignity, and —inspired by the example of the free tribesman—liberty itself. No one, to repeat, was forced to obey without his own assent. (This has such deep roots that modern rulers have at times been unspeakably brutal to force the assent of the people. What is often, with tragic consequences, called "ungovernability" is really an age-old independent-mindedness.)

The community regulated by the shari'a can thus be said to also guarantee its members a substantial extent of negative freedom. For this is how we must interpret the freedom of all Muslims to disobey their rulers and the distancing of the rulers from the affairs of the community (more on that in the next chapter). But it is the personal and communal aspects of positive freedom that the spirit of the shari'a has most concern for. The shari'a is meant to regulate a community that, like the book that is its ultimate reference, juxtaposes the mundane with the transcendent, or sets the tone for a daily rhythm of life ever near transcendence. Not only is the path of individual persons toward God open in Muslim communities, but there are constant reminders of it. The possibility for individual Muslims to extend their being into the infinite openness and experience the other end as a felt response that suffuses the infinite with meaning is there, over and above the fact that nothing in principle is supposed to obstruct it, as an explicit calling. Later on we shall see how different orders that people with different spiritual temperaments were free to join were within easy access, orders that housed teachers who had gained accepted credentials with regard to their own spirituality.

We have seen that positive freedom is associated with transcendence. Muslim communities underline, more than anything else, their association with transcendence. For nothing is more central to the Muslim consciousness than the one God. Moreover, because the history of Muslim communities is a clear and detailed example of how communal wisdom accumulates, and because it is just this kind of shared cumulative wisdom that enables those who have access to it to move forward through life as the terrain that circumscribes it grows wider and psychological, moral and spiritual hurdles increase, then the shari'a symbolizes an enabling community par excellence. All the freedom one gains through belonging to a community of whose shared and cumulative possibilities one may then partake is there for Muslims aware of their inheritance. And at the limit, where the communal and personal aspects of positive freedom are joined in the same final anchor, that community not only enables Muslims to move purposively through transcendence; the community itself is defined in utterly purposive terms. It is expressly there as the best possible human approximation of a divinely ordered community. And it attunes individual Muslims, through rituals, movements, attitudes, and habits of mind, heart, body, and soul, to life near the beyond.

If past and present are hard to separate owing to the continuity of the paradigm on which Muslim communities converge, the personal and communal aspects of positive freedom are equally hard to separate. For personal positive freedom—even at the zenith—never leaves the community behind, and the community, in the persons whom it relates each to the other and each to God, is never oblivious to what at any rate is one form of personal positive freedom.

Communal Extremism in Islam:
The Case of Ibn Taymiyya

There are times when the more zealous among the guardians of Islamic communities gain the upper hand, usually amid combat against incipient domestic or external threats, but also simply because they wish to make their presence felt and be satisfied that their surroundings conform to what they take to be the Muhammadan paradigm. These periodic eruptions often distort the community for a mythical Islamic purity the imposition of which has always been oppressive and occasionally murderous. The lapidary notion of Islamic soundness perpetrated by the zealots, in its utter disregard for historical and cultural change, and its resonance within the hearts of individual Muslims, can lead only to destructiveness, all the more so as the centuries go by at an accelerated pace away from the Medinan experience that hence waxes utopian. It is difficult to imagine how much has changed, subtly or coarsely, when one contrasts Medina in the early seventh century with Muslim communities in, say, Turkish or Persian lands a thousand years later. To literally will the reversal of all that change is to sanction a bloodbath. In fact, this will has never been carried through to its logical conclusion. But even its preliminary effects have made countless individual Muslims, who would normally seek refuge in the community from the excesses of the state, sadly find themselves in real or imagined flight from their erstwhile protectors.

Such rigid Islamic perspectives of the communal paradigm are the outgrowth of the tradition established by the piety-minded at Medina in the context of early imperial wanderings from original Muhammadan ideals. Less than half a century after Muhammad's death, however, such conservatism could hardly bode ill. On the contrary, it may have prevented ambitious rulers and local leaders from bringing Islam down to their level as a mere instrument of power. At a critical time for Islam, when its lands suddenly encompassed many different countries and peoples and its armies were constantly on the move, its integrity was preserved by individuals who knew at firsthand what the companions of the Prophet had experienced, and whose piety was an example to Muslims threatened with the allure of imperial lassitude.

We have seen how the piety-minded at Medina managed to set broad principles within which the shari'a has unfolded ever since. But we have also seen how these principles themselves underwent two series of subtle transformations in parallel with the changing civilizational complexion of Islam. After a few generations of subtle movement, even if in the true spirit of the direction ordained for it, change becomes noticeable. Some Muslims then find themselves disturbed—for the societies in which they live are now seen to diverge from the original paradigm, of which a meticulous record has been kept. Why, then, can they not accept a dynamic notion of faithfulness, one that recognizes certain historical and cultural inevitabilities and thus allows subtle but ultimately noticeable departures from the recorded version of the paradigm? Why are there always zealots, or conditions that create them, in whose eyes a community is only Muslim if it literally conforms with Muhammad's at Medina, in defiance of all that must happen to it over a very long time?

All communal extremists have in common the doctrine that if something is neither in the Qur'an nor the hadith, nor has been mentioned by the companions (nor, sometimes additionally, by the four founders of Sunni jurisprudence, nor by the first Sufis), then it is an illegitimate innovation. One quick look at real Muslim communities today, and one beholds their universal illegitimacy according to that doctrine. This is indeed what the hero of contemporary Islamic revolutionaries, Sayyid Qutb (1906–66), upheld.[46] There are many reasons for such residual lapidary notions of Islamic communities. In the first place, they have an atavistic quality. For the Arabs in pre-Islamic times, in common with some other ancient peoples, believed that what is true and just "must accord with, and be rooted in, inherited opinion and custom."[47] On these grounds the Meccans initially objected to Islam. Their ancestors had said nothing about Paradise, Hell, and Judgment Day as Muhammad had spoken of them.[48] From their point of view, Islam was an illegitimate innovation, a bid'a. This attitude was then transposed into Islam. Meccan and Medinan theologians, now Muslims, would sternly dismiss any departures from the Qur'an, hadith, and the practices of the earliest generation of Muslims. "Sunna" itself originally referred to inherited opinion and custom in pre-Islamic Arabia, and was later introduced to Islam.[49] From then on, there have always been individuals among the Sunnis in whom this attitude survived intact, even though almost all the Sunnis accepted, however reluctantly, the gradually changing norms, habits, and textures of their societies.

At any given time and place in the Sunni Muslim world, then, there have been those unwilling to legitimize, and occasionally willing to wage war against, any changes effected since the seventh century. Their presence has not always been felt. Their numbers may dwindle to insignificance under certain conditions. But should a foreign threat loom, their ranks swell, for conservatism is never stronger than when a community feels itself on the defensive. The first large-scale disaster for Islam came with the Mongol invasions in the thirteenth century, the most recent with the European conquests and subsequent Western domination. In response to both disasters, some Muslims attributed them to departures from the Medinan paradigm, called for a return thereto, and found an audience stunned into sympathy by the weakness that had befallen their communities.

Apart from foreign threats, there are dynamics internal to the Arab

Muslim world that magnify the power of the communal extremists. The simplest of these is when heterodox practice gets out of hand or is perceived as such. Throughout Muslim lands, for example, cultic tendencies have evolved around local saints and their tombs. Although they were mostly tolerated, they were easy to single out as rallying points by zealots on the rise.[50] There also is the quite different pattern of settled or urban areas extending their power to the countryside, in which case urban orthodoxy gained the ascendancy over rural heterodoxy.[51] A large-scale instance of this can be observed in the evolution of the Ottoman Empire, which in its early centuries was tolerant of heterodoxy to the point of occasionally actively promoting it, and ended up enforcing orthodox Sunnism after the Empire had expanded and its rulers came to see it as a classical Islamic caliphate. Sunni narrowness was also the consequence of prolonged conflict with the neighboring Safavids, who were in power in Persia and had exploited heterodox groups within Ottoman territories.[52] Finally, there is the case of fighting off a non-Muslim threat to Muslims within territory under their control. For instance, the syncretism of Akbar, the Mughal emperor who ruled in the Indian subcontinent between 1556 and 1605, was fought by a revivalist movement led by Shaikh Ahmad Sirhindi (1564–1624) amid concern that Hindu influences were creeping into Islam.[53]

The remarkable bravery and persistence shown by many leaders of movements intended to restore Islamic communities to their original purity contributed further to their resonance among Muslims, especially in troubled times. From early in the ninth century onward, a succession of charismatic individuals risked their lives for their puritanism, from Ibn Hanbal, whom we shall say more about in the next chapter, through 'Abd al-Mu'min Ibn 'Ali in the Maghreb (ruled 1130–63), Ibn 'Abd al-Wahhab (1703–87) in Arabia, 'Abd al-Qadir in Algeria at the time of the French conquest (1830), and the Mahdi who rose against the British in the Sudan late in the last century, to Sayyid Qutb and Khomeini in our time.

Ibn Taymiyya (1263–1328) belonged firmly to that tradition of heroic Islamic zealots and was intellectually the most brilliant of them and an inspiration to subsequent movements like Wahhabism and contemporary revolutionary Islamism. His birth was immediately preceded by the rolling back of the Crusades and the Mongol invasions. Baghdad was sacked in 1258; and had the Mamlukes not stopped Hülegü's armies at 'Ayn Jalut in southern Palestine, they would have also overrun Egypt. In 1269, Ibn Taymiyya was taken to Damascus with his family after the devastation of his hometown, Harran, now part of southeastern Turkey. With the memory of the Crusades, and the Mongols at Syria's doorstep, he could hardly have been more conscious of Islam's military vulnerability and its political repercussions. As if that threat were not enough, he was also discouraged by the corruption of the Mamlukes, who ruled the Near

East at the time. For they ruled with the combination of pragmatism, expediency, and intimidation characteristic of durable military regimes, and were therefore willing to depart from the shari'a whenever it suited them. They had managed to co-opt the religious scholars and were free to introduce legal secularization. Besides, the Mamluke ruling class was either Turkish or Circassian, perceived as foreign by Arab subjects. It comes as no surprise that Ibn Taymiyya, himself an Arab, saw the Mamluke regime, and all those who owed allegiance to the Mongols, as infidel governments that ought to be overthrown by means of *jihad*.[54]

Under all the foregoing pressures, it is understandable that Ibn Taymiyya should have concerned himself exclusively with the strength and survival of Muslim communities or, in his terms, the Muslim *umma*. He believed that the plurality of opinions within Islam would sow discord and weaken the community. No such plurality could thus be tolerated. Islamic legitimacy could be directly rooted only in the original teachings of Islam, found in the Qur'an and the hadith.[55] The same motives made him assert boldly that theology and philosophy have no place in Islam. His refutations of the concepts and arguments developed by Muslim theologians up to al-Ash'ari (873–935) follow the same pattern. They are to be rejected because they occur neither in the Qur'an nor in the hadith, nor in anything said or written by the companions of the Prophet, the early followers, the four founding jurists, or the first Sufis.[56] Moreover, no discussion is permitted about any difficulties that may arise when the Qur'an is interpreted literally. For instance, when it is mentioned that God sits on His throne, He does so in a manner that befits Him, period. It is useless to debate if God must then be viewed anthropomorphically or if the passage is to be read metaphorically or symbolically.[57]

Ibn Taymiyya's uncompromising positions, and his open advocacy of holy war against the infidel regimes, which putatively included the Mamlukes in whose territories he lived, led him to spend many years in prison. He died in captivity in the citadel of Damascus. His personal hardship must have contributed to the harshness of his judgments and opinions. His suffering and death for his vision of Islamic purity and communal felicity made him a heroic figure for many Muslims ever since. Despite the opprobrium heaped upon him by the authorities and the danger to those seen to support him, large crowds turned up at his funeral.

There is a tragic quality in movements that act with great zeal and courage against injustice, corruption, decline, and invasion, and wind up as tyrants over the communities so dear to them. We are familiar with the excesses of Wahhabism and contemporary Islamism. But even outside the Sunnism typical of these, we find examples of such tragedy in Islamic history. Two cycles of misfortune that struck at the Maghreb are instructive. The first began late in the ninth century with a high-minded Shi'ite campaign, led by Isma'ilis who were headquartered in Syria in a small town between Homs and Hama. This missionary wave was the third in the area, and it is noteworthy that all found a sympathetic response, such was the readiness of oppressed or marginalized Maghrebi groups to rally around sincere men of piety and learning. The Isma'ili regime established there eventually became the famous Fatimid dynasty that ruled in the Near East between 969 and 1171. In the region where it achieved its early successes, however, it had turned so brutal that Sunnis took the unprecedented step of joining a sectarian group of Muslims, known as the Kharijites, themselves largely failed harbingers of an Islamic utopia, in rebellion against the Fatimids barely half a century after their missionary activity had begun.[58]

Two centuries before Ibn Taymiyya's lifetime, another reformer who studied in Cordoba and the Orient returned to his native Morocco to establish an Islamically "pure" community. Ibn Tumart (ca. 1080–1130) was a Berber whose advocacy of a return to Islamic sources was so rigid that he recognized only the Qur'an, hadith, and the practice of the companions of the Prophet as sources for the Law and rejected all established schools of law and the use of personal opinion and the exercise of legal judgment, *ijtihad*. The following actions of his were recorded:

1. He insisted that true Muslims ought to impose punctilious religious observances on other Muslims.

2. When he saw men and women mixing in the streets during Ramadan, he dispersed them.

3. He threw the local emir's sister "off her horse when he saw her in the streets unveiled."

4. He denounced the use of musical instruments and "other marks of pleasure-loving."

5. To create a politically and militarily cohesive force, he purged his own community by having thousands killed.

6. He installed himself as the supreme head of the community "who conducted religious instruction and acted as custodian of the faith, arbiter of moral questions, and the chief judge."[59]

Ibn Taymiyya might not have condoned such excesses. But there is an internal logic according to which the active promotion and subsequent enforcement of an Islamic vision like his leads to systematic violence. Any kind of thought that sees the life of the community frozen by laws, general or detailed, directly derived from sources centuries old, whose context may have also been culturally profoundly different from other regions where communal practice must be legitimized, radically denies the inner dynamism natural to all culture and natural human resistance to the kind of conformism that reaches into all aspects of life. Muslims, as will become clearer in much of what follows, have not only found an ingenious accommodation between the sanctity of their sources and the changing complexion of their realms, as we have seen in the two transformations undergone by the three main principles that direct the derivation of their laws. Many Islamic currents gradually emerged so that Islam became congenial to all sorts of personalities and temperaments, and various ethnic and cultural groups. The broad and flexible framework implicit in the Qur'an has been adapted to natural human differences and idiosyncracies that not even modern totalitarianism, for all the technology of control at its disposal, could level. To radically deny what in the lives of individuals and communities, over time and vast areas of our world, cannot forever be fixed in the sources and lore of early Muslims, and for that denial to power concerted action, is to incite the annihilation of Islam's arborescent history and countless individuals for good measure. In our day, to enforce a vision so much at odds with contemporary reality, and so comprehensive, is tantamount to totalitarianism.

At the practical end of visions that seek the restoration of threatened communities in lapidary sources, squads of moral enforcers attract the usual unseemly types to oversee the rectitude of their brethren. Much as the virtues of communities have been extolled in this book from the standpoint of positive freedom, those virtues are not destined for most Muslims in the event that they must live by the ideas of Ibn Taymiyya or like-minded reformers. The strength and solidarity so ardently sought by him for the community would not issue from conviction, but from fear of thuggery. Whoever does not agree with that Islamic vision would no longer possess the elements of positive freedom that flow from belonging to a vibrant community—for one would no longer be treated as a person, but as an object that must ceaselessly satisfy a moral and legal checklist; one would no longer inherit the enablement to pass through potentially disorienting dilemmas that result from the freedom of choice that all human beings intrinsically have, but is obliged to mimic an anachronism; and one would no longer feel genuinely in the neighborhood of transcendence, but of the terror inevitable in a community that officially denies the existence of time and place. Whatever positive freedom one is capable of under such conditions is attributable to secret residues within the hearts and souls of Muslims otherwise forced into habitual hypocrisy.

Even Iran at the height of revolutionary fervor, and Saudi Arabia, whose rulers must impose an Islam inspired by Ibn Taymiyya, are now unable (or unwilling) to take what they officially espouse to its logical conclusion, such is the resiliency of human color and character (as we shall see in the last chapter). Outside Arabia, there has never been an enduring Islamic regime since Ibn Taymiyya's death that acted fully according to his preferences. But his legacy has been a looming presence, with adverse effects on the options that Islamic societies might otherwise have offered to individuals who, given a slight chance, would accept them with alacrity. Let us briefly review three instances of those effects.

1. The change in the attitudes of Ottoman rulers after the expansion of the empire has already been mentioned. But earlier in this discussion, emphasis was made on the domestic dialectics of the centralization of Islamic belief and practice. Here, we may turn to a specific factor that had nothing to do with raison d'état. There has always been a fanatical class of ʿulama in Ottoman society who regarded all intellectual sciences, mysticism, poetry, music, and dancing as impious. These were typically lower-ranked scholars who had considerable influence over their local communities.[60] Sometimes, the movements that sprung from those ʿulama were strong enough to be seen as a threat to public order, thus leading the government to act against them.[61] One of the leaders of these movements, a certain Kâdizâde (d. 1635), preached that all practices introduced since the time of the Prophet were heretical! He declared the use of tobacco, the drinking of coffee, and any kind of song and dance contrary to religious law. He demanded the abolition of mathematics and the intellectual sciences from the medreses. Such pressure led the Ottoman sultan, Murad IV, to issue fanatical decrees and have them ruthlessly enforced.[62] Short of that, fanaticism restrained Ottoman society and brought it eventually to the point where a determined and uncompromising group of secularists could abolish it and decree its reordering along nonreligious lines based on the modern European model.

2. The mystical movements, always a source of expansiveness and diversity in Islam, were themselves, when not repressed, often gradually pushed by circumstances to reconstitute themselves in a spirit closer to that of Ibn Taymiyya. Those circumstances included the domestic and foreign threats already alluded to that were pivotal in a general Islamic retrenchment. But the presence of fanatics who were never comfortable with almost all Sufis increased the chances that the reconstitution would not be in the traditionally open-minded and open-hearted spirit normally associated with the mystics. Naqshbandis, perhaps the most powerful Sufi order in modern times, emphasized the shariʿa more than any other mystics and were openly hostile to Shiʿism.[63] (This is not necessarily the case today.) A Kurdish Naqshbandi, whose mission took him from his homeland to Damascus, was so harsh in his insistence on the importance of strict obedience to the shariʿa and his fanaticism toward non-Muslims that he offended the urban "Sunni idea of broad tolerance for the sake of peace, unity and order." He is said to have refused to enter the Church of the Holy Sepulchre because "he who enters a church is like him who enters a house of fire."[64]

3. In recent decades, a situation has emerged, especially in the Arab regions of the Muslim world, where despotism, corruption, and the specter of foreign domination are such that, with the memory of Ibn Taymiyya and other heroes of Islamic revivalism always alive, it was inevitable that a new movement would surface, with additional borrowings from

modern revolutionary activity. In Nasser's concentration camps in Egypt, there was fertile ground for Sayyid Qutb's extreme condemnation of modern society and writings that call for a vanguard to actively restore sovereignty and worship uniquely to God. Such revolutionary action would rectify the cumulative errors into which Islam had strayed ever since little more than a generation after the Prophet's death elements from Byzantine and Sassanid culture were assimilated into Islam.[65] Qutb continues to be an inspiration to many Islamic revolutionaries.

In the current epitomized by Ibn Taymiyya, we observe a tendency that, in its solicitude for Islamic communities, undermines their well-being because of its failure to recognize historical and cultural dynamics, and individual autonomy and idiosyncracy. It has generally not contributed to the freedom of Muslims. It has made them ill-prepared to encounter modern Europe constructively and confidently. It has stifled the free expression of many possibilities that Islam could potentially embrace. And it has caused much suffering for many Muslims.

The strength of a community, and its crucial role in the enhancement of the positive freedom of individuals, does not lie in strict conformism with ancient sources, but in its ability to subtly metamorphose in the spirit of those sources. This is why in the theoretical discussion about the communal dimension of positive freedom, vibrant communities were stressed. Islam has currents within it that could lead either to funereal or vibrant communities, and we are now ready to turn to more promising and on the whole more influential currents within it as we come to appreciate the Islamic components of the synthesis with modernity that is the necessary context for freedom in the Arab Muslim world. We begin with the middle of the road.

Al-Ghazzali's Effective Embrace of Positive Freedom

There had been successful efforts centuries before al-Ghazzali's birth to steer a moderate course between contending Islamic currents. One of the most enduring compromises between rationalism and traditionalism, and between those who stood for freedom and the determinists, was thought out by al-Maturidi (853?–944) at Samarqand. Such broad outlooks were available to al-Ghazzali (1058–1111), who then extended the compromise to embrace mysticism. He has since been viewed as the leading classical figure of the middle of the Islamic road.

One does not leave Hodgson or Lapidus's work with a contrary impression. But some scholars have recently questioned the importance attributed to al-Ghazzali.[66] It is not clear how far they can pursue their argument. It is certain, however, that they will have set themselves an unenviable task. Here are but three citations, among so many possibilities, spanning nearly a century of writing on Islam.

Ignaz Goldziher, in a lecture that he delivered early this century, and with a strong reputation for impeccable scholarship until this day, firmly asserts that "since the twelfth century, al-Ghazzali has been the final authority" for orthodox (Sunni) Islam. His work has been accepted by the consensus of the community, *ijma'*, and has been made sacrosanct, to the point that to condemn it is to commit what in Islam is the serious offense of breaching the ijma'.[67]

Nearer the middle of our century, H. A. R. Gibb described al-Ghazzali as "the great theologian" who, "in his most important work, demonstrated the truly Islamic foundation of Sufism, and reconciled both with the argument that orthodoxy without the revivalist leaven of Sufism was an empty profession, and Sufism without orthodoxy dangerous subjectivism."[68] Later in another essay, he reminds us that although theological systems have a greater effect "upon the thought of the religious leaders than upon the thought of the general community ... [their] influence, mediated through ulama, preachers, and teachers, affects and directs the religious attitude of all faithful Muslims."[69]

To understand just how profound an effect al-Ghazzali had on Muslim life, we turn to the more recent work of the Turkish historian Halil Inalcik. He reveals in no uncertain terms that Ahmed Taşköprülüzâde (1495–1561), the Ottoman encyclopedist whose division of the sciences was followed in the curricula taught throughout the empire's schools, was a follower of al-Ghazzali.[70] Moreover, this was not much of a surprise because "[b]y the Ottoman period, al-Ghazzali's thought dominated Sunni Islam." Inalcik can even trace the influence through a chain of acknowledged masters directly linked to al-Ghazzali.[71]

We do not doubt that al-Ghazzali has been the leading classical thinker for the scholars at al-Azhar for the past two hundred years or so, nor that he is given prominence in the Persian schools. Whatever the scholars who seek to demote al-Ghazzali eventually manage to persuade us of, there is no escape from the centrality of the synthesis between orthodoxy and mysticism to Muslim civilization and the evidence that points to al-Ghazzali as the first to have won over the Muslim authorities to the idea of such a synthesis. Even if such evidence could change with the disinterment of manuscripts as yet unchanced upon by an unsuspecting goatherd, tour guide, or vacationing engineer, the centrality of that synthesis would remain intact. Some regions in the Arab Muslim world, for instance in parts of Arabia and the Maghreb (especially postliberation Algeria) may prefer to emphasize orthodoxy; others, for instance, in Central Asia, Anatolia, and Iran, may tilt toward mysticism. But both elements will generally be there to complement each other. Without undue concern for hypothetical changes in historical scholarship, let us then turn to al-Ghazzali at least as an excellent example and probable originator of the Islamic mainstream's most powerful and enduring synthesis.

Al-Ghazzali lived at the height of a kingdom that had brought some order to the central Muslim lands amid a particularly brutal and chaotic period in Islamic military and political history. The popular longing for order, and the external threat posed by the Crusades, have certainly influenced al-Ghazzali's political thought and his relations to the Seljuq state. So did the state's vigorous support for Islamic institutions. These will be given due consideration in the next chapter, for they belong alongside the allegation that al-Ghazzali's legacy is quietism when Muslims are faced with despotism. Here, we shall concentrate on al-Ghazzali's transcendence of his historical particularity. For al-Ghazzali epitomized the timeless tendency we have noted in Islam with respect to freedom and reason: reason firmly embedded in a communal outlook, itself meant to approximate a divinely inspired order; and freedom gained through the inexhaustible possibilities of an Islamic life at once true to itself and dynamic, spurred by a succession of encounters with otherness.

In his famous autobiography, *The Deliverer from Error* (al-Munqidh min ad-Dalal, with the ordinary sense of *dalal* as "going astray" also to be kept in mind), al-Ghazzali early on announces his willingness to suspend confidence in tradition and gain knowledge from only what the mind can accept with certainty.[72] His search for certainty, however, leads him to doubt at two levels. He doubts his senses, because of many experiences in which it is possible to discover that things are not as they seem. (It is not because of our senses that we know the sun to be larger than the earth.) But then, if reason helps dispel us of sensory illusions, what if there were a higher faculty relative to which the rational would turn out to be illusory? What if, just as we distinguish awakeness from dreams, there were another state relative to which being awake is like having a dream? Al-Ghazzali found he could doubt all necessary truth, with no science on which to found it.[73]

Contemporary epistemologists, singularly meticulous as they are, will find room for improvement in al-Ghazzali's skeptical argument. It does not concern us here whether al-Ghazzali produced an airtight argument for the limitations of reason (although we must not forget that al-Ghazzali's doubt preceded Descartes's by five centuries). What matters is al-Ghazzali's recognition of reason's limitations. Today, the view that we must reach a point where it is no longer possible to demonstratively establish our knowledge is widely accepted (and is related to the case made for the background or life world at the beginning of this chapter). We do not always know how we know what we know, but often in such situations, we do not doubt that we know. We have also seen how, when it comes to what we can establish with the help of reason, it does not amount to very much. Reason is dependent, much more than is still admitted, even in physical science. Whatever the shortcomings of al-

Ghazzali's argumentation, he is right in reaching an impasse once he chose to establish certain knowledge or necessary truth with his reason unaided.

Al-Ghazzali knew, as we now know, that reason needs an authority beyond it. He pointed out the means for the recognition of that authority at both ends, with regard to the authority itself and the faculty or gift within each one of us that enables us to find it. Turning first to the authority itself, we recall that the shared endeavor to gain truth and wisdom, especially when it comes to decisions heavily overlaid with a moral or spiritual dimension, spares individuals, who often are not up to the whole endeavor all by themselves in any event, of the need to start from scratch each time. Communal tradition is in part an inherited wisdom about things difficult of access to almost everyone, and sometimes impossible for an individual to attain. Some things are only known when they withstand the test of much longer than a lifetime. For Muslims, the criteria for distinguishing truth from falsehood are there in the Qur'an, the hadith reports (chronicles), and the shari'a. These, painstakingly validated or derived respectively in the case of the reports and the shari'a, consistently with the eternal guidelines revealed in the Qur'an, could not be contradicted by al-Ghazzali. We thus notice, in al-Munqidh as elsewhere, al-Ghazzali's unconditional acceptance of all that there is in the main Muslim sources.

Because the Qur'an, the hadith, and the shari'a define Muslim communities, encompassing the paradigm that runs through them all as well as the changing "prosody of their existence," al-Ghazzali's position is a strong endorsement of the communal basis for the truth and knowledge that elude reason—and the freedom that is gained within such a community. So the authority that reason needs beyond itself is seen to reside in the community. But he knew, through his own example, that more restless, inquisitive, enterprising, and independent-minded individuals would not be satisfied if the matter were left at that. Whatever the community embodied had to be attainable by other means, for, after all, the community comprised persons inspired by a real example, persons whose conviction had initially been won over by that example. The authority of the community, then, is validated by the events that took place at its inception, and individual recognition of the meaning of those events. We shall presently see, starting with individual recognition, how these converge and then dovetail with the communal bedrock for reason.

The recovery of certainty came to al-Ghazzali in the wake of two months of sophistry, which he significantly described as an illness rather than a reasoned position, thus in need of a cure and not yet another elusive argument. God cured al-Ghazzali from the illness of sophistry, so that his spirit regained health and moderation, and rational necessities were once more acceptable and trustworthy with certainty, which did not occur through the formulation of a proof or the proper arrangement of words, but thanks to a light thrown by God into the breast. And that light is the key to most of what is known. Whoever believes that disclosure [or unveiling, *al-kashf*] depends on independent proof narrows the wide realms of God's mercy. For when the prophet of God (God's prayers and peace be upon him) was asked about the meaning when He, be He exalted, said "Whosoever wants God to guide him, let him seek comfort[74] in Islam," he replied "It is light that God throws into the heart." Then it was said: "And what is its sign?" And he replied: "Turning away from the realm of vanity and the return in repentance to the realm of immortality." And it is also he, God's prayers and peace be upon him, who said: "God, be He exalted, created people in darkness and then sprayed them with His light . . . God blows whiffs[75] in the days of your lives, so expose yourselves to them."[76]

We may associate the light that al-Ghazzali believes God throws into the breasts of all individuals with the ability, for instance, to recognize what transcends sensory experience and rational arguments. This transcendence, as was noted earlier, is pivotal to the exit from the narrow realms to which freedom would be confined were nothing but the rational and the sensory acknowledged.[77] Al-Ghazzali naturally found the source of our repeated encounters with the transcendent in pure transcendence, God. And he remained consistent with the ancient Greek doctrine that like identifies like—our knowledge of transcendence and transcendence itself must be organically linked. The link is between God and the light that He throws into human breasts. His statement about the consequences of admitting only what is susceptible to independent proof as knowledge rings prophetic in the light of what has happened when a whole civilization took it upon itself to restrict itself to such admission. Al-Ghazzali saw such restriction as a narrowing of "the wide realms of God's mercy." In our context, God's mercy must be understood as the limitless extension of the possibilities of human being, a mercy that constantly lifts individuals out of narrowness and calls them to the expanses of transcendence. Thus in a few lines, al-Ghazzali encapsulated and anticipated the unexpected narrowing of the realm of freedom should knowledge be confined to the independent judgment of individuals with recourse only to reason and what is given to the senses.[78] They are a measure of the foresight won when one can contrast the expanses of transcendence with their opposite, as al-Ghazzali surely could, when one has the humility to admit that it takes far more than reason to experience that contrast. Finally, we see the characteristic placement of such profound insights in a setting of legitimating citations from the Qur'an and the hadith reports. Al-Ghazzali found citations that ensured the consistency of his insights with the cumulative communal outlook, which he unwaveringly endorsed.

This device, however, was not aimed at appeasement. A devout Muslim like al-Ghazzali expects to find whatever insights he may gain, however profound or ingenious, reflected in the scriptures, perhaps with some interpretive help (but not too much and certainly not fancifully). The scriptures themselves are seen as the font that can draw the outreach of persons without end. And when insight rises to the prophetic, that can be reflected as well—for in Muhammad, Islam has its nonpareil prophet (although it took some time for the cult of Muhammad to become what it had in al-Ghazzali's time). On the other hand, a devout Muslim such as al-Ghazzali would not want his insights to undermine the well-being of his community. Even if they seemed at variance with the scriptures (which he would, to repeat, not expect), he would be at pains to show their consistency with that well-being. In such attempts much room was made for ingenuity.

All at once, then, al-Ghazzali came upon an indispensable individual capacity and its place at the heart of major Islamic sources. The light within human breasts, through which one recognizes transcendence just as one sees gardens with one's eyes and formulates proofs with one's reason, originates in the same God who speaks in the Qur'an through Muhammad. The prophet who founded the paradigm community at Medina received the same light, abundantly, as that by which individuals transcend what is given their senses and reason. The authority that rests in the community, *so long as it sustains the presence of the paradigm,* issues from the same light by which individuals can find for themselves the authority that reason needs beyond itself. This outlook has convergence written all over it. But it subtly encourages the individuals who are up to it to seek their own lively path to the recognition of authority beyond reason and distinguishes between the inward individual experience of recognition and outward obedience to authority. Truth is the same, the authority is the same, but the difference is clarified between their acceptance and the existential encounter with their origin.

This is retrospective in al-Ghazzali's case. In the *Deliverer,* having announced the presence of that divine light in his breast, he works his way upward to the convergence between individual experience and the authority that rests in the community. With the help of the divine light, al-Ghazzali can now examine the standing of theology, philosophy, and mysticism with regard to truth. Theology, he believes, cannot furnish what withstands confusion, but is a source of good arguments in support of orthodoxy.[79] Al-Ghazzali, we may recall, did not want to blindly accept tradition. So theology could not answer his questions. Neither could philosophy, because its province is the (logical) derivation of a Creator from a close study of his creation. This obscures the importance of faith and God's moral authority. If moral philosophy tried to compensate for what metaphysics failed to accomplish, then this too was not good enough, for whenever moral philosophy offered something valuable, it seemed that the Sufis already possessed it. Otherwise, it was not valuable, if not downright false.[80]

Al-Ghazzali found truth in the mystical life. That truth, however, is most difficult to put in words. To express it verbally is to falsify it.[81] The only means to attain the transcendent truth of mysticism is to follow the path (suluk) already trodden by mystics and to "taste" (tadhawwuq, roughly, to directly experience) the various stages that one reaches on the way.[82] So to listen and learn can be only ancillary to living the life that leads to the truth. The truth, when it is fully known, must be lived rather than demonstrated (just as one knows health and hunger far better through living them than through definitions).[83] The attainment of mystical truth, as we shall further examine shortly, is not a random or capricious affair. Mystics in Islam have outlined detailed disciplines toward it over centuries. These disciplines may differ in detail from one mystical order to another, but the stages on the way are common, as is the ultimate goal of mystical experience.

Now comes a crucial turn in al-Ghazzali's argument. The guarantee that mystical experience itself does not go astray is prophecy, in particular the prophecy of Muhammad.[84] This guarantee refers to the agreement between the Prophet's vision and that of mysticism. But al-Ghazzali goes further than the externals of agreement to introduce an agency integral to both the Prophetic vision and mystical experience that ensures their harmony. He believes that mystical experience is guided by a light emitted from the Prophet's niche.[85] Mystical experience, in turn, allows its disciples to partly envisage the Prophet's encounter with God and thus acknowledge it firsthand.[86] In fact, al-Ghazzali openly shows his preference for this kind of acknowledgment to that by which it depends on miracles and the certainty that they happened.[87] The vision of the Prophecy is thus at least partly repeatable through mystical experience (and prayer)[88] just as we validate (some but not all) scientific knowledge through repeatablity.

The central event of Islam, then, is recaptured by those Muslims willing to subject themselves to certain disciplines. The light by which the Prophet organized his Medinan community guides individuals centuries removed from his lifetime to the same vision. Al-Ghazzali thus saw the Prophecy and the personal quest for its vision as dynamically interactive, each authenticating the other. It must be emphasized, however, that the Prophetic vision is *independently* attained in mystical experience, and the Prophet as guarantor for it is an *independent* fact that does not wind its way into the inward individual path toward the Prophetic vision. Another independent fact, the light from God common to the Prophet and the humans who partly attain his vision, is what makes the vision the same in both cases. Al-Ghazzali fully regards the vision to reveal an independently existing reality made accessible to humans through an independently existing agency. That humans often do not encounter that vision or encounter it in varying degrees, even when their efforts are sincere, is entirely attributable to their uneven endowment with that agency. The presence of that vision in the life of the community compensates for that unevenness.

Because it is the fulcrum of the search for truth, al-Ghazzali finds it necessary to make a case for prophecy, specifically that of Muhammad. His vision, after all, is Islam's final reference. First, al-Ghazzali argues that just as experience with medicine allows someone who has never met him to identify Galen as a doctor, and experience with jurisprudence allows an analogous identification of al-Shafi'i as a great jurist (faqih), so do Sufi mystical experience and sufficient reflection on prophecy allow the identification of Muhammad's prophecy as the culmination of prophecy.[89] Next, al-Ghazzali points out the difference between the illnesses, cures, and medicines for each of the body and the heart or soul. We are familiar with those that pertain to the body. As for the heart or soul, the prophets are its doctors. For its illnesses, they prescribe prayer and worship.[90] Al-Ghazzali then chastises those who refuse to go beyond what they can see or reason about. Had they been told of something small that eats up a whole town and then consumes itself, and had never seen or heard of fire, they would not have believed it. Natural phenomena sometimes occur in ways that defy common sense. (This rings so true today, with what we learn from quantum physics or microbiology.) Why is it not also possible to accept cures for the heart under the eye of Prophecy?[91] Finally, if people accept the results of science from others without finding out for themselves, why not extend the same trust to prophets? And why, if they obey the doctors of the body, do they not obey the doctors of the soul?[92]

The typical modern reader who, like al-Ghazzali, does not want to start out with a traditional outlook will instinctively criticize him at many points. None of al-Ghazzali's arguments about prophecy are demonstrative. They simply appeal to common sense, and rely on "the light thrown by God into human breasts." Theology and philosophy are rejected almost summarily. It seems wanton, for instance, to dismiss all the accomplishments of moral thought as either repetition of what mystics know, or worthless and false.

However, the reader who stays with such criticism, which is fairly leveled at al-Ghazzali, misses the point of the argument. It is doubtful that al-Ghazzali expected to *demonstrate* the authenticity of a prophecy. One need not be too intelligent or wise to realize that demonstration does not belong to such an argument. It is impossible to prove to someone who is tone-deaf that a work of music has unusually appealing melodies. If melodies with near universal appeal are lost on tin ears, so are more subtle musical highlights lost on common ears. The full appreciation of a work such as a late string quartet by Beethoven is the province of a few. The merits of these works cannot be demonstrated—yet they have not been doubted ever since listeners became accustomed to their unusual sound and form.

We have noted the ubiquity of transcendence in human experience.[93] Nevertheless, there always are human beings who strongly deny that anything transcendent exists. The more common manifestations of transcendence are hardly as elusive as the kernel of a late Beethoven string quartet, yet elusive they are to some of us. To these, the presence of transcendence can never be demonstrated. The rest can never doubt it. The capacity to recognize transcendence may be compared to that to appreciate music. There is a point at which it is either there or not. But like music appreciation, it can be cultivated to a considerable extent. Only a few human beings will never be able to appreciate any music. The same is true for the recognition of transcendence—had it not been that much prejudice is implanted against such recognition in our time, whereas, if anything, music appreciation is encouraged.[94] The reverse was true in al-Ghazzali's time. In many places, not many appreciated music because, like Ibn Tumart, they sullenly declared it to be impious and forced others away from it. But the recognition of transcendence was commonplace.

The recognition of transcendence, let alone mystical visions and prophecy, must begin with *acknowledgment*. If one refuses to acknowledge transcendence, one can certainly not recognize it. Now, just as we speak of musicality, perfect pitch, and other gifts that distinguish levels of involvement with music, so can we speak of an analogous gift through which we recognize transcendence. Al-Ghazzali called it "the light thrown by God into the breast." To not lose sight of what al-Ghazzali had within reach, we must stress his apprehension of how transcendence is recognized—that this must rely on a special endowment. It is natural for al-Ghazzali, as it would be for many religious persons, to associate that endowment with God and to behold its lightlike character. Moreover, just as we identify peaks in musical composition and performance, so is it possible to identify peaks in the encounter with transcendence. We recognize different levels of spiritual awareness and intensity among individuals, and historical breakthroughs in opening up humanity to transcendence. The greatest breakthroughs have been identified with the likes of Laotzu, the Buddha, Jesus, and Muhammad. As we all know, their encounters with transcendence have had astonishing power and endurance. If musicians can better appreciate what goes on in the best works, then those who have expended much effort on their spiritual lives can better fathom what Jesus and Muhammad and others have bequeathed. Not much imagination is needed to extend this to the point of the authentication of prophecy.

When we turn to al-Ghazzali's near summary dismissal of theology and philosophy (which, to be sure, had dire consequences), we again ignore the value of his argument by staying with its weaknesses. Plato, for one, has surely made monumental contributions to the encounter with transcendence. Philosophy appears to be the worse for it whenever the vast realms it encompasses in his dialogues is narrowed. But in our time, a gulf has indeed emerged between the search for truth and living the truth. If Socrates could describe philosophy as a way of life in his time, it is virtually impossible to do so in ours. Whether al-Ghazzali anticipated or helped instigate that gulf is an interesting question.[95] Given the gulf, however, it is important to emphasize the priority of one's mode of being, how spiritually aware and alive one is, as opposed to how well one argues, if the problem at hand is how one should live. This kind of truth al-Ghazzali most sought. And as regards the problematic of this book, we have come across positive freedom as *inward* expansiveness when its personal aspect was discussed. This was tied to the encounter with transcendence. Now, philosophically, one can make a strong case for positive freedom. But positive freedom itself depends on something that philosophy cannot give, as long as philosophy is defined through *externals* or the search for (outward) truth. Positive freedom depends on a personal process whose adumbration is now typically (but not necessarily) associated with literary and religious writing. In this respect, Plato is seen as a religious thinker, despite the anachronistic separation of the religious from the philosophical in his work and the wanton disruption of its continuity entailed by that attitude.

A similar argument can be made for theology. But it must also be pointed out that the best theological writing, from Saint Augustine to Karl Rahner, though it obviously cannot *provide* the spiritual states in which the truth resides, can surely *inspire* their advent. Thus, if al-Ghazzali could not find what he needed in theology, it was because of an illegitimate expectation. Theology cannot be dismissed for what it cannot possibly accomplish. On the other hand, whatever it does accomplish, in its finest examples, can enhance the attainment of the truth which Al-Ghazzali sought above all. Perhaps for both theology and philosophy, what al-Ghazzali leaves behind is a valid distinction between the *articulation* of the spiritual life (including its stages and the vision that gives rise to it) and *living* it. To that extent, philosophy and theology are definitely on one side of the divide. But their potential is not thereby worthy of belittlement; for it can very well flow smoothly into the other side.

If the negative side of al-Ghazzali's work is the temptation to curtail intellectual life, which we shall deal with more extensively in the next chapter, then the constructive part of his legacy is an integrated outlook that brings both aspects of positive freedom into its fold. It does so first through openness to what lies beyond reason's compass and acknowledgment of a special endowment ("the light thrown by God into the breast") of those privileged in their access to transcendence through an abundance of that divine light combined with spiritual diligence. It places the prophecy of Muhammad at the head of that privileged group and regards his vision as the final reference and guidance for individual quests. And just as Muhammad built a paradigmatic community at Medina inspired by the prophetic vision, so is the community continuously brought back to that vision many years hence through the light of its spiritual leaders, a light in principle given all, who may then partake of the Prophecy to their best ability. And all along, al-Ghazzali upholds that community and its scriptures.

If al-Ghazzali's outlook were reflected in Muslim life, then the community would enable each individual to enjoy the freedom it gives as such, in which persons are always taken to be persons related to other persons, in which all share the fruits of a cumulative encounter with transcendence (including the equality and justice decreed by that encounter), in which the individual has a secure identity and moral mooring; and each to gain the inward expansiveness, if he were so inclined, that is a result of a steady personal encounter with transcendence, all the while protected from narcissism or the unnoticed descent into the abyss with which solitary mystical types are threatened.

The Personal Dimension and the Limit of Positive Freedom Revisited

We have noted the origins and transformations of the communal paradigm earlier in this chapter and have seen how from the very beginning the seeds of great possibilities for the realization of positive freedom in a communal context have been planted. Now we shall turn to the other end of the Ghazzalian outlook. Al-Ghazzali, as we saw, preferred to authenticate the Prophecy through personal experience rather than reliance on tradition. In the end, he returned to the community to which he never lost his loyalty. However, through a personal vision he saw the value of that community and the truth that resided within it. If his own vision was limited, then he trusted that of other Sufis: "[Al-Ghazzali] did not have major mystical experiences, but he had enough to convince him that there was indeed a sort of awareness that could not be reduced to Aristotelian syllogism and yet carried its own conviction; enough, indeed, to convince him that the claims of more advanced Sufis could be trusted." [96]

The personal vision in question here involves a special case of what was previously described as "the limit of positive freedom" (pp. 144–46). It is the culmination of "a whole person's orientation toward transcendence" (p. 140) and reflects the freedom gained when one's being flows toward the unfathomable in a manner nevertheless experienced as directed. Each time that discussion referred to such a limit, nothing much was said, partly because of the difficulty of saying anything about it, but also because the proper place for a more sustained effort is here, as a general prologue to a brief account of its Islamic transpositions.

First, then, we shall see how others have described the extension of human being toward the unfathomable in a manner nevertheless experienced as directed and in the process gain a few glimpses of positive freedom at its limit. We are no longer at a point where what is said can even begin to appeal to those who completely shut themselves off from transcendence. This is not to give license for speculation anymore than it makes sense to say that music or poetry are speculative. It is rather that one usually introduces a musical work to another with the expectation that the other has some appreciation for music already. We shall once more traverse art on the way to a religious sketch of the unfathomable and the limit of positive freedom in its vicinity.

The world, as we have seen (pp. 134–42), is full of things and happenings that point beyond the physical: melodies, marvelous creatures, exceptional natural scenery, literary and poetical language, architecture, kindness, compassion, generosity, prayer, and worship. We can therefore think of a zone where the (physical) world flows into another, with the shape of the boundary visible and ever-present to the senses and the soul, and outlined in works of art and human deeds. Few have portrayed this boundary zone with greater skill and conviction than Proust. All the more noteworthy is the occurrence of this following passage in a work that continuously displays the aesthete's worst excesses, so infuriating are the detail and self-absorption at times. These exercises in aesthetic self-indulgence lend credence to the author's titanic struggle to overcome them and literally will the morass of his labyrinthine art into the domain of the transcendent. This passage comes across with great force because it appears just when the reader is near despair over the possibility of deliverance.

Certainly, experiments in spiritualism offer us no more proof than the dogmas of religion that the soul survives death. All that we can say is that everything is arranged in this life as though we entered it carrying a burden of obligations contracted in a former life; there is no reason inherent in the conditions of life on this earth that can make us consider ourselves obliged to do good, to be kind and thoughtful, even to be polite, nor for an atheist artist to consider himself obliged to begin over again a score of times a piece of work the admiration aroused by which will matter little to his worm-eaten body, like the patch of yellow wall [in *View of Delft*] painted with so much skill and refinement by an artist destined to be forever unknown and barely identified under the name Vermeer. All these obligations, which have no sanction in our present life, seem to belong to a different world, a world based on kindness, scrupulousness, self-sacrifice, a world entirely different from this one and which we leave in order to be born on this earth, before perhaps returning there to live once again beneath the sway of those unknown laws which we obeyed because we bore their precepts in our hearts, not knowing whose hand had traced them there— those laws to which every profound work of the intellect brings us nearer and which are invisible only—if then!—to fools.[97]

The exact manner of Proust's portrayal of the boundary zone is not beyond dispute. But the perception of works and deeds way beyond what a physical view of the world and a functional view of life suggest, which lies at the heart of the passage just quoted, signifies a genuine encounter with transcendence by way of its most accessible presences. Such an impassioned turn to excess—and the very idea of the metaphysical ever-present in our neighborhood is an excess—is also a sign of transfiguration. The perception of transcendence as an excess is related to that of transcendence as a gift. And the world takes on a radically different aspect within those who behold its transcendent dimension as a songlike gift. The freedom to experience the world as shot through with the transcendence with which it resounds is the ascent to the positive essence of freedom. For the world of everyday experience gives way to an infinity made meaningful by an apparently ordered realm beyond. The world opens up dramatically—and is then gently and steadily reordered from another point of view. Positive freedom streaks ahead through the dramatic opening and gradually gains a sense of its direction as an otherworldly reordering begins to assert itself. Our everyday world becomes an infinitely larger place in the deepest sense of the word, and it shows in the inward expansiveness, expressive possibilities, and changed perception that follow. The free person is also one free to ground his relationships with others in that other world eulogized by Proust, "based on kindness, scrupulousness, self-sacrifice" and, we may add, untold love and generosity. In retrospect, a world dead to its transcendent other seems as a domain for slaves.

The transfiguration through which individuals become free passes through the boundary zone where the physical becomes porous to the metaphysical. The extent to which the metaphysical permeates the physical varies greatly, between the faintest glint and effulgence. Physicists have recently described the universe as seamless. That description would be fitting if it withstands the test of time. For the world is metaphysically seamless. Wherever its physical limits may be, they fade into the metaphysical.

The physical domain is thus not separated from the metaphysical by a sharp frontier. Between the domains lies a boundary zone. We have just noted the general interaction of the physical with the metaphysical.

The sphere of this interaction defines the boundary zone. The particular case reflects the wide variance of the degree and quality of this interaction. Thus, as the transcendent begins to unfold in the life of a person, the material (or immanent) does not shrink instantly into a well-bounded domain now viewed from the outside, but gradually gives way as one becomes increasingly immersed in transcendence. The edges of the physical, always cracked because of the relentless run of everyday experiences that point beyond them, eventually develop the crevices through which one's existence intermingles more easily with the metaphysical.

Human life is never totally confined to immanence. It is always open, if only through doubt and negative assertions, to transcendence. Once this openness is positively affirmed, given the fluid nature of the boundary between the immanent and the transcendent, a further point is suggested at every level—in nature, in art, in science, and in moral and religious life. These intimations of a further point to reach, wherever one may be, describe utter freedom. One grows toward the furthest reaches of humanity and always feels the surrounding immensity, at times as if there were too much! This freedom would be absurd were it not for the possiblity to sense direction in this growth—a direction that is not automatic, not formulaic, not necessary, built only on the ineffable conviction that one moves through the immensity as if guided by an invisible hand.

The first intimation of the invisible hand that guides one through the immensity where freedom fully comes into its own will again be gleaned from the work of Proust. I have briefly mentioned music, with regard to the openness of its signification, in the foregoing chapter.[98] The time has come to consider the direction of the unified work of a great composer, indeed the source of its unity. Much as the simplest melody already signifies transcendence, the vast reach of an oeuvre such as Beethoven's last string quartets (or Bach's *St. Matthew Passion*) into the metaphysical underlines the depth and extent to which Beethoven was really at home in the domain of freedom. But Beethoven's expression of this was not the same as, say, Schubert's or Fauré's. Nor was it possible for him to explicitly lay out the features of that domain. (If anything, his late quartets are shocking in their defiance of the metaphysical's alleged ineffability.) Every time the metaphysical is present in a work, in a life, in a life's work, it is present anew and uniquely. This is the consequence of its elusiveness to final expression, its peculiar aliveness, and above all its *radical otherness*. The Word must ever remain open. The one domain seems as many.

Thus Proust speaks of the composer Vinteuil, one of the fictional characters in his novel probably modeled on a cross between Franck and Fauré, as a native of an unknown country, which he himself has forgotten, and which is different from that whence another great artist, setting sail for the earth, will eventually emerge.

Composers do not actually remember this lost fatherland, but each of them remains all his life unconsciously attuned to it; he is delirious with joy when he sings in harmony with his native land, betrays it at times in his thirst for fame, but then, in seeking fame, turns his back on it, and it is only by scorning fame that he finds it when he breaks out into that distinctive strain the sameness of which—for whatever its subject it remains identical with itself—proves the permanence of the elements that compose the soul. . . . A pair of wings, a different respiratory system, which enabled us to travel through space, would in no way help us, for if we visited Mars or Venus while keeping the same senses, they would clothe everything that we saw in the same aspect as the things of Earth. The only true voyage of discovery, the only really rejuvenating experience, would be not to visit strange lands but to possess other eyes, to see the universe through the eyes of another, of a hundred eyes, to see the hundred universes that each of them sees, that each of them is; and this we can do with an Elstir [the painter], with a Vinteuil; with men like these we do really fly from star to star.[99]

There is a tension in these wonderful passages between the transcendent world that draws the work of a great artist ever closer to itself and the world of the individual artist that appears to fall back upon itself. This tension is characteristic of Proust's struggle to leap out of his narcissism. For our purposes, we should concentrate on the sense of an oeuvre, especially when expressed in a symbolic medium as potent as music, wandering deeper into transcendence. We should try to empathize with the moment when a composer feels in harmony with that domain, as if his music issued directly from it and he grasped that this were so. (We therefore also have before us another instance of the moment when the eternal and the historical intersect, and we may read Proust's phenomenology as a detailed and empirically reproducible introduction to the ultimate encounter between eternity and history at the core of the great monotheistic faiths.)

The invisible hand is present, then, in the composer's sense of return to his "native country" deep within the domain of freedom. It is also present in the sense of being in touch or in tune with the regions within that domain to which one has access. And what is true for the great composer such as Beethoven, what is true for all great art, is potentially true in the lives of persons, for whom great art has its ultimate worth because it holds up a "measure" for one's own transcendence. But this is not the only way for there to be a "measure" (and here we must leave Proust's overdependence on art behind). We can transpose Proust's celebration of great art directly to the realm of religious experience, equally for the anonymous person who reaches into transcendence and for those whose mystically gained freedoms have become the summit of our religious lore.

The religious believer who belongs to and accepts one of the principal monotheistic traditions will readily identify the invisible hand as God's work.[100] And since he believes God has revealed Himself to him, he knows a few things about Him. On the other hand, if, like al-Ghazzali, one is compelled to take the initiative to (at least for a while) distance oneself from the comfort of tradition, an opportunity is created for a fresh examination of certain notions about God, say His mystery.

Believers and unbelievers alike often complain about the mystery commonly attributed to God. But if God is nevertheless present to the person who finds Him mysterious, the mystery gains immeasurable value as a boon of freedom. For if God's presence clarifies the meaning of the unfolding of transcendence in a person's life, His withdrawal behind what remains mysterious to an individual gives him the freedom to extend his existence as far as it can go and in a manner unique to it within the transcendent domain. Mystery can thus be regarded as an essential feature of a presence-at-once-withdrawn that accommodates limitless yet meaningful freedom. If God were transparent to the everyday world, the realm of freedom opened up would be closed. A considerable element of mystery relative to the everyday is essential for there to be the kind of freedom that has long been known to us. Mystery may be a source of endless frustration for its constant flight from the everyday mind; but it is everything that makes the mind more than a calculating machine. The paradox of mystery is mirrored in a human paradox: humans at once cherish freedom, yet, in their thirst for total transparency (still the impulse for modernity's pursuit of knowledge), they act as if to stifle it.

Nicholas Berdyaev was a philosopher who particularly appreciated freedom. He was therefore incensed at the very idea of demoting mystery, especially that attributed to God.

> God is not to be thought of on the analogy of what takes place in society or on the analogy of what takes place in nature. We cannot think in determinist terms in relation to God. He determines nothing. Nor can we think of causality. He is not the cause of anything.
>
> Here we stand face to face with Mystery and to this Mystery are applicable no analogies with necessity, with causality, with domination; with causality in natural phenomena, with domination in social phenomena. Analogy is only possible with the very life of the spirit. God is certainly not the cause of the world. He certainly does not act upon the human spirit as necessity. He certainly does not pass judgment as judgment is in the social life of man. He certainly is not a master, nor authority in the life of the world

and of man. None of these sociomorphic and cosmomorphic categories are applicable to God. God is Mystery, a Mystery towards which man transcends and with which he enters into communion.[101]

Berdyaev's theological views are quite unorthodox. They conflict with institutional religious doctrine. The extremity of his emphasis on God's mystery, however, is justified when set against modernity's predictably futile rush toward transparency, and the repreated, vain efforts since ancient times to imprison God within human conceptual limitations. Less extreme and more orthodox than Berdyaev, but no less appreciative of mystery, is the Catholic theologian Karl Rahner. His concern is not to celebrate mystery to the point of an impassable distance between humans and God. Rahner astoundingly converts God's mystery into God's fatherhood. He shifts the focus from the distance of mystery, which he first acknowledges and justifies, to the mystical sense of a caring envelopment of the human reach into transcendence. The mysterious remains mysterious. But rather than a mystery utterly out of reach, it is experienced as a positive, responsive mystery.

> The God of the philosophers is no "Father," but the incomprehensible ground of all reality which escapes every comprehensive notion because he is a radical mystery. This is always only the beyond, the inaccessibly distant horizon bounding the small sphere we are able to measure. He certainly exists for us also in this way, as the unanswered question that makes possible any answerable one, as the distance which makes room for our never-ending journey in thought and deed. But does this ineffable being which we call God exist only in this way? That is the question. True, the distance which philosophical theology establishes between God and ourselves is still necessary to prevent us from confusing God with our own idols, and thus it is perhaps more than philosophy, it is a hidden grace. But the question whether God is only unapproachable ineffability must be answered in the negative. He is more, and we realize this in the ultimate experience of our existence, when we accept it without rejecting or denying it under the pretext of its being too good to be true. For there is the experience that the abyss protects, that pure silence is tender, that the distance is home and that the ultimate question brings its own answer, that the very mystery communicates itself as pure blessedness. And then we call the mystery whose customary cipher is "God"—Father. For what else are we to call it?[102]

Repeated readings of this remarkable passage will show the depth of Rahner's comprehension of positive freedom at its limit, which has been described as "limitless yet meaningful freedom" relative to our ordinary conception of freedom. The passage holds within itself the totality of the experience of freedom without bounds, but within an infinity whose apparent muteness conceals a wealth of presences. At either end, it also holds the two fundamental aspects of that totality: withdrawal (as mystery, in which there is more room than human being can ever expand into) and presence (as God the Father, concerned with Creation).

If the quotation from Berdyaev emphasizes withdrawal (as the occasion for limitless freedom), and that from Rahner comprehends withdrawal and presence (as the occasion for limitless yet meaningful freedom), what follows from Chesterton's *St. Francis of Assisi* emphasizes presence, in particular the divine presence and its liberating effect on the man thereby transformed into a saint. The liberation is by way of a changed perception of the world, along the lines previously discussed, but here taken to its limit. For the everyday world is now no longer experienced only as a much broader and fuller world as a result of the appreciation of transcendence, but the order is reversed. Transcendence is beheld as springing forth from its source rather than leading up to it. The world is seen and lived in from a transcendent point of view. Positive freedom changes from a striving to an irreversible condition.

> The transition from the good man to the saint is a sort of revolution; by which one for whom all things illustrate and illuminate God becomes one for whom God illustrates and illuminates all things. It is rather like the reversal whereby a lover might say at first sight that a lady looked like a flower, and say afterwards that all flowers reminded him of his lady. A saint and a poet standing by the same flower might seem to say the same thing; but indeed though they would both be telling the truth, they would be telling different truths. For one the joy of life is a cause of faith, for the other a result of faith. But one effect of the difference is that the sense of a divine dependence, which for the artist is like the brilliant levin-blaze, for the saint is like the broad daylight. Being in some mystical sense on the other side of things, he sees things go forth from the divine as children going forth from a familiar and accepted home, instead of meeting them as they come out, as most of us do, upon the roads of this world.[103]

Sufism and Unlimited Positive Freedom in an Islamic Context

Chesterton's depiction of the saint's transformed perception, so that he relates to the world not as pointing to transcendence, but as springing from it, is often found in the works of Sufis. They not only see the world as a child of God, but, in their closeness to God, reenact the motive for Creation, which is often held to be love. Fakhruddin 'Iraqi (ca. 1213–89) called God "King Love."

> King Love desired to pitch His tent in the desert, open the door of His warehouse, and scatter treasures to the world;

> then raised His parasol,
>   hoisted His banners
> to mingle Being
>   and nothingness.
> Ah, the restlessness
>   of enrapturing Love
> has thrown the world
>   in tumult! [104]

To rise expansively above the material world and throw oneself open to transcendence is seen, in this passage, as called forth from the beginning. The very existence of the world is a loving effusion that turns the chasm between being and nothingness into a creation ever since restlessly turned beyond itself. The chasm is not filled with any old thing, but with treasures from the divine storehouse. And so responsiveness to the divine must be natural to creation, or to some of it. These few lines combine limitless freedom with guidance. The world is clearly boundless because of the boundlessness of what it everywhere evokes; yet the evocations all originate in and continue to signify the source of the loving effusion.

In the last section, we met in the quotation from Rahner the attempt to reconcile mystery with providence, and the realization that mystery allows freedom limitless room while providence assures the free person that the abyss is not cold, indifferent, mute to his outlook and entreaties. If we continue the same "divine flash" that we started above, we first see how 'Iraqi highlights the element of mystery or hiddenness.

> But if He had not done so [i.e., pitched His tent in the desert, etc.], the world would have slumbered on, at rest with existence and nonexistence, at ease in the retreat of Vision where "God was, and nothing was with Him."

> In those days
>   before a trace
> of the two worlds,
>   no "other yet imprinted
> on the Tablet of Existence,
>   I, the Beloved, and Love
> lived together
>   in the corner
> of an uninhabited
>   cell." [105]

In Sufi metaphysics and theology, there is recognition of a divine reality before which any entification is possible. Even "Being," which they have used, is, strictly speaking, a delimitation. They were aware of this, and insisted that one keep in mind the utter unentifiablity of the divine reality, even before it can be called "God" or "Creator." Thus the Beloved and Love, as well as whatever it has become possible to distinguish, all "lived together in the corner of an uninhabited cell." That "they" have come out of that cell does not negate the continuing resistance of the divine reality to all delimitation. Whatever entifiable presence we are faced with is something lovingly revealed to us, always underlaid with mystery. This sense of utter and enduring mystery is a token of respect for an absolutely transcendent God, which God is in Islam. Such is the respect for the absoluteness of God's transcendence that emphasis is repeatedly made on the extent to which nothing whatsoever can be said of Him, not even "Him."

That anything should spring forth from such forbidding hiddenness can only be an act of love. 'Iraqi, having paid homage to God's mystery, continues his second "divine flash" in dramatic contrast by turning to the essence of providence, which is God's love for His creation.

> But suddenly Love the Unsettled flung back the curtain from the whole show, to display Its perfection as the "Beloved" before the entity of the world;
>
> > and when Its ray of loveliness appeared
> > at once the world came into being
> > at once the world borrowed sight
> > from Love's Beauty, saw the loveliness of Its Face
> > and at once went raving mad;
> > borrowed sugar from Loves' lips
> > and tasting it at once began to speak.
>
> One needs Thy Light
> To see Thee.[106]

These lines repeat the sense of a world in tumult faced with the immensity and intensity of its Animator. There also is the kernel of a theology of language: speech is seen as a primordial response to the divine presence, and as one of its gifts. Language thus does not grope for transcendence and thereby remain seamless, but is a transcendence from the beginning, necessarily seamless, only gradually fixed in the myriad specific and precise usages dictated by practice. (One can almost sense 'Iraqi using language consistently with his vision of its origins.) Thus, freedom of expression does not bend language to its will, but is there as soon as language exists. To speak is to be free from the laws and obstructions of the material world. Language is a symbol of the expansiveness built into the nature of creation. Finally, there is reference to what we have discussed when al-Ghazzali searched for an authority beyond reason: the light thrown into the breast, that can identify other divine presences through likeness to He who bestows it.

By the time 'Iraqi tried to put some of his spiritual outlook and experiences into words, Sufism had become a highly developed tradition. It had already reached a double culmination in Ibn 'Arabi (1165–1240) and Mawlana Jalaluddin Rumi (1207–73). 'Iraqi knew Rumi personally. Ibn 'Arabi's work was transmitted to 'Iraqi directly through Ibn 'Arabi's foremost disciple and interpreter, his stepson Sadruddin Qunawi (d. 1274). All these meetings took place in the Anatolian town of Konya. However the modern reader may react to writings such as 'Iraqi's, he must note that they were the outcome of generations of spiritual quests of the utmost sincerity combined with a disciplined elaboration of concepts, categories, doctrines, and allegories that spared subsequent Sufi authors the need to write in an intellectual vacuum.'Iraqi thus had a considerable intellectual repertory at his disposal. For all the ineffability of his goal, he could count on a milieu familiar with his vocabulary and references.

Among the Sufi doctrines that have bearing on the openness of the corporeal to transcendence and its presence in the world, and ultimately on the ground of freedom, are the "isthmus" and the "perfect man." Sufi ontology not only divided the world into visible and invisible entities, or the corporeal and the spiritual. It also posited intermediate entities, standing between angels and pure intellects on the one side and corporeal bodies on the other. They have the luminosity of spirits, but can also appear in corporeal shapes. They thus form an isthmus between the spiritual and corporeal worlds. "Without the isthmus the Spirits in their pure luminosity and subtlety would be completely cut off from the Corporeal-Bodies in their unmixed darkness and grossness." [107] In Sufi ontology, there is an overall sense of an intermediate existence that bridges the gap between immanence and transcendence, indeed comprehends them. The isthmus that comprehends the actual spiritual and corporeal worlds is a posterior reflection of a more fundamental isthmus, that which bridges and comprehends both nonentification and entification as such. The first isthmus stands where out of the abyss of God's utter otherness and unknowability there emerges the most primordial entification, that by which we can even begin to call ultimate being "God."

Thus the notion of a world permeable with transcendence, and a zone in which they intermingle, is elevated to an ontological status in Sufi metaphysics. It is an isthmus, both primordially and in all concrete instances of visible bodies with a spiritual luminosity, for which the name "image-exemplars" has been devised. Theirs is a world of the imagination, "within which spirits become corporealized and appear to prophets and saints as visions." [108]

Much more complex and comprehensive is the doctrine of the perfect man. Here, we are not to think of any actual individual, but "a metaphysical and cosmological priniciple that embraces the whole of creation and is man's ontological prototype." [109] This principle decrees that God created the world through the perfect man, "and ultimately this means that the whole of creation is in one sense identical with him." [110] In particular, the perfect man encompasses the three worlds just mentioned, namely, the spirit world, the corporeal world, and the world of image-exemplars (or the isthmus), and the other two among the five divine presences distinguished: God's knowledge, in which all of reality and its archetypes are seen or beheld by God before they become outwardly manifest; and the archetype of the perfect man himself, or the perfect man's nature as such. [111]

This is not the place to explore the doctrine of the perfect man further. What is crucial for our discussion is its consequence for specific human beings: they are held to be individual "microcosms," in which all these levels are reflected. Every human being is body, spirit, an isthmus that comprehends the two, a creature of God (with access to some of His knowledge), and an (imperfect) outward manifestation of the perfect man. Hence, even though this hardly ever happens, nothing in principle stands between human beings and the whole of creation. Nothing, in fact, stands between humans and God. And it is for humans to live up to the infinite possibilities of their ontological reality. The freedom inherent in that reality must terrify whoever realizes its extent. Small wonder, then, that Sufi aspirants should be put through an arduous course in preparation for its full exercise. And small wonder that the Sufis have given freedom in Islam its fullest expression.

> The most crucial test for the actual realisation of means to attain freedom in Islam has been the degree to which it has been able to keep alive within its bosom ways of spiritual realisation leading to inner freedom. And in this matter of central concern, as far as man's entelechy is concerned, Islam has been eminently successful. Over the ages and despite all the obstacles which the gradual darkening of man's outward nature has placed before authentic spiritual paths, Islam has been able to preserve intact to this very day ways of attaining freedom in its absolute and unconditional sense, that is in the sense of complete detachment from everything except God, which is in fact exactly how Sufis have defined freedom or *hurriyyah*. Its spiritual techniques and methods, contained mostly within Sufism, are doors which open inwardly to the only freedom which is real and abiding but which is imperceptible to the outward eye. Any discussion of the concept and reality of freedom in Islam must take into account, besides outward manifestations of freedom on the plane of action, the inner freedom which is related to the experience of being itself, and which transforms us in such a way that outward forms of freedom gain a completely different meaning for us. [112]

Ibn 'Arabi and the Expression of
Unlimited Positive Freedom

As the vista of Islamic options spreads out before us, we see at one end a rigid view of the community, without much room for maneuver around individual and historical irregularity and surprise, and less still for freedom as such; in the middle, a more fluid terrain in which the identity and stability of the community are cautiously reconciled with the open-endedness of human life; and at the other end, an expanse so vast it appears to span the horizon and the beyond as it holds fast to the essentials at the heart of the community, recognizes and makes the most of their suppleness, and thus unites Muslims in a tumultuous and ecstatic turn toward the unnameable yet ever-present and caring infinity.

We have already glimpsed unlimited positive freedom in an Islamic key when we read the three passages from 'Iraqi in the last section. Now we can consider it somewhat more systematically. No mystical thinker has articulated a more comprehensive and integrated outlook, ranging with ease over cosmology, theology, ontology, metaphysics, morality, epistemology, hermeneutics, and soteriology, than Ibn 'Arabi. From such a corpus of intimidating scope, and thanks to the recent scholarship of William Chittick, we can cull those ideas and insights most relevant to making the strongest case for the possibility of unlimited positive freedom in Islam.

It must be kept in mind, however, that it is impossible to present Ibn 'Arabi's thinking in a logically satisfactory manner, for it consistently defies all logic as it soars repeatedly into the spiritual order. One can only highlight some of these points and hope that the reader will attempt to visualize the interconnectedness between them. Like all mystical thought, Ibn 'Arabi's ideas cannot, in the end, be abstracted from the faith and experience that support them. At the very least, one must read his work imaginatively. Hopefully, his significance for Islam,[113] and especially for the possibility of freedom in its context, will inspire the effort it takes to begin to get some sense of what he is trying to express.

The doctrine of the *isthmus,* as a mediating entity standing between the corporeal and the spiritual, or the seen and the unseen, was introduced in the foregoing discussion. We find it used at every level of mediation between such pairs in the thought of Ibn 'Arabi, from the most general to the most particular. The Arabic for "isthmus" is *barzakh,* and it is more appropriate to use the Arabic term henceforth. Most generally put, the barzakh is the dividing zone between being and nothingness.[114] It is one of three fundamental termini of knowledge, all of which are infinite.

1. Nondelimited or pure Being, which refers to Being at such an original and originating level that it is inconceivable that any definite thing

whatsoever can be attributed to it other than its perfect fullness and self-sufficiency.

2. Nondelimited or pure Nothingness, which is Nothingness so total that nothing more can be said to clarify our conception of it.

3. A Supreme Barzakh, or a Universal Divide with one face toward Being and the other toward Nothingness, in which all possible things, all things other than nondelimited Being and nondelimited Nothingness, have their being or existence. Ibn 'Arabi produces the abstract argument that the Supreme Barzakh is necessary because all pairs of contradictories, such as the ultimate pair of Being and Nothingness, need a separator that enables us to distinguish one terminus from the other. Thus, like Being and Nothingness, the Supreme Barzakh is immutable because its essence is to stand as a separator between a pair of immutable contradictories.[115]

Ibn 'Arabi also offers a more poetic origin for the Supreme Barzakh. It springs from the mystical belief that God created the universe out of love and that all things have dwelled with Him in immutable form since time immemorial. Propelled by that belief, which one also finds in Hinduism, Judaism, and Christianity, Ibn 'Arabi has the vision of all that dwells with God yearning to exist and God responding to that yearning out of love. (One must always mentally replace "God" with "nondelimited Being," for "God" already places some limit on a more primordial presence.) Just as the first sign that we yearn for love is a sigh that is the initial motion toward the beloved, so does the Cosmic Breath become manifest in a Cloud whence all particular beings come forth. This Cloud is none other than the Supreme Barzakh, now beheld as the Breath of the All-Merciful (*Nafas al-Rahman*). For to allow creation to come forth may be conceived as an act of mercy. Breath is also a vapor that relieves constriction in the breast, and a vehicle for words—so the Breath of the All-Merciful relieves Him[116] of the clamor of a universal desire to be, and is a vehicle for His Words, each of which becomes a creature.[117]

So portrayed, the Supreme Barzakh, the Cloud, or the Breath of the All-Merciful becomes a "cosmic matter" in which the ultimate meaning of all things can take on a definite shape and become corporealized. Apart from the Supreme Barzakh, "barzakh" is used to denote all kinds and grades of mediation between being and nothingness. For instance, an alternative description for the immutable poles between which all things are is "pure light" and "absolute darkness." All intermediate degrees of luminosity are barzakhs.[118] So seen, every single thing known to us and knowable by us, lying as it does between pure light and absolute darkness, or being and nothingness, is itself intermediary and hence also a barzakh.[119] The whole of existence, which includes all creatures, lies suspended between the absolute poles and mediates between them. Creatures are neither completely spiritual nor completely corporeal, but somewhere in between. Human beings are closer to spirituality than orchids, orchids closer than boulders, and all further than angels. But nothing, not even volcanic ash, is entirely devoid of spirit or luminosity. This status can be ascribed only to nothingness or absolute darkness.

Besides the cosmic dividing zone between pairs of absolute poles, there is a faculty that corresponds with such primordial mediation. That faculty is the imagination, which is of three kinds depending on the extent of its reach.

1. Corresponding with the Supreme Barzakh, and in some sense identical with it, is Nondelimited Imagination, which embraces the entirety of existence. We may say that all that mediates between being and nothingness is God's Imagination. So God's Imagination and the Supreme Barzakh are one.

2. Less encompassing than the divine imagination that spans being and nothingness, but still independent from that of human beings, is what Ibn 'Arabi calls "discontiguous imagination." This level of the imagination corresponds with the world of "image-exemplars" already mentioned, or the intermediate world within the Supreme Barzakh that spans the world of spirits and the corporeal world, the world in which prophets through visions and dreams communicate with angels and ordinary mortals with the absent and dead.

3. The human imagination is called "contiguous imagination" by Ibn 'Arabi, and it issues from the discontiguous imagination and therefore in its nature allows humans to expand their being beyond the corporeal into the imaginal realm and thus toward the meaning of things.[120]

The imagination, then, as the mediating faculty between sensory things and their meaning, has the aspect of a barzakh.

> The *barzakh* is the widest of presences and the Meeting Place of the Two Seas (Koran 18:60)—the Sea of Meanings and the Sea of Sensory Things. The sensory thing cannot be a meaning, nor can the meaning be a sensory thing. But the Presence of Imagination—which we have called the Meeting Place of the Two Seas—embodies meanings and subtilizes the sensory thing. It transforms the entity of every object of knowledge in the viewer's eye.[121]

However obscure those fundamental elements and their elaborations in Ibn 'Arabi's Sufi metaphysics may seem to us, we can, formally speaking, notice a fit between the various descriptions. The world is a bridge that pours out of ultimate being into the abyss of nothingness, remains suspended between the two, and contains within itself every possible grade of suspension relative to its nearness or distance from the two absolutes. Alternately, God's Imagination spans over the abyss of His primordial gaze into nothingness, and brings forth every grade of the imagination between His own and that of the humblest creatures. The continuity of the world and the imagination allows those who have that faculty to be, in principle if not in practice, radically open to the entire domain of the imagination, which at the limit corresponds with the Supreme Barzakh. Besides the formal coherence of this perspective, we may notice its momentous implications for human freedom. For what, if not inherent freedom, can we attribute to beings who have a faculty (the imagination) systematically linked with the whole cosmos and thus potentially allowing them to bring the whole cosmos into their purview? To meditate on the ontological position of human beings is to realize the full extent of their freedom. Human freedom is grounded in the very manner that we are primordially constituted and located in the order of things.

As we approach the more specific manner in which Ibn 'Arabi's thought links up with the twofold definition of positive freedom central to this work, we must come to terms with one more principal theme unlikely to resonate among moderns: the role of Divine names or attributes. Muslims believe they know some of God's attributes because of the names He has revealed in the Qur'an. For instance, God is all-knowing, the giver of life, the merciful and compassionate. Furthermore, a saying of the Prophet asserts that there are ninety-nine such "most beautiful" names of God. Ibn 'Arabi goes on to devise an ontology from these names. Briefly, he believes that all things have their roots in one or another name of God. The only difference between things is the intensity with which they reflect the attributes implied by those names.[122] What distinguishes human beings from the rest of creation is that *all* the names of God, although not to a perfect degree, are reflected in them at once. God placed within each human being every one of His attributes. In human beings they are gathered, whereas they are scattered in the rest of the cosmos.[123] This is what it means to say that we are created in the image of God. The moral consequences of such an ontology are enormous. For it means that the moral plateau human beings aspire for is not extraneous to their condition, but is *ontologically* constitutive of their being. Human beings are simply made in a way that potentially allows them to cultivate and attain excellence of character. All the qualities that they need to develop are already planted within them. Human moral identity is thus connected with the whole fabric of existence and its originator, and its perfection becomes the fulfillment of all creation. (So we are back with the doctrine of the Perfect Man that we have also encountered.)

If Charles Taylor speaks of our gradual and painstaking experiential discovery of the moral map drawn within ourselves, and Kant speaks of the affinity we have for moral ideals, Ibn 'Arabi portrays us as essentially endowed with every attribute that we need to strive for toward human perfection, and implies further that the perfection of all the divine attributes, to be found in the archetypal Perfect Man, posits a perfection beyond good and evil (for not every attribute associated with God is within the bounds of the moral). From Ibn ʿArabi's vantage point, one that he shares with other mystically inclined Muslim authors, the archetypal Perfect Man corresponds with the primordial Muhammadan reality. Muhammad is seen here as a prophet when all things still dwelled with God, before the creation of Adam, long before he became embodied. And so the Word in his possession is all-comprehensive, its Book comprehending all scriptures and books, its Law all revealed religions [124] (keeping in mind that the Book is not identical with the Qurʾan, nor the Law with the shariʿa, but the Qurʾan and the shariʿa are respectively translations into human language of the Book and the Law).

The Muslim community is hence seen to be rooted in the archetypal Perfect Man in whom all the divine attributes are gathered and perfected. The message delivered by Muhammad, the man encountered by the first generation of Muslims in the flesh, is a human rendition of the Word that has eternally dwelled with God. The paradigm that forms the outline of Muslim communal life is then seen to be a reflection of the divine order.

The more concrete pillars of Muslim life, the Qurʾan, hadith, and shariʿa, are themselves integrated into Ibn ʿArabi's thought, which he insists is consistent with their content at all times and believes to have been the fruit of a divine favor that allowed him to penetrate into their inner meaning. Ibn ʿArabi believes that the literal text of the Qurʾan must always be respected. It is possible to understand the Qurʾan only if one comes to it with faith, fears God, has fulfilled the requirements of the Law, and respects those who have already established themselves as interpreters of the Qurʾan. Only then can one feel free to interpret it in a new way, and only if the new interpretation is in harmony with those made and acknowledged before.[125] To illustrate Ibn ʿArabi's regard for the Qurʾan, he asserts that to regard God in a manner other than He appears in it, for example, rationally, is to worship a god created through rational considerations. If one really believes in God, however, then one accepts Him as He revealed Himself.[126] Chittick states flatly in the preface that all Ibn ʿArabi's teachings are based on the Qurʾan and the hadith, and that he fully respects their literal meaning.[127] One can estimate his regard for the hadith through ascribing the status of Perfect Man to the reality from which the embodied Muhammad had emerged.

As for the shariʿa, Ibn ʿArabi finds its existence to be most natural, for everything has a scale over it: logic over reason, grammar over speech, and so on. God generally "sends down" (yunazzil, the same term used in Arabic to denote how the Qurʾan was given to humans) everything in a known measure. The scale ruling over human beings is there for justice. There is indeed a cosmic sense of justice, or order, that depends on the divine scale. "Were the Real[128] to let the Scale drop from His hands, the cosmos would immediately be annihilated...." [129] Without the shari'a, the human version of God's justice, man would be lost in a universe fraught with ambiguity. The Law enables man to return to the Center of his being. [130]

We therefore see in Ibn 'Arabi a recognition no less than al-Ghazzali's and even Ibn Taymiyya's of the sanctity of the community. For him, the Qur'an, the hadith, and the shari'a are unassailable. But the difference between them could not be greater. For Ibn 'Arabi does not merely assert the sanctity of that triad, but also sees it in the light of his utterly open-ended view of the cosmos, as three instances of crystallization that are nevertheless continuous, *in a living manner,* with pure Being: the Qur'an with the Word of God, the hadith with the example of the Perfect Man, and the shari'a with divine justice and the cosmic order. Only their surface is lapidary. But they are lapidary inscriptions in a medium shot through with the infinite. Humans are free to travel through this medium as far as they are ready and able to go. The community itself has this feature, which we now see as characteristic of Ibn 'Arabi's thinking. It has a facade frozen into a paradigm, behind which it is thrown open toward the divine embrace. Thus life within the community has this charcteristic also: it is spread over the spectrum ranging between the poles of rigid, almost automatic formalism, and mystic rapture. Every individual life is layered and urged toward open-endedness. If Ibn 'Arabi does not contest what in the hands of others are incarcerating inscriptions, then in his eyes, they are inscriptions that signify unlimited realms and invite those who hold them sacrosanct to advance toward the infinite. They are words, deeds, and rituals that appear carved in stone, but in truth hold passageways to the heavens. What one makes of them depends on the maker, be he inclined to the stout, stern, dour world of dull, provincial mullas or the freedom of birds and gods at play.

Thus Ibn 'Arabi clearly distinguishes himself from those who limit themselves either to the Law (the scripturalists) or reason (the philosophers), for the Law denies many things (such as the validity of mystical experience often denied by the scripturalists), and reason denies what lies beyond its grasp, whereas the mystical perspective, gained through "unveiling," embraces all things and acknowledges each for what it is.

> We live with the present moment. With reason we deny what reason denies, since then our present moment is reason, but we do not deny it by unveiling or the Law. With the Law we deny what the Law denies, since our present moment is the Law, but we do not deny it by unveiling or by reason. As for unveiling, it denies nothing. On the contrary, it establishes each thing in its proper level. He whose present moment is unveiling will be denied, but he will deny no one. He whose present moment is reason will deny and be denied, and he whose present moment is the Law will deny and be denied. [131]

Ibn 'Arabi's thought is more radically synthetic than al-Ghazzali's. Unlike al-Ghazzali, he does not see mysticism as something in conjunction with living according to the scriptures. Rather, to live truly according to the scriptures becomes a mystical experience. Besides his emphatic acknowledgment of the Muslim community by rooting it directly in pure Being, the Perfect Man, and the scale of the Law that reflects God's vision of the order of things, we find much support in Ibn 'Arabi's thought for the three elements of positive freedom that may be realized in a vibrant communal context. (And since only vibrant communities enable individuals to be positively free, it must be pointed out that Ibn 'Arabi's communal perspective, far from the ossified attitude of the literalists, bursts with vibrancy because it integrates the communal paradigm dynamically with the ultimate source of life, creativity and order.)

1. As far as the moral identity of individuals is concerned, which is necessary to enable them to exercise their freedom of choice meaningfully and advance through the dilemmas and obstacles posed by life to grow in cumulative fashion, toward a fuller existence, rather than disperse themselves aimlessly over choices never really made, that identity is present in the very constitution of human beings. In them, all the divine attributes are gathered. They are beings granted a special dignity, made in the image of their creator. This defines who they morally are and where their moral growth may lead. All revealed texts, as well as the practical methods developed to realize human potential, are thus expected to find a natural empathy among their intended audience. And the whole civilizational edifice that rises around those revelations—and the practices, narratives, temples, shrines, and smaller artifacts that they inspire—eventually contains daily, detailed reminders of the moral identity of the individuals who belong to it.

2. Another element of the positive freedom in a communal context rests in a community's ability to maintain individuals near transcendence, so that they are ever aware of a realm more vast and offering greater sustenance for one's inner being than human beings can accommodate, so that they experience their freedom as truly limitless. That Ibn 'Arabi's thought supports this is evident in every glimpse we have had of it. For an individual who sees all things in active suspension between pure transcendence and nothingness beholds a ubiquitous threshold for transcendence. The community, like all things, can be regarded as a barzakh, yet another face of the infinitely varied bridge that spans the two poles of ultimacy. In a way peculiar to each community, there is lore, scriptural or symbolic, concrete or abstract, urbane or folkloric, that expresses its transcendent component and makes this a living presence for the individuals in whom it also resides. (It should come as no surprise that this resembles what has just been said regarding moral identity. For within Ibn 'Arabi's world, no radical separation between any two things

is possible, except for pure Being and absolute Nothingness. In between, within the Supreme Barzakh, distinctions that we make are no more than shedding different light on different aspects and regions of a cosmic, continuous entity.)

3. The third element of positive freedom in a communal context has to do with the recognition of each individual as a person, rather than, for instance, relative to his social or economic function. Here, it seems that Ibn ʿArabi's outlook does not allow for the individual autonomy essential to any meaningful notion of personality, joined as all things are within the Supreme Barzakh. Yet it does. In the first instance, Ibn ʿArabi, unlike mystical extremists, affirms the reality and dignity of all created things. He asserts that God wants us "to stand up for them."[132] In particular, since human beings are specifically addressed by the Law and are created in the image of God, their acts surely belong to them.[133] Otherwise, if they were powerless to act, God would not *enjoin* human beings to pray, be patient, and so on.[134] He would simply *program* them to that end. Chittick sums up Ibn ʿArabi's position on individual autonomy and freedom of action as follows:

> [H]uman beings are not puppets in this show. They are actors, which is to say that they possess the capacity, albeit limited, to direct the flow of their own unfolding. It is true that God has precedent knowledge of their choices, but they have no such knowledge. Whatever choice they make has a real effect upon their becoming. For example, if a person sincerely asks God for "increase in knowledge," he opens himself up to greater knowledge, since God answers prayers. Knowledge is light, and light is existence; greater knowledge means a greater capacity to manifest existence.[135]

If to such endorsement for individual freedom we were to add the individual's creation in the image of God, we would have a fairly substantial concept of the human person and could derive its inviolability from the pinnacle assigned by God to human beings within the Supreme Barzakh.

Now that a viable concept of the person has emerged from Ibn ʿArabi's thought, we may move toward the personal dimension of positive freedom. Besides the endorsement for the autonomy of the individual (and all individual things, for God saw it fit to create them and find a place for them in the order of being), there are specific references to the different faces of the meaningful infinite that defines unlimited positive freedom. There is first of all the general affirmation of the infinity of creation within the compass of human knowledge and experience, which issues from the endless nuances of suspension between Being and nothingness inherent in the spectrum of barzakhs, and the unfathomability of the Supreme Barzakh that is forever able to replenish "the waves on its surface."[136] For there is no end to the variety in which pure Being becomes manifest within a medium. To put the matter differently, the words of God (that become things) can never be exhausted. Whatever knowledge is gained by us lets us know that there is more to be gained. Similarly for experience. Ibn 'Arabi has mystical knowledge and experience in mind. Thus "the seeker of knowledge is like him who drinks the water of the sea. The more he drinks the thirstier he becomes."[137] There is potentially no limit to the knowledge we can gain, because God, who is especially close to humans in whom all His attributes are gathered, has deposited all things in us that have also been dispersed throughout the cosmos. As we fully awaken to our reality, the whole cosmos gradually comes within reach.[138]

Once again, we see how the whole universe is potentially encompassed by man and lies within the range of the Perfect Man who calls individual human beings toward his all-comprehensive embrace. This has become known as the "microcosm theory," according to which each human being is a reflection of the entire universe and (potentially) a fulfillment thereof. It is hard to conceive of a more radical notion of human freedom (or dignity, which in our time forms a solid basis for an Islamic transposition of human rights).

The unlimited positive freedom implied by Ibn 'Arabi's outlook has been apparent throughout the foregoing exposition of its relevant aspects. The whole cosmos is so made as to be turned toward the infinite and moreover suffused with it. Human beings can infinitely extend themselves not only because they exist in such a cosmos, not only because they can represent it mentally to themselves, but because within themselves they bear the distillation of all creation and can thus mirror it. All the principal threads that spring forth from the heart of transcendence are woven into the human fabric. We are called explicitly toward unbounded, pure Being in our very constitution.

In identifying what he calls the "Muhammadan reality," which dwelled with God before creation, with the Pefect Man, the Perfect Man's embodiment in the historical prophecy of Muhammad is hence seen by Ibn 'Arabi as an occasion to transfigure human life and turn it decisively toward pure Being and perfect freedom. The community is no longer seen as a static expression of recorded revelations, chronicled sayings and deeds, and written laws, but a collective creative reach, revolving around a privileged prophecy, toward utter transcendence. Muslim communities under the influence of Ibn 'Arabi's joyful vision are stirred with the torrents of life that have ceaselessly poured forth from the unfathomable depths of Being into the abyss of nothingness. The whole Islamic edifice then becomes strung above its multifarious mundane facade and fastened tightly at the Center of all being so that every Muslim fundament shows, if viewed from the side, an infinitely elastic interior between a static surface at the front and the final Origin at the back.

Ibn 'Arabi's absolute dynamism, wrought strictly within Islamic themes and forms, did not fail to gain a wide following among Muslims. In the Ottoman Empire, his popularity cut across all social classes. The scholars at the religious schools followed his teachings from the earliest times. At their head again stood Taşköprülüzâde, the pivotal figure in Ottoman scholarship.[139] The actual founder of the Ottoman system of religious instruction, Mehmed al-Fanari, was himself a follower of Ibn 'Arabi. Turkish translations were made and several commentaries written. Ibn 'Arabi was also highly regarded by the Ottoman intellectual elite and the masses. This goes back to the Seljuq period, when the sultans welcomed scholars and mystics from Iran and Central Asia and their cities became brilliant centers of mystical thought. Konya, as we saw in the last section, became the center for three of the greatest mystics of Islam, the other two besides 'Iraqi being Rumi and Sadruddîn Qunawi. As a token of respect, less than a year after the Ottoman sultan Selim conquered Syria in 1516, he had a mausoleum built on Ibn 'Arabi's tomb in Damascus, and a mosque next to it.[140]

While Ibn 'Arabi's influence has waned in modern Turkey because of the secular extremism of the early republican regime, it has hardly vanished. Its remnants have nurtured the thought of a leading modern Turkish author to whom we shall turn later as a harbinger of freedom in the contemporary Arab Muslim world. And Ibn 'Arabi's memory is vivid in rural Anatolia.

Because the Shi'ites, apart from their wariness of mystical claims of union with God, have generally been favorably disposed toward mysticism, the proclamation of Shi'ism as the state religion by the Safavids in Iran early in the sixteenth century started a chain of events that eventually led to a nationwide reverence for mystical thinkers, above all Ibn 'Arabi and Suhrawardi. To this day, the curriculum of higher learning at the religious schools assigns a prominent place to the work of Ibn 'Arabi. Because the Safavids extended their rule into parts of Central Asia, and the Turkic peoples there were already responsive to mystical ways, Ibn 'Arabi's popularity can be said to include much of the Turco-Persian regions within the Arab Muslim world. And because the Turco-Persian cultural sphere has also penetrated the Indian subcontinent under Moghul rule, and India herself has a great ancient and homegrown mystical tradition, Ibn 'Arabi's reputation and influence could spread eastward.

So far as the Arabs are concerned, it is somewhat ironic that Ibn 'Arabi, who himself was an ethnic Arab, appears to be much less popular. This has much to do with the attacks of Islamic revivalists and Islamic and secular modernists on mysticism as "retrograde" and an obstacle to national liberation, strength, and progress. We cannot dwell here on the highly charged political context that made such narrowmindedness expedient. But Ibn 'Arabi has quietly retained some influence in certain circles in Egypt and Syria, and has long been an inspirational figure among rural mystical orders in Africa, for instance, in the Sudan.[141] This unfortunate country's fanaticism, however, has nothing to do with him.

A Note on the Origins and Methods of Sufism

Just as we have seen how Islamic communities are set against a specific paradigm with definite historical origins, and just as principles have been formulated that regulate the derivation of rules to enable and ensure the fidelity of a community of Muslims to the paradigm (without losing sight of a changing reality), so can we find a historical origin for Sufism that defines and sustains its Islamic character, and a complex of orders in which various disciplines have been elaborated to save a potentially boundless human freedom from dissipation. The reader unsympathetic to mystical experience, provided he is not irremediably hostile to it, will therefore find much to distinguish Sufi writings from rants and ravings, and genuine Sufi teachers and masters from charlatans. For one to go beyond reason in Islam, there are reasoned ways.

Islamic mysticism is one among several versions of Islamic piety. In general, the turn to piety followed disillusionment with the excesses of the courtly society. For all the refinement and beauty of the poems, palaces, words, and manners that blossomed around the rulers within the empire, there was always a sense that this violated the spirit of Islam. For Islam had been especially concerned with shunning an external magnificence that might distract man from God. There was never supposed to be an Islamic courtly life in the first place—for Islam is uncompromisingly egalitarian. Having accepted the caliphal court and its satellites as an imperial fact of life, Muslims had to turn elsewhere for moral and spiritual examples. This turn intensified when the court's excesses were not only aesthetic.

> The glitter of the court and its refinement were founded at last upon pride and greed, upon torture and murder, upon innumerable falsehoods of word and deed. Nor could any privileged circles in Islamdom fully escape a like indictment. There were those who longed to break through the everyday round of life, however beautiful, to confront the realities of the universe in the deepest realities of their own beings, to confront its awesomeness with their own immensity of hope, and find a radical commitment which should claim the stakes of life and death. Some individuals devoted their whole lives to such an effort; many others, happy to cultivate the surface as best they could, nonetheless supported the more committed ones sufficiently to make them a force in the world. Thus personal spiritual concern became one of the most active forces in the high culture of the Muslim cities.[142]

Muslims did not have to look very far for their inspiration. The Qur'an itself provided many passages whose inner meaning, if uncovered, could open windows to the "spiritual states out of which the words had been formed."[143] The mystics were particularly impressed with a passage in the Qur'an that depicts a primordial covenant between God and humans:[144]

> When thy Lord drew forth
> From the Children of Adam—
> From their loins—
> Their descendants, and made them
> Testify concerning themselves, (saying):
> "Am I not your Lord
> (Who cherishes and sustains you)?"—
> They said: "Yea!
> We do testify!" (This), lest
> Ye should say on the Day
> Of Judgment: "Of this we
> Were never mindful":
>
> Or lest, ye should say:
> "Our fathers before us
> May have taken false gods,
> But we are (their) descendants
> After them: wilt Thou then
> Destroy us because of the deeds
> Of men who were futile?"
>
> Thus do We explain
> The Signs in detail;
> And perchance they may turn
> (Unto Us).[145]

The goal of mysticism is a return to that covenant, which Sufis have seen as uniting God with human beings even before their creation. (We can therefore see Ibn 'Arabi's and 'Iraqi's sense of a primordial link between the world and God as linked to the mystical interpretation of this Qur'anic passage). The Sufi séances of *sama'*, "the 'spiritual concert' which [they] employed as a means of opening themselves up to the inrushes of knowledge and awareness,"[146] are intended to bring about a state in which the soul regains the resonances of the Primordial Covenant.[147]

The central Qur'anic experience, from a mystical point of view, is the *mi'raj*, the Prophet's nocturnal journey referred to in the following verse: "Glory to Him who by Night took His servant journeying from the sacred mosque to the distant mosque, *Al-Aqsa*,[148] whose precincts We have blessed, in order to show him our revelations. He is the One who hears all and sees all." [149]

There are many references to this nocturnal journey in the chronicles, and Molé considers it the basis of the Sufi's ecstatic experience.[150]

A third Qur'anic reference important to the Sufis is to "the day of increase," on which God's elect are promised joys beyond those of the common paradise and an encounter with His essence.[151] A hadith report also speaks of how God entirely fills the being of the elect, so that they see, hear, touch, and speak through Him—a state ardently sought by the mystics.[152]

Two other features of the Qur'an gave rise to mystical experience. One was the texts that assert that the face of God is everywhere, or that signs have been put in nature and the human soul so that God's presence may be recognized;[153] the other was the effect that the recitation of the Qur'an could have on pious worshipers. The tone of the Qur'anic language, if properly recited, is enchanting and itself a medium of the higher awareness and understanding sought by Sufis.[154]

By means of the Qur'an, the broad elements of Islamic mysticism are thus available: a primordial covenant that assures the eternity of humanity's essential relatedness to God; the ubiquity of God's presence and the signs that lead back to Him; Muhammad's nocturnal journey that set a precedent for ecstasis; the promise of a full divine presence to those worthy of it; and words whose recitation helps bring about the spiritual state necessary for the full experience of God's presence and the return to the immediacy of the covenant.

A series of concrete events have enhanced the mystical potential already present in the Qur'an:

1. Foremost is the example of Muhammad himself, who is known to have spent long periods in contemplation. The Sufis tried to imitate him with the help of the many chronicles gathered about his life, deeds, and sayings other than the revelations collected in the Qur'an. They hoped to regain the conditions under which he was the recipient of those revelations.[155]

2. Hasan al-Basri, who died barely a hundred years after Muhammad in 728, was a contemporary of the rapid expansion of Muslim realms to form an empire. He worried that the lures of conquest might threaten the true Muslim life. He thus became an ascetic and later assumed a prominent place in Muslim devotional lore.[156]

3. As the body of rules derived from the main principles that guaranteed the fidelity of Muslim communities to Muhammad's Medinan paradigm continued to grow, there was less and less room for innovation. For every rule that was there, the domain for individual judgment was diminished. Meanwhile, Muslim theology, much like the European scholasticism that followed it, had reached a point where much of its energies

were devoted to hairsplitting discussions. Those who sought an inward expansiveness in Muslim life therefore had to look elsewhere, beyond "spiritual legalism and theological sophistry." And in turning to mysticism, they could evolve a spirited discourse.[157] Through mysticism the spirit returned to the law and theology became more metaphysically adventurous. Another problem arose from the theologians' emphasis on the radical difference between man and God, which closed off the windows of immediacy opened through Qur'anic passages such as that which testifies to a Primordial Covenant. The need for immediacy in the Muslim's relationship with God eventually found an outlet in Sufism.[158]

4. The encounter with other religious traditions, especially Christianity, because of the Muslim conquests also influenced the early Sufis.[159] Many converts to Islam in the formative period were originally Christians, Mazdeans, Manicheans, or Buddhists, and could not have forgotten their traditions and attitudes overnight. As a result, Islam bears the stamp of the "pre-Islamic religious substrate."[160] A particular influence line traced by Molé shows a striking similarity between some heterodox movements within the Monophysite and Nestorian monastic orders and certain Sufi ways.[161] This is especially so for ascetic Sufis, above all those who behaved in an antisocial manner to incur the wrath of society and ensure the purity of their motives by denying themselves all earthly reward and praise.[162] This movement became known as the *malamatiyya*, derived from the Arabic word *malama*, which means "blame." Its members then were the "people of blame." (Another ascetic tradition that influenced Islamic mysticism was already there in Khurasan, and may have had its roots in Buddhism, which prevailed in eastern Iran before the Islamic conquest.)[163]

5. The Hellenistic world that flourished at the time of the Muslim conquest of the Near East seeped through Islamic mysticism in several ways. There was to begin with the general idea of the two orders, the one visible, the other invisible, and the two kinds of people who follow two kinds of prescriptions respectively tied to the two orders: one external, the other internal. This idea had found a Christian expression recorded in an ancient work of Christian spirituality entitled *The Book of Degrees*. It was also common to all neo-Platonic movements. Such currents linked up with Gnosticism, and the symbiosis eventually found its way into the thought of the mystics of Islam, who subsequently developed a great esoteric tradition of their own.[164] The second largest group of Muslims, the Shi'ites, believe that Ali and his heirs, the Prophet's only legitimate successors, are privy to an esoteric knowledge because of their special relationship with God, and are thus in a unique position to mediate between man and God. The Shi'a emphasis on the Qur'an's inner meaning made them receptive to Sufism, except for Sufi claims of union with God.[165] The Hellenistic substrate could thus find a permanent home in

Shi'ite circles and remains resonant to this day in the intellectual and spiritual culture of the classical centers of learning in Iran.

Because of the early Sufi impulses, centered in piety and devotion on the one hand and rebellion against the constrictions of legalism and scholasticism on the other, the only knowledge that mattered to mystics was that important for a better religious life. Amid this antiintellectualism, idiot savants were seen as Sufis. It thus became easy for magicians and tricksters to dupe their followers. In time, the Sufis attacked such charlatans and realized that knowledge of the shari'a was necessary to set them apart from genuine mystics, whose task was now seen as inward spirituality *in the context of Muhammadan law.* It was also preferred that Sufis have a normal profession.[166] Junayd (d. 910) and others expressed the new ideal as action in accordance with "God's orders and laws understood in their deepest spiritual sense without denying their outward forms." [167] The Sufis thus not only accepted the performance of ritual prayer, fasting, and the pilgrimage to Mecca, but often did so with great enthusiasm. Many made the pilgrimage several times. And they believed that "mystical training would be useless and meaningless" without minimal religious obligations. These included the recitation of the Qur'an.

But the Sufis did not turn to the shari'a to ensure the authenticity of their quest for external or utilitarian reasons alone. More crucially, they held the outward forms of Islam to contain broad gateways to a life of piety and freedom once their inward meaning was uncovered. The outward forms were a necessary and fertile datum without which the Sufis would face a void. Schimmel describes the shari'a as the "soil out of which their piety grew." [168] For the Sufis, Nasr writes,

> freedom means to gain an inner detachment through the help of the revealed forms, whether they be cultic or artistic, forms which are outwardly limited but open inwardly towards the Infinite. Sufis, therefore, have always[169] been the most rigorous in the observation of forms, in regard for the *Shari'ah* and its meticulous practice; yet they have "broken" these forms from within and attained complete freedom. They have, moreover, done so not in spite of the revealed forms but because of them. No one can transcend what he does not possess. The Sufis transcended forms not by rebelling individualistically against them but by penetrating their inner dimension which because of the sacred character of these forms opens unto the Infinite.[170]

Apart from the intrusion of charlatans on a noble undertaking when it became too closely identified with antiintellectualism (which we no longer find in the mystical thought of Ibn 'Arabi), the immensity of Sufi freedom carried its own dangers with it. For though the Sufis sought to liberate themselves from the various inhibitions, prejudices, habits, and regulations, especially if adhered to for their own sake, a tendency to which traditionally minded Muslims have been wont to succumb, they realized that to liberate themselves from these totally, to the point of rejection, would inevitably turn freedom to license. The liberation they sought was not a plunge into randomness and absurdity, but freedom under the influence of a "spirit of universality and truth." So they sought guidance in those who exuded that spirit. The seekers were called *murids*, and their teachers or masters *pirs* or *shaykhs*. The pir-murid relationship therefore became very important.[171]

As for how the pirs themselves gained their status, there were informal but elaborate methods of certification. They include the reputation of a local Sufi master or saint, some of which is rooted in an aura or blessing bestowed by God, but much of which has to do with the saint's actual deeds, his knowledge of the various stations and states through which his disciples must pass to become mystics, and his wisdom and psychological acumen so that he can judge what goes on within the souls of his disciples and help them with their problems.

Among the various stations and states distinguished by Sufis are: repentence, renunciation, trust, poverty, patience, gratitude, contentment, fear, hope, contraction, expansion, love, gnosis, annihilation, and subsistence.[172] Each of these was defined dialectically over several generations, until it became better understood what each involved. For instance, renunciation in the extreme may mean that the Sufi must not accept anything not fashioned by himself, including food. (This is still upheld by Druze shaykhs in Mount Lebanon.) The idea is to stay away from whatever may pollute pure intentions. If a government is regarded as corrupt —as governments often are—then whatever is made by it or with its help is stained. However, the Sufis soon became aware that extreme renunciation has its own pitfalls. One may take to long fasts and sleeplessness for the strange pleasures that they bring. Furthermore, outward renunciation may mask inward greed. Renunciation was eventually seen as a means to an end. It is not so much an extreme renunciation of bodily needs as the realization that they do not really matter that is a necessary step on the way to mystical fulfillment.[173]

A similar sophistication was shown in the understanding of the other stations and states. Poverty, for example, was first interpreted to mean the refusal to possess anything. But when this threatened to become an end in itself, the concept of poverty was turned not to wealth as such, but to how one related to wealth. Poverty came to mean a detachment from wealth rather than the attempt to prove that detachment at all times.[174]

In general, we notice an early tendency to interpret the meaning of the stations and states in an exaggerated manner that nearly obscured the ultimate aim of each, then the return to a more reasoned interpretation of each as a temporary measure to discipline the mystic on his way. With time, more importance was given to attitude, say, toward food or wealth, than to the actual outward condition in which the mystic found himself. This dialectical process of discovery culminated in a sophisticated and psychologically advanced theory and practice of spiritual growth and nourishment.

Besides their deepening understanding of each station or state, the Sufis distinguished between a station and a state. A station can be arrived at by a man through his own striving. A state, in contrast, is given only by God's grace. The Sufis then noticed that certain stations prepare the seeker for certain states in the normal course of a mystical quest; but it is also possible for God to land the murid in a state beyond his present station through His grace.[175] Given these distinctions, the Sufis could discuss and debate the relative importance of stations and states, whether something is a station or a state, and their chronological order. In this way, different Sufi paths emerged, each in an order or *tariqa* (literally "way"). How these tariqas edified the communities in which they were located, and how the Sufis within them graced the lives of Muslims often under terrible outward conditions, will be discussed in the next chapter.

6

The Roots of Unfreedom
in the Arab Muslim World

Prologue

The transposition of the entire nexus of problems associated with freedom in the Arab Muslim world has so far been restricted to classic figures that have epitomized the various options available to Muslims. This does not mean, however, that we have transposed these problem only to the past. For we have seen the importance of continuity for Muslim life and thought, one regarded as unbroken from the time that Muhammad established his community at Medina. Islamic history telescopes, and so every figure central to the tradition is permanently absorbed into it. The respective emphases of Ibn Taymiyya, al-Ghazzali, and Ibn 'Arabi continue to correspond with the main currents one finds among Muslims devoted to Islam, even if a modern current has grown out of them, or alongside them. Just before the emergence of the modern current, Albert Hourani could hence describe the three circles of culture found throughout Muslim societies as follows: The narrowest circle was that of the ruling élite, which included some religious scholars who were state officials; wider was that of the urban culture shared by religious scholars, craftsmen, and merchants; and widest of all was that centered in mysticism.

> The widest circle of culture was that which included all those who participated, at one or another level of understanding, in the attempt of the Sufis to lead a life of devotion derived from the Qur'an and Hadith and directed towards acquisition of experiential knowledge of God. Generations of teachers and masters had gradually evolved the practices and rituals through which this life of devotion could be sustained: in particular, the *dhikr*, or recollection of God, practised alone or in company, silently or aloud, and accompanied by movements of the body or rhythmical breathing which could by repetition help to free the soul from the distractions of the world. Gradually, too, there had evolved a mystical theology, a description and explanation of the descent of the world from God through a series of emanations, and the ascent of the soul, moved by love, through various

213

stages towards knowledge of God; the multifold imagery through which this vision of the arcs of descent and ascent could be portrayed was perhaps the most vital part of the shared culture of eighteenth-century Muslims. In one or other of the Islamic languages it was still being refined.[1]

Hourani's reflections on the situation in the Arab Muslim world in the eighteenth century are significant, for they allow us to glimpse its character and direction just before the fateful encounter with Europe and to see what would persist in the same spirit for all the new ideas and attitudes made necessary by that encounter. Given the main circles of culture delineated by Hourani, we can once again appreciate the extent of the field of influence for any successful, recognized attempt to bring Muslim orthodoxy, theology, and mysticism together, as in their different ways al-Ghazzali and Ibn 'Arabi did. Ibn Taymiyya's influence, for its part, endured to the extent that those mainly preoccupied with the unity and solidarity of the community held sway. This increased as the ascendancy of Europe at the expense of Muslims unfolded.

The communal extremism exemplified by Ibn Taymiyya, we may recall from the previous chapter, does not bode well for freedom. Ibn 'Arabi's joyful gaze does. Yet many modern critics, looking back from the lamentable conditions that generally prevail in the contemporary Arab Muslim world, see in Islam itself a hindrance to freedom or, at any rate, the middle-of-the-road Islam that had one of its best representatives in al-Ghazzali. Here, then, we shall be concerned with such claims. Because the voices of poets are more easily and readily heard among the Arabs, immeasurably more so than professional intellectuals, and the Arab world displays all the dimensions of unfreedom that need to be examined throughout the Arab Muslim world, it may be appropriate to begin with the words of its most profound and brilliant poet. Besides, poets are freer to express themselves openly. Their popularity protects them from their potential persecutors. Nizar Qabbani, for instance, a very popular poet whose language is accessible to almost any Arab, has relentlessly attacked Arab tyrants (often through thinly veiled allusions), corruption (especially that which followed the wealth generated by the rise in the price of petroleum), orthodoxy of every sort (including religious and linguisitic orthodoxy), and the oppression of women (whom he dauntlessly urges to express themselves, to live and love, with abandon).

Adunis's portentous poem on al-Ghazzali, then, will send us on our way to uncover the roots of unfreedom in the Arab Muslim world.

*Selections from Adunis's Attack
on al-Ghazzali in Verse*

A flutelike caravan, and palms
like sinking ships in the eyelids' lake
A caravan—comet
made of the stones of grief
whose moans are drawers
filled with God and the sands:
This is al-Ghazzali.

He comes to us in a planet
nestled by our women,
who from its radiance
fashion clothes, pearls and dreams.
The fall begins in the cities of al-Ghazzali
[Qur'anic] proof and speech are settled [2]
brows get stuck in the dust—
in the cities of al-Ghazzali—
a spark that has no place
and the wind like a camel.

And after a seeker is silent or loses his way,
he is drawn by the herb of questions to know:
Every stream
whose source or mouth is in the cities of al-Ghazzali
becomes a cistern of tears
and turns in the waterwheel of the lips or in the ribcage:
    "And the homeland open like a shroud
    is a dove slaughtered in a spring
    in which I saw a nation . . .
    in which I saw the moon effaced
    from the faces of children,
    and the shattered, deposed age,
    and the convulsive age to come"

The fall begins in the cities of al-Ghazzali
The street trembles like a curtain
and age like a dagger
dives beneath the neck,
and the beacon like a black drape.

At every moment I destroy
the cities of al-Ghazzali,
I roll their stars and put out their skies:
    "The dawn is like a child
    Seven black spears

Seven boundless skies
Wandering in its footsteps."

And the dead enter and leave
from a green tunnel—in the cities of al-Ghazzali
They come through words
that moan, through saltlike paths, through a book
that dies, whose covers
are dance and daydreams
and the dead enter and leave:
    "and the sun in their robes
    is a yellow maiden
    whose breasts are painted with hearts,
    with bloodstone, brimstone and mysteries[3]
    Every night, she is swept
    by the rapture of flight[4]
    She engulfs the swords and the years,
    and, every moment, miscarries"
and the dead enter and leave . . .

Travelers . . .
"Where are you going?
You will not arrive, for this road does not
pass through Damascus, and the morning
is drawn by idols and ghosts."
Travelers wandering aimlessly in the night—
Where are they going?
From the corpses of their ancestors they carry talismen
and the strayings in their feet are a road
and the sands in their faces are eyes.
    (I fastened my clothes
    and came to the desert
    the lightning flash stood, led by
    Gabriel, his face like Adam,
    his eyes planets
    and his body that of a mare. And when
    he saw me
    he shook like a fish
    in a net)—.

I am certain, this is the age of
reincarnation-illumination:
The sun is the eye of a cat
and oil is the head of a camel
adorned with robe and dagger,
and whenever, on my way, I favour
a dove or a flower

or hide in a sign between the light and
myself, and lean like a spring through a stony path,
in my eyelids sprouts a bullet,
and whenever I say I love water
and the age to come, and all things
and whenever I try to build or have built
beneath the suns of the water
a roof,
in my veins appears
a bullet . . .

. . . And whenever it occurs to me
to enjoy the air and plant myself
like grass in the city of soil,
explore space and flight,
inhabit the dawn of winds,
in my clothes sprouts
a bullet—
a bullet—
and whenever I ask
and the question breaks within me, and I tilt
like a branch, or I resolve to float
in the layers of the sun and the air
yielding like water,
in the letters and intent appears
a bullet—
a bullet—
and the green trees on the way
are fire without victim
whose ashes remain
in the hearth of speech
and waft to the child that sleeps
a dream,
and to the child that awakes
a notebook of sorrows and songs . . .[5]

Toward an Interpretation and Evaluation of Adunis's Poem

"The Eighth Sky" is an astonishing work by any standards. It mixes poetry with dramatic passages mostly in poetical prose. In the original Arabic, it reverberates with sounds and melodies in harmony with the melancholy and near despair. These are carried in its tones before the various layers of meaning begin to surface. These layers cannot be dealt with extensively in the context of this work, but some mention must be made of each. One meaning stands out and remains insistent throughout the poem: the sense of a deep and broad condition of ruin in the cities that have lived in al-Ghazzali's image. "The fall *begins* in the cities of al-Ghazzali."

The passages translated here deliberately leave out the resolution of the poem, whose spirit belongs to the concluding chapter. It can nevertheless be anticipated as we distinguish three levels within the poem. Mostly, there are depictions of the conditions in the cities of al-Ghazzali, seen from the standpoint of a wandering universal soul whose presence becomes more pronounced as the poem unfolds. This universal soul in turn has access to an otherworldly point of view that defines the remaining two levels. The first, always between quotation marks, is a series of esoteric, semioracular commentaries, visions, and prophecies; and the second, always between parantheses (of which I have included only the first), is a series of encounters in the hereafter with Gabriel, and Muhammad and other prophets, also in esoteric language. The universal soul, which Adunis has chosen as his narrative viewpoint, can travel freely across space and time, and across the boundary that separates the sensory from the nonsensory and the temporal from the eternal. This enables him to combine an unequivocal condemnation of the temporal (especially the contemporary situation) with how it may be seen from an eternal perspective. It also enables him to imagine a supernatural power to intervene and contribute to the salvation to come. The poem then drives relentlessly toward a pagan-mystical redemption. The sun is throughout used as a metaphor for (or in place of, the ambiguity left intractable in the poem) a divine or otherwise transcendent illuminatory presence.

The more one is familiar with the esoteric tendencies in Islam, particularly among certain sects such as the 'Alawis and Druze, the more one can appreciate the origin and meaning of otherwise impenetrable scenes. In Adunis, we find that poetic license blends with an elaborate esoteric and mystical tradition. This is part of the astonishment one is left with: concrete scenes and events freely merge with a mystical perspective having pagan overtones. Let us from here on remain with the concrete, for there we can begin our search for the roots of unfreedom in the Arab Muslim world. In this poem, Adunis would like us to end the search with al-Ghazzali. We, however, must consider the best available historical works to see where it does end, and thence to cull the contemporary turn to freedom.

Here, paraphrased, are some of the images Adunis impresses upon us: an overriding confusion, wanderers, people who have lost their way, with the illusion of guidance, but guided by no more than talismen carried from the corpses of their ancestors (the conventional Islamic outlook and code?); a quagmire, people stuck in the dust or unable to see because of the sand in their eyes (and so blinded that they take the sand for eyes); pervasive grief and mourning, where a beacon seems draped in black, words moan like the doleful tunes played by a solitary flutist (which returns us to the opening image of an entire people filed into the shape of a flute, which, "played" by the universal soul, sounds the same, long, doleful notes), where every stream turns into tears, and joy is wiped off children's faces; and despair, for whoever still has hope, curiosity, loves nature, or wants to redeem the situation ("to favour a dove or a flower," ask questions, enjoy the air and the sun, or grace the towns with verdure) is thwarted, mercilessly ("a bullet, a bullet"). And in the last few lines translated, we have the rudiments of a transfiguration. The notebook of sorrows and songs is carried to children from the ashes of dead trees. The history, anatomy, and root of confusion, quagmire, grief, and despair are made known to the coming generations, which will rise against the prevaling order to liberate and redeem themselves, urged on by the mystical poet.[6]

The Deplorable Condition in the Cities of al-Ghazzali

For about a hundred years before al-Ghazzali's birth in A.D. 1058, the Islamic state that had peaked in the early 'Abbasid era, under the inspired if frequently brutal caliphate of Abu Ja'far al-Mansur, Harun al-Rashid, al-Ma'mun and al-Mutawakkil, had been in decline. The powerful central state, which could influence events in the remotest regions of a vast empire and rule directly closer to Baghdad, had gradually given way to local powers. The state in fact had contributed to its own demise as much as the warlords, generals, princes, and tribal chieftains who had been undermining it. For instance, near the beginning of the ninth century, in the war between two of Harun al-Rashid's sons, al-Amin and al-Ma'mun, al-Ma'mun needed help from a lord in Khurasan to defeat al-Amin. As a reward, the lord became governor of Khurasan and his sons were given the right to succeed him. The state had hitherto rotated governorships to maintain centralization. So Al-Ma'mun himself created a local dynasty. Such local dynasties, however, had to be stopped from gaining too much power. Counterbalancing forces were thus created, usually consisting of Turkish slave regiments centered in garrison cities. The soldiers there became primarily loyal to their officers. With time, these officers realized they could act with impunity and became warlords. Both the local dynasties and the forces created to offset them became autonomous centers of power. Both were directly instituted by the state.

Meanwhile, in an environment of bureaucratic corruption and the greater need to pay officers and soldiers by distributing land to them, the landholdings grew larger as smaller landowners preferred to join the new landlords in order not to pay to the tax bureaus. These large landowners were soon in a position to deal directly with the central government and negotiate a payment of fixed fees. The countryside thus became a patchwork of tax farms where finance, security, and agriculture were locally controlled. Ties with the countryside were further weakened because prominent positions in the central government now went to the sons of (urban) scribes instead of members from strong provincial families, and later to merchants, always highly influential in citied areas of the Arab Muslim world, whose wealth was needed more than ever for state investment.[7]

In such an economically, politically, and militarily fragmented state (with the fragmentation exacerbated by various Shi'a revolts that were often successful), traders shifted routes to more secure areas and the government could no longer support agriculture and manufacturing as before. Rampant impoverishment resulted. Wealth was lopsidedly transferred to merchants who traded with luxury items. The Arab Muslim world was largely at the mercy of petty despots, no longer restrained by the bureaucratic complexity and strong peasantry and bourgeoisie of the old central state. They ruled by virtue of their military prowess alone and were eager to prove it at every opportunity, be it against their own subjects or their neighbors. Those in an area controlled by a despot were treated brutally in military courts. Imposition of the death penalty was commonplace and immediate. And the despot, to keep his soldiers content, had to expand his economic base. He could only do so through attack on the nearest despot. And so, despots were constantly at war with one another.[8] For people who lived under those conditions, there was, as Hodgson put it, injustice, cruelty, ugliness, falsehood, hunger, physical illness and deformity (especially in old age), blindness, famine, and pestilence. "Many anecdotes," he wrote,

> show that, if not too pressed by their own troubles, many people were inclined to treat kindly even the animals that lived among them, down to the despised dog. But the dog's role in the village was to be watchdog (to alert people to any stranger's presence) and scavenger, and he was held to that role: dogs did not become pets; the children in the streets found it amusing to throw stones at them, and few adults would check them. In consequence, the dogs grew up curs, almost destitute of the endearing qualities that, in lands where they were better known as helpers in hunting or herding, made them so highly respected. Too many human beings grew up in much the same way.[9]

Much has changed since al-Ghazzali's lifetime, much of it for the better, but the scenes of despots at war with one another and with their own people, and of poverty and destitution among too many, have a timeless (if not preordained) quality that vindicates Adunis's choice of the universal soul as narrative point of view, and gives the free passage between the medieval and the modern in his poem an aspect of genius (Adunis's choice of the universal soul is also consistent with the fact that Islamic history telescopes). The foregoing quotation from Hodgson shows that Adunis, if anything, restrains himself where, to those unfamiliar with the history, he may seem to exaggerate. The cities in "The Eighth Sky" were indeed al-Ghazzali's—in the sense that al-Ghazzali lived and died in a land replete with such cities. But whether they were his work's progeny is another story, one we must next turn to.

Sources of Edification for People under Deplorable Conditions

Edification Through Community Life and the Positive Influence of the Shari'a

The desperate, atrocious conditions that many had to endure under the despotic regimes that mushroomed in the middle period of Islam were dignified "with phrases that reminded [Muslims] of [their] ultimate commitments."[10] They lived in a milieu that reverberated with the calling to turn acceptance of a terrible material predicament toward spiritual betterment. Many took up that calling. This calling could by itself neither feed nor intellectually enlighten them. Islamic life, however, tied as it has always been to the sacred and the profane, provided the scriptural and legal basis for informal arrangements that could often, if not regularly or reliably, water parched bodies and minds.

If the mental routes of escape from oppression teemed with superstition, so that people imagined fantastic turns in their fortunes (genies that could just as well turn princes to statues as bequeath palaces unto fishermen, or magician-taught princesses who would bestow favors upon paupers, as the *Thousand and One Nights* tells us); and people willingly submitted to the power of amulets and sorcerers, enhanced by tales servant girls told the children in their care; if such were the prevalent means of mental flight, more sophisticated lore could also find its place among the many seekers. For Islam allowed and encouraged a continuum of levels of thought, which ranged from the best philosophy in an intellectual center to whatever of it reached the village sage. The countryside was associated with the high culture of the cities, and this facilitated the free travel of philosophical and other ideas. How much of the high culture was absorbed depended entirely on the ability of those to whom it was carried. No ceiling was imposed. And amid great official caprice and cruelty, it was possible for anyone to find a sage within easy access and seek solace or guidance.[11]

The lowly were also relieved from their bodily want during the many secular and religious feasts that punctuated the oppression. Weddings were occasions for banquets and cash handouts, for all villagers were entitled to share in the happiness. Religious festivities were also such occasions. Ramadan, a month long and a central part of the Muslim calendar, was celebrated with food and joy by night, and piety and contemplation by day. The shari'a urged Muslims not to associate their piety with mechanical and general almsgiving, which would be a literal application of the *zakat*, but with how much they gave to the needy.[12]

Wherever there was deprivation, in rural and underprivileged urban areas alike, relief was mediated through various communal forms. Those who shared the same craft or trade, for instance, had their shops alongside one another, shared the same neighborhood, joined the local men's club, and were affiliated with the local sporting team. They helped one another when in need. Such expressions of solidarity were also to be found in the extended family, in which all members shared in the fortune and misfortune of the leader.[13] These informal institutions were often drawn, as we shall presently see, into the Sufi orbit. For the Sufis not only furthered spiritual life but also provided other means of edification.

The shari'a itself, while it did not specifically legislate the acts that were a source of edification for the lowly and oppressed, promoted values that encouraged them: communal solidarity, family life and autonomy, care for the needy, knowledge of the world and its ways (both theoretical and practical), patience when faced with adversity and piety. If it could not guarantee a good life overall for everyone, the shari'a nevertheless enabled the lowly to rise above their socioeconomic allotment and become spiritually, psychologically, intellectually, and, occasionally, materially better off.[14]

Besides the various ways in which individuals could transcend their situation, they enjoyed considerable liberties, partly because of the shari'a's direct influence and partly because of the peculiar political conditions of the period. First of all, Muslim institutions themselves achieved much independence because they could support themselves financially. This was possible because land and buildings were donated to those institutions, which could then count on income from rent. The donations have since become known as *waqf* endowments (so important today that many countries in the Arab Muslim world have a ministry for the waqfs). The waqf endowments cemented the social groupings held together in various ways often reflected in the shari'a. They furnished private means to run and maintain schools, mosques, shrines, hospices, wells, and fountains, and care for the poor and those who suffered personal emergencies.[15] (This again has much contemporary relevance, not only with respect to traditional waqfs and the social services supported by them but also the tendency, especially in underprivileged urban areas, in countries such as Egypt and Algeria, to circumvent the state in the provision of essential services. In such areas, not only are mosques and schools privately paid for, but food cooperatives and some utilities as well).

Financial independence furthered the tendency for Muslim institutions to limit the power of the state and create a climate that nurtured societies in their image. In these societies, the shariʿa guaranteed norms, rights, and liberties such as the following:

1. Any Muslim could move to any other area throughout Islamic lands and be guaranteed the same position he had earlier.[16] (People in the *Thousand and One Nights* are constantly on the move. Craftsmen, clerics, or viziers, they continue their occupations as they travel from Egypt to northwestern China without disruption.)

2. The shariʿa generally guaranteed an open social structure and mobility for the individuals within it.[17]

3. Common norms for city life also found their way into the shariʿa. Ties between different groupings in different cities were strengthened (which made it easy for travelers to pick up where they left off in their previous city).[18] The shariʿa in fact saw each city as a particular case of a communal life common to all Muslims. It completely disregarded political boundaries.[19]

4. Egalitarian expectations were consolidated by the shariʿa. It denied the bureaucracy control over tradesmen and their associations. It consecrated the break in the hold of the agrarian gentry and the attendant social stratification.[20] It insisted that peasants, regarded by privileged urban classes as little more than beasts of burden, be treated as equals and that a relief fund be set up to help them.[21]

Against a backdrop of stalemate between the two wealthiest social groups (merchants and landed families), and the weak political power of the military rulers who took advantage of that stalemate, the foregoing amounted to a significant degree of individual freedom (besides the communal freedom already discussed in both its general and Islamic aspects). No one was required to submit except to what the shariʿa imposed. In return for that submission, the lowly were far better treated than they might have been, in the end free to seek better fortunes elsewhere if they did not get relief often enough. Those in flight from the brutality, however privileged, could continue as before in friendlier Islamic parts. States could intervene in the lives of their subjects to a very limited extent. The Islamic institutions that attenuated the atrocious conditions had their own means to support themselves and thus act consistently with the shariʿa's decrees. And the door was open to all Muslims to partake of some intellectual enlightenment and much spiritual betterment, even if not very many crossed the threshold.

Edification Through the Work of the Sufis

The origins of Sufism and the highest expression of personal freedom, which Sufis exemplified, have been discussed in the previous two chapters. Here, we turn to the reflections of the piety and inward freedom that

Sufis could attain on the community at large. By the time the aforementioned conditions spread throughout much of the Islamic world, when warlords warred among themselves and treated subjects to their whims, each community—each neighborhood in each city and each village—had had, besides the mosque, a house known as a *zawiyah* where the Sufi masters and their disciples lived, devotional services were held, instruction given, and wanderers lodged. The Sufis in a certain zawiyah belonged to the same order (as those in a Carmelite or Benedictine monastery would). Many laymen and sometimes whole (probably informal) associations of craftsmen[22] were associated with a given order. For all these—laymen, disciples, wanderers, and masters—the zawiyah was a center for *religious* life, the more so in contrast with worship at the mosque, which had by then become a state function.[23]

The Sufi orders had also spread throughout Islamic lands, so that an international network of orders coexisted and criss-crossed with other institutions that had grown, with the shari'a's blessings, heedless of national boundaries. The houses that belonged to such orders became independent channels in their own right, with their own financial resources, where the affiliated could seek shelter and support. Each order was usually physically centered in the founder's tomb, and personally in the latest handpicked successor, to whose headquarters distant masters and zawiyahs were subordinated.[24] Through their networks, the Sufis could influence the spiritual course of Islamic communities and, overall, make life better for those who came into contact with them.

Because Sufis cared only for the heart's inner disposition, they were not conformists who required that true Muslims should everywhere submit to the same outward modes. They tolerated local differences, even between Christianity and Islam, so that, for instance, they encounraged Christians and Muslims who shared the same craft to fraternize.[25] The Sufis, because their indifference to material attachments freed them to travel extensively, had become knowledgeable about the world and realized that the harsh conformism of the 'ulama was unrealistic and a function of their (relatively) limited exposure. The Sufis also gave social groupings spiritual direction, something untouched by the shari'a because it dealt only with relations between individuals. Thus Sufis became actively involved with craftsmen and men's clubs, and tied these to their network.

Many different people could be accommodated by the Sufi network, for besides the tolerance and worldliness of Sufis, a great variety of orders and a complex hierarchy reflected spiritual advancement from the bottom up. The zawiyahs welcomed, as has been mentioned, laymen and wanderers besides the mystically inclined. Among the laymen welcomed were those interested in esoteric speculation, those who felt the proximity of God in the presence of persons who clearly exuded what they stood for, superstitious villagers, craftsmen, and members of men's clubs. All these could be variously touched by the piety and compassion of the Sufis.[26]

From a spiritual point of view, Sufism could be described as "a vast complex of practices and theories and hopes," in which each person partook at his own level. Apart from the immediate spiritual effect this had on individuals, "this whole personal and social and imaginative complex ... became the starting point for the creative works in philosophy and literature that Sufism inspired and carried with it throughout Islamdom."[27] There were also deeds. Sufis helped people with their ordinary moral problems[28] and did their utmost to assuage those with whom they had come into contact. If people could not attain the same mystical heights as the Sufis, they took note of the changes these heights had wrought in those who had attained them. A Sufi whose outlook changed because of mystical experience was typically free from envy, lust, or anger, and enjoyed a broad perspective and a calm self-acceptance. This reflection of mystical experience in everyday attitudes won over the affection of the populace. It showed them the nearness of a religion that could seem remote in the hands of the scholars.[29] It answered the yearning for the personal validation of mystical experience, one that Sufis were willing to share with others. And personal validation is always more resonant (and far more potent) than the mere affirmation of the creed or the events central to a religion.

Amid the outward adversity, and alongside the norms and ordinary communal safety nets that nevertheless assured a better life for politically and militarily hapless subjects, we can imagine the international network of Sufi orders as a vast, independently existing, concretely expressed spiritual presence that edified those whose lives intersected with it. Their number was large and their variety great. Not only is it wrong to say that in the cities of al-Ghazzali, those who still had hope, curiosity, loved nature, or wanted to redeem the situation were mercilessly thwarted. On the contrary, it seems that wherever they turned, they could find a zawi-yah or run into a Sufi. Wherever one might have been in the sea of suffering, the thread of redemption was always near.

Freedom, Edification, and al-Ghazzali

The freedom discussed so far has little to do with the outward conditions in which communities live. Only rarely do these conditions turn so evil that the community itself falls apart. All too often in this century, we have seen individuals within communities turn viciously against one another in a climate of fear and suspicion. However, it has only become possible to systematically keep watch over a population in modern times. It is a disease that began in Europe and has since spread sporadically to other parts of the world. Certain areas of the Arab Muslim world have not been spared. But on the whole, Islamic communal solidarity has been strong enough to withstand the most destructive consequences of technologically empowered systematic repression. We may thus safely assume that in earlier times, the main elements of communal freedom—the recognition of persons as such, the provision of cumulative wisdom for broad guidance and purposiveness in one's choices, and the collectively recognized turn toward transcendence—were substantially there for Muslims for all the illness, hunger, and brutality that they at times had to endure. We have seen how that communal bedrock concretely manifested itself in institutionalized charitable acts and guaranteed rights and liberties. However able militarily and politically powerful rulers might have been to fling their subjects about like broken toys, they could hardly do so in practice on any significant scale without incurring the wrath of a community whose obedience, after all, they needed. Communal institutions persistently attempted to ensure that even the lowliest be treated as full human beings. These attempts often bore fruit.

If the freedom gained through communal life persisted through outward adversity, then personal positive freedom, as an inward expansiveness that rises toward a boundlessness experienced as lovingly guided, did not suffer in the least. It thrived. The Sufis had gained acceptance throughout Islamdom, so that their houses could be built everywhere, and many different spiritual paths could be offered to various seekers. This inward freedom, whose heights surely only a few reached, was neverthless shared. Those individuals freed by the boundlessness of their vision and the fullness of their spiritual lives, immune to any outward adversity, were often active in their communities. As has been mentioned, their outreach included not only seekers of the mystical way, but many laymen. They drew as many people as they could toward their bounty. Those who could not partake of it directly were touched by it in some other way. Alongside the agents of brutality, and untouchable by them, were agents of kindness and compassion.

Modern critics who habitually have eyes only for outward conditions are advised, if they cannot go further, to note *all* outward conditions. Adunis does not depart from the facts available to us in his depiction of al-Ghazzali's cities. He simply overlooks a strong counterforce to that which obsesses him. Had he noticed how the community and the Sufis attenuated the harsh conditions, his attention might have shifted to the source of that attenuation, namely, the solidarity and inner thread of the community and the transcendence that grounds them.[30] We are fortunate to have a record of laws and deeds that reflected a more elusive reality. One might look at these as a mirror for a transcendence that modernity often finds unintelligible or unrecognizable.

It should also be clear by now where al-Ghazzali stood relative to that positive counterforce. His support for the community was never in question. He unconditionally accepted the scriptural sources for the laws that sustained communities in the image of the Muhammadan paradigm. As for the limitless font of personal freedom, al-Ghazzali recognized that too. As we may recall, he gave priority to the *personal* validation of religious truth (through mystical experience) over those validations that were possible in theology, philosophy, or Isma'ili esotericism. He believed in the convergence of that personal validation with the Prophecy. Its status could thus hardly be higher. In fact, as a result of al-Ghazzali's endorsement of the Sufi way, the acceptance of Sufism, already on the rise, accelerated. The presence of a zawiyah in every community owes much to al-Ghazzali. Whatever edified those who lived in al-Ghazzali's cities was most definitely dear to his heart and was reinforced by his work.[31]

We do live in modern times, however, and though it is crucial for modernity to remain conversant with the moral and spiritual dimensions of freedom, which are the essence of freedom and for which modernity has partly arisen, one must also heed outward conditions. For these, thanks to the technological revolution, can acquire such power and complexity as to limit access to the spiritual dimension of freedom and weaken the moral fabric that situates it communally.[32] Modern technology, especially communications, allows (but does not dictate) unprecedented play with hearts and minds toward quiscence, conformism, and spiritual apathy. The technology of surveillance and law enforcement (which includes the sham laws imposed by illegitimate regimes) results in communal fragmentation and mass intimidation. The technology exists to visit moral, spiritual, intellectual, and certainly bodily and environmental devastation upon a land. This is the nightmare in Adunis's poem, a nightmare brought on in part by the extension of medieval practices and attitudes to a more recent time, when the power of states has grown tremendously. One can no longer simply accept outward conditions and count on various attenuating and edifying presences, given the greater force and pervasiveness of those outward conditions in modern times. Now that modern technology allows the fairly comprehensive herding of multitudes in both subtle and coarse ways (and the rapid recession of the coarse "version" makes it incumbent upon us to underline the subtle), be it through turning them respectively into passive consumers or passive political subjects, political quietism and intellectual elitism are likely to have disastrous consequences. Modernity imposes a new kind of vigilance. For instance, never before have people needed to sift so carefully through torrents of information that far exceed the human capacity for absorption and to discriminate among such disparate standards within that information. Never before have the means of deception and disinformation become so nearly airtight. Never before has so much knowledge been necessary simply to choose meaningfully, which is true for significant as well as trivial choices. Never before have the means for diversion been so potent and multifarious. And never before has so much unfreedom been disguised as freedom.

These concerns, common in the centers of modernity, have percolated to the Arab Muslim world. There, it is more a matter of resistance to the temptation for states to gain political and intellectual monopolies, a temptation made possible by modern technology. The people of the Arab Muslim world are more likely than not to face coarse rather than subtle attempts at herding. But liberation from the coarse may only herald the arrival of the subtle. Sooner or later, the political and intellectual vigilance required in the centers of modernity will also be a requirement elsewhere. In any event, political and intellectual elitism can no longer be easily offset by the substantial breathing room afforded by the community and the Sufis. This is not only because of complex diversions from the spiritual dimensions of freedom and the centrifugal pressures on community life. It is also because Sufism has been heavily suppressed by the state in various parts of the Arab Muslim world, and the community has lost much of its vitality because decisions made centuries ago have gradually but relentlessly turned into the elements of a regressive conformism (although not in as simple and linear a fashion as is usually believed).

It is fanciful to see al-Ghazzali as anything other than an agent of kindness and compassion in a brutal age. Whatever edified people then, he wholeheartedly embraced. However, the political quietism and intellectual elitism that have become incompatible with modern realities may also be attributable to him. In that sense, we may naively regard a politically quiescent and intellectually constricted population to be his legacy, in the face of regimes nowadays tempted to control political and intellectual life to the greatest possible extent. (These can no longer be monopolized as was feared in the Soviet Union's heyday; it was probably an exaggeration, given human nature and resourcefulness, to think that they ever could). In truth, to be fair to al-Ghazzali, we need to have some idea about the context in which he espoused political quietism and intellectual elitism. For it was hardly the kind to inflict consequences as dire as those that al-Ghazzali's position would cause today.

Political Quietism as a Root of Unfreedom

'Abdul 'Aziz ad-Duri reviews the various factors in the rise of authoritarianism in Islam, some of which we have already come across. He reminds his audience that the pre-Islamic Arabian ideal, which carried over into the early Islamic period, was for the chief to be regarded as first among equals, and for him to be chosen by a consultative body.[33] This had to change for the following reasons:

1. The expansion of the Islamic empire made it impractical.[34]

2. The tribal nobility, which could earlier choose a chief in harmony with the preferences of the populace, lost touch with the ordinary members of the tribe and their interests because it had turned into a wealthy landowning class.[35]

3. The power of the merchants grew to the extent that they dominated urban culture. Merchants typically have a great interest in stability, and would much prefer long periods of authoritarian rule to political chaos provided their trade is unfettered.[36]

4. The 'Abbasids came into contact with the Sassanian tradition of absolute monarchic rule, to which they had in any case been disposed.[37] (One should also add that the 'Abbasids' immediate predecessors, the Umayyads, were hardly averse to imposing themselves whatever the cost.)

Meanwhile, Islam had had more than its share of tribal, sectarian, and dynastic strife. From the time of the schism between 'Ali and Mu'awiya, which ended violently in 661 in Mu'awiya's favor and was to culminate in the Shi'a-Sunni divide, barely a few decades would pass before the next major rebellion or civil conflict. Long before al-Ghazzali was born, the yearning for political stability had become very strong. So was the sense of futility faced with of the cost of revolt against unjust rulers and the failure of the leaders of successful revolts, once firmly in power, to act more justly than their predecessors. All this had led to the now famous (or infamous) doctrine: obedience to those in authority *(Ta'at awliya' al-'Amr)*. This doctrine has its basis in the Qur'anic injunction to obey those in authority;[38] only the Qur'an, when it speaks of authority, does not necessarily have warlords and other despots in mind.

Some accounts suggest that the habit of obedience to those in authority was also acquired because of a political and institutional vacuum left by the shari'a. For the shari'a did not recognize any corporate group that would bridge the gap between the individual (or the family) and the whole community (the *umma*).[39] Muslims might have formed such groups on their own initiative, but they did not find any intermediate institutions that they could inherit from late Antiquity, for the cities they conquered had already been in decline.[40] When they did form autonomous urban groups, these remained informal, and were more like an interregnum between dynasties whose ebb and flow had become erratic during the long period dominated by the aforementioned warlords. In other words, homegrown urban autonomy was more a makeshift political measure in the absence of central power than a permanent institutional restraint on its exercise.[41]

However, the foregoing view is not without its critics. Yahya Sadowski has recently argued that whether the state in the Arab Muslim world had been dominant or not, and society strong or not, has fluctuated in the positions developed by classical orientalists and their successors according to the changes in their perception of the prerequisites for democracy. When democracy is believed to require an assertive population that instinctively limits the state's propensity to dominate, Muslim societies are found afflicted with quietism; and when democracy is thought to demand the voluntary ceding of much power to the state, so that production may expand in orderly fashion, Muslim societies are judged too assertive to be made governable.[42]

Although such arguments are illuminating in their own way, and highly entertaining, their fixation on a relative position makes them obscure the difficult matter of ascertaining basic facts. Relativism appears urged by the examination of the work of scholars who consciously or not have failed to exhibit sufficient impartiality in their studies of Islam, especially in the context of current popular discussions about how and whether to secure new conquests for democracy. But relativism leaves us none the wiser regarding the issues of institutionalized corporatism and quietism as such, and the relationship between them. So for our purposes, and without any undue preoccupation with questions surrounding the propagation of democracy, we may be reasonably confident that a significant degree of quietism did prevail and became habitual, regardless of the relative formality or informality of the corporate groups that are known to have existed.

Obedience to authority, however, was never meant to be blind. In theory at least, those in authority had to be chosen (or otherwise approved) by the most *knowledgeable* men. In Islam, this had a special meaning. "Knowledge" meant "knowledge in the ways of the Prophet." In general, it meant those best fit to choose leaders who would lead the community as had Muhammad and his immediate successors.[43] Even that was much in dispute. Some thought knowledge to rest firmly in scriptures, without undue exegetical excursions. Others thought it rested in a divinely given ability to interpret the true meaning of the scriptures, particularly the Qur'an.[44] But all the disputants had in common some notion of authority based upon the transmitted presence of the Prophet.[45] The dispute was over the manner of transmission.

Thus al-Mawardi (d. 1058) believed that the caliph, the supreme authority, ought to be chosen by those who have a clear sense of justice and the learning and wisdom that enable them to choose well. In principle, nothing prevented the number of those who chose to be as small as one. A person generally acknowledged to embody all the Islamic requirements for an informed choice of caliph could do so as well as a hundred. This was neatly consistent with the reality of caliphs (in theory the most just and wise of men, but only in theory) choosing their own successors, usually one of their children. In view of that, the caliph's qualities were emphasized. He had to have a clear sense of justice, the capacity to exercise independent judgment *(ijtihad)*, good senses and organs, the courage to protect his flock and fight its enemies, and concern for the political interests of the community. On the other hand, al-Mawardi acknowledged the right to oppose a deviant caliph (without specifying the permitted methods of opposition).[46]

To these al-Ghazzali added a few ideas of his own. He insisted, aware of the long history of strife within Islam, that the caliph must not be removed by force. Furthermore, the caliph must be respected because his choice finally derives from God's wisdom and grace, and not from the learning and wisdom of those who select him. (This is one of the points where al-Ghazzali is a little hard to take, and perhaps was himself too taken by his preoccupation with orderly succession. Not many believers would have been able to sustain their faith if they seriously believed their caliph to have been actively chosen for them by God.) Al-Ghazzali extended these to local sultans and kings, whose authority (as we have seen) had become politically and militarily irresistible in his lifetime. Sultans and kings ought not be deposed either. Nevertheless, they ought to lend their ear to the learned and wise.[47]

Classical Islamic political thought, however, had peaked in the work of al-Ghazzali's contemporary and friend, the Seljuq vizier Nizamulmulk (1018–92). Nizamulmulk had been asked to recapitulate the past conduct of princes and kings for the benefit of his new master, Sultan Malikshah, son of Alp Arslan, the founder of the Seljuq empire. Nizamulmulk's ideas were the culmination of the gradual revival of Persian political institutions under the patronage of the Samanids, the Ghaznavids, and the Seljuqs.[48]

In the first instance, Nizamulmulk advocated an absolute monarchy: the king or sultan rules by divine right. His function is to "bring order out of chaos, and to maintain peace and justice." The ultimate objective of the monarchy is to "create and maintain wholesome conditions so 'that the people may live with comfort under the shadow of [its] justice.' " The king must therefore be obeyed by his subjects, because he gives them peace and prosperity after they had been deprived of them in "punishment for their sins."

There were practical reasons for Nizamulmulk's unequivocal support for absolute monarchy. The territories conquered by the Seljuqs were full of people among whom the idea of kingship was popular. The Turkish concept of tribal leadership prevalent among the Seljuqs (who were Turks), which breeds instability because of its complex and ultimately divisive rules of succession (among other problems), needed to be replaced with an ideal more conducive to stability, a goal that had become an obsession. And nomadic tribal political organization had to be recast in a form compatible with imperial exigencies.

Nevertheless, absolute monarchy did not entail absolute license. Muslim law, as a divine Law, was as binding on the king as on any of his subjects. The king was merely "an instrument for enforcing that law." To be able to do so, "it is obligatory for the king to seek knowledge in religious matters, and to comply with, and make arrangements to carry out, the commands of God and the traditions of the Prophet, and to pay respect to religious scholars."[49]

As Nizamulmulk puts it elsewhere, "the most virtuous thing for the king is to uphold the right path."[50]

Nizamulmulk constantly insists on the religious character of the king's authority and of the king's need to live up to it. The outstanding moral virtue of the king is hence his justice (rather than, say, his power and glory). The king must rule for the good of his country, is responsible for the welfare of his subjects, is personally accountable to God, and should appoint moral, God-fearing individuals to *all* posts.

When all these qualifications are considered, it becomes difficult to see how Nizamulmulk in any way supports tyranny. For him, absolute monarchy could only be a means to an end, one that he truly held noble. And lest anyone should doubt his position on tyranny, he even warns of its practical consequences: "A state can continue to exist notwithstanding impiety, but it cannot exist with tyranny."

Moreover, the subjects had rights. For instance, they were free to air their grievances to the king, who was required to grant them a public audience twice each year. Subjects were also free from the power of landowners and other heavily advantaged men, for all were equally beholden to the king.[51]

The modern reader hence ought to proceed with great caution before drawing any conclusions about Nizamulmulk's thoughts in relation to contemporary tyranny in the Arab Muslim world. For modern tyrants have offered no religious or moral leadership and inspiration to their unfortunate subjects, nor have they fulfilled any of the obligations specified by Nizamulmulk. Even the order they have provided has been diseased and is usually a veneer for myriad latent disorders. And one must bear in mind Nizamulmulk's emphatic rejection of tyranny as such, no matter what the rationale. (It is also somewhat ironic that though *all* subjects were entitled to an audience with Nizamulmulk's absolute monarch, few individuals today have access even to corporate executives ranked a few degrees higher than themselves, let alone the highest government officials.)

For all that, as might be expected, those in authority were not there in accordance with publicly professed Islamic ideals. In the time of al-Mawardi, al-Ghazzali, and Nizamulmulk, they were there by brute force. That the three thinkers persisted in laying out the ideals that ought to direct the choice of rulers was not a charade. It reminded the community of those ideals and indirectly showed what their actual rulers lacked.

The ideal ruler is presented as ethical, just and God-fearing, but the unspoken motive for the composition of these literatures is that actual rulers are capricious, willful, self-serving, and tyrannical. The unspoken contrast symbolizes the deep conflict which is experienced in the soul of every individual and in the body of society—the conflict of unbridled passion and unrestrained exercise of power, and moderation and self-control. It also symbolizes the ever-present conflict in society generated by family antagonisms, tribal wars, factional struggles, conquests, and the rise and fall of regimes, as opposed to the hope for peace. The ruler signifies not only order but the quest for order in a society composed of self-seeking human beings and groups.[52]

One must also keep in mind that the aim of all Muslim writers, even when they dealt with the political dimension, was for there to be a favorable climate for individual moral and religious perfection. The qualities of the ideal ruler reflected that perfection.[53] We saw this in the thought of Nizamulmulk. But in the absence of rulers who approximated the ideal, the next best thing was for them not to rule over very much. If rulers were corrupt, then at least an unwritten pact would keep them from meddling in individual aspirations to moral and religious perfection.

Haroun al-Rashid may symbolize the golden age of the caliphate and be an embodiment of the apogee of its power. Yet already then, the caliph's role had been restricted. He was to lead prayer in the mosques, holy war, and the pilgrimage, and ensure justice in the courts, security in the streets, and safety from foreign attacks. The articulation of the positive content of the social order and the good life was left to religious scholars and family traditions.[54] The result was a "division of labour" between the caliph and the piety-minded (whose legacy, as has been mentioned, is the shari'a). The caliph had no jurisdiction over the areas circumscribed by the shari'a.[55] The famous Muslim historian al-Tabari illustrated this division in specific incidents that he related and which imply that individual action can circumvent authority at most levels. Given his further implication that justice is guaranteed by individual action rather than by government, one is left with the conclusion that there is no need to usurp it.[56] The modern reader can thus appreciate that quietism in such a context was not a consequence of fatalism, weakness, or deep psychological inhibitions, but of the realization that justice could be attained by means other than open rebellion. These means had partly taken the form of widespread employment of cunning and guile to wrest one's dues, as the popular culture amply enshrined in its literature—and as indeed one still finds today in the behavior of many individuals, within all sectors of the population, who need to protect themselves and their interests from the whims, suspicions, lust, greed, and envy of despots (and from the state, for they do not yet believe, perhaps for good reason, that it can work for rather than against them).

We have seen how the autonomous application of the shari'a was further supported by the financial independence of the institutions that lived by its tenets. Land was declared permanently free from state control, and the rent from it, and other revenue, was used to support religious schools, mosques, hospitals, caravansaries, and individual charitable acts.[57] Cultural autonomy was backed with financial autonomy. Such autonomy was accentuated once the grand era of caliphs faded and warlords and other petty local rulers emerged whose power rested on military strength alone. These rulers limited their responsibilities to defense, law, and order. Religious, economic, and legal life were largely left alone.[58] Once the caliph's military and political power had diminished, and as if to consecrate that development, he came to be viewed as the moral and legal symbol of a unified, international Islamic society.[59] But already in the reign of Haroun's son, al-Ma'mun, the caliphate had lost religious primacy because of al-Ma'mun's failure to decide the outcome of sectarian and doctrinal strife.[60] As a measure of the extent to which political and cultural affairs had become separated, the shari'a recognized a single Muslim society regardless of the (shifting) political boundaries, in which each Muslim was guaranteed freedom of movement and whatever position he had established before.[61]

Precisely because of weak states that by al-Mawardi's, al-Ghazzali's, and Nizamulmulk's time had become military regimes, and because of their high turnover, there was much room for the development of institutions that would survive the politico-military flux—and the incentive to do so. We have seen, for instance, how a vast network of Sufi houses became centers for spiritual life and how the community could reliably support its members in myriad ways. The state was almost irrelevant to the life of the community. Islamic society really came into its own under a panoply of transient and marginal regimes.

The narrowness in the reach of the authorities, and the positive social content that unfolded in the vacuum, leads us to all sorts of questions. How, for instance, did the peasantry cope with the brutality of the regimes that ruled them (given that the aforementioned Islamic institutions touched urban communities far more than the rural)? And how could crucial decisions be reached in the absence of strong state institutions?

The peasants, whose conditions were ideal for rebellion if modern criteria were applied, had several means of escape. They could return to pastoralism, for they often had kinship ties with pastoral groups. The regions that supported pastoralism were never far from even the most cosmopolitan urban centers. They could join the soldiery, always in need of new recruits amid the constant feuds. They could flee to other areas or live off an abundance of marginal lands that could temporarily yield crops. They could find refuge in fortified mountain villages that warlords found too costly to subdue. They could take up a trade for which no connections or great skills were necessary. And they could hide their surplus produce and feign misery and destitution. In general, peasants were shrewd, played by the rules, and knew where the way around them was open.[62]

As for the formulation of policy, whenever a city faced a major decision, say, which rival power to side with, it was usually possible for those who were informally held to represent its interests—'ulama, qadis, and neighborhood and family headmen—to reach a consensus. The cities in the period of petty despotism could function with neither a bureaucratic chain of command nor political customs held to be immemorial.[63]

Under all the foregoing political conditions, what, then, did it effectively mean for al-Ghazzali (or any other well-meaning Islamic thinker such as Nizamulmulk) to affirm the legitimacy of the actual caliphs as well as the local kings and sultans (the warlords), to the extent that he rejected the use of force in their deposition no matter what? What did it mean for him to preach obedience to those in authority?

We now know the following about actual rulers in al-Ghazzali's time:

1. They were expected to rule in the name of Islam. This entailed that they not impede the evolution and workings of Islamic institutions. We have seen that these indeed became the real centers of urban life throughout Islamic lands.

2. The caliph had already come to be seen as a moral and legal symbol of Islamic unity rather than the supreme political and military leader. Loyalty to him meant loyalty to the community's Islamic ideals.

3. By implication, this diminished the value of the actual political and military authorities, whose rule therefore had no legitimate (and hardly any actual) bearing on Islamic institutions, other than to give the institutions still more room to create and sustain communities in their image. (The Seljuqs under Nizamulmulk's influence were a noteworthy exception to this, as we shall see below.)

To these, we may add another significant development. Al-Ghazzali's support for Sufism meant recognition of the authorities esteemed by Sufis. In that period of Islam, the Sufis throughout Islamdom, from different orders, came to recognize a single person as the living axis around which the whole spiritual life of Islam revolved. He was a living reflection of the Perfect Man, and had the most perfect knowledge of God among his contemporaries. The pinnacle of the hierarchy of saints, masters, and disciples was known as the *qutb* ("pole" or "axis"). He was the true caliph. The identity of qutbs was kept secret to protect them, but the names of actual Sufis have been associated with supreme spiritual leadership.[64] Although nowhere do we find explicit reference in al-Ghazzali to the qutb as true caliph, there is an important sense in which al-Ghazzali would acknowledge the authority of the qutb. And given the simultaneous decline of the public institution of the caliphate, it does not stretch the imagination to transfer obedience at least in part to the qutb and remain within the spirit of al-Ghazzali's work.

Apart from the meaning of al-Ghazzali's affirmation of the legitimacy of temporal authority, which includes sound Islamic rule one way or another, point 3 above gives us a clue as to the effective meaning of al-Ghazzali's political doctrines. Al-Ghazzali knew that since the caliphate's decline, Islamic institutions were free to develop virtually unmolested by the political authorities, all the more so when the authorities had literally nothing to offer besides brute force. Thus the combination of obedience to those authorities, the injunction that they preside over a sound Islamic order, and the independent growth and jurisdiction of Islamic institutions that these entailed given the actual conditions, gives al-Ghazzali's doctrines the following effective meaning: To obey those in authority, to decline the use of force against them, and to insist that they act in the best interests of the community is—again, given the actual nature of the prevailing regimes—to support the autonomous development of Islamic institutions without end. It is to preach the independent aspirations of the community for the moral and religious perfections stipulated or implied by Islam. It is, in short, an indirect boon to the autonomous individual and communal drive toward those perfections.

The question now arises whether these are not in contradiction with al-Ghazzali's support for the strongest state to emerge in Islam's middle period, namely that led by the Seljuqs. For al-Ghazzali's support for the Seljuqs laid the ground for the conversion of Islam to a state religion and the eventual loss of much of the autonomy it had so carefully and persistently cultivated as first the deviant behavior of caliphs and later their waning power had made it essential for Islamic institutions to go their separate way. By Ottoman times, religious scholars had become state bureaucrats and (especially by late Ottoman times) their careerism as blatant as that of their bureaucratic peers.

The Seljuqs had come to power in Baghdad in 1055 (after having established themselves in Khurasan in 1038), just three years before al-Ghazzali's birth. His life coincided with the height of Seljuq power. He was, as we have seen, a friend of the Seljuq's greatest vizier, Nizamulmulk. The Seljuqs needed to establish their legitimacy among all their Muslim subjects. Because most were Sunnis, they fervently advanced the cause of Sunnism. In particular, they gave far greater state support than hitherto to the establishment of religious schools (madrasas) and mosques, and the promulgation of all four Sunni schools of jurisprudence. Every major city within the Seljuq domain had an endowment for a madrasa-mosque complex.[65] Through the madrasa system, masterminded by Nizamulmulk, the Seljuqs hoped to create a homogeneous bureaucracy with solid Sunni credentials. The old paradigm of fellowship among Muslims, long impracticable in view of the imperial expansions, and already transformed from personal relations between all Muslims to personal relations between all Muslims of repute to personal relations between all ʿulama,[66] was further transformed to camaraderie among madrasa graduates who manned the bureaucracy. The ʿulama were well on the way to officialdom, their opposition diluted, their interest vested in the state.[67]

From al-Ghazzali's point of view, these did not seem to be negative developments. On the contrary, if his ultimate concern was the moral and religious well-being of Muslims, and the state took it upon itself to support the institutions that cultivate such well-being, more strength to the state. No Muslim thinker rejected the state as such, but only to the extent that it failed to further the cause of Islam. This failure had become so habitual before the rise of the Seljuqs that it engendered the lowest expectations from the state on an Islamic plane. A state that enthusiastically supported Islamic institutions, to the point of a rapid increase in the buildings that housed them and official doors opened everywhere for the graduates of religious schools, could therefore only be welcomed. It is all too human not to have foreseen the consequences of allowing the state a leading role in the promotion and support of Islam (which ironically had always been publicly professed as the ideal, but tacitly discarded because of the reality of state policy, which had thus meant tacit endorsement for the separation of state and Islamic institutions). In the early days of Islamic officialdom, it was natural to be more Islamic than official.

It was not lost on al-Ghazzali that the Seljuqs, besides their Islamic credentials, provided a long lost political stability. After generations of endless feuds between petty despots, their arrival as a powerful, stable state was a relief. Besides, al-Ghazzali had the highest regard for the wisdom and benevolence of Nizamulmulk.

It just happened that the Seljuqs' rise coincided with al-Ghazzali's life and that they did what Islamic rulers were supposed to do—at least with regard to some of their policies. This must not be forgotten in the interpretation of the effective meaning of al-Ghazzali's political doctrines. One must remember the nature of the authorities to whom he preached obedience, just as one must be mindful of the conditions when authorities were Islamically deviant and judge what the political doctrines entailed in that case, as has been done above.

How we interpret the meaning of al-Ghazzali's affirmation of the injunction to obey those in authority and the legitimacy of the rulers—caliphs, kings, or sultans—thus depends on what the rulers were like. A state such as the Seljuq, perceived to have real Islamic credentials, would merit substantive obedience. On the other hand, a state with only brute force to recommend it would in practice, in the hearts of its subjects, be obeyed within the strict limits of that force. Because obedience in this case does not extend in any meaningful way to what matters to the community (moral and religious perfection), then substantive obedience is effectively diverted to those who have the community's true Islamic interests at heart. Historically, this gave rise to the informal institution of religious scholars. For when people began to realize, fairly early in ʿAbbasid times, that the caliph for all his majesty had lost touch with the Islamic interests of his Muslim subjects, they began to recognize individuals within their immediate surroundings, known for their piety, uprightness, and learning, as community leaders. And when, much later, these in turn had a vested interest in the state and no longer served their flock properly, the Sufis rose to further prominence. Either way, whether obedience to the state was substantive because of its genuine Islamic credentials, or a mere formality because of its brute presence, the ultimate aim of obedience was the promotion of the moral and religious betterment of Muslims and the good of their community. (There is no doubt that unscrupulous or unimaginative religious leaders, officials, and scholars frequently exploited the obedience that they preached to maintain their positions, which rested in some measure on their hold over Qurʾanic exegesis. At other times, they preached obedience to curry favor with rulers whom they feared.[68] Their objective was not to further Islamic life and ideals. But such deviance does not undermine the reality of the importance of furthering Islamic life and ideals in the eyes of Muslims and their willingness to pledge obedience to those whom they perceive to act accordingly. Modern critics disturbed by repeated exploitation of that reality sometimes unfortunately find themselves pushed by their abhorrence of exploitation to deny the reality that had made it possible.)

On all the foregoing counts, with the (metaphysically unnecessary) assumption that Muslims are forever stuck with the injunction to obey those in authority, the injunction does not apply today. If Adunis laments the atavistic tendency toward political quietism, then the drastic change in the context for quietism ought to assuage him. We need not examine the modern state too closely to realize that no matter what direction it takes, it does not merit traditional Islamic obedience. In the first place, the modern state is immeasurably more powerful than the Seljuqs ever were. If it so chooses, it can meddle with Islamic institutions to great effect. Nasser was able to turn Sunni Islam's most venerable center of learning into a rubber stamp for all his major decisions. A few decades earlier, Atatürk severely restricted the activity of Islamic institutions by decree, to the point that competent religious scholars soon became scarce. The Algerian military recently incarcerated every prominent member in the admittedly extremist and occasionally fanatical Islamic opposition movement. If the modern state decides to suppress Islamic expression or channel it along official lines, it has the means of enforcement. In the event, to obey those in authority quite literally means to obey those who undermine (paradigmatic) Islamic expression. The ultimate aim of quietism is foiled when the modern state harnesses or suppresses Islamic institutions.

On the other hand, if the modern state is itself Islamic, then the sheer power at its disposal and the complexity of the decidedly secular affairs that it has to manage (the economy, for instance) will invariably corrupt its Islamic thrust. We are fortunate to have witnessed the Iranian revolution as an illustration of this dynamic. Another good example is what happened to the Islami Jami'at-i Tulaba movement in Pakistan. Originally it was established as a student movement in affiliation with the Jami'at Islami party, which was committed to setting up an Islamic state in Pakistan inspired by Mawdudi's ideas. The early thrust of the Jami'at-i Tulaba was therefore the furtherance of Islamic ideals. A few years of political activism, however, made it pursue politics for its own sake.[69]

Let us recall that in the days of much weaker Islamic states, say, in their support for Islamic centers of learning and their embrace of the graduates from these centers, a process was set in motion that turned religious scholars relentlessly toward their bureaucratic careers at the expense of their religious vocation. Already then, it was clear that a state religion would steadily favor the state over the religion. If this was the logic of change under weak states, how must it be now that they are much stronger? Mardin's study, *The Genesis of Young Ottoman Thought*, often cited in this book, can be read as a close account of how an Islamic state that sought to revitalize itself in the name of Islam against the encroachments of its European (and by then nominally Christian) adversaries became far more a state than Islamic. It is no accident that the first secular republic on Islamic soil emerged in Turkey. The late Ottoman and republican Turkish experience is a classic example of how the logic of modern statehood unfolds. The Ottoman-Turkish state became modern by distancing itself, at times radically, from Islam.

In medieval times too, many states explicitly founded to further the ideals of Islam have turned away from them. In the Maghreb, a series of such disappointments may be summarized as follows:

> While contributing towards making Islam the religion of the whole of the Maghrib, the reformist religious movements which appeared in the Maghrib between the eighth and twelfth centuries failed to realize the religio-political ideals which they proclaimed, and they invariably led to the coming of power of dynasties which subordinated the realization of these ideals to the requirements of maintaining power.[70]

We need not dwell on the details of such developments here, but Abun-Nasr's work does delve into them and presents to us the spectacle of Rustamids, Fatimids, Almoravids, and Almohads promising Islamic utopias and ultimately delivering despotism. Even the religious scholars, long a refuge for the populace from the burdens of harsh rule, were eventually co-opted by the state: "Through becoming the allies of the rulers, the Malikite scholars of the Maghrib lost the dynamic vitality which had characterized them in a previous age, when they represented the religious consciousness of the community in opposition to the state."[71]

The modern state must be preoccupied with the management of the economy, health, education, communications, transportation, scientific research, and so on. These are far too extensive for even the most powerful state to manage. The state increasingly is forced to restrict itself to setting guidelines as the activities that had brought it to the fore grow in complexity. All these activities put together have a limited bearing on the core moral, social, cultural, and religious orientation of the population (not so limited in education, much more so in transportation). The modern state can do no more than define its relations with the institutions that nurture the orientational core of individual existence. It either provides ample room for them to flourish, or (whether benignly or not) it oversees policies that undermine them and risks the scourge of apathy, alienation, and nihilism (which is the lesson of the catastrophe that the inner cities of the United States have become). In either case, the modern state cannot begin to cope, besides its almost impossibly complex managerial activities, with actively shaping the institutions that nurture moral and religious life. From an Islamic point of view, obedience to the modern state has different meanings depending on how it relates to those institutions. If it allows them a congenial environment, then obedience means the promotion of (paradigmatic) Islamic expression (however modified). If not, then obedience is Islamically self-undermining. Republican Turkey began with hostile relations between the state and religious institutions, but has slowly moved away from that hostility to what may be termed a crossroads. We ought to remember that because republican Turkey has frequently held open elections in the last forty years, obedience to the state entails the freedom to vote the opposition into office. Obedience is transferred gradually to rules rather than rulers.

To return to Iran, the Islamic state there was certainly meant to be Islamic. However, the stringent managerial demands of modern statehood soon made it clear that those who had the "best" Islamic credentials were rarely those most competent to occupy their positions in the state. (The disastrous performance of the Iranian military in the initial phases of the war with Iraq is a case in point.) For the state not to be undermined beyond repair, the Islamist rulers of Iran have had to accede to the logic of modern statehood (thus the restitution of many of the Shah's top officers). Conversely, the attempt to link Islam organically with the modern state can only undermine the Islamic component. It involves Islam in labyrinthine managerial and bureaucratic problems that exhaust its moral and spiritual energies. And it presents Islamist officials with the many temptations of the power at the disposal of modern states. For Islamists to hold such power is for them to relinquish the distance that enables them to ensure its just employment. Obedience to such an Islamic state is then likely to undermine paradigmatic Islamic expression.

The days when Muslims naturally evolved the conception of an Islamic state and preached obedience to its leaders are initially bound with the unique Medinan situation and its immediate outpourings, when the state was also a community. Thus, the best interests of state and community were identical. Loyalty to the state was loyalty to the Islamic communal vision, which entailed individual moral and religious perfection for its members. Nothing could be further from community than the modern state. The very history of modern statehood bespeaks antagonism to traditional community life. Already in Seljuq times, and certainly in Ottoman times, the state had become more of a mechanism than a community. Today, the model the state tends to is a highly elaborate mechanism, despite all sorts of human imperviousness to mass mechanization (corruption is an instance of this, besides being a result of greed). In its essence, the modern state is hostile to Islamic communal ideals. Theoretically, an Islamic modern state is an oxymoron. Practically, it spells disaster for Islam (and so would the obedience of Muslims to it).

The modern state, preoccupied as it must be with secular managerial problems, has no positive contribution to make to Islamic self-expression. This rests firmly in the hands of Islamic institutions or, in the event that the institutions have lost touch with individual Islamic aspirations, with the emergent new leadership that no doubt will transform these institutions (more on this in the next chapter). And it is to them that those whose ultimate aim is the good of the Muslim community ought to pledge obedience (or trust and loyalty, perhaps more appropriate virtues in a rebellious age). Their goal would then be to ensure that the modern state leave sufficient room for Islamic expression. (As for what contemporary Islamic expression might be, it is a very large and multifarious problem yet to be worked out by Muslims, about which a few ideas will be suggested in the next chapter).

Once the original context for Muslim political thought is clarified and contrasted with the contemporary situation, it will be widely realized that political quietism is either inapplicable or its meaning has shifted so radically as to make vigilance unavoidable. To obey those in authority indeed leads to much unfreedom (politically and Islamically, whether the state is secular or Islamic), not because al-Ghazzali, Nizamulmulk, and others preached it, but because of how much the conditions under which they preached it have faded. Obedience today, above all in the best interests of the Muslim community (whose leaders surely know that the modern state is a fact of life and that wherever we go from here, it will not be back to a time when the state and the community were identical), means obedience to the rules governing the functions of states that allow a congenial environment for Islamic expression. This is where *both* Turkey and Iran may arrive from opposite directions.

We may now recast the effective meaning of the injunction to obey those in authority as follows:

1. The expression of a long-standing yearning for political stability.

2. The consecration of an imperial-authoritarian reality.

3. Obedience to the ideals of Islam that states were generally too weak to undermine, and thus obedience to those who informally embodied the ideals, both as communal and spiritual leaders. These leaders also were "those in authority."

4. Obedience to heads of states that were not disruptive of traditional community life, which was referred to an original state at Medina in which state and community were identical.

Now that the modern state seriously disrupts traditional community life, has turned into a complex of systems and mechanisms either neutral or subtly hostile to religious expression, and has enormously increased its power and scope, obedience can be only conditional on such states allowing room for the expression of the Islamic ideals mostly for which obedience had been preached in the past. Obedience is thus transferred to the rules governing such states and the institutions that promote Islamic expression. To attempt this promotion by Islamizing the modern state will cause the corruption of Islam because of the profound differences between the modern state and the state at Medina, and because the state today is bound to be modern in the sense of comprising a complex of systems and mechanisms that prevent it from being a community in any meaningful sense of the word. Any unconditional obedience to the modern state, be it secular or Islamic, entails disaster for Islam—and freedom. And in no way can the classical injunction to obey those in authority, if its meaning and context were properly understood, be interpreted as unconditional support for the modern states that have emerged in the Arab Muslim world—so that the responsibility for political unfreedom cannot be transferred to the classical mentality, which was appropriate well beyond its time frame and in certain important respects still is, but to the failure to come to grips with the modern reality. Both religious scholars and secular thinkers share in that responsibility. It must also be remembered, however, that the classical mentality seemed appropriate for so long that for scholars trained in the classical tradition to see that its political aspect has largely run its course takes more time than is realized. The habits that obstruct coming to grips with the modern reality are there for good reason. Those freed from such habits are therefore bound to feel much impatience, as Hanafi does, an impatience that sometimes blinds the moderns to the classical reality.

Al-Ghazzali, Modernity, Intolerance, and Intellectual Unfreedom

Hassan Hanafi, in an essay that was cited near the beginning of this book, launches a visceral attack on what he perceives to have been al-Ghazzali's debilitating effect on reason in the Arab Muslim world.

Al-Ghazzali's attack on the intellectual sciences in the fifth century since the Hijra, his annihilation of philosophy, his hostility towards every rational civilizational current, his rejection of all the Islamic sciences including those of *kalam* [theology] and *fiqh* [jurisprudence], and with the exception of the mystical sciences, his destruction of the way of theory and his call to take up the way of mystical experience, his abandonment of truth to follow the mystical path, and his criticism of human knowledge in the eager expectation of otherworldly knowledge—all this was the beginning of the destruction of reason, which is the instrument of dialogue.[72]

It does not befit an appeal for the unfettered use of reason, however passionate, to smother the adversary with hyperbole. Whatever Hanafi states in final terms ("annihilation," "destruction," "rejection," and "abandonment") at best corresponds with a much milder negative outlook in al-Ghazzali. For instance, as we have seen, al-Ghazzali does not reject philosophy and theology in toto, but only insofar as they cannot deliver the most important truth. This truth, he believes, comes through mystical experience. And so to take up the way developed and articulated by the Sufis is not meant to be a "destruction of the way of theory," but an extension of theory's limited potential. And it most definitely is not an "abandonment of truth," but an uncompromising search for the highest truth attainable by humankind. Finally, one cannot sensibly speak in such stark terms as "the destruction of reason." Reason, as integral to the human makeup, exists as long as human life continues. Its free use can be curtailed. Its expression can be limited. It may be overpowered by the irrational (to be distinguished from the *non*rational, a quality better attributed to mystical experience and the ultimate basis for the appreciation of art. Irrationality, on the other hand, is what we may attribute to superstition, mob rule, or the grossly unrealistic mass expectation of a military victory). It may be abused. But it is there all the same.

This does not mean that al-Ghazzali's clear sense of priorities and his (by modern standards) excessive solicitude that these be reflected by the community of Muslims did not eventually help turn the intellectual ground fallow. G. F. Hourani, for instance, evaluates how reason and revelation are related in Ash'arism as "revelation supplemented by dependent reason."[73] Al-Ghazzali followed the Ash'ari creed and saw the relationship between reason and revelation in exactly the same way. Al-Ghazzali's views on ethics illustrate his demotion of reason: "Obligation" is defined as what God commands and backs with rewards and punishments.[74] "Good" and "evil" are respectively defined as what is fitting for the ends of the next life and what hinders their attainment.[75] "Obligation," "good," and "evil" cannot be applied in a manner known by the human intellect.[76] And so on. As a result of this attitude toward reason and the human intellect, given the prominence of Ash'arism and Ghazzaliism in the middle of the Islamicate continuum, G. F. Hourani finds that today in the Arab Muslim world, there is a lack of popular initiative to propose state reforms and organize secular groups such as labor unions or political parties. To these, we may add a climate of intellectual stiflement where issues that are believed to have been resolved once and for all are concerned.

Before we assess the extent of intellectual freedom within Islam, however, it is necessary to heed the view that Islam has of itself, and how it relates to other currents. Here is how Seyyed Hossein Nasr describes the confrontation between Islam and rationalism.

> Rationalism, basing itself on the exclusive validity of judgement of the human reason which is but a reflection of the Intellect, tends towards the secular by nature, because human reason, although real on its own level, is but a limitation and dispersion of the Intellect and to that extent is rooted in that illusory void which separates our existence from Ultimate Reality. This rationalism, based neither upon Islamic revelation nor on other inspired doctrines which are largely gnostic and illuminationist rather than rationalistic, was for several centuries the main source of potential secularism in the cultural life of Islam. It manifested itself primarily in the form of various philosophical and theological movements. . . . [Eventually], the danger of the suffocation of spiritual life under rationalism was curtailed. . . . [T]he spiritual principles of Islam met secularism in its most basic form, and in restricting its influence enabled the Islamic world to continue its life upon the foundations established by the Quranic revelation.[77]

Thus the assessment of the extent of intellectual freedom in the Arab Muslim world depends on the perspective and expectations of who makes that assessment. If the requirement for intellectual freedom is that Islam yield to secular rationalism (and Nasr is correct in stating that rationalism, in the mechanistic sense to which it is often reduced, can be only secular), then intellectual freedom demands that Islam become unrecognizable to itself. From this standpoint, the choice is effectively put forward as one between intellectual freedom and Islam. The secular rationalist cannot see Islam as compatible with intellectual freedom. On the other hand, if the dependence of reason on revelation in Islam means that there can never be free discussion about all sorts of things, then Islam makes unrealistic—and ultimately unrealizable—demands on the human propensity for free expression and rational argumentation. So the overly solicitous Islamist also effectively presents Islam and intellectual freedom as mutually exclusive. He cannot see intellectual freedom as compatible with Islam. But neither secular rationalism nor an overly solicitous Islamism are tenable; for the one overestimates its independence, while the other underestimates the independence of those whom it patronizes. We have already come across a lengthy argument that pointed out the limitations and unavoidable dependence of reason. We saw that the cry for sovereign reason ends up as an endorsement for whatever flourishes when reason overtly declares its independence (and covertly becomes an instrument in the hands of the newly ascendant forces). So though it is true that a certain current in Islam (and Nasr does not represent that current) understands by the dependence of reason, in Islam's case on revelation, that reason should never be freely used whenever a verdict has been given by revelation, or even when one has been deduced (often through a spurious argument), then to oppose this current as Hanafi does is to perpetrate all sorts of illusions about reason's potential and to undermine intellectual freedom itself—this besides the fact that the impossible would be expected from Islam. Unchecked rationalism could well suffocate spiritual life, just as an overbearing and overly defensive view of the sustenance of spiritual life could suffocate intellectual life.

But what was the situation like in al-Ghazzali's time and immediately thereafter? Just as many modern accounts of intellectual life in the Middle Ages are exaggerated, for they fail to acknowledge the lively debates that took place and the great Renaissance (and later) works that they made possible, so is it inaccurate to attribute intellectual unfreedom to the period here under consideration. Abu-l-'Ala' al-Ma'arri was a poet who died in the year of al-Ghazzali's birth at the age of eighty-five. Throughout his life, he was a severe critic of injustice and hypocrisy and a proponent of the highest moral standards. He freely judged rulers and religious scholars from that vantage point. He ridiculed formal religious dogmas and valued as pious only those who helped their fellow men.[78] Far from being persecuted or ostracized, Abu-l-'Ala' remained the most prominent notable in his town until his death. Someone like Abu-l-'Ala' would not be countenanced by today's secular dictatorships. But because he is well known throughout the Arab world, it is possible to invoke his name as a slightly veiled criticism of contemporary rule and rulers.

There are many other examples of dissent deep into the "middle period" of Islam (usually 845–1248 C.E.). Ibn al-Rawandi (d. 910) espoused a naturalism that every Islamic creed regarded as heretical. As if that were not enough, he is said to have believed in the superiority of a Manichaean dualism over monotheism and in the eternity of the world rather than its creation by God. These beliefs could hardly be further from the Islamic view, and it is usually considered blasphemous to even utter anything that unquivocally departs from monotheism. He went so far as to parody the Qur'an and ridicule Muhammad.[79] And yet there is no record of any measure having ever been taken against him, nor even that he was dismissed on the ground of madness (a common ruse to evade the wrath of the Islamic authorities).

One of the most respected classical Islamic philosophers, Abu Bakr al-Razi (d. 925 or 932), was a religious skeptic who also held doctrines and views that should have sent him to the gallows had intellectual unfreedom really been on the scale alleged by some modern critics. For instance, he professed the transmigration of the soul;[80] he believed that the soul can be purified only by philosophy; and

> in perfect consonance with his rationalistic premises, had rejected outright the concept of revelation and the role of the prophets as mediators between God and man. He reasoned that prophecy was either superfluous, since the God-given light of reason was sufficient for the knowledge of the truth, or obnoxious, since it has been the cause of so much bloodshed and warfare between the one people (presumably, the Arabs) who believed itself to be favored with divine revelation and the other less fortunate peoples.[81]

Al-Razi too was not harmed. The case of al-Hallaj, the most famous among those put to death by Islamic authorities because of their heretical pronouncements, is itself instructive. For though al-Hallaj refused to recant his claims to have attained the kind of union with God that enabled him to declare "I am the truth," no longer distinguishing between himself and God in the use of the "I," and though he chose not to feign madness to escape the consequences, thirteen years passed between the order to institute proceedings against him and the day of his execution. The Islamic imperium was altogether different from our contemporary scene, where "intellectual unfreedom" evokes images of arbitrary arrest, show trials, and secret executions after dark (Al-Hallaj's arrest, trial, and execution were orderly, perfectly legitimate according to official laws that had wide popular approval, and a highly public affair). It is worth remembering that Bayazid al-Bistami, whose pronouncements were no less extravagant than al-Hallaj's (and perhaps more so), lived out his days unmolested by ascribing his utterances to madness, continued to have a strong following, and has since assumed an eminent position in the pantheon of Islamic mystics.

As for al-Ghazzali himself, *al-Munqidh* makes it clear that given the nature of the audience, any appropriate method is acceptable for bringing its members closer to the truth. But the same work warns against the dangers should philosophical or mystical truths fall into the wrong hands. So what we have is a mixed situation: methodological pluralism is endorsed in the name of religious truth. If theology works for some and Sufism for others, if one kind of philosophy works here and another there, if an eclectic mix is favored by some and strict scripturalism by others, so be it.[82] In this sense, we can ascribe a significant measure of intellectual freedom to a milieu influenced by al-Ghazzali's thought. However, because he wants to ensure that no one would be led astray through immersion in an inappropriate discipline, he recommends that philosophy, for instance, be restricted to initiates. Sufism and esotericism are naturally restricted and not much emphasis is needed on that. As a result, although all different temperaments were catered to, so that those more attuned to philosophy could feel as much at home as those more attuned to mysticism, the various disciplines, paths, and methods wre sequestered. If within each there was dialogue, there was hardly any exchange between the disciplines. This was a clearly restricted environment and in that sense, al-Ghazzali wrote a prescription for intellectual unfreedom.

The limited intellectual freedom allowed by al-Ghazzali must be seen against its proper background. Al-Ghazzali had to persuade the representatives of an extremely conservative but popular trend in Islam to open up. These were known as the hadith folk *(ahl al-hadith)*. They recognized only the authority of the Qur'an (interpreted literally) and reports about the life and sayings of Muhammad transmitted by or in the name of his associates (also interpreted literally). No further source or faculty (such as reason) could be used to determine Islamic soundness. The hadith folk came to see the community as God's blessing and the Qur'an as His eternal speech. These could not be disturbed by any questioning. They believed that God was immediately present in the laws of the community, directly derived as they had supposedly been from the Qur'an and the hadith reports. (The hadith folk did not, for instance, allow the use of analogy or independent judgment in the derivation of laws.) They radically opposed the mystical quest for God, sainthood, art, incense, and messianism because all these, in their view, cloud the face of God. Instead, because the Qur'an is something of God Himself, they believed that God's speech was on their tongues when they recited the Qur'an.[83]

With time, buoyed by their popularity because of the courage shown by one of their members, Ibn Hanbal, who had resisted al-Ma'mun's attempt to impose an opposing (and somewhat rationalistic) interpretation of Islam as a state religion, the hadith folk (later known as the Hanbalis) gradually subdued the creative imagination.[84] Al-Ghazzali spent many years in Baghdad where, more than two centuries after Ibn Hanbal's brave stand, Hanbalism was still very influential.[85] He later recognized, as we have seen, the significance and truth of mystical experience and sought to secure its legitimacy. This was a considerable achievement in a Hanbali-influenced city.

The Sufis, meanwhile, had accepted the shari'a not as routine, but only if it could be validated through its inward meaning and purpose. They had minimized the differences among religions, even to the extent of accepting pagan worship as the best approximation of the truth for certain people. They had revered Jesus as a prophet of the inward life, who revealed the beauty of God and the love we ought to have for Him.

The inward expansiveness within an infinity, experienced as directed, as has been argued, is the ground for the freedom, spontaneity, and responsiveness of mystics. Sufis always sought truth beyond what they had found. This temperament collided with the Hanbali sense of responsibility toward the community and their aversion to whatever bore the slightest hint of delimiting God. Hanbali attitudes led to conformism and the stiflement of creative dialogue for communal unity, coherence, and continuity. These, from a Hanbali point of view, would be undermined by Sufi freedom and spontaneity, albeit for the direct experience of the central mystery of Islam—God's oneness. Hodgson belives it very difficult to resolve such a conflict.[86]

Nevertheless, al-Ghazzali succeeded in making official the growing mass acceptance of Sufis, which had run contrary to the mass following of the Hanbalis.[87] Some changes were effected. For instance, instead of the Sufis following only those laws whose inward meaning and purpose could be validated, all laws were declared valid in this way, and the work was then to uncover the validation for each. This is the position of *The Revivification of the Religious Sciences*. There may have also been an internalization of the openness that Sufis showed toward other religions. But the essence of Islamic mysticism was left intact. Eventually, whoever was inclined toward mysticism found a house within easy access where he could be trained at the hands of a recognized master. We have seen how the spread of a network of Sufi paths throughout Islamdom edified a population under adverse conditions.

Al-Ghazzali not only had to face Hanbali influence. Many other obstacles lay in the way of intellectual openness. Rampant despotism and brutality had only just been replaced by a relatively strong and benign central state. But the state had its own demands, among them the homogenization of the bureaucracy that would underpin it. There was also the memory of recent Isma'ili-led revolts, which sundered the community and set its members against one another, as though to effect the Apocalypse and Judgment Day. These added to the obsession with communal unity and coherence, and thus strengthened the Hanbali cause. Finally, there were the Crusades. When all these circumstances are combined— Hanbali influence, the rise of the central state under the Seljuqs, the memory of communal strife, and a (Western) Christian war on what by then had long been Islamic territories—it is remarkable that al-Ghazzali could effect a milieu in which there was free intellectual discussion at all. Judged in the context of the conditions under which he worked, al-Ghazzali left far more room for intellectual growth than another wellmeaning thinker might have. His thought was a decisive departure from the Hanbali school, the real force of intellectual darkness in Islam, on every plane. Unlike the Hanbalis, for instance, al-Ghazzali supported the use of independent judgment. In response to those who may ask how one decides without a text, given that the use of independent judgment may lead to conflicting decisions regarding the same case,[88] al-Ghazzali

invoked the example of a contemporary of the Prophet, whose position
he paraphrased and expanded upon.

> "[We] judge by the text when a text is there, and by independent judg-
> ment [*ijtihad*] when it is not. Indeed we act like heralds should they be far
> from their leader [imam] in the remotest parts of the land, where one can
> not judge by the text, for finite texts can not absorb an infinity of incidents,
> nor can one consult with the imam concerning each incident, for by the
> time one traverses the distance and returns, the consultee dies and the
> consultation becomes useless. Whoever is perplexed regarding which way
> to face Mecca has no other recourse than to pray in a manner judged by
> himself, for by the time he travels to Mecca in order to know the direction,
> he misses the hour of prayer. Hence, it is right to pray in the wrong direc-
> tion based on what one supposes to be the right." And it is said: "Whoever
> errs in his independent judgment is rewarded once, and whoever judges
> correctly twice."[89]

Al-Ghazzali also endorsed the study of science, theology, philosophy,
and esotericism, under certain conditions, to be sure. And he wholeheartedly supported the Sufis. Adunis, Hanafi, and other modern critics would
do well to see the extent of al-Ghazzali's accomplishments under circumstances in so many ways inimical to the creative imagination and intellectual freedom. The problem is not that al-Ghazzali did not go far enough
for intellectual freedom. He could hardly do more, although we must
remember the anachronism of judging al-Ghazzali's work in such terms
as its contributions to intellectual freedom, for he lived in a time with
different priorities and a different outlook. Al-Ghazzali's positive influence on intellectual life in his time was the outcome of his general concern
for the Muslim community, his quest for truth, and his own curiosity.
Al-Ghazzali's contemporary critics might then note the balance between
the conservative and the creative in his work, trace the developments
that would later tip the balance in favor of the conservative, and emphasize the creative in our modern situation. The judgment of al-Ghazzali's
work depends on whether he is seen as having surmounted many forces
of intellectual darkness or whether, because he had to contend with these
forces, his work is too conservative for another era, in which it arrests
rather than fosters intellectual life.

It is not as though al-Ghazzali grudgingly compromised with the conservatives of his day. He had a genuine conservative streak himself. If he
accepted the authority of scriptures and the hadith reports, saw the whole
shari'a as underlaid with an inner meaning, and promoted the good of
the community, it is because these were his own beliefs. But there was
more to al-Ghazzali than these. His claim to have sought the truth wherever he might find it appears sincere. So is his enthusiasm for the Sufis.
Al-Ghazzali's credentials among conservatives enabled him to expand

the horizons of discussion and spiritual life among them. His genuine conservatism was complemented with a genuine openness. What, then, was accomplished within the limits that he set, other than expanded recognition of Sufi orders?

One must keep in mind that the work done in fields thenceforth open only to those with the necessary qualifications, with the idea of shielding it from the uninitiated, became increasingly esoteric. Its masters took pains to ensure that the uninitiated could not understand it. A language of symbols evolved, which was used in metaphysics and some sciences, in Shi'ite interpretations of the Qur'an, and in Sufi theosophical works. All these were artificially made difficult of access.[90] Thus it is very hard for outsiders to appreciate them.

> Islamic intellectual life turned from rationalism to a form of knowledge based on intuition and illumination. It subsequently produced many sages who have preserved this tradition of wisdom, although to this day it remains almost completely unknown to the outside world. Moreover, while the purely gnostic teachings of Ibn 'Arabi spread throughout the entire Islamic world, the *ishraqi*[91] theosophy and the later schools, which combines it with the teachings of Ibn 'Arabi and also the Peripatetics, developed almost wholly in the Shi'ite world. This latter tradition of wisdom, of which Mulla Sadra is perhaps the greatest representative, has since remained mostly within the boundaries of Persia. The Persian world has served as its home, even though it has journeyed occasionally westward to the Arab countries and especially eastward to India.[92]

This Persianate mystical philosophy was to have a decisive influence on what is known as Islamic modernism, which came to the fore in the latter half of the nineteenth century. It has been firmly established that the man widely considered the movement's spiritual father, Jamal ad-Din "al-Afghani" (1838/9–1897), was himself a Persian who studied and appreciated Islamic philosophy as taught in the traditional madrasa system.[93] In one of his philosophical writings, his thought reveals how much it owes to Ibn 'Arabi, for instance in Afghani's view of the Qur'an as the first teacher of philosophy because it is an infinite work that also contains the most fundamental unifying principles (which makes the Qur'an the repository of metaphysics, to the extent that metaphysics is the study of first principles). He then goes on to make the analogy between the Qur'an's letters, words, lines, pages, and the interpretation thereof with respectively individuals, species, races, microcosms, and (general) movement (or change),[94] in the spirit of the mystical conception of all things and their interconnectedness as being already contained in the Book of Heaven, of which the Qur'an is an Arabic version. Although such ideas may seem remote to contemporary readers from the modernist concerns for which Afghani is better known, such as his call for Muslims to embrace technical progress, he indeed saw Islamic philosophy, as he had come to know it in Persia, as a basis for homegrown Islamic reform;[95] and it remained the broader framework and the inspiration for the more specific material reforms that he preached.

If the Persianate mystical philosophy remains arcane to outsiders (although this is finally beginning to change with recent publications[96]), then less effort is required to appreciate other intellectual accomplishments. Scientific thought in general did not decline. Innovations were made in mathematics, optics, astronomy, and chemistry.[97] Furthermore, now that the canons of the Arabic language and grammar had become well established, pre-Islamic philosophical and scientific traditions absorbed, the shari'a developed, the various schools of jurisprudence defined, and libraries built with the support of private endowments, a mélange could flourish: works of literature were imbued with philosophy, theology, and the shari'a, while philosophical, historical, and scientific works were also great works of literature. The Sufis contributed intellectually because they "provided a wide field of free development for the exceptional individual."[98] They were tolerant enough to accommodate various intellectual views embedded in several religious traditions.[99]

The question, however, still stands: If, as Nasr himself admits, intellectual discussion at the highest level and the freedom that accompanies it (for the initiates, at any rate) were mainly restricted to the Persian sphere of influence, which followed Shi'ism in modern times, what are we to make of the vast regions of the Arab Muslim world untouched by that efflorescence? Might *this* not be part of al-Ghazzali's legacy?

After all, al-Ghazzali did say, for instance, that philosophers are heretical insofar as they deny the resurrection of the body, claim that God knows only universals and not particulars, and that the world has always been there and will always be there.[100] He termed as unbelievers those who study the physical world and the creatures that inhabit it closely, and thus deduce the presence of a Creator. For their sin is the failure to attribute moral authority to the Creator and find their way to Him through faith.[101] He accused moral philosophers of having adopted whatever is true and worthwhile in their work from the Sufis.[102] Political philosophers had nothing valuable to add to what God has revealed in His books.[103] He did affirm that people should acknowledge the truth in the work of philosophers even when it is mixed with falsehood, for it is wrong to dismiss a truth because of the character of its author.[104] Nevertheless, as has been mentioned, he did not wish for philosophy to fall into the hands of those insufficiently trained to be able to sift the truth through the many falsehoods. Finally, the title of his classification of the different philosophers speaks loudly: "The Different Kinds of Philosophers and the Stain of Unbelief That Encompasses Them All."[105] No stigma is graver in Islam.

This is not the place to speculate on whether al-Ghazzali felt so strongly about all philosophers, or whether he sought to appease the conservatives and allow at least initiates to pursue philosophical studies. The tone of his words is unmistakable. And it comes as no surprise that throughout the Sunni-dominated regions of Islam, the study of philosophy, science, and mathematics receded (for even these last two he warned against lest people be misled by the ease with which truth is demonstrated within them to conclude that it can be so demonstrated in other fields, thus undermining their truths).[106] It is not unfair to read those passages in al-Munqidh as discouraging free intellectual inquiry.

Let it be mentioned in fairness that another great Islamic thinker who is usually very well thought of in the West was at least as vehement and explicit as al-Ghazzali in his readiness to drastically limit intellectual freedom for the community's perceived well being. For Ibn Khaldun frankly asserted that the community ought to be left in peace through strict outward conformism, and hence that philosophy and theology could be persued only as an elite activity by those so disposed. He dismissed the philosophers because they did not begin with faith, but rationally sought after knowledge otherwise given in revelation, a knowledge he claimed they had held inferior. Philosophers also deserved censure because they did not live up to their own scientific standards in their metaphysical theories. Even theologians, Ibn Khaldun believed, were useful only in the event of a threat to orthodoxy from "dangerous innovators" such as the Shi'ites or the Mu'tazilites. Once the threat has been warded off, the community would no longer need theologians, for its beliefs would be secure without rational support that, in any event, cannot be scientifically grounded in the theological domain.[107] Because Ibn Khaldun lived at a time that provided a historical view of forces that had undermined a community still threatened by Timur in the east and advancing Iberian Christians in the west, he felt that priority must be given to whatever empowers a community, whatever is necessary for its survival and strength. This is not acomplished by a philosophical or rational justification of the faith, but by protecting the multitudes in their faith through unquestioned obedience to the law and the rulers who are there to uphold it.[108]

On the other hand, while al-Ghazzali can be fairly said to have discouraged free intellectual inquiry, his support for the Sufis (which Ibn Khaldun in contrast was less eager to show) opened up a different avenue for intellectual freedom. This seems to have been followed most consistently and eagerly by those within the Persian cultural orbit. For there, in a climate overflowing with ideas about "a spiritual order situated beyond the limited experiences of common everyday life,"[109] it was possible to pursue a wide variety of philosophical and scientific studies with the implicit assurance that they would somehow converge upon truth and ultimate reality. The Shi'ite-Persian milieu seems to have opted for intellectual openness within the framework of spiritual and religious soundness. The Sunni milieu, on the other hand, especially when it distanced itself from Sufism, lived by a more rigid definition of religious soundness, and let this decide the limits of intellectual pursuits, which, subsequently, were relegated to insignificance.

Both trends were al-Ghazzali's legacy. But the divide was not so simple. The magnificent mosque-madrasa complexes of Central Asia and the great Moghul civilizational thrust into northern India were wrought by Sunnis. In both cases, however, Persian culture was influential. When we consider the Moghuls, the additional presence of Hindu culture must not be downplayed. After all, most of the people ruled by them were Hindu. In Sunni-dominated areas without other influences, intellectual life suffered the most. Such was the fate of much of the Arabic-speaking world. And because both Hanafi and Adunis belong to this world, their indignation over al-Ghazzali's legacy, much as it may veer toward historical inaccuracy, is quite understandable and is *partly* justified.

The extent of the intellectual limitations that became endemic in the Arab world can be illustrated in many ways, perhaps no more poignantly than through the degree to which two eminent Islamic modernists, Muhammad 'Abduh and Rashid Rida, were sufficiently ignorant of certain basic facts and important scholarly and creative developments to embarrass themselves more often than they might have. Like their peers, they were burdened with the sheer volume of materials handed down to them by their own tradition, and thus believed they already had more than they could handle, never mind Christian, Jewish, and other scholarship. They were also more concerned with the purification of their own heritage than with initiation into novel studies of history and religion that had begun to appear in the West a hundred years earlier. But the result was that Rashid Rida felt free to state unequivocally that Europe owed her liberal culture and scientific efflorescence *entirely* to Islam, nay even Japan, in its drive to Westernize, could be said to owe its successes to the long-term consequences of the Christian encounter with Muslim civilization during the Crusades. The usually more cautious 'Abduh also attributed European rationality and modern civilization to the Christian-Muslim encounter in the Near East as well as in Spain. Europe, 'Abduh believed, owed all her civilizational merit to Islam.[110] To cite just two more examples: Both 'Abduh and Rida did not reject, and Rida further embraced, the so-called Gospel of Barnabas, a work without historical foundation believed to have been authored in the Renaissance, because they could not find anything in the Qur'an that contradicted it;[111] and Rida rejected philosophy as useless and confusing in the absence of the Qur'an and could evaluate and compare the two based only on the *number* of people each had been able to guide.[112] We might easily dismiss such extravagances were it not for the fact that 'Abduh's major work is still highly regarded by Islamic and *secular* modernists in the Arab world,[113] and both he and Rida, his self-proclaimed disciple, continue to inspire many moderate Islamists. We hence expect too much equanimity from the best educated non-Islamist contemporary Arab intellectuals, caught up like Hanafi in a ferocious cultural struggle, and rightly indignant over the foregoing shortcomings, if we insist that they dissociate these as much from Islam as an outsider can.

Al-Ghazzali, in his time, contributed much more to advance intellectual life than he might have. But away from his time, his legacy has been mixed. The scientific and other intellectual work mentioned by Hodgson quickly faded in mostly Sunni-dominated regions of Islamdom. This, however, is not the only factor that narrowed the scope for discussion. An entirely different development, ironically tied to the same modernity incessantly used as a judgmental reference for the criticisms leveled at the Arab Muslim world, made free dialogue harder still. So we must turn briefly to the relevant consequences of the intensity of the Arab Muslim world's confrontation with modernity, especially as experienced through the colonial thrust into its territories.

One of Islam's remarkable successes has been the durability of an equilibrium between two opposite currents within it.

> On the one hand, [Islamization] has consisted of an effort to adapt a universal, in theory standardized and essentially unchangeable, and unusually well-integrated system of ritual and belief to the realities of local, even individual, moral and metaphysical perception. On the other, it has consisted of a struggle to maintain, in the face of this adaptive flexibility, the identity of Islam not just as a religion in general but as the particular directives communicated by God to mankind through the preemptory prophecies of Muhammad.[114]

Geertz speaks mainly from his firsthand knowledge of Morocco and Indonesia. What he says here can nevertheless be extended to the whole Arab Muslim world. The most recent and comprehensive scholarship, which includes many references to works containing insights gained through years of fieldwork, confirms this. Lapidus's *A History of Islamic Societies* and Hodgson's *The Venture of Islam* are cases in point. How did modernity affect that equilibrium?

Modernity has brought about both fragmentation and uniformization. Just as societies and economies have become more complex in their composition, and individuals are more conscious of the choices available to them, so has the globalization of the world economy facilitated (and to some degree necessitated) the oversimplification of culture and civilization. From one point of view, once solid and coherent communities are falling apart and people are increasingly clustered around their varied individual interests. From another, the global dissemination of cultural conformism has become possible and the clusterings are taking on a worldwide sameness. Communal fragmentation and cultural conformism (based on truncated worldviews) have equally eroded the sway of older traditions and lifestyles.

These changes have contributed to the tendency to oversimplify Islam and spread it uniformly throughout the Arab Muslim world faced with the forces of fragmentation, now much more highly visible than before. Such is the soil that has first nurtured scripturalism, then revolutionary Islam (that Geertz also calls "fundamentalism"). What we refer to by 'Muslim fundamentalism' is a late stage of an ongoing retrenchment in the name of maintaining Islamic identity (the second of the opposing currents just mentioned).

The premodern equilibrium has been upset by modernity for two reasons. First, how Islam was far more variegated than its official articulations indicate, easier to tolerate when self-consciousness was relatively dormant and different communities that called themselves Islamic were hardly in touch with one another, not only became much more apparent, so that it alarmed those more concerned with the maintenance of an Islamic identity. But (now turning to the second reason) modernity itself, with a new rhythm of life that did not generally favor careful, subtle, and broad cultural self-articulations, pushed the drive to maintain an Islamic identity toward the only Islam that could be sustained at a fast tempo: some kind of literalism (or fundamentalism), to become everywhere the same because the scriptural sources are the same. The ascendant narrow views of Islam are thus a reflection of both the centripetal and centrifugal tendencies in modernity.

Those more concerned with the maintenance of an Islamic identity perhaps always felt uneasy about the reality of Muslims who did not entirely conform with their vision.

> In Indonesia as in Morocco, the collision between what the Koran reveals, or what Sunni (that is, orthodox) tradition has come to regard it as revealing, and what men who call themselves Muslims actually believe is becoming more and more inescapable. This is not so much because the gap between the two is greater. It has always been very great, and I should not like to have to argue that the Javanese peasant or Berber shepherd of 1700 was any closer to the Islam of Ash-Shafi'i or Al-Ghazali than are the Westernized youth of today's Djakarta or Rabat.[115]

But the divergence in modern times has become impossible to ignore and has been compounded by the other fragmentational tendencies engendered by modernity. Those who seek to preserve the unity of Muslims, symbolized in the identity of their articulation of Islam, are thus greatly fearful of fragmentation and hence less likely than ever to tolerate heterodoxy and free discussion. Today, we see Muslim revolutionaries typically eagerly embrace the applied sciences, where hardly any discussion about the techniques thereby acquired are likely to give rise to dissent. At the same time, they are intolerant of the slightest questioning regarding their views of Islam (and of any other group that has a different view of things). The Islamic version of modern cultural oversimplification and conformism has its own twist. Rather than subtly put sophisticated and genuinely pluralistic discourse under pressure, it tries to stamp it out altogether as it responds with alarm to the many signs, real and imagined, of communal disharmony and disintegration.

Geertz himself provides detailed examples of the rise of Islamic currents that had no patience with Islamdom's traditionally broad civilizational horizons. Before the middle of the nineteenth century, heterodoxy had been an outstanding feature of Indonesian cultural and religious life, as the country had become a meeting place for Islam and a homegrown Hinduism. The influence of Muslims who had taken Islam to mean certain legal, moral, and ritual demands had been limited. But then, much improved transportation accelerated traffic in two directions: more could make the pilgrimage to Mecca; and religious ideas dominant in Mecca could spread more quickly to Indonesia. It so happened that a revivalist Muslim group had become dominant in Mecca. Their ideas, which were austere, extremely conservative, and often fanatical, were transmitted to religious scholars and students who then returned to Indonesia determined to refashion its Muslim life in their image. They built schools and hospices. Their social network attracted peddlers who then took revivalist Islam into the interior much as merchants had first brought Islam to the archipelago's shores. The base of revivalism expanded. Its hostility to heterodoxy grew. Eventually, the hostility encompassed all foreign influence. The xenophobia was fed by the increased violence with which the Dutch, who ruled Indonesia at the time, put down a stream of insurrections. What finally emerged early in the twentieth century was a kind of scripturalist Islamic nationalism.[116]

In Morocco, there was the same dual aspect of the emergent scripturalist Islamic nationalism: local heterodox Islamic traditions were declared to be worn out and heretical; and war was being waged against colonialism and the rise of European power and influence.[117] Geertz goes on to tell how this tendency (temporarily) lost out in both Morocco and Indonesia, because they both, respectively in Muhammad V and Ahmad Sukarno, had brilliant national leaders whose credentials were also solid from the standpoint of their old traditions. But Sukarno was eventually overthrown in a coup that claimed hundreds of thousands of Communist and other left wing victims. The new regime then waged a genocidal war against the Christians of East Timor.

The modern history of Algeria reveals the influence of similar currents, but the outcome is dramatically different. Islam in Algeria, before the French invasion and occupation of 1830, had been largely rural. It had become centered in saints who had played a number of roles among the various tribesmen, from regulating the use of land for grazing and settling political disputes to instilling an immediate sense of participation in Islamic life by illiterates and near heretics. The saints did not ascribe great importance to political events. They treated the French attempt to fully incorporate their land benignly, sometimes cooperating with the colonial authorities. The French colonization, for its part, urbanized the Algerian population at a fast rate. With greater access to literacy, Algerians came into contact with the revivalist current emanating from Mecca, and the reformism of modernist religious thinkers such as Afghani and 'Abduh. The Islamic nationalists of Algeria then rejected the rural saints and their culture on two grounds: they were unfit to advance the cause of national liberation; and their Islam was questionable.[118] The ferocity of the French encounter with Algeria ensured that Algeria's traditional culture would not survive the drive for independence. The only alternative in Algeria henceforth was between Islamic and secular nationalism. Secular nationalism appears to be in steep decline. Both have shown no tolerance for genuine dialogue. The outcome is there for all to see.

The Algerian case gives us further cause for reflection. For modernity did not singlehandedly contribute to a polarization that culminated in intellectually intolerant national liberation movements. It coincided with a latent local aversion to heterodoxy and a desire to instill new life in Islam quite apart from its helplessness faced with European expansionism. In the heat of battle, the perceived corruption of local Islamic traditions and institutions was magnified into the resolve to radically transform Islamic life and thought. We see this attitude reflected, more passionately than ever, in every Islamic revolutionary movement throughout the contemporary Arab Muslim world.

Two historical examples are instructive here. The first is the well-known Wahhabi uprising in Arabia. Its leader, Muhammad ibn 'Abd al-Wahhab (1703–87), sought to overturn religious ignorance and renew Islam. He happened to follow the Hanbali school of jurisprudence, which as we have seen is by far the most restrictive on intellectual freedom (and indeed almost every other freedom as well). Albert Hourani suggests that he went even further than traditional Hanbalism in his rejection of Sufism. This contributed to the narrowness of Islamic life in much of Arabia after the success of the Wahhabi uprising. To this day, Saudi Arabia follows the Wahhabi adaptation of Hanbalism and regards Sufism with extreme suspicion.

Another renewer of the Islamic faith, while less known than ibn 'Abd al-Wahhab outside scholarly circles, is by no means less important: Sheikh Ahmad Sirhindi (1564–1624). Sirhindi was concerned about the syncretism eagerly promoted by the great Moghul sultan Akbar. So he sought to restore Islamic purity in response to heterodox practices that resulted from combining elements from both Islam and Hinduism. He rejected all innovations (or departures from the traditional practices encoded in the shari'a in the spirit of the early Medinan community). He purged Sufism from all non-Muslim influences and insisted that the Sufi restrict his pursuits to the inspired experience of the Law as given by God, and avoid what was over and above the Law. And he preached the inviolability of the shari'a, so that the test for perfection and inner purification of the Sufi was "sincere observation of and submission to the divine Law." [119] Sirhindi then helped spread the Naqshbandi Sufi order, to which he belonged and which subsequently bore the personal imprint of his teachings, further into India, from which it thence spread to Istanbul and Anatolia and, later, to Kurdistan, the Caucasus, Syria, Mecca, Sumatra, Java, and Borneo, through a remarkable series of personal transmissions.[120]

The essay that Albert Hourani wrote about the Naqshbandis does not only trace the rise of the order in the context of Islamic renewal but also links it with two other developments that contributed to the narrowing of Islamic intellectual horizons. For by the time the order had spread to Istanbul in the latter half of the fifteenth century, it became favored by the official religious scholars who had had the recent struggles between the Ottoman state and heterodox Sufis very much in mind.[121] Hourani adds the insight that once an imperium becomes conscious of itself as such, attitudes change. When the Ottomans suddenly found themselves, after a rapid succession of military victories, as guardians of Islam, they perceived the responsibilities that issued from that role as entailing a much more conservative view of their religion. Established empires favor orthodoxy, and the Ottomans were no exception. The Naqshbandis' spread to Istanbul coincided with the apogee of Ottoman power. Their strict adherence to the tradition made theirs a welcome presence (made more welcome still by lingering bitterness toward heterodox Sufis who had allowed themselves to be used as pawns by the Ottomans' most persistent and dangerous adversary up to that point, the Safavids of Persia. Note that it is the Safavids who had earlier destroyed the Naqshbandi presence in Iran and part of Central Asia, where it had originally thrived, so that we may see the Naqshbandi ascent within the Ottoman Empire as also the means to get back at the Safavids). By the eighteenth century, the Naqshbandiyya were "popular with men of every class." [122]

The other pertinent development was the threat presented to the Arab Muslim world from Europe. Islam, in Hourani's words, had become "a society threatened in its beliefs, autonomy and self-confidence."[123] The Naqshbandi program, as seen through the positions of Sirhindi adumbrated above, could then reinforce Muslims in their resolve to defend their faith and realms. This convergence is perhaps too obvious by now for us to dwell on it. But it must be clearly distinguished from modernity's tendency to narrow the scope of speech and discourse because of its dual centripetal-centrifugal effects. For we are today all too familiar with the phenomenon of Islamic retrenchment, which translates itself into extremism, faced with foreign influence and power now perceived greater than ever. Indeed, the whole complex of convergences has been spiraling since the days of Sirhindi; for contemporary Islamic revolutionaries also struggle against the corruption, ineptitude, and cruelty of their rulers regardless of the foreign factor, rulers whom the former judge to have consistently made serious departures from Islam.

Before we recapitulate the main strands running through the limitations on intellectual freedom in the Arab Muslim world, some mention must be made of one further modern development that has intensified the polarization still more. It is the sense that people are no longer held by the beliefs that they cherish and therefore are more desperate than ever to hold them. The shift, as Geertz puts it, is one from religiousness to religious-mindedness.

> A few untroubled traditionalists at one pole and even fewer radical secularists at the other aside, most Moroccans and Indonesians alternate between religiousness and what we might call religious-mindedness with such a variety of speeds and in such a variety of ways that it is very difficult in any particular case to tell where one leaves off and the other begins. In this, as in so many things, they are, like most of the people of the Third World, like indeed most of those of the First and Second, rather thoroughly mixed up. As time goes on, the number of people who desire to believe, or anyway feel they somehow ought to, decreases much less rapidly than the number who are, in a properly religious sense, able to.[124]

The doubt that afflicts Muslims in countries such as Morocco and Indonesia is not directed at the *validity* of religious belief, but at "its depth, its strength, its hold upon them."[125] The response to such doubt is much greater emphasis on the celebration and appeal of belief, rather than its content. The response is to transfer the validity of beliefs from their "intrinsic coerciveness" to "their hallowedness—their spiritual reputation rather than their spiritual power."[126] It is very difficult to illustrate this shift to appreciate its effect on individual Islamic revolutionaries, whose devotion to their own sketch of Islam is at times almost painful to watch. It would be best for us to return to consider personal positive freedom from a mystical viewpoint and imagine the gap between immersion in that freedom and the will to exercise it (say, on having read several moving accounts about it and perhaps encountered a few individuals who exude something of the sort). No amount of willing that freedom, however eloquently one affirms it, can begin to substitute for its exercise. The intuited elusiveness of a freedom desperately willed, given its continuous absence, may shift to a frenzied cry for the various images one has of it. These will continue to prove unsatisfactory. And the cry will grow more frenzied.

Something similar may be taking over the hearts and minds of contemporary Islamic revolutionaries. Their sense of the value of religion is sincere. But modernity has exiled them from the ease and immediacy of true religious immersion. Islam is so rich with reminders of religiousness that they cannot fail to have an inkling of what they miss. So they try, hopelessly, to realize themselves religiously by means of the symbols of religiousness. Today's Muslim revolutionaries are terrified when confronted with serious questions (in a manner that traditional scholars and Sufis would not be), because the meaning of their lives rests not on a whole in which they fully participate, but on their *idea* of that whole. Such instability is not to be taken lightly. For the longing to be religious in a Muslim milieu is deeply felt and widespread. And without the true fulfillment of that longing, the tragic consequences of the Sisyphan struggle to hold on to its images will remain a fact of life throughout the region. The most visible consequence is the steady unwitting descent of those images into the sphere of parody and caricature—which is what the Islam of militant Algerian extremists amounts to. The only disagreement I have with Geertz concerning a most subtle and profound point put forward is whether the shift from religiousness to religious-mindedness is indeed inevitable. For it can equally be argued that as long as human nature remains recognizably the same, the essential qualities that supported religiousness are still there. And if, as Geertz and many others believe, religiousness is contingent upon being actively brought up into a religion, then one may see the tide of religious-mindedness as a historical corrective toward an environment more congenial to religiousness.

Given the many tracks along which intellectual freedom has become restricted in the Arab Muslim world, it may be useful to recapitulate them. They may be neatly divided into two groups, the first defined by the internal dynamic, and the second by foreign intervention.

The internal dynamic has the following dimensions:

1. A long conservative streak within Islam that has its origins in the efforts of the piety-minded Medinan Muslims to preserve the Prophet's community faced with Umayyad corruption. A literalist devotion to the first Muslim community later combined with several puritanical movements in various parts of the Arab Muslim world, and heroic individual feats faced with tyranny and heresy, to create an enduring Islamic conser-

vatism, really an ultraconservatism with a latent fanaticism running through it. Ibn Hanbal, Ibn Tumart, Ibn Taymiyya, Ibn 'Abd al-Wahhab, and Mawlana Khalid al-Naqshbandi have all been mentioned. Their inheritors are today's Islamic revolutionaries.

2. The rise of strong central states that have found it expedient to promote orthodoxy. Both the Seljuqs and the Ottomans initially looked on with approval at pluralism and heterodoxy. Both later turned much more conservative when they established themselves as the supreme protectors of the Islamic faith.

3. Reform movements that were motivated by the rejection of syncretism (for instance in Akbar's India), the alleged Sufi disregard for the shari'a (in many areas within the Arab Muslim world), or the rulers' serious deviations from the Islamic faith. This dimension is not exactly the same as the first dimension above, for not all reform movements necessarily had the ideals of the peity-minded at Medina or the Hanbalis in mind. Sheikh Ahmad Sirhindi, though imposing extensive limitations on Islamic life and discourse, cannot be easily included in the ultraconservative tradition. Furthermore, these reform movements later took on the added feature of the fight against foreign intervention, which we turn to next as we consider the four dimensions of the external dynamic.

4. The exasperation by colonial encroachment and later domination of the latent drive for strict orthodoxy among Islamic conservatives and reformists, who led the fight against the European powers. This is repeated in the present struggle between Islamic revolutionaries and local powers perceived as beholden to the interests of the United States. To the extent that this struggle drives fanatics and extremists to the forefront, it narrows the scope for intellectual life. The biggest casualties of those protracted struggles on the Islamic front have been the Sufis, who like all mystics had always been a force of openness and tolerance in Muslim societies. In fact, even Sufism has been narrowed down within itself if it is true, as many believe, that the most powerful Sufi order today is the Naqshbandi.

5. The tendency within modernity to oversimplify in the face of cultural complexity, and to penetrate other societies with a model of universal conformism. This tendency has created an Islam in its own image, one that has a substantial meeting ground with, but is not identical to, Islamic ultraconservatism and earlier Islamic reformism. We now have an oversimplified Islamic current structurally incapable of absorbing the subtleties and pluralism that Islam had long cultivated.

6. The modern assault on the security and stability once widely enjoyed by those with religious faith. This has engendered the frenzy that accompanies the descent from religiousness to religious-mindedness, where to be "religious" has become to loudly affirm (and impose) the symbols of religion rather than to quietly and assuredly grow inwardly

in one's faith. Because it is precisely in their outward aspects that religions (and currents within them) differ most radically from one another, this shift to religious-mindedness invariably breeds a far more intolerant ambience than that found in a culture permeated with religiousness.

7. The despotism, corruption, ineptitude, and collaborationism that have become endemic to modernizing regimes. These have bred an appropriate revulsion that has further magnified the influence of the Islamic revolutionaries. For not only are they more vocal in their opposition to those vices or have shown more preparedness to fight against the regimes that exhibit them but they have also built alternative networks to set an example for others.

The Status of Christians and Women: Concluding Remarks

The Status of Christians and Freedom in an Islamic Milieu

To single out Christians for discussion here is not meant as a slight to other religious groups that have lived under Muslim rule, such as Hindus, Buddhists, Jews, and Baha'is. It is rather that the Christian-Muslim divide has generally been more protracted than the others and has had more international ramifications. This continues to the present, despite the disproportionate attention given in the media to the conflict over Palestine since 1948. For there are actual or potential crises in the Balkans, Nigeria, the Near East (including the Sudan), the Caucasus, and Central Asia (and possibly Western Europe) on the one hand, and the growing polarization between the so-called Christian West (which is really a global civilizational trend that can no longer be called "western" and is not fundamentally Christian either) and the equally so-called Muslim fundamentalists (who are by no means strongly representative of Islamic civilizational currents)—a polarization that is nevertheless given the glamorous appellation of "Christian-Muslim conflict."

In a work more exclusively devoted to the relations between Muslims and non-Muslims in those lands politically controlled by Muslims, it is necessary to discuss all combinations. But besides the rationale just cited (which is not enough to justify leaving out the serious and important problem developing in the Subcontinent), there is only enough room here for discussing one such case with an example that in certain respects sheds light on the others.

A cautionary note is necessary given the passions that have long surrounded the encounter between Christians and Muslims, passions that have fostered strong prejudices that often shape their opinions of one another. It is extremely difficult to treat this matter fairly, but this account aims not to be unfair for lack of trying. Before one involves oneself in the problem of freedom for Christians in the Arab Muslim world, one would do well to keep in mind the status of non-Christians in lands politically dominated by Christians until modern times. This certainly does not justify any Muslim abuses against Christians but is rather intended to put some perspective on such a controversial issue. The truth is that historically, and *in general*, Muslims when they were in control treated non-Muslims better than non-Christians were treated when Christians were in control. For a long time, and except for the Jews whom they regarded—with much mixed feelings reflected in inconsistent attitudes and treatment—as their biblical forerunners, Christians did not even tolerate the *presence* of any other religious tendency, let alone that others enjoy certain freedoms. Prior pagan practices were violently ended, occasionally with genocide committed against certain groups, sometimes to the extent of the attempt to ensure that no physical evidence would survive them (which is why it is so difficult, for instance, to say much about Mithraism and, had it not been for discoveries in China and Central Asia, Manicheanism as well). We are familiar with the expulsion of Muslims and Jews from Spain, and the decimation of Native Americans across the Western hemisphere by European Christians who often saw the former as subhuman. Horrid acts were likewise committed against dissenting Christians, be they Monophysites and Nestorians in the East or Cathars and Knights Templar in the West. (Disenchanted Nestorians and Monophysites would later welcome the conquering Muslim armies and assist them in further conquests.) Nothing of the sort ever happened under *religious* Muslim rule. The Armenian genocide took place, significantly, in the *nationalist* era, as did the starvation of the Lebanese by the Young Turk regime during World War I, the massacre of Assyrians by the Iraqis in the 1930s, the present massacres in the Sudan, and those widely feared to be in Nigeria's future (besides the Nigerian attempt to starve the Christians of Biafra into submission at the end of the 1960s). These confirm the disparity, for they force one to ask why those Muslim-perpetrated atrocities (mostly against Christians, who have been strongly identified with the new order) occurred in the past hundred years and never before.

It is true that today, non-Christians are *legally* guaranteed their freedom in lands where modernity has advanced furthest, and which are demographically dominated by (at least nominal) Christians. Muslims, Jews, Buddhists, and others in the United States enjoy more freedom perhaps than any minority in the past under a different kind of regime. But the United States is a product of the Enlightenment. Politically, there is a radical separation between state and church. One can not therefore compare a secular with a religious system if the intention is to judge the relative tolerance of one religion toward another. Under a secular regime, all religions are supposed to be equal. The interesting question is what religion offered the more tolerant religious regime. Historically, between Christianity and Islam, there is no doubt that Islam is heavily favored by the facts.

Another thing to keep in mind is the asymmetry in how Christianity and Islam view one another. Muslims hold Jesus in special regard, a position repeatedly affirmed in the Qur'an. They acknowledge the Immaculate Conception, Jesus' triumphant entry into Jerusalem, the miracles he performed, and the Resurrection (noting that they do not, and could not if they are to remain Muslim rather than become Christian, acknowledge the Crucifixion and the Holy Trinity). On the other hand, because Islam arose several centuries after Christianity, it is understandable that Christianity should have no prior awareness of Muhammad's prophecy. Although Christian officials have largely become far more broad-minded, it does not help that Christians repeatedly intimate, even now that Islam has long established itself as a legitimate world religion, that Muhammad's was a false prophecy or that Islam is little more than a reformulation of a combination of Christian heresies. If Christians are unhappy with the inadequate portrait of Christianity given in the Qur'an, how is it then with Muslims who are never sure whether their religion is even *acknowledged* by Christians in their hearts? Contrasted with the unwavering refusal of Muslims to consider Christianity apart from the limits set for it in the Qur'an is the Christian tendency to treat Islam with misunderstanding, denigration, and disdain. These may be rooted in the succession of Christian retreats faced with centuries of Muslim gains. But what about today, when the Muslims very much feel on the defensive?

We now have the proper setting to proceed with an analysis of the situation in which Christians find themselves in the Arab Muslim world. We shall follow the problematic relations between them in historical order, beginning with the Qur'anic verses and early Islamic ideas that had set the initial tone for those relations, the events that later pushed them toward their more negative aspect, and the polarizing pressures that followed the encounter with modernity. The reader can then distinguish between those restrictions on Christian freedom in the Arab Muslim world genuinely rooted in Islam and those more attributable to factors with which Muslims as such had little or nothing to do.

The Qur'an itself, unless it be interpreted with imagination and generosity of spirit, and scholarship were to provide the exact context for all relevant verses, unfortunately leaves Muslims apt to pursue ordinary avenues of exegesis with mixed feelings. On the one hand, it exhorts tolerance, famously:

> Let there be no compulsion in religion: Truth stands clear from Error: whoever rejects Evil and believes in God hath grasped the most trustworthy Hand-hold, that never breaks. And God heareth and knoweth all things.[127]

This verse is often adduced by those who believe in coexistence, and is usually dear to the hearts of Muslims conscious of the accusations leveled at them by their opponents. But much in the Qur'an is prima facie inconsistent with the foregoing verse, both generally and with regard to the Qur'an's view of practicing Christians. Two passages are worth citing to illustrate the general inconsistency.

> Those who reject Faith and do wrong,—God will not forgive them nor guide them to any way—
> Except the way of Hell, to dwell therein forever. And this for God is easy.[128]

How can there be no compulsion in religion if those who reject it are certain to spend an eternity in the flames? Reading these two verses, one concerned about his ultimate fate will feel quite compelled. The Qur'an also tells us:

> It is He Who hath sent His Apostle with Guidance and the Religion of Truth, to proclaim it over all religion, even though the Pagans may detest [it].[129]

It does not stretch the imagination to interpret this verse as at least encouraging an active effort to convert all non-Muslims to Islam, for the "Religion of Truth" means "Islam" in this context, and is set apart from *all other religion* (including pagan religions, but implicitly also Judaism, Christianity, Hinduism, and so on). Everything then depends on how "active" the effort is. It could easily degenerate into compulsion, for God, asserts the Qur'an, has proclaimed Islam over all religion.

When we consider the Qur'an's specific treatment of Christians, we find that it often portrays Christians either in a manner unacceptable to them or directly attacks them for what they profess, which the Qur'an takes to be a departure from, and a willful distortion of, the faith that God had given to *Christians*. Only rarely is there a verse that unambiguously preaches a more open-hearted attitude.

> Say ye: "We believe in God, and the revelation given to us, and to Abraham, Isma'il, Isaac, Jacob, and the Tribes, and that given to Moses and Jesus, and that given to [all] Prophets from their Lord: We make no difference between one and another of them: And we bow to God [in Islam]."[130]

Other verses that exude a friendly mien are aimed at Christians who offer good prospects for conversion.

> [N]earest among them in love to the Believers [i.e., the Muslims] wilt thou find those who say "We are Christians": Because amongst these are

Men devoted to learning and men who have renounced the world, and they are not arrogant.[131]

From an ordinary Muslim perspective, arrogance has been identified with the refusal to be open to conversion to Islam. And certainly, in the wake of the already mentioned persecution of Eastern Christians by the dogmatically victorious Western Christians in the three centuries before Islam came into being, many Christians would satisfy Islamic criteria for not being arrogant. But for most Christians who took the Incarnation and Crucifixion very seriously (besides the Christian beliefs acknowledged by the Qur'an), the Qur'an offers mostly reprobation.

> They do blaspheme who say: "God is Christ the son of Mary." But said Christ: "O Children of Israel! Worship God, my Lord and your Lord." Whoever joins other gods with God,—God will forbid him the Garden, and Fire will be his abode. There will for the wrongdoers be no one to help.[132]

Blasphemy is no light matter in Islam. Note that this verse occurs in the same sura as the preceding quotation, and is close to it in the actual order of appearance. Clearly, some Christians blaspheme while others are very close to Islam. But we are not concerned here with the real meaning of the relationship between God and Christ in the eyes of a great Christian theologian or mystic (or a so-called Christian heresy), but with how most Christians who take their faith seriously view that relationship. Conversely, we must consider popular Muslim reaction to that general Christian view given Qur'anic verses such as that just quoted rather than the perception of a great Muslim theologian or mystic (or a so-called Muslim heresy) who understands that Christians affirm the unity and uniqueness of God as much as he does. Against the background of popular religious sentiment, conflict is unavoidable when a verse such as Qur'an 5:75 and the expression "Mother of God" are taken literally and without an attenuating contextual exegesis—as is bound to happen in most cases. On the Islamic side, popular sentiment would not be discouraged by the exhortation to Muslims that they

> [t]ake not the Jews and the Christians for your friends and protectors: They are but friends and protectors to each other. And he amongst you that turns to them (for friendship) is of them. Verily God guideth not a people unjust.[133]

Because Christians depart so far from the true Religion (another synonym for Islam), they (together with the Jews) must be fought unto submission.

> Fight those who believe not in God nor the Last Day, nor hold that forbidden which hath been forbidden by God and His Apostle, nor acknowledge the Religion of Truth, (even if they are) of the People of the Book, until they pay the *Jizya*[134] with willing submission, and feel themselves subdued.[135]

The only way that Christians can be on the right path from an Islamic point of view is for them to see Christ in Qur'anic terms:

> Christ Jesus, son of Mary was [no more than] an apostle of God, and His Word, which He bestowed on Mary, and a Spirit proceeding from Him: so believe in God and His apostles. Say not "Trinity": desist: it will be better for you: For God is One God: Glory be to Him: [Far Exalted is He] above having a son. To Him belong all things in the heavens and on earth. And enough is God as a Disposer of affairs.[136]

We have come across the emergence of the piety-minded Medinan Muslims faced with imperial distortions of "pristine" Islam.[137] It should not surprise us by now that the piety-minded found enough Qur'anic support for their wish to purge Islamic life and culture from all other influences. They saw Islam in increasingly exclusivist terms in response to the threat of heterodoxy within the expanding imperial realms. This eventually meant more rigorous discrimination against non-Muslims. We can sample this through how Christians (and Jews) were treated during the reign of the caliph 'Umar II (717–720 C.E.), a man whose election was secured by the piety-minded at Medina, who thereby showed just how influential they had become.

> [W]hile scrupulous justice was extended to them, within the terms set by the Arab conquest, Christians were made to feel inferior and to know 'their place'. It is likely that some of the humiliating sumptuary laws that later were sometimes imposed on the wealthier dhimmi non-Muslims . . . were sanctioned by 'Umar II: that Christians and Jews should not ride horses, for instance, but at most mules, or even that they should wear certain marks of their religion in their costume when among Muslims.[138]

'Umar II was a caliph much admired by Muslims for his piety and uprightness. And it is precisely these that led him to treat Christians and Jews in a manner that could hardly have endeared him to them. For he had much in his religious sources to recommend the practices that he endorsed. From then on, there has continuously been a current within Islam whose followers would treat non-Muslims with similar (or worse) discriminations. This current passed through leading Islamic figures such as Ibn Hanbal, Ibn Taymiyya, Ibn 'Abd al-Wahhab, and, more recently, Sayyid Qutb, the Ayatullah Khomeini, and Hassan Turabi.[139]

It is remarkable, then, that for all the pervasiveness of an influential Islamic puritanism that often yielded to fanaticism, for all the foreign threats that amplified its presence, and for all the political and military dominance by Muslims in the lands they had conquered, it took centuries before Christians would convert in large numbers and, even then, we have few reports of forced conversions on a significant scale. The poll tax itself was unusually mild. Only able-bodied males were required to pay it, and the amount involved was typically a pittance. The tax was effectively a symbolic payment in recognition of *pax Islamica.*

That the real situation was much better for non-Muslims than the harsher Qur'anic assertions might have allowed speaks loudly about the people involved in Islamic rule. More than six hundred years after the conquests, most of the population in the Near East, for instance, was still Christian (if we exclude Egypt. In Iran, mass conversion took place about three centuries after the conquest). It is perhaps unprecedented that the bearers of a universal religion with a strong sense of its superiority should have won so many battles so decisively and yet have not imposed their faith on their subjects. That they chose not to do so may have had sociological and economic dimensions, but one can not in all fairness refrain from attributing this extraordinary fact to something in the nature and humanity of the people in power—and of Islam itself. It is difficult to resist reminding the reader one more time of the comparative situation when Christianity was victorious.

The story of what finally led the Christians to minority status in the Near East is itself indicative of the benign, tolerant quality of much Islamic practice. For that change was entirely a result either of Muslim reaction to events initiated by non-Muslims or institutional developments that favored conversion for structural reasons (rather than reasons specifically attributable to the Muslim religion). A few such developments deserve mention.

> The first mass conversion of a Middle Eastern population took place in Egypt in the middle of the ninth century. A massive Coptic peasant rebellion was crushed in 832. In the wake of the rebellion bedouins attacked Christian villages; money was extorted from the church. Under pressure of communal defeat, bedouin attack, and the impotence of the church, Christian loyalties were subverted. In regions which had been partially settled by an Arab population, such as the eastern delta and parts of upper Egypt, mass conversions to Islam took place. Other parts of Egypt, however, especially the western delta region, remained Christian.[140]

One must pay attention to all the factors involved. Opportunistic bedouin reprisals in the wake of a crushed rebellion are not to be confused with Islamic severity; and the weakness of Eastern churches, deprived of support from the West and left stagnant in the new Islamic milieu, contributed as much to the Christian decline as the rise of Islam itself. It is still (pleasantly) surprising that the response was far from total. Not only were the Christians of the western delta region and parts of upper Egypt (among others) left unmolested—but many survive there to this day.

Meanwhile in Iran, conversion took place mostly because of the collapse of the old order and endemic instability in the guise of frequent warfare and chaos across the countryside, which made Persians responsive to the proselytizing activities of Sufis, Shi'ites and Mu'tazilites, and the multifarious stability that Islam would bring them—in both this world and the next.[141]

The structural changes can be summarized as follows: Because the Near East became mostly Muslim by the end of the Seljuq period, and the Seljuqs originated as nomadic Turks, we must go back to the most unlikely first cause in this particular chain. In the seventh to eighth century, the T'ang dynasty in China prevented an eastward push by nomadic Turks facing demographic pressures, so instead they began what was to become an inexorable westward drive that would take them all the way to Constantinople. The nomads, while still in inner Asia, through their cultural and commercial relations with settled peoples, then came into contact with Muslim merchants, scholars, and Sufis. The Sufis were active and quite successful proselytizers. So the nomads, as they approached what was then the Islamic heartland (which has since shifted eastward, at least with regard to demographic weight), were not denied entry by the Muslim "border guard" known as ghazis. The parallel decline of the 'Abbasid dynasty (discussed near the beginning of this chapter) enabled one group of such converted nomads, the Seljuqs, to establish a powerful central state in Baghdad in 1055 C.E. But they faced a skeptical population, for Turks were seen as alien by Arabs. So they were eager to demonstrate their Islamic soundness and did so through their massive support of a state system of schools (madrasas) and mosques that followed the four recognized schools of Sunni jurisprudence. Meanwhile, faced with the arbitrary rule of the warlords finally pushed aside by the Seljuqs, the 'ulama had emerged as community leaders rather than just informal spiritual and moral leaders. Christians whose churches no longer had the means and intellectual vitality to support them, and faced with growing social and economic deprivation, followed those 'ulama and converted. The Seljuq state formalized that situation: the only means of intellectual, social, and economic advancement was to be part of their state system. To do so, one had to be Muslim. A tendency already in motion snowballed. Most of the people within the Seljuq domains were to become Muslim.[142]

Many have the impression that the Christian flight into Islam was hastened in the aftermath of the Crusades. However, the various accounts we have of Muslim actions and attitudes throughout that interlude once again reveal just how resistant to barbarism Muslims generally were. As late as a century after the first Crusade, Muslims still did not see Christians as their enemies; indeed, they locally joined Christians in alliances against other Muslim forces whose intentions they did not savor. Early successes against the Crusaders were more likely to have been motivated by the desire of warlords and princes to expand their domains than that to expel the Europeans. When the tide at last turned in favor of an openly anti-Christian Muslim underground, its members were subordinated to the political elite: no reprisals were permitted. The conversions that did occur on a large scale were therefore a result of the trend already discussed: the defeat of the Crusaders resulted in an expansion of the central state that structurally tilted the balance toward the adoption of the Muslim religion. This was politically consolidated by the Mamluks, who had also defeated the Mongols (in 1260 C.E.) and saved the Levant from their scourge. The Mamluks, entirely composed of a non-Arab military caste originally brought into service as slaves, were keen to affirm their Islamic credentials. We are back with the rationale of the Seljuq state and its (unintended) influence on Middle Eastern religious demography.[143]

From then on, the Christian position grew steadily worse. Their decline in Anatolia illustrates this poignantly: "Before the Turkish migrations, the Greek, Armenian, Georgian, and Syrian population of Anatolia was in the vast majority Christian. By the fifteenth century more than 90 percent of the population was Muslim. Some of this change was due to the immigration of a large Muslim population, but in great part it was due to the conversion of Christians to Islam."[144]

The conversions largely took place because the Christian churches were left in disarray, not least owing to the confiscation of church revenues and properties, the exclusion of bishops from their sees, and the abandonment or destruction of monastaries, schools, hospitals, and orphanages. Muslim actions were directly responsible for these. But in the Balkans, the Muslim conquest had different consequences. Turkish migrations were on a much smaller scale, and the Balkan Orthodox Church was far stronger, helped in part by the Ottoman decision to preserve and safeguard it after the capture of Constantinople in 1453 C.E. Christianity could hence flourish there and remains the dominant religion today.[145]

Modernity has paradoxically contributed to the long Christian decline in the Near East. Initially, despite the memory of the Crusades, Muslim-European relations (which are always reflected in local Muslim-Christian relations) were not hostile. In the eighteenth century, despite their negative attitude toward Islam, the European imagination was stirred by the need or urge to travel to distant, exotic lands, and newly wealthy Europeans sought to add items to collections that filled their mansions and palaces. The Muslims were driven by their sense of an ascendant force to be faced and feared to learn more about Europeans and their lands; so they mingled freely with them and those who lived among them (usually local Christians). The secrets of European power thereby acquired were later translated into practical steps, through modern engineering methods, military science, printing presses, and so on. Alas, by the end of the eighteenth century, the Europeans became quite conscious of their power and before long, in an all-too-human manner, imposed it. Their individual demeanor changed correspondingly from benign acquaintance and curiosity to distance and disdain.[146] Muslims hence experienced political, military, economic, social, and personal humiliation, and resentment built up against the greatest beneficiaries of European preponderance: Near Eastern Christians. This explains the outrageous and otherwise insane pogrom perpetrated against the Christians of Damascus on July 9, 1861, just when the Druze-Christian conflict in Lebanon had been winding down (and which itself had been fed, but not entirely caused, by European meddling). Violence or the fear thereof then spread to every Christian community in Syria, Lebanon, and Palestine. Some reports mention that entire villages converted to Islam in Palestine to avert persecution.[147]

To the widespread sense of humiliation and defenselessness among Muslims must be added the factors that have contributed to the narrowness of Islamic possibilities in modern times recapitulated at the end of the previous section of this chapter: the tendency of the struggle against Western dominance or hegemony to increase the clout of fanatics; the similar effect of local despotic regimes enjoying the power at the disposal of the modern state; modern conformism and oversimplification (reflected in a conformist and oversimplified revolutionary Islam); and the erosion of faith and its replacement with the symbols of faith (which enables many to measure their fidelity to Islam through their aversion to Christians, Hindus, or Jews).[148] If these have all led to less freedom for Muslims, one can only imagine the consequences for non-Muslims. It seems that how a Muslim treats others depends on the depth and breadth of his understanding of Islam, and a certain amount of confidence in its world standing.

The Status of Women and Freedom in an Islamic Milieu

Modern society teems with those who obsessively devote their energies to a single issue at the expense of their own humanity and that of others. We must therefore be wary of allowing our discussion to be compromised by the success that fanatics have recently had in casting the relevant discourse in their image. When it comes to dealing with the status of women in the Arab Muslim world, we must above all avoid anachronism. An enormous amount of literature deals with the present dynamic of this issue, to which there is nothing to add here. However, some historical points are worthy of mention to properly evaluate the Islamic component of how women have generally fared in the domains under its sway.

One well-known fact bears repetition. The prophet Muhammad himself was *employed* by a successful businesswoman several years his senior, a woman whom he subsequently married and who bore him several children. Her name, as every Muslim knows, was Khadija. From this fact alone, two important conclusions may be drawn. No Muslim who disrespects women and who denies them work can claim to follow the example of the prophet of Islam; and no modernist overwhelmed with the feminist agenda can claim that women in the regions later under Islamic rule were previously structurally subordinated (else how could Khadija have assumed a prominent place in the caravan trade?).

That women indeed found themselves in a subordinate position in the Arab Muslim world has a complex cultural and sociological explanation. Moreover, they were not subordinate in the sense that we automatically attribute to the word today, and their subordination was not ordained in the Qur'an in an unqualified manner:

> Say to the believing men
> That they should lower
> Their gaze and guard
> Their modesty: that will make
> For greater purity of them:
> And God is well acquainted
> With all that they do.
>
> And say to the believing women
> That they should lower
> Their gaze and guard
> Their modesty; that they
> Should not display their
> Beauty and ornaments except
> What [must ordinarily] appear
> Thereof; that they should
> Draw their veils over
> Their bosoms and not display
> Their beauty except
> To their husbands, their fathers,
> Their husbands' fathers, their sons,
> Their husbands' sons . . .
> . . . and that they
> Should not strike their feet

In order to draw attention
To their hidden ornaments . . .[149]

We notice, first of all, that modesty and the "lowering of their gaze" is commanded of women and men, and that this is ultimately for turning their attention to God rather than to one another (which is characteristic of Islam)—and not for governing "power relations" between them. Second, we notice that the list of people to whom women could "display their beauty" is fairly extensive, especially if one should consider the size of families and the extent of their intertwining in Arabia (and throughout much of Africa and Asia today). Finally, what women must do about their exact appearance, to conform with those Qur'anic commands, is left vague and most definitely does not entail the kind of veil typical of Saudi Arabia, Afghanistan, or Iran (where, as we shall see in the next chapter, the *chador* has turned increasingly flamboyant). What, for instance, is that aspect of feminine beauty and charm that "must ordinarily appear" so that it is exempted from deliberate concealment?

These verses suggest a similar rationale to that given in the foregoing discussion about Muslim-Christian relations. The Qur'an does not encourage Muslims to suppress women, but Muslim men inclined to do so can believe themselves supported by it without wild flights of fancy. They can, if they so wish, enforce a literal interpretation of "lowering one's gaze" and understand veiling in a more stringent sense than that implied by the Qur'an. But the Qur'an, and Islamic teachings on the whole, *improved* the lot of women. Women were given certain inheritance rights, for instance, and were allowed to retain possession of property they had owned before their marriage. Above all, Islam urged men to treat women with respect, to regard them as human beings rather than mere belongings (which was typical of pre-Islamic Arabia). This meant an invaluable change in attitudes from what women had known before. That the *practice* of Muslims has often been at variance with the spirit of Islam[150] has to do with other facts, which we briefly turn to next.

The various modes of puritanical behavior, which is never far enough from fanatical outbreaks, all seem traceable to the concerns of the piety-minded at Medina once Islam ruled over an empire and thus became hostage to imperial logic. We have examined the ensuing distortions suffered by Islam on the political and intellectual planes, and have seen how it affected Muslim-Christian relations by the time the imperium had evolved into a strong central state under the Seljuqs. The position of women in Islamic realms was also pushed in a negative direction, so that the piety-minded beheld Qur'anic ambivalence, even if pervaded with a positive underlying spirit, as consecrating subordination. Not given to festive outpourings even during the best of times, the guardians of Islam were dismayed with the song and dance that swept through Mecca with the wealth gained in conquest, and ill at ease with the sight of sirens and the sounds of love lyrics—so they decreed the separation of men and women during the ritual circumambulations of the *Ka'ba*.[151] A little later, Islam itself had an unintended consequence prejudicial to women, for the egalitarian practice encouraged by Islam created conditions that made well-born women mingle freely with men and women from lower classes. Those women then began to veil themselves to mark themselves off. Before long, the well-born segregated from those with humbler origins (and those judged to engage in less noble pursuits). The shari'a never made that segregation explicit. On the contrary, having recognized the Islamically dubious grounds for that segregation, the veil was not permitted during the *hajj*, precisely because it had become a mark of social distinction.[152]

Meanwhile, a more insidious reality was to impose itself on Islamic life. The regions under Islamic rule mostly coincided with an environment where social status was constantly in flux. This is because the economy of the vast arid stretch between the Atlas mountains of Morocco and the eastern end of inner Asia did not permit long-term social hierarchies nor wealth to endure over several generations. The men in those arid zones thus had to rely disproportionately on their "honor," an attitude allowed by geography and the endemic misery of the middle period of Islam to carry over from tribal society. Male honor rested mainly on two things: revenge as fixed by family feuds; and sexual mores. A man largely came to identify his wealth with the degree to which he was secure in possessing his woman (or women). The jealousy entailed was so pathological that access to women was steadily reduced to almost nil. Strict veiling became the norm. Separate quarters were built for women to head off the remotest possibility of a chance encounter with a stranger. For the upper class, these quarters were the infamous harems. The severity of the measures to possess his women became such that to even mention them to a man in conversation was considered indecorous. One can only imagine—quite easily, nowadays—the deformations and perversions that followed on the sexual plane.[153]

Muslim clerics were powerless to stop these severe distortions of the position of women in Islam. Many tacitly acceded to them, being after all part of the same culture. But the Islamic religion is not responsible for such abominations. What happened is clearly the dark side of a culture's triumph over the limits imposed by religious strictures (and indicates the bright side of the strictures when faced with some of what human beings left to their own devices are capable of).

For all that, women were far from reduced to silenced playmates. The social scene acquired such complexity that one must resort to highly informal accounts to describe how they managed to retain an influential position. Although not engaged in public life, women, through the mere exigencies of social and economic life, made themselves quite indispensable. Through guile and psychological games common in male-female interaction, they could bear strongly on their husbands and sometimes dominate them. Sexual blackmail was not unheard of. The veil was not universally worn. Usually, urban and middle-class women were veiled; working, peasant, and nomadic women were not.[154]

If we turn briefly to the contemporary situation, we hence do not find *Islamic* atavisms in the revolutionaries' attempt to draw the veil over women and their freedom of expression, but ancient, quasi-tribal attitudes that have endured *despite* of Islam, and have, like many other negative developments, become reinforced through the encounter with modernity. The specifics of this encounter are often written about. To mention some: There is the insecurity of rural folk in urban areas, where they need to assert their identity in what comes across as a disorienting milieu to them; greater attachment to the symbols of Islam (especially the coarser among them) to confront the perceived incipient hegemony of modern popular culture; fear of and opposition to the "West" (which leads to the affirmation of what most sets Muslims apart from the "West"); and the narrow-mindedness and fanaticism bred within modernity itself that, as has been repeatedly mentioned, have their reflections in the Arab Muslim world.

Concluding Remarks

In the previous chapter, we have seen how the profoundest expressions of positive freedom have been consistently possible within Islamdom. Positive freedom, in its core communal and personal sense, was indeed fostered by explicitly spelled out Islamic attitudes. In this chapter, however, we see that Muslims and others ruled by them suffered a number of significant unfreedoms. There was overall pain and misery at the socioeconomic level and because of the arbitrary and brutal hand of despotism. There was a great lack of political freedom. Intellectual life left much to be desired. Women were systematically oppressed. Christians and other non-Muslims were often allowed to suffer benign neglect or worse. All these unfreedoms linger, more or less residually, in the contemporary Arab Muslim world.

But it is egregious to root all the foregoing unfreedoms firmly in Islam. In many cases, Islam had to grudgingly coexist with developments it could do nothing to arrest. We have seen how the politico-military decline of the central lands of Islam had an internal logic quite unrelated to Islamic beliefs, laws, and attitudes. Political quietism, on the other hand, though it owed much to the Islamic preoccupation with civic peace, was transferred first to authorities that were so unfaithful to Islamic ideals as to merit no obedience from Muslims at all, and then to modern states that in their very nature could not possibly be Islamic. If political quietism became a central political tenet of Islam, that was under conditions that have changed so much as to make it moot. To the detriment of a more fruitful Islamic turn, the revolutionaries have made this discovery and have since dominated the activist Islamic scene. The restrictions on intellectual life perhaps owe more to Islam than the others. But Islam, as is well known, invites its followers to seek knowledge and learning wherever they may find it. The narrow view on intellectual life, for which al-Ghazzali bears *some* responsibility, developed in intense adversarial circumstances and survived in the ensuing uncompetitive climate that usually follows the long wake of decisive victory. Despite the uncompetitiveness, the legacy has been twofold: fallow grounds in some areas, broad intellectual-spiritual horizons in others, respectively and very roughly along the Sunni/Shiʻi, non-Persianate/Persianate divide. Women were mostly oppressed for social and cultural reasons that Muslim communal leaders, themselves belonging to that cultural background, saw it fit not to oppose. When the oppression became extreme, as in the case of the harem, Muslim religious authorities simply did not have enough power (or will?) to stop the practice. The oppression of Christians must be seen not only in the context of Islam's self-professed superiority over other monotheisms, for it claims to correct or complete them, but in that of the frequent warfare between the two domains and of how non-Christians were treated in lands ruled by Christians. The oppression of Christians has some roots in Islamic attitudes and practices, but it is hypocritical to divorce this from comparative situations. In this regard, the fate of Christians under Islam is decidedly better than it might have been. Only now are Christians under serious threat because of the ferocity of the Islamic encounter with modernity, which narrows Islamic horizons while it threatens the communal existence of Muslims and the solidity of their faith, and of which Christians (often unfairly, but not always without foundation) are seen as the agents. Contemporary Muslim intolerance of non-Muslims has much to do with factors that extend this intolerance to the breadth and subtlety of Islam itself. Islam itself ultimately stands to lose the most from successful Islamic revolutionary action.

7

Toward Greater Freedom in the Contemporary Arab Muslim World

The Intellectual Approach

The question of freedom in the Arab Muslim world is tied to that world's encounter with modernity. From modernity's standpoint, Islam may appear to circumscribe a realm of unfreedom. From Islam's standpoint, that same modernity seems a threat to cherished values, traditions, and ideals. Each emphasizes a different sense of freedom. The more positive the freedom, the more it has a home in Islam; the more negative the freedom, the more it is stressed and promoted by the more powerful and influential among those who have been acting on modernity's behalf.

The initial encounter between Islam and modernity could only be harsh. At the time, modernity rode the wave of Enlightenmentarian ideals of sovereign reason, individual freedom and choice, and voluntary association. If it took Islam time to see through the consequences of those ideals, it was quick to intuit their alienness. Only recently do we come across the renewed clarification of traditional Islamic positions: the authority of reason is not final, only God's. Freedom (in the negative sense) and choice must be constrained by the good of the community. This in turn is regarded as an integral whole rather than an aggregate of atomized individuals. There can be only that much compromise between Islam and the Enlightenment. Thus, so long as modernity did not question the Enlightenment, it was impossible for Islam to adopt it. Muslims who tried appeared less Muslim for doing so. And those who tried to reaffirm their Islam appeared more obscurantist as modernity's presence became more pronounced in the Arab Muslim world. Modernity's utter failure to understand Islam—to the extent that it held fast to the framework of the Enlightenment—and the force with which it intruded upon Islamic life were particularly repugnant. So were the practice of driving human energies with ruthless organization toward technological innovation and the improvement of material life, and the visible signs of social dissolution.

277

Since then, a series of developments have significantly reduced the gap between Islam and modernity. The presuppositions of the Enlightenment are unraveling. Its theoretical pillars have been eaten away by two centuries of criticism and the discovery that even physical science does not mainly advance through the independent use of reason. Its practical consequences at the environmental, social, moral, and spiritual levels are opaque only to its fanatical supporters. On another plane, modernity's geographic presence has become more diffuse. It has become intermeshed with life almost everywhere, so that the geographic congealment of civilizational alternatives (and hostilities) will soon become impossible. The spread of modernity and the elucidation of its erstwhile presumptions have changed the tone of its encounter with traditional civilizations—or, in the case of Islam, simply "other" civilizations, for it is incorrect to identify a religion with Islam's potential only with the traditional. For Islam to merge with modernity today no longer implies that it submit to modernity. It means the revolutionary opportunity for an Islamic modification of a modernity endemically nostalgic for the social, moral, and spiritual core heavily eroded by a prodigious economic, military, technological, and demographic upsurge. Conversely, Islam has no alternative but to take a constructive stand toward modernity, which has penetrated Islamdom irreversibly and is now a local factor everywhere. The modern imperative is reinforced by the new economic reality, several breakthroughs in communications, and increased global interdependence.

Just as Christianity is reemergent in the face of an exhausted and demoralized modernity (for all its muscle), so can Islam find strength in its preservation of the domain of moral and spiritual freedom (although this is an insufficiently explored potential owing to the sterility caused by retrenchment in the face of modernity's initially alien and hostile guise, and by an internal process of stagnation). The idea is for Islam, without ever turning its back on the core positive freedom to which it has been so congenial, to transpose such freedom to a more robust and pluralistic environment, where core positive freedom can thrive and an adequate response be made to the clamor for other freedoms. Thus, Islam can promote the freedom of women from the traditional manner in which they have been oppressed (which, as we have seen, has less to do with Islam than is commonly assumed). But it can also discourage women from uniformly following identical career paths as men in view of the horrendous social and communal price exacted where a rather simplistic notion of equality between the sexes has become institutionalized. It can encourage freedom of thought and dynamic intellectual exchanges without turning relativism into an unspoken creed; for intellectual freedom need not entail that people utterly lose their moral bearings, and certainly not that the opinions of children be so esteemed that they grow up unable to handle real arguments or make up their minds when faced with real choices. It can support freedom of expression while actively ensuring that the ability to discriminate is not thereby lost; for the freedom of expression without discrimination breeds an undiscriminating populace. Islamic society need not run the risk of no longer knowing where to draw the line by yielding to the hysteria that to draw it anywhere is to draw it everywhere; and so Islam can teach that tolerance does not mean the refusal to disagree strongly with what is strongly disagreeable.

The foregoing gives us a tentative idea of what Islam's meeting ground with modernity may look like once it is better defined. In the meantime, the shock of the initial encounter between Islam and modernity continues to divert their interplay from moderation. Early retrenchment reverberates and has become magnified in the activities of the Islamic revolutionaries. And the early rush into modernity has contemporary advocates in Muslims who range from apologism on behalf of Islam to renunciation, and non-Muslims blissfully ignorant of the extent of modernity's limitations. The conflict between these adversaries gains the headlines, gives the semblance of perpetual civilizational war, and makes the prospects for freedom in the Arab Muslim world fairly dismal. At the same time, the more civilized encounter is gradually shaped between modernity's revisionists and Muslims able to grasp their momentous revisions, follow Islam meaningfully, and deal constructively with modernity. These are engaged in what is more properly termed a dialogue rather than a conflict. If the profundity of this dialogue is given sufficient expressive scope by the contemporary global situation—and it is by no means clear that such will be the case—then the transformation that alone can sustain the freedoms aspired for will be effected.

Assuming that the battle between the fanatics of modernity and Islam does not scorch the ground for freedom, each unfreedom expounded upon in the previous chapter can turn to freedom as follows:

Contra Despotism and Socioeconomic Misery

These can recede along two different axes. Several global developments have made despotism less tenable than ever. Despots can no longer control the flow of information as before. Borders can no longer be tightly sealed. Access to other ways of life and viewpoints is constant. Centralized economies can have only a limited success, so that much state revenue must depend on some form of private enterprise. International pressure, despite inconsistent application and occasionally questionable motives, is routinely brought to bear on rulers who openly abuse their people.

The current situation does not favor despots—not the crude, tangible sort, at any rate. However, it may look upon the gross socioeconomic inequity with indifference. Here is where Islam comes in. For Islam is clearly on the side of social justice and condemns the callous treatment of the less fortunate. It stipulates help for the needy. And in view of the inapplicability of the traditional injunction to obey those in authority, for several reasons,[1] it can rally the populace against rulers who continue to act unjustly. It has become Islamically legitimate to match the greater power of the modern state with greater resistance from Islamic institutions and individuals in the event that the state is unjust. Islamic activism need not take fanatical and, in their own way, despotic forms. It can move peacefully and gradually through the formation of informal alternatives to the state. Where Muslims financially supported by the private sector can build and run their own schools, hospitals, mosques, cooperatives, and even utilities, the state becomes irrelevant. This had been the case to some extent in Algeria,[2] for instance, before Islamic activism turned more confrontational and now, thanks to the government crackdown, has become more extreme than the Iranian revolution was at its height. Also, the informal marginalization of the state is, as has become more widely known, well under way in Egypt.

Contra Political Unfreedom

Traditional Islamic political thought was articulated in difficult external circumstances, so that ideals were more a reminder to Muslims and their rulers of how things might (and should) have been rather than a call for action. The injunction to obey those in authority for at least a semblance of political unity, which really was a symbol of the unity of the community of all Muslims, directed them to live with what was given and concentrate on their moral and religious lives. Such thought, to its credit, holds before itself the principle that a morally and religiously sound population will effect a state that reflects this. Sound states, however, were not common throughout the Arab Muslim world. And there is widespread disaffection with the present state system.

The modern period has introduced the idea that political unfreedom is not necessarily something given, in the sense that one should live with it as best one can. The situation can be changed. Collective action can win political freedom for all. This has not escaped the people of the Arab Muslim world. So far as the Islamic frame of mind is concerned, we have seen how it would be disastrous, given the much greater power and intrusiveness of the modern state, to continue to espouse quietism. We have also seen how the attempt to Islamize the modern state will eventually compromise Islamic aspirations. Given that the modern state in its very makeup and as one situated in a complex tangle of intertwined states cannot be genuinely Islamized, nor can Muslims unquestioningly obey the heads of modern states without severe consequences, it seems that the authorities to whom obedience has been traditionally pledged will split into independent Muslim bodies that act as watchdogs and apply pressure on the state whenever necessary, and a system of government deemed just and fair. On both counts, political freedom will be significantly greater than at present—otherwise resentment will turn explosive, especially when faced with the apparent international reluctance to promote Muslim self-expression as has been done for others in Latin America and eastern Europe, a reluctance regarded by Muslims as haughty, hypocritical, and derisory.

The new Islamic political philosophy will require a reinterpretation of the doctrine that Islam is a religion and a state. Taken literally, the doctrine becomes self-undermining for Islam, for it insists on the Islamization of an un-Islamizable modern state. "State," however, surely has no constant meaning ranging equally over Muhammad's Medinan community, the Islamic empire, and the contemporary system of states in the Arab Muslim world. If the Medinan paradigm was a state, and it could be usefully applied as a model to keep the imperial state well within the ideals of Islam, the modern state is far too different for "state" to have anything other than an analogous meaning at best when used for the various political formations throughout the history of Islam. Hence, if Islam has been a religion and a state, and it has definitely been so in the case of the first community of Muslims, and partly so in the empire's heyday, it is not so today—not because Islam is no longer a religion and a state in the absolute, but because the meaning of "state" has changed beyond recognition since the days of the Revelations. Muslim thinkers and jurists are thus faced with defining "state" in a historically plausible manner, to ensure that one of Islam's central doctrines stands without losing its applicability. A return to the more genuine sense of "state," as condition (halat), as some Shi'ites now advocate (although these same Shi'ites do not yet appreciate how far the modern state would not serve Islam well if Islamized), may be a step in the right direction, combined with the clear demarcation of the different meanings of "state" and what exactly is meant by the doctrine. Such a development has the added benefit of defusing the apprehensions of non-Muslims for whom an Islamic state, traditionally interpreted, still means the institutionalization of various unfreedoms.

The framework for political freedom need not replicate liberal democratic thought. Although it is impossible to Islamize the modern state, Islamic bodies (and other religious bodies for that matter[3]) may be far more politically influential than the Church is in western Europe and North America. And while a process may be developed in which the aspirations of the people are fairly represented, it need not rest single-mindedly on the mechanics of elections. There is much room for imaginative political thought, given the universal longing for political freedom, strong Islamic sentiment, and several groups of non-Muslims in the Arab

Muslim world whose rights must be respected, from the fifty million Christians in Nigeria to the large mainly Confucian Chinese minority in Malaysia.

Contra Intellectual and Cultural Unfreedom

The greatest obstacle to intellectual and other freedoms in Islam is the controversial notion of "innovation" or bid'a. Once the communal model for Islam had been worked out more than a thousand years ago, anything that departed from it was rejected as an (illegitimate) innovation. From the standpoint of the Medinan paradigm, based on the small community built by the Prophet and his first associates, details about which had become known to later generations through meticulously tested (if sometimes nevertheless spurious) reports about the founders' words and deeds, "innovation" and "illegitimacy" are synonymous. How then can there fail to be severe restrictions on Islamic life, above all on creativity?

There are several ways around this restriction, none of which would require its express renunciation. Each revolves around the meaning of the key terms to be interpreted, "paradigm community," "reports" (about the Medinan community), and "innovation" (not in the absolute, but always relative to the paradigm community).

In chapter 5, we saw how a code emerged to regulate personal and social life in accordance with the Medinan paradigm. More important for our purposes here, we saw how the three principles in which the code was grounded were transformed as the nature of the Islamic domains changed, from a single community at Medina to a vast Islamic empire containing a non-Arab and (at the time) non-Muslim majority. For instance, the final reference for the approval or disapproval of an act shifted from direct appeal to what Muhammad or his contemporaries did, first to the Qur'an (thus replacing a personal with a textual reference), and then to the Qur'an and the reports that supplemented it (which were ideally the unadulterated transmission across several generations by reliable men of the actions of Muhammad and his contemporaries). So a personal reference became a textual reference augmented with chronicles of varying reliability. The very ground for the derivation of the code that preserved the communal paradigm was allowed to shift with the changing political and cultural realities of Islam as it expanded into other domains. It can thus be argued that though there has been little Islamic expansion in modern times (other than in Africa), the reality of the Arab Muslim world has changed dramatically in the past two centuries. The modern upheaval represents at least as radical a break with the premodern situation as imperial Islam did with the Medinan community. If once, the three principles that grounded the code that allows Muslims to live by the Medinan paradigm shifted, then surely they could shift again given an equally compelling justification. The intersection of Islam with modernity provides such justification. This does not mean that the essential ideals promoted by the code are no longer valid. These, as we have seen, were the greatest possible protection of individual rights, protection of the weak against the strong, the rejection of usury and fraudulent business exchanges (or exchanges heavily tilted in one party's favor), regard for personal dignity, equal rights for women, the proper performance of prayer and pilgrimage, fair inheritance, and a just criminal law. Many of these ideals are timeless. How can it ever be outdated to value dignity or individual rights? How can it become undesirable to have a fair criminal law or protect the weak against the strong? The only change can be in the specific content assigned to those ideals. Depending on the concepts central to those ideals, change spreads across a continuum. This ranges from relatively changeless concepts, such as "dignity," to concepts that retain a core content but otherwise shift, such as "individual rights," to those whose content may change substantially, such as "women's rights" or "just criminal law."

The purpose of the code itself, which is to promote the good of the community as envisioned at Medina, cannot retain the same meaning. The less communities resemble, or can conceivably resemble, the Muhammadan community at Medina, the less they can adhere to its letter and the more they must turn to its spirit. To the extent that the Qur'an is closer to the spirit and the reports closer to the letter (which is not always the case), this may leave much room for the articulation of the good of the community in modern times consistently with the Qur'an but perhaps not so mindful of those reports that clearly pertain to the letter.

Certainly when al-Ghazzali was concerned with the good of the community, he did not think of it as frozen in time. When, for instance, he thought about the role played by the community in providing truth, wisdom, and guidance for its members, he appealed to "the living community," which "made [him] . . . somewhat careless of proper isnad documentation in citing hadith reports. It was the present community, not that of Marwani times or even Medinan times, that played the role of guarantor."[4]

It was just as well that al-Ghazzali did not worry about the establishment of the reliability of the reports. For these could rarely be demonstrated to have been transmitted through an unbroken chain of reputable and reliable men leading all the way back to Muhammad. Reports were more often accepted on much weaker grounds. Some were invented by pious men who assumed that whatever was good for the (living) community must have been said by Muhammad himself. A report was "transmitted" that approved of such a practice.[5] There thus are two ways in which the contemporary community can be brought in harmony with the reports. Either mould the reports to conform with the contemporary conception of the good of the community, as has been done in the past without objection, or ignore all those whose ascription to Muhammad and his associates is in doubt—which means most of them. Either way, there is no solid ground for the reports to continue to impede a more dynamic vision of the communal good.

Based on the foregoing, what does it mean to reject something because it is deemed an innovation? What would innovation be relative to? Surely not the Medinan community as it literally was. For the entire Arab Muslim world is living a multitude of innovations, and irreversibly so, relative to the life of the first community of Muslims. So divergent from this is the contemporary situation that little more than a mythology can arise around the prototype. Innovation can no longer be denied relative to the Medinan paradigm in the literal sense. "What should be placed in question is not, if you will, the original perfection of these norms as they were revealed, but the modality of their temporal application."[6] But what, then, is the spirit of the Medinan paradigm? This can be fathomed by Muslims steeped in the Qur'an and their rich lore (as we shall see in the latter part of this chapter). Mostly, however, the spirit cannot specify the letter. Earlier in this book, when we first came upon the shifts in the principles that grounded the derivation of the code, the idea of "change that somehow leaves [Muslim] life attuned to its enduring spirit" suggested itself. This is possible. Hard as it is to recapture the details of the Medinan community, Islam endured continuously through the Qur'an and the unbroken *presence* of Muhammad and his associates (never mind the specifics of that presence). What we have here is an intuitive and spiritual continuity, guaranteed by an unchanging text. The determination of communal forms and laws given these must be a creative endeavor. The entire contemporary situation of the Muslim community is one that *demands* innovation. Bid'a can no longer mean the summary dismissal of innovative work, for the good of the community now depends on it, but the reminder that innovation remain within the spirit of Islam. It can no longer mean frozenness in time, but must be relative to a combination of the eternally valid and the constantly changing.

The Islamic ideal must therefore turn to something like "modern communities infused with the spirit and consistent with the distillation of the Medinan paradigm." If the good of the Muslim community depends on such a turn, then to deny it is a transgression equivalent to earlier departures from the paradigm when it was relatively well defined and viable. The very articulation of the turn will involve much *ibda'*, or creative brilliance, a word etymologically related to bid'a and cast aside when bid'a was a serious offense.

To illustrate how the new turn might be applied to specific innovations, consider the cinema and television. The cinema is literally an innovation. Thus literally minded Muslims are inclined to ban the cinema (which also calls up the periodic Muslim aversion to pictorial representation, especially in Arab lands). On the other hand, directors such as Tarkovsky, Kieslowski, Olmi, Bergman, and Bresson have proved that great religious movies can be made, every bit as edifying as any other religious art. Films can also deal sensitively and beautifully with the general human condition, take on difficult philosophical themes, narrate historical epics to tremendous effect, and entertain children constructively. They can entertain neutrally. And they can entertain destructively. Any Muslim jurist in tune with the contemporary good of his community would find it ridiculous to ban the cinema altogether and, in some cases, harmful to the community (for the community would be deprived of worthy enrichment through an easily accessible medium). At most, he would recommend the prohibition of films that serve no other purpose than the flagrant exploitation of sex and violence and that satisfy and nurture the basest instincts. He may caution against harmless, but also "useless," entertainment (although he would thereby be insensitive to the need for such diversion and the value of its enjoyment). But all the rest is surely compatible with the good of the community.

Similarly for television. One can only decry the dross heaped upon passive viewers and subtly shaping their minds, or how television disrupts gatherings, so that people no longer talk to one another, but are drawn to the displays before them. Ordinary healthy conversation and storytelling are compromised by television in the living room. But the wholesale condemnation and prohibition of television would not only be unworkable but also ludicrous. The content of what is broadcast depends on the broadcasters, and can equally be harmful, neutral, or beneficial to the community.

More generally, because the contemporary situation of the Muslim community calls for innovation through and through, a profound change in intellectual life recommends itself. Innovative thought needs surroundings that continuously encourage free and creative thought. Again, this does not mean that Muslims ought to encourage secular fanatics who interpret freedom to mean their freedom to desecrate the sacred, sometimes in unimaginably vulgar ways. The rise of secular fanatics who overinterpret their consitutionally guaranteed freedoms can only feed religious fanaticism and is ultimately a cause for unfreedom. Muslims can find their way to a more delicately balanced conception of what the freedom of thought and expression involve.

Among the intellectual problems to be worked out is the role of reason. This book repeatedly emphasizes the dependence of reason and warns that to promote the ultimate sovereignty of reason is effectively to cede authority to whatever thrives under such conditions, notably the materialistic view of human life and aspirations combined with a morality based on self-interest. Because Kant and other major figures could in their day take for granted a modicum of good moral and communal sense (Kant was of course committed to more than this), they could be excused for not seeing where the ideal of the ultimate sovereignty of reason might lead. We may recall that Kant saw far beyond the prevalent understanding of "reason." In retrospect, the ideals of the Enlightenment are viable, from a broad human perspective, only if good moral and communal sense prevail. And these can prevail only when they are the object of an explicit commitment and there is awareness of their origin or foundation and conviction in the validity of these. Islam is therefore favorably positioned inasmuch as it naturally views reason as dependent and affirms revelation as the higher authority. If anything, Islam is prone to the other extreme. The Islamic equilibrium then is for the realization to come about that the dependence of reason on revelation does not entail the rejection of, for instance, the possibility that intelligent discussion of moral values, the nature of faith, the limits of the empirical world, or transcendence may profoundly enrich cultural life, and that such discussion bears fruit only when minds frolic in myriad intellectual fields. Furthermore, the definite center on which Islamic life converges, and the unalterable textual nature of the revelation, need not entail that the objects of serious moral, religious, and philosophical discussion have been laid out comprehensively, and with such finality that no more than minor interpretive work remains necessary. To do so is to imprison Islamic thought, and consequently a major portion of cultural life, in necessarily transient embodiments of a revelation whose depth and open-ended, encompassing nature demand repeated dynamic interpretations. To deny this is to cause the inevitable disembodiment of a temporal set of views about the revelation from the revelation they had embodied. This is one of the crisis areas of Islam. The intellectual faculties on which dynamic interpretations are contingent have been allowed to fall short of the task at hand, thus causing spasmodic jumps between static interpretations that have lost their vitality and dynamic outbursts that are not really interpretations of the revelation at hand. Hence the culturally barren duel between out-of-touch traditionalists and up-to-date fanatics, a duel that has not obliterated more thoughtful and viable alternatives, but has made the context for their articulation as distant as it is urgent.

Reason is not the sole agency of the renewed intellectual and cultural drive in Islam. Just as one must acknowledge that the dependence of reason on revelation does not entail the virtual incarceration of reason, so must one insist that reason does not have a monopoly over intellectual and cultural openness. If the power of reason is in the organization and clarity of thought, then thought would be sterile without the further contributions of the imagination, intuition, insight, and certain aptitudinal qualities. (For one cannot escape from aesthetic, moral, or metaphysical aptitudes that cannot be further explained but are crucial to the shaping of the relevant outlooks.) These are often neglected in the modern emphasis on reason, or reduced to the narrow terms in which they can be rationally presented and appreciated (which amounts to the fundamental lack of appreciation of what they are). They may in turn be empowered with grace and driven by faith. They constitute a fluid and vast middle terrain between reason and revelation. Like all other middle ground, they tend to vanish whenever there is polarization. They are often absent in the discourse of secular intellectuals throughout the Arab Muslim world whose usual appeal away from the constriction of outworn interpretations of the revelation is to reason. And they are hardly more in evidence in the work of Muslim revolutionaries and that of the more conservative traditionalists. Ideally, intellectual and cultural freedom in Islam seems to hinge on the open use of reason generally turned toward revelation, with the infinity between them significantly bridged by the imagination, intuition, insight, and one's own aesthetic, moral, and spiritual aptitudes. And for such freedom to bear fruit, the insistence on the explicit convergence of everything upon revelation is harmful.

Given such intellectual freedom, this reflects on what has been discussed concerning political freedom. For it would become easier to disseminate and exchange ideas regarding the status of the injunction to obey those in authority and the famous credo "Islam is a religion and a state." And to aniticipate, it would become possible to deal with the condition of women and non-Muslim minorities in a way that would result in acceptable positions.

Contra Unfreedom for Women and Religious Minorities

The scriptural obstacles to the more equitable and respectful treatment of women are not intractable. The Qur'anic basis for the oppression of women seems to rest on verses like those at 24:31.[7] Much hinges on how *zinatuhunna* is interpreted. Yusuf Ali takes it to include both natural beauty and artificial ornaments, with emphasis on natural beauty.[8] Cragg, on the other hand, translates the word as "their charms."[9] What is meant, for instance, by urging women to refrain from displaying their charms? Does it have the same meaning from one millennium to the next? Against a cultural background that supports the habit of viewing women as the possession of their men, to be guarded as strictly as possible from male "predators," the temptation to use the passage in the Qur'an to confine women to their private quarters and cover them from head to toe whenever they venture outside is hard to resist. Such a mentality will dust all sorts of chronicles about the early Muhammadan practice in support. If, however, women are less obsessively viewed in terms of pride of possession, which makes their least exposure compromise the "honor" of their men, then the same Qur'anic passage might (1) simply be taken in an advisory capacity or, at least, (2) be interpreted to mean that women should not unsettle the men with whom they mingle through excessive displays of their charms. In a few cases, any display of any female charm will capture the attention of some men. But to ensure that this never takes place, one must practically stop women from living. Surely the Qur'an did not intend that. The verses at 24:31 can be aimed, if they are judged to have continuing literal relevance in our context, only at specific situations that might poison relations between the sexes—for instance at work.

More daring Muslim jurists, especially faced with changing public mores they are powerless to stop, might extend the hermeneutic exercise of determining the meaning of a pivotal term to the whole passage in relation to the context for revelation—and decide that in the contemporary world, it no longer represents an improvement for women to have them live by a strict, or even moderate, interpretation of the verses at 24:31. It very likely leads to oppression. But just as Islam profoundly improved the condition of women at the time of the revelation, not least because the Qur'an also implored men to act more chastly and modestly and set boundaries for philandery, and just as the Qur'an became the vehicle for that improvement, so can Islam through the very same Qur'an see to it that women are no longer oppressed and the cultural traditions that have supported that oppression are no longer to be met with inaction, silence, perfunctory protestation, or furtive support.

The problem, then, appears to turn on two breakthrough points. The first is the general difficulty of whether a specific Qur'anic injunction whose *literal* content is clearly anachronistic might be overruled without violating the Qur'an, and the second is the struggle against a deeply rooted cultural habit that has caused too much harm to too many people in the region. Again, this does not mean that the relations between the sexes must resemble those where women's liberation has become institutionalized. Muslims do not need to swing to the other extreme and undermine the family, which Islam has consistently and successfully supported, or confuse men and women so ludicrously that they are made to see their sex as acquired!

The first breakthrough is easier than one might think. The ground for the admission that certain Qur'anic injunctions no longer apply because of changing circumstances is there in the Qur'an itself. The Qur'an openly describes how its own verses may supersede one another.

> When we substitute one revelation
> For another,—and God knows best
> What He reveals (in stages),—
> They say, "Thou art but a forger":
> But most of them understand not.[10]

> None of Our revelations
> Do We abrogate
> Or cause to be forgotten,
> But We substitute
> Something better or similar.[11]

In the same spirit, if the specificity of a verse is such that it could refer only to a specific time and culture, and not to all times and cultures, which would make it impossible for that verse to be superseded within the Qur'an given the actual temporal and cultural context of the revelations, then it can be argued that the specific content of the same verse would be different today, that indeed it would have to be different. And this would be Qur'anically inconsistent only to literalists. Besides, such an interpretive exercise would not undercut the authority of the Qur'an because most of its verses are not constrained by a time-and culture-bound specificity. On the contrary, the failure to understand the nature and implications of time-and culture-bound verses that specify conduct in detail, through the insistence that they are literally eternal, would, faced with the insurmountable gap between them and the contemporary cultural reality, itself undercut the Qur'an's authority *among Muslims*. The ideas put forward here extend to the entire spectrum of problems that result from time- and culture-bound verses in the Qur'an.

The issue of Muslim relations with other religious minorities throughout the Arab Muslim world is perhaps the most inflammatory and must be treated with care and sensitivity. To begin with, the current global situation does not favor an attenuation of the most persistent confrontation line of them all, that between Islam and Christianity. Those who celebrate the global village do not realize that precisely that vision terrifies Muslims, who like many others fear for their identity. Because the apparently relentless drive toward the global village has originated in at least nominally Christian lands, it is possible for Muslims to perceive yet another source of enmity between themselves and Christians. This can only compound the by now explosive Muslim resentment over how their domains have been systematically dominated by what to them are Christian powers (even though, again, the sense in which these powers are Christian has been increasingly nominal). The unabating condescension and superiority with which official Western pronouncements pertaining to the Arab Muslim world are intoned have made matters worse still. That some Christians in the Arab Muslim world, themselves ripe for a reassertion of their aspirations, have echoed the tone of those pronouncements and assisted in the penetration of modernity has been enough for the less subtle among the Muslims to see all Christians in their midst as a fifth column—economically, militarily, and culturally.

In the previous chapter,[12] we have come across the paradoxical tendency of modernity to at once act centrifugally and centripetally upon those societies it has penetrated. We have seen how Muslims fearful of fragmentation narrowed the realm of difference even among Muslims as they regrouped to confront the European powers. We have also seen how an internal dynamic, combining imperial or state logic with the reaction against heterodoxy, had already begun to limit Islamic options. If Muslims thus became intolerant of genuine debate among themselves, how could they be expected to treat non-Muslims? And if non-Muslims were further perceived as agents of fragmentation, then their prospects seemed unenviable. Add to this the related problem that has also been mentioned, namely, the growing distance between Muslims and their own religious experience. As we saw, the greater the distance, the greater the dependence on the perpetuation of the *images* of religious experience. This involves the sometimes mindless application of the strictures and other externals of religion, often vulgarized, as many Muslim revolutionaries tend to do. The more the outward manifestations of Islam gain in importance, the less it becomes possible to accept those who are obviously and unavoidably outwardly different, namely, non-Muslims. Some manifestos issued by extremist Muslim groups appear to strive for an outwardly exclusively Muslim society consisting of individuals who mimic a coarsened and superficialized Islam. Such an unfortunate abandonment of the inward implications of religion is among the progeny of modernity.[13]

If the foregoing were the only factors at play, then non-Muslims (and a great many Muslims) do not have much to look forward to. We have seen the rise of Jewish, Christian, and Hindu militancy. In its own right, the creation of a Jewish state in the Arab Muslim world has further narrowed the logical lines of Islamic statehood, already under the various pressures that have been mentioned. (The corrupting influence of this vicious circle on the Jewish religion and traditions is also noteworthy.) In Lebanon, we have witnessed an armed rebellion on behalf of its Christians spearheaded and peopled by men as far removed from the Christian vision and values as one can imagine, and frequently contemptuous of these. In some other Arab countries, notably Egypt, the Christians are under much more pressure than before; but where, as in Egypt, armed rebellion is out of the question, they are at a loss over what to do and contemplate emigration as a more realistic option.[14] Nigeria, which for a while has effected a workable framework for the coexistence of its Christians and Muslims, perhaps mindful of the cost of civil war after the Biafran tragedy, is at a critical juncture. Meanwhile in India, where Muslims are a sizeable minority, and which shares a long border with two of the most populous Muslim countries, Hindu militancy has been on the rise and is diminishing the prospects for communal peace (although one ought not underestimate the resiliency of the tolerant streak within Hinduism). Even the once successful and admired model of power sharing in Malaysia between Muslim Malays and ethnic Chinese may be under some threat, albeit remote at this time because more easily abated.[15]

How can non-Muslims expect freedom under those circumstances, when we remember that many Muslims also feel compromised in their self-expression? From a Muslim point of view, the key once again lies in the depths of the crisis described in the previous section. The revitalization of Islam itself demands a visionary framework that restores the full implications of its original openness and open-endedness. Because the Islamic condition calls for creativity and inventiveness at a fundamental level, there is no room, as far as the community's future well-being is concerned, for platforms that reduce Islam to a coarse aggregate of externals and Muslim life to conformity with these. In other words, the narrowness that equally makes non-Muslims *and other Muslims* suffer and impoverishes their lives is incompatible with contemporary *Islamic* expression in the serious and far-reaching sense. Islam did not become a great world religion, nor will it continue to be one, because of a parody of itself.

As part of the fashioning of the new dynamic framework, we have seen how prior shifts in the principles that ground the Islamic code justify further shifts under equally compelling circumstances—and modernity represents just such a compelling reason for further shifts. The principle that concerns us here is that which had originally described the mission of the Muhammadan community as that of "the extension of its rule over all infidels, to ensure that God's true ways obtain everywhere."[16] This shifted long ago, when Muslim leaders had to consider the vast numbers of non-Muslims who had come under their control, first to the consensus of the community (a tacit demotion of proselytization because of much increased Muslim self-confidence), and then to a consensus based on reports about the first Muhammadan community and the current vision of Islam (which is consistent with the tolerance and even the acceptance of non-Muslims). These shifts tacitly overrule the literal application of the Qur'anic injunctions at 9:29 and 9:33 that respectively call for subduing all non-Muslims within reach of the Islamic armies and preach universal proselytization.

What has happened since then has surely brought the realization to Muslims that the earliest possible date for the conversion of all humanity to Islam is the end of time. For they can see hardly any further advance of their religion relative to Christianity, Hinduism, Buddhism, Confucianism, Judaism, and several forms of animism. All they can hope for is to regain some of those who have turned to agnosticism or atheism from within their ranks. The recognition of this worldwide religious equilibrium is augmented by the communications revolution. Nothing Muslims can do will insulate them from global trends, ideas, attitudes, and fashions. Whether non-Muslims share the same apartment buildings with them or live an ocean away, their presence will still be felt. For whatever Muslims cannot adopt or embrace, they will have to find a modus vivendi. Non-Muslim communities in their midst can hence in no way undermine their pursuits—if these be directed toward an authentic Islamic revitalization. On the contrary, the dialogue that follows true religious coexistence can contribute only favorably to those pursuits. With regard to materialism and communal disintegration, all religious persons can find themselves pretty much on the same side.

The principle among the three that have grounded the Islamic code, and which had started out as a call for universal proselytization and conversion when the geographical scope of Islam had been very limited and internal dissent might have been fatal, and which then changed to consensus of the community based on the Medinan paradigm and the current vision of Islam, can now be turned to encompass the shifts brought about by modernity. It is necessary to at once preserve Islamic unity and the good of the community while recognizing the world religious equilibrium and the futility of "purging" Muslim lands from non-Muslims under the illusion that this would advance the cause of Islam. The wording of the principle does not really need much change: It is a matter of reinterpreting key concepts. For instance, it may be possible to represent the unity and good of the community through Muslims whose credentials are determined according to broader and more open criteria than before. As we shall see, a Muslim scholar today need not be the direct analogue of the Muslim scholars of yesterday—nor need he reason and interpret the traditional sources in the same way.

All along, there has been a still more solid basis for coexistence. It is found in the Qur'an itself, which repeatedly specifies that Christians and Jews must be protected and given all sorts of rights and freedoms. Muslim fanatics who attack Christians and Jews transgress the highest authority in Islam. In this regard, Islam has largely been historically more tolerant than other religions enjoying similar power. The Qur'anic specifications were quickly extended to Mazdeans and Zoroastrians, and then to Hindus, Buddhists, Confucians, and the pagan star worshipers of Harran. There is both a scriptural basis and a strong precedent for the official and institutionalized tolerance of other communities among Muslims. And to its credit, Islam developed the precedent when under no earthly compulsion to do so. Given the temporal finality of the world religious equilibrium, and the dynamic and open nature of the contemporary situation, there is no reason—certainly not in principle—why the attitude of tolerance cannot metamorphose into acceptance.

If skeptics continue to emphasize Qur'anic verses like 9:29, one might point out, besides the fact that their literal interpretation has long been tacitly brushed aside in a climate of unquestioned Islamic legitimacy, that other verses might altogether supersede them in the new context. Thus the famous verse that affirms freedom of religious choice (2:256) may be judged to gain precedence over 9:29, given the reality of a world religious equilibrium and cultural openness, and vast Muslim domains that ensure that Islam is no longer in its infancy and thus unable to brook divergence. One could judge that 9:29 was there to help Muslims off to a secure start in the real world, and that 2:256 was there to make the world under Muslim control even better. Muslim practice has sometimes overwhelmingly reflected that supersession long before it has become evident—and necessary. The wisdom, pragmatism, and humanity of the early (and middle) Muslims will hopefully not be lost on their descendants.

The status of Muslim-non-Muslim relations is in flux, caught between the potential for communal pluralism and harmony—against which nothing stands that would violate Islamic beliefs, sources, and practice—and the thrust of various global trends toward ethnic narcissism and strife. Among Muslims themselves, the more their situation favors a thoughtful response, the freer they are to develop a broad and dynamic communal framework; and the more they are made to feel discriminated against and on the defensive, the stronger the fanatics for whom the fact and forms of assertiveness overwhelm all else will become.

The brute direction of the world situation unfortunately appears to favor the steady and rapid erosion of the ground for thoughtful interaction. Non-Muslim attitudes toward Muslims have been neither favorable nor helpful for a long time indeed. The Muslim religion has been repeatedly the target of gross misrepresentation and verbal sacrilege. Highly visible to Muslim multitudes is the political hypocrisy that routinely makes them the shortchanged party. All kinds of writers in the Arab Muslim world, whatever their differences, are united in their outrage over the apparent singling out of Muslims with regard to the enforcement of the ban on nuclear proliferation. The injustice surrounding how Israel was created and the long chain of related events have also been a symbol of universal Muslim grievance. The rush to "liberate" Kuwait while Bosnia-Herzegovina was allowed to be partitioned and devastated by its Serbian (and sometimes Croatian) neighbors suggests another chapter in a lesson that has not been lost on Muslims. Principles apply only where real economic or strategic imperatives exist.

Unless there is a decisive change in non-Muslim attitudes toward Muslims—a just and lasting peace in the Near East and the firm rejection of the suffocation of Muslim life in the Balkans would go a long way in signaling a turning point—the buildup of fear and resentment can sour relations between Muslims and others possibly to the point of no return. On the other hand, with greater equanimity by the powers of modernity, the problem of freedom for non-Muslims in the Arab Muslim world can be decisively solved, for its internal logic has a remarkable quality. The conditions of freedom for non-Muslims in the Arab Muslim world are closely tied to the conditions of freedom for the Muslims themselves.[17] The more Islam comes into its own and flourishes, attuned to (but not compromised by) the modern reality, the more other communities within Islamdom will enjoy the breathing room for the articulation and expression of their own aspirations.

The Practical and Popular Approach

Everywhere in the Arab Muslim world, there are many signs impossible to miss that people who consider themselves Muslims are quite untroubled by their open rejection of those injunctions and rules that are specific, irrelevant to the heart of Islam, and obviously anachronistic, counterproductive, or harmful. For the official spokesmen to persist in the implication that such rejection entails practices that constitute serious violations is for them to risk the consequences of too close an association between Muslim religious belief and certain scriptural passages that address specific conduct, for instance the Qur'an at 24:31 (the verse that eventually helped justify the unjust treatment of women). The insistence on that association may lead the millions of Muslims who reject the conduct urged in the passages in question to lose their reverence for the scriptural sources, including the Qur'an, and perhaps turn agnostic or atheist. It may also lead other millions of Muslims for whom the affirmation of Islam and the Qur'an come first to reduce their affirmation to the easy and shallow path of adherence to the conduct specified. Either way, Islam is the loser. The loss is predictable because it is rooted in a false identity. A religion as comprehensive and profound as Islam cannot be staked on practices that the more thoughtful can see have run their course, and which can never begin to amount to a religion in any plausible sense of the word, nor be a gateway to it. An Islam staked on what is unworthy of it endangers itself. Thus, many Muslims who defy the strictures that have become unworthy of Islam, so long as they are not yet driven toward indifference by fanatics and unimaginative traditionalists who loudly tell them otherwise, ironically affirm a worthy Islam, while those who believe they affirm it by holding fast to a segment of tradition's outer shell bring Islam down to their level. As the polarization intensifies, Islam loses the opportunity for the articulation of an official framework that sustains its worthiness in a contemporary context. The sooner the articulation, the more secure *both* kinds of rebellious Muslims will feel about their Islam. The battle between the two rebellious groups, and the struggle to find an official Islamic accommodation for both, is the most important within the Arab Muslim world.

Because we are dealing with a popular dynamic here, one that is politically and intellectually amorphous but is highly influential in the life of Muslims today, our access to it is informal. Fortunately, access is also simple and direct. The description of the elements of that dynamic, in which Muslims repeatedly reject some of their scriptural injunctions and act freely without waiting for their official spokesmen to catch up with them, can be pieced together by anyone who regularly follows the events of the Arab Muslim world, and are most visible to those at the scene, travelers and locals alike. Popular defiance is not restricted to Islamic strictures, but also regards all sorts of other political, intellectual, and social prohibitions. The following examples will reflect the multifarious defiance and display various free actions that circumvent or brush aside the official unfreedom.

1. The eyes of modernity's leading powers have recently been on Saudi Arabia, which, after Oman, is the most closed Arab Muslim society of them all. Films and videotapes are banned in the kingdom. But those Saudis who can afford it have large screens in their homes for private viewing. This has been the case for decades. With the advent of video technology, there is no way to stop salesmen from circulating tapes purchased abroad.

The modern history of Saudi Arabia has been officially rewritten. So sensitive is the subject that some crucial records are said to have been destroyed. Nevertheless, a Saudi writer has produced a massive historical novel that chronicles the kingdom's rise with the house of Saud at the helm. Whenever the author seems to be on solid ground, fiction barely disguises fact, often not at all. He otherwise resorts to imaginative speculations that frequently match eyewitness accounts. Abdulrahman Mounif's pentalogy, *The Cities of Salt,* is banned in Saudi Arabia and most Arab countries. But it can be bought by all Arabs abroad, or in Beirut and Damascus, and thus reach its intended audience anyway. A bookseller in London has described it to me as a "best-seller."

As for all the social restrictions that have made Saudi Arabia notorious, one need only take account of the behavior of Saudis abroad or, again, in the privacy of their homes, to evaluate their assimilation to official Saudi life. And here, we are not concerned with compulsive gamblers and their ilk, but with those for whom Islam means much and yet suffocate under what legally constitutes Islam in their country. There are many in Saudi Arabia, some of whose true feelings were made known to a worldwide audience by the women who drove their cars through the streets of Riyadh. No one quite knows how many believing Muslims suffer under what passes for Islam in Saudi Arabia. And many of their excesses can be excused considering the suffering.

The Saudi authorities, like many unyielding at heart but intelligently aware of the contemporary situation, act paradoxically. For instance, they pay for a station for Washington, D.C.'s large and growing Arab community that features talk shows where all sorts of subjects tabooed in the kingdom are freely discussed: dictatorship, personal problems of a romantic or psychological nature, women explaining their illnesses (sometimes in graphic detail) to a male general practitioner, and so on. Once, the moderator of a weekly review of the major political events broadcast on Sundays signed off by noting what day it was, wished followers of the Roman and other Western churches a happy Easter, a happy Palm Sunday to Orthodox Christians, and a happy Passover to Jews. This is remarkable for a kingdom that is officially severely intolerant toward the other monotheistic faiths.

2. The phenomenon of discussion far freer than allowed by both Islamic and secular authorities has spread throughout the Arab Muslim world. Although the wide audiences of magazines and radio shows enjoy greater social and cultural freedom than is officially suggested, limited audiences can extend their leeway even to the political sphere. Thus a forum on freedom and democracy, with some speakers espousing controversial and radical views, can take place in Cairo and be sponsored by a prestigious center that has received much money from the Iraqi regime. On the other hand, because the airwaves do not recognize political boundaries, inflammatory poetry and music easily reaches audiences whose governments would prefer otherwise. Nizar Qabbani's later poetry may not be of the highest literary quality. But it repeatedly breaks political and sexual taboos, relentless in its rousing condemnation of dictators and the plight of women. Qabbani had already written poetry that must have occasionally shocked some people when he made a tour throughout the Arab world and lectured on poetry—with allusions to his deepest concerns that were hardly lost on the audience.[18] Here, we come across a combination of phenomena. Besides the free travel of broadcasts and booklets, poets, singers, and comedians like the Syrian Dorayd Lahham can rise to such popularity that few governments would dare refuse them entry. Thus another door to freedom is opened for those who wish to cross the threshold.

3. The ease of travel and the globalization of communications have exposed unprecedented numbers of travelers from the Arab Muslim world to other alternatives. The ideas, habits, attitudes, and trends thus encountered are not necessarily adopted indiscriminately (although they often are). But people from all walks of life meet directly with what they might know indirectly through broadcasts and hearsay. When they return to the Arab Muslim world, if they are unhappy with the official position, they can back up their intuitive cynicism with a concrete picture of what changes they would like to see. The global intersection of cultures is now unavoidable, and people can no longer be expected to accept that their official version is the best. They need to be convinced that it is so. And if they find certain particulars preferable elsewhere, they are bound to clamor for some reform. For instance, people from the Arab Muslim world may take a strong liking to writing letters to the editor in which

one can speak one's heart and mind. This practice has nothing to do with Islam or traditional culture in the Arab Muslim world. To adopt it would not run contrary to these. It would simply worry those who prefer sycophancy. Many other practices, though they may have geographically originated in the West, are really part of an emergent universal culture. They add to the means of contemporary self-expression. They are largely not meant to supplant local traditional frameworks.

4. The worldwide intersection of cultures and the ease of travel have also helped transport many among those who would engage in the liveliest and most far-reaching discussions in the Arab Muslim world to places where they can pursue their activities more freely. Beirut was such a place before the Lebanese civil war began in 1975 (it continues to offer the widest selection of books among any Arab city). London, Paris, and Washington, D.C., have become major centers of Arab Muslim discussion. Participants are stirred to greater extremes by exile and the lack of social restraint. And the written or broadcast record of their work, which trickles back to their native lands, flows into an oppositional current thus made all the stronger.

5. Whatever people might say about Islam's intolerance for public mirth and the visual arts (largely based on false impressions fed by morose groups of revivalists who occasionally impose their will on local Muslim societies), millions of faithful Muslims enjoy the cinema, television comedies, the theater, and festivities of song and dance throughout the region. Egyptian films are popular throughout the Arabic-speaking world (and the cinema is loved throughout the region), Muslims in the Subcontinent have adopted the great Indian musical traditions, satirical plays freely abuse and condemn the authorities with an allusive language familiar to the audience and sometimes make fun of everything,[19] Um Kulthum's stature hardly needs mention, and love songs are heard everywhere, from revolutionary Iran's clandestine markets to Algerian cafés. These are not new upsurges, but are the contemporary form of an expressiveness that has always been there. And they are joys in which Muslims who believe in Islam participate in far greater numbers than would please their sterner religious leadership.

6. The Islamic revolutionaries, for all the nonsense they sometimes promulgate (say, about music or the cinema being "un-Islamic"), and the freedom they would curb if in power, are themselves a good example of free action at the popular mass level. They openly reject political quietism, and have taken the cause of action against state injustice, corruption, and impotence into their own hands. Occasionally, they have risen to heroic confrontations with brutal regimes that destroy entire neighborhoods to quell dissent without blinking. Such heroism is reminiscent of Ibn Hanbal's brave stand against al-Ma'mun, which has never been forgotten, and will galvanize those fed up with the present state of things.

7. It would be fitting to end these illustrations with what has been going on in Iran in the past few years. Iran has been consistently maligned in the Western press, brandished as a pathetic island of doomed retrenchment. Thoughtful observers of the area have long known the Islamic revolution to hardly merit such facile dismissal. Already at the beginning, in early 1979, Iranians were freer than hostile reports by their adversaries suggested. In a report recently published in the *Washington Post*, the striking manner in which Iranians have stamped their social preferences on an officially conformist landscape has finally become available to a wider readership. According to the report, whoever wishes to circumvent the ban on alcohol (an enduring symbol of the reduction of Islam to a number of anachronistic, oppressive, or irrelevant strictures) makes it at home and brings it to parties in jerricans. Women, though not permitted to swim with men, can sunbathe in their bikinis "under guard" in some areas reserved for them. Videotapes circulate as they do in Saudi Arabia. The report adds:

> Two years ago, Iran's film industry began making movies about love again. Cinemas, by some fluke, have always escaped the government's attempts to segregate the sexes. While men and women—even married couples—must take separate cable cars on the ski slopes of the Elburz, they are allowed to sit side by side in a darkened movie theatre.
>
> Yes, young men do take their girlfriends to the movies, said Hamid Taqavi, an Iranian reporter. "We can't put a policeman for every individual in Iran," he said. "But I, as a religious man, I wouldn't take my girlfriend to the movies because I think *it* starts with the movies." "It" needed no elaboration.
>
> "This is a river—they can't stop it," said an Iranian woman. "You cannot separate men and women. They were created together."
>
> Every week, the Islamic censor uses a thick black pen to blot out female necks, breasts and arms in the photographs of Newsweek magazine. But stores selling Persian handicrafts have shelves full of traditional drawings of women with flowing hair, bare arms and breasts—usually locked in an erotic embrace with a wild-eyed lover.[20]

Yet it would be hasty to conclude that all free action flows against strictures supported by the revolution and (increasingly sporadically) enforced by zealots. In certain respects, the revolution itself has been a harbinger of freedom. Many women have been liberated from their cultural shackles by the Islamic upsurge.

> "We were just like puppets," before the revolution, said Sakineh Nouri, a 33-year-old volunteer at the Bader Health Center in Shahr-e-Rey, a low-income neighborhood in southern Tehran. "The most important thing," a fellow volunteer, Shahnaz Ghanavati, 30, said, "is the participation of all